# CAMBRIDGE LATIN AMERICAN STUDIES

59

# ROOTS OF INSURGENCY

*For a list of other books in the*
*Cambridge Latin American Studies series*
*please see page 275*

# ROOTS OF INSURGENCY

*Mexican regions, 1750–1824*

BRIAN R. HAMNETT

*Senior Lecturer, Department of History, University of Strathclyde*

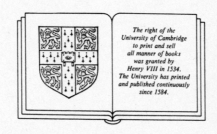

The right of the
University of Cambridge
to print and sell
all manner of books
was granted by
Henry VIII in 1534.
The University has printed
and published continuously
since 1584.

CAMBRIDGE UNIVERSITY PRESS

*Cambridge*

*London   New York   New Rochelle*
*Melbourne   Sydney*

Published by the Press Syndicate of the University of Cambridge
The Pitt Building, Trumpington Street, Cambridge CB2 1RP
32 East 57th Street, New York, NY 10022, USA
10 Stamford Road, Oakleigh, Melbourne 3166, Australia

First published 1986

Printed in Great Britain at the University Press, Cambridge

*British Library cataloguing in publication data*
Hamnett, Brian R.
Roots of insurgency: Mexican regions, 1750–1824.
– (Cambridge Latin American Studies; 59)
1. Mexico – Politics and government – 1540–1810
2. Mexico – Politics and government – 1810
I. Title
972.02    F1226

*Library of Congress cataloguing in publication data*
Hamnett, Brian R.
Roots of insurgency.
(Cambridge Latin American Studies; 59)
Bibliography: p.
Includes index.
1. Mexico – History – Spanish colony, 1540–1810.
2. Mexico – History – Wars of Independence, 1810–1821 –
Causes. 3. Insurgency – Mexico – History – 18th century.
4. Insurgency – Mexico – History – 19th century. 5. Mexico –
Social conditions – To 1810. 6. Mexico – History, Local.
I. Title.   II. Series.
F1229.H36 1986   972'.02   85–26929

ISBN 0 521 32148 4

# Contents

# Maps

# Acknowledgements

At various stages, Christon Archer, Paul Vanderwood, Linda Arnold, Guy Thomson, Jan Bazant and John Lynch gave me their time and advice, and were prepared to discuss or read what I was trying to convey. In Guadalajara, I was particularly grateful to Carmen Castañeda for guiding me towards the appropriate archives of that city. D. Salvador Gómez kindly enabled me to work in the Guadalajara municipal archive, of which he is the director. Representatives of the Executive Power in the States of Jalisco and Puebla facilitated access to their respective notarial archives, and in the latter case also to the Registro Público de la Propiedad y Comercio. I received ready assistance from the directors and staff of the Archivo de la Casa de Morelos and the Archivo del Ayuntamiento in Morelia, Michoacán. The municipal president, Ing. Ruiz Béjar, enabled me to work in this latter archive, of which the *encargado*, D. Antonio Chávez, helped to orientate me. In Puebla, I was fortunate enough to gain admittance to the archive of the Cathedral, through the kindness of its *encargado*, Padre J. Manuel Martínez.

The Social Science Research Council in London generously funded my research in Mexico during the summer months of 1977, 1978 and 1979. The British Academy financed research in Guadalajara, Morelia, Puebla and Mexico City for the period July to December 1982. The Carnegie Trust for the Universities of Scotland enabled further secondary and bibliographical research to be undertaken at the Bancroft Library, Berkeley, California, in January 1981. Initial research findings were presented and discussed at the University of Edinburgh Economic History Seminar (1977), at the University of Bielefeld (West Germany, 1978), at the University of Calgary (Canada, 1981), and at the Conferences of the Society of Latin American Studies held in Manchester (1978) and Bristol (1980). The ensuing discussions contributed in no small way to the clarification of themes presented in this book. My colleagues at the University of Strathclyde listened patiently through two delivered papers at the Department of History Senior Seminar in 1979 and 1983, and offered their helpful criticisms. Dr Madeleine Tearse and Dr Anita Prazmowska read sections of the manuscript of this book and made several valuable suggestions for improvement. Mrs Jean Fraser kindly typed drafts of the manuscript and Mrs Irene Scouller expertly completed the final version on the word processor. I am grateful to Dr Miles Oglethorpe for assistance in producing the maps.

I doubt anything could have been written at all, without the company of my Mexican friends in those crucial hours after the archives had closed their doors.

*Strathclyde*                                   BRIAN R. HAMNETT

# Weights and measures

## Land

| | | | | |
|---|---|---|---|---|
| sitio de ganado mayor | = 5,000 × 5,000 varas | = 41 caballerías | = |
| | 1,755 hectares | = 4,388.9 acres | |
| sitio de ganado menor | = 3,333 × 3,333 varas | = 18 caballerías | = |
| | 780 hectares | = 1,928.4 acres | |
| caballería | = 1,104 × 552 varas | = 42.8 hectares | |
| fundo legal | = 1,200 × 1,200 varas | = 101 hectares | |

## Dimension

| | | |
|---|---|---|
| legua | = 5,000 varas | = 5,572.7 metres |
| vara | = 0.836 metres | |

## Capacity

| | |
|---|---|
| fanega | = 5.5 litres |
| carga | = 2 fanegas |

## Weight

| | | |
|---|---|---|
| arroba | = 25 libras | = 11.5 kg. |
| quintal | = 4 arrobas | |

## Money

| | |
|---|---|
| peso | = 8 reales (silver) |
| marco | = 8 pesos 4 reales (silver) |

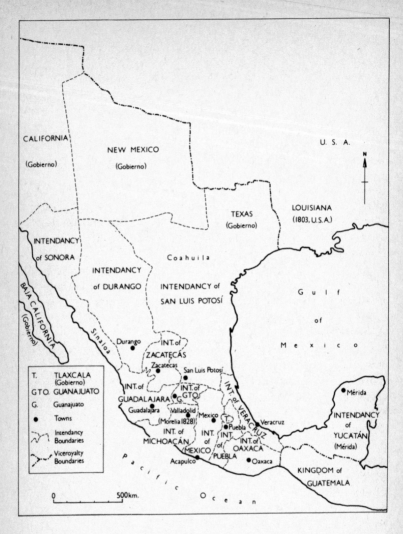

Map 1 The viceroyalty of New Spain in 1810

# Introduction

There is a need for a fresh view of the process of Independence in Latin America. This has become particularly important, in view of the increasing interest in the formative period of national development during the first half of the nineteenth century.[1] Furthermore, recent studies of the late colonial period in the Viceroyalty of New Spain (Mexico) have placed an emphasis on the regional context of economic developments, and it has now become possible to compare and contrast social conditions among and within the provinces.[2] Few such works, however, have examined the 'Independence period.' Their conclusions have rarely been projected into the complex processes of regional change that accompanied and formed part of the Mexican revolutionary movement of the 1810s. It is the purpose of this book to examine the regional dimension of the process of Independence, particularly in its social aspects. The focus will be upon the protracted insurgency that developed from the initial, failed attempt in 1810 to overthrow Spanish peninsular rule by a revolutionary uprising. The intention here is to make the connection between the social tensions of the late colonial period and those of the nineteenth-century Mexican Republic. The War of Independence (1810–21) constituted a broader expression of the limited popular discontent which from time to time erupted in the periods both preceding and following it. Stripped of the nationalist casing, the struggles of the 1810s often subsumed earlier conflicts and foreshadowed later ones. Very few works, to date, have attempted to make this connection.[3] As a result, it has proved difficult for historians to determine exactly how the Latin American Independence movements relate to either the colonial or national experience of the countries concerned. We have, accordingly, been left with the traditional periodisation, which ends the colonial period at 1810, and begins the national period at some stage in the early 1820s. This has meant that the decade of the great upheavals has become a period in itself,

apparently unconnected to what preceded or followed it – if it was, in
fact, dealt with in specific relation to either of them at all. The
underlying continuities have only sketchily been appreciated.[4] It is
perhaps feasible to argue that the struggles of the 1810s formed one,
albeit turbulent, aspect of the broader period, 1650–1850, that
stretches from the post-Conquest era to the Liberal Reform Movement
and the early stages of 'modernisation'.

Most traditional histories of the Independence movements have
focussed on the national dimension, rather than the regional. The
earliest historians traced the developments of the Mexican nation. In
many respects, their historical reconstruction of events formed part of a
general endeavour to create a sense of nationhood, which could not only
contrast with the colonial past, but also transcend the regional component elements of the newly independent sovereign state. Historical
interpretation provided the means whereby national consciousness could
come into existence. In that sense, the works of Lorenzo de Zavala, Fray
Servando de Mier, José María Luis Mora, Carlos María de Bustamante,
and Lucas Alamán complemented the contemporary European historical
tradition of tracing the development of nation-states.[5] Such historians
had little interest in regional identity, which represented a potentially
centrifugal force. On the whole, they stressed the national elements in
the struggle of Mexicans for political liberation from Spanish Imperial
rule. From their founding efforts emerged the powerful modern trilogy
of 'Independence – *Reforma* – Revolution.'

Even so, geography and settlement patterns provided a natural basis
for regional sentiment in New Spain, as in other Spanish American
territories. Distinct regional characteristics and problems, moreover,
explained the different responses to government policy. Little effort is
required to demonstrate that a multiplicity of particular regional and
local issues characterised political life in the colonial and national
periods. These, in any case, were the usual features of pre-modern or
modernising societies. What needs to be explained is how a political
entity such as New Spain managed to cohere at all. The explanation does
not appear to lie in coercion, since no effective police force controlled the
whole extent of territory, and military force remained largely non-
existent until the 1770s. The explanation probably lies in the common
interests that transcended regional differences and enabled the political
and economic system to function at a national level. A major dynamic
was the revival of silver-mining, stimulated by the investment of
mercantile capital. These networks of interest, however, did not
supersede the reality of regional economies, but served to connect region

to region, and region to centre. Although this ensured that each province was not entirely autonomous, we cannot, nevertheless, speak of a 'national economy' in the sense of an integrated infrastructure and market. The relationship between locality, province and centre that made such cohesion feasible still remains inadequately understood. Yet, despite the potential centrifugal tendencies regularly apparent, neither New Spain nor independent Mexico was simply the sum of its component parts. It was a functioning economic system with a central political power that was not negligible, even after 1821.[6] Government in colonial Spanish America did have at least some significant impact on society, if only by virtue of the religious symbolism and dynastic legitimacy upon which it was founded. Appreciation of such points should provide a greater understanding of how pre-modern government functioned.

## Realities and perceptions

A general deterioration of lower-class living standards in a number of regions appears now to be an established fact for the fifty or sixty years preceding the outbreak of the insurrection of 1810. If we add to this the sense of grievance amongst the Spanish American professional classes at the lack of opportunities for them in bureaucratic office and government, then we have a potentially inflammatory social combination. Much, however, depends on our understanding of contemporary perceptions of grievance. In the latter case, these have been given considerable attention in the literature to date, beginning with the Mexican nationalist historians of the post-Independence period. In the former case, less has been said, if only because source materials of lower-class grievances are not easy to come by, since, by definition, such social groups did not belong to the articulate élites. Nevertheless, repeated litigation over land, labour, water rights, pasture, and traditional customary practices indicated lower-class consciousness of a deteriorating or threatened position. Conflict – usually in the form of peasant land invasions, landlord enclosures or abuse of labour – brought these tensions to the surface. In most cases, the perceived causes of social deprivation were the actions of entrepreneurial-minded landowners or of the merchant–investors who operated in the localities. These long term social grievances should, of course, be separated from the short term impact of dearth in 1808–10. The latter was the action of natural agencies, rather than of human, and, accordingly, involved a different mechanism of response. Appeals to the supernatural represented the traditional response to terrestrial calamities. When, however, human agencies sought to benefit from such natural catastrophes, then perceptions altered once more to focus upon the evil-doers. Perceptions of human causes of material deprivation often led to the identification of the source of mischief, and the transfer of the social grievance to a political plane.

The problem on the political plane was for the provincial creoles to find a common cause with the lower classes, and, once having done so, to provide the leadership in a common movement of opposition. Hatred of the Europeans (*gachupines*) provided such a rallying cry, sanctioned as it were, by the symbolism of the cult of the Virgin of Guadalupe. Religion provided not only clerical leadership but a moral justification for the source of legitimate dissent.

When examined in regional terms, the economic growth of eighteenth-century New Spain reduces itself to the expansion of particular sectors of the economy in specific areas. The chief of these were the mining, cereal and livestock sectors of the centre-north-west, principally the plateau known as the Bajío, central Guadalajara, and the mining zones of Guanajuato, San Luis Potosí and Zacatecas. Even so, the diocese of Puebla still produced the second largest diocesan revenues after the Archbishopric of Mexico, and greater than those of the diocese of Michoacán in which the Bajío was situated. During the long periods when warfare and blockade disrupted transatlantic trade, particularly between 1795 and 1808, the woollen industry of Querétaro and the Bajío towns, and cotton manufacture, chiefly in Puebla and Guadalajara, also grew. A number of recent scholars have pointed to the connection between economic expansion and recovery of population. D. A. Brading argues that the rapid economic growth of late Bourbon Mexico, a major facet of which was the striking revival of the silver-mining industry, rested upon the demographic recovery prior to 1760. For the period, from c.1660 until the 1720s, Brading suggests a rate of population growth of 2.5 per cent, falling to 1 per cent between 1727 and 1736, and to zero after 1760.[7] Eric Van Young attributes the expansion of the regional economy of Guadalajara to population increase. There again the rate of demographic growth appears to have been greater in the earlier part of the century, from 1710 to 1770, though the increase in the population of the city itself took place after the 1760s, partly as a result of migration from the countryside.[8] Nevertheless, the city of Puebla still remained New Spain's second most populous urban area after Mexico City itself. Sherburne Cook and Woodrow Borah, in their estimates for the broadly defined west-central region of Mexico, point to a rate of population increase above 2 per cent for each decade of the eighteenth century after 1710, with the highest rate in the 1760s at 2.69 per cent. Thereafter, a gradual fall occurred to 2.4 per cent in 1790–1800, followed by a substantial drop to 0.69 per cent in the 1800s. The rate of increase sustained between 1710 and 1800 was not reached again until the 1940s.[9] The rate of population growth in the Guanajuato–Querétaro zone was greater than in the rest of New Spain. There, as we shall see, increasing demand for foodstuffs altered conditions of labour.[10]

Writing in 1955, E. R. Wolf drew attention to the recovery of both population and economy after the late seventeenth century, but stressed the regional application of this phenomenon. The principal zones affected were those located beyond the northern limits of pre-Columbian Meso-America, regions, that is, characterised by distinct cultural patterns from those of the more heavily indigenous central and southern zones of New Spain. The Bajío and the mining zones were cases in point. Wolf pointed to the interrelation between agriculture, mining, and textiles as a significant contributory factor to economic growth. Inter-regional relationships stimulated and reflected this new activity. Bajío cereals, for instance, supplied both the Mexico City grain market and the northern zones. Regions in the north, such as San Luis Potosí, Zacatecas, or Coahuila tended to become the economic hinterland of the expanding centre-north-west.[11] John Tutino argues that the area from Querétaro to San Luis Potosí became closely integrated into the central Mexican social and economic system during the eighteenth century.[12] Jan Bazant's examination of San Luis Potosí's landed estates highlights the orientation of their products to the urban markets of Querétaro and Mexico City.[13] The Guadalajara region clearly illustrated this connection between the growth of the urban area and the development of the hinterland. Ramón Serrera's examination of the regional economy suggests the primacy of urban demand, to which the wool trade and the cotton industry responded. The growth of the market helped to determine the degree of specialisation in the surrounding zones. Serrera stresses that the rise of Guadalajara in the later eighteenth century shows a clear case of an expanding regional economy in which silver-mining was not paramount in determining the pace of growth. The contrast with Guanajuato was striking.[14] The rapid growth of the city of Guadalajara during the eighteenth century, from 1,500 to c.40,000 inhabitants, particularly in the 1760s when the population doubled, was the cause and effect of the expansion of government and commerce. The urban demand for wheat placed heavy demands on the rural maize economy and its traditional Indian-peasant cultivators in terms of land usage. The growth of the rural population meant that after the 1780s, Indian villages could no longer count on a maize surplus.[15] In the Guadalajara zone, moreover, in contrast to the Bajío, an Indian village society still remained intact at the end of the colonial period, in spite of serious encroachments. The majority of the sixty-two Indian villages of the Intendancy of Guanajuato, however, had already lost or sold their lands by the end of the eighteenth century. Most of their population worked on the private estates.[16]

Quite clearly two different worlds existed on either side of the Río Lerma, which had been the northern boundary of the Aztec Empire. Claude Morin emphasizes this contrast in his examination of the diocese of Michoacán during the eighteenth century. The region north of the river had been the preserve of the barbarian tribes or *Chichimecas* in the pre-Hispanic period. The southern zones, corresponding largely to colonial Michoacán, had been settled by Tarascan cultivators. Given the absence of Indian-peasant communities north of the Río Lerma, the new Hispanic municipalities tended to consist of modest farmers. The open area of the Bajío remained under free-ranging livestock until demand increased for cereals in the expanding mining communities of the adjacent regions. Within Michoacán itself, considerable sub-regional variation existed between villages which still possessed the legal minimum of 600 *varas* of land circumference (101 hectares) at the end of the eighteenth century, and those which did not. One-fifth of all the Intendancy's villages no longer possessed this *fundo legal*. All such villages were located in the triangle between Pátzcuaro, Zacapu and Cocupao. Those villages which continued to possess the *fundo legal* or more could be found in the Sierra Tarasca, where private estate owners had little interest in the poor grasslands of the pine-clad hills. Almost all villages from which part of the legal minimum had been taken were located north of a line through Valladolid, Zacapu and Tlazazalca, on the plain of Zinapécuaro and on the shores of Lake Pátzcuaro. This was the principal area of hacienda cereal production, with a large non-Indian component in the population, an area of fertile soil, access to water supply and in proximity to the main urban markets.[17]

In the Altos de Jalisco, vitally located across the route between Guadalajara and Zacatecas, no significant indigenous population group competed with the pioneering advance of Hispanic settlement in the sixteenth century. A series of small villages emerged, a different pattern of settlement and landownership than elsewhere. The social basis of the region lay in its small-scale properties known as *ranchos* and its cattle *estancias*, rather than in large-scale proprietorship. Beneath the *rancheros* were share-croppers and rural workers, though no really sharp social or economic distinction separated them from the former. From the earliest times of defence against marauding *Chichimecas*, it had been possible to speak of a kind of '*nacionalismo local*' in the region. The Altos grew in response to the mining zones, for which they provided foodstuffs. This regional interdependence reinforced rather than debilitated local characteristics and enabled the consolidation of local power groups opposed to central government incursions.[18] Van Young points to the increasing importance of the Altos and the Bajío as wheat suppliers to the city of Guadalajara in the late eighteenth century and early nineteenth century.[19]

On the Bajío estates, land was frequently rented to tenants and small farmers, since proprietors generally did not reside on their haciendas. Hacienda lessees (*arrendatorios*) and resident labourers (*gañanes*), moreover, were complemented by associated families (*arrimados*) and temporary labourers. The status and condition of the two latter groups were considerably below that of the *gañanes*, who were paid wages and a maize ration. *Gañanes* could earn as much as three pesos per month. They tended to be few in number in the Bajío, and, in fact, hacienda owners were often indebted to them rather than vice versa. Given their situation, *gañanes* were in a relatively favourable economic position, in comparison to that of the hard-pressed tenant. This view is confirmed by Bazant's study of mainly livestock or mezcal haciendas in San Luis Potosí. On estates within a reasonable vicinity of the provincial capital, the resident workers, referred to as *peones acasillados*, received a monthly wage and a weekly maize ration. This security made them, in effect, a relatively privileged group within the rural labour force. The absence of a pre-colonial Indian structure in San Luis Potosí explained the predominance of the large estate there, and the demand for resident labour. Tutino's comparison of social relations in San Luis Potosí and Querétaro emphasises the importance of rural employment in the former and of rental arrangements in the latter. He argues that employment gave rural families greater security in adverse times such as those of the 1800s, but that in Querétaro, in contrast, the economic problems of that decade led to the destabilisation of conditions on the land. Such regional differences, despite similar social systems, helped to explain why estate residents responded differently towards the issue of insurgency in the 1810s. Furthermore the surplus population created a pool of migrants competing for temporary jobs. In Querétaro, at any rate, the temporary labour force oscillated between the land at planting and harvest time and the city's textile workshops (*obrajes*) during the rainy season. Temporary labourers on the land, moreover, sometimes sub-rented from existing tenants.[20]

Despite the varied structure of rental arrangements and different labour practices, the hacienda owners tended to control access to arable, pasture and water supply. Tenant restlessness, coupled with surplus manpower created a potentially volatile situation in the centre-north at the beginning of the nineteenth century. As haciendas, often through the investment of mercantile capital, developed into more commercially viable units, lesser proprietors, such as *rancheros*, found themselves increasingly squeezed out. The *ranchero* sector encountered a problem of lack of available land during the half century before 1810, at a time of increased population. The *rancho* is always difficult to define, especially since it was sometimes an independent entity and at other times a dependent part of an hacienda. In both the Bajío and Guadalajara, the estimated number of *ranchos* was high in relation to the total number of haciendas, and showed that, prominent as the latter were in the central grain-producing zones, their hegemony was not unchallenged in the less fertile areas or in upland regions such as the Altos de Jalisco.[21]

Long term economic changes in the centre-north-west contributed to the deterioration of living standards among lower social groups. By the end of the eighteenth century, the increasing prosperity of the Bajío, cereal cultivation along entrepreneurial lines, and the greater abundance of the labour force enabled hacienda owners to exercise greater pressure on the work force. There was a tendency towards rent increases and the replacement of traditional customary rights by cash payments. This process formed a parallel development to the replacement in the mining industry of the traditional share-out or *partido* system, in accordance with which mine workers took away some of the ore as part of their salary. From 1790, the Guanajuato mines went over to a wage system.[22] Such trends in social and economic relations had profound repercussions among both industrial and rural workers, and helped bring about a consciousness that status and conditions were deteriorating, as a result of identifiable causes. Tutino argues that pressure by private proprietors led to some evictions or migrations from estates. Such actions interrup-ted family continuity on the land. Increasing economic demands in the form that they took in the Bajío were perceived as threats to the peasant community as such. These trends in the late colonial decades in the eastern Bajío created a fertile ground for rebellious sentiments when imperial and environmental crises struck together from 1808 to 1810.[23] In central Guadalajara, the hacienda dominated the rural economy.

With the intensification of cereal cultivation and the rise of urban demand in the late eighteenth century, land values rose, sometimes spectacularly. Since grain farming required a regular labour force, changes in the recruitment of labour and the inducements offered to it resulted. Furthermore, the recovery of the Indian population of the Guadalajara lakes region increased pressures on land area and usage. Land suits grew in number and bitterness in the latter half of the century.[24] For the Indian population, 'the perceived cause of the increasing strain was the active encroachment on peasant resources of a growing rapacious capitalist agriculture which happened to be in the hands of the whites'. The conditions of the Indian village population and of the rural lower classes worsened in the late colonial period, specifically in the countryside around Guadalajara. Commercial agriculture, rising prices, relatively stable wages, population growth, inability of the peasant sector to benefit from increased market demand – these were the contributory factors. Possibly they helped to explain the growing evidence of rural violence in this period.[25]

Many estates in the Querétaro zone attempted to reduce their resident workers to a more subservient condition. Tutino's view is that they were never wholly successful, and that insurgency during the 1810s demonstrated 'that estate residents had yet to be driven into easy or absolute submission to the colony's great landed families'. The tighter social structure in San Luis Potosí perhaps helped to account for the lesser popular impact of insurgency there and the availability of recruits for the Royalist militia.[26] Querétaro was, of course, a highly urbanised zone. By the end of the eighteenth century, more than half the population of the eastern Bajío lived in cities. In the city of Querétaro itself, the growth of population beyond the capacity of the economy to absorb the excess labour force, led to serious social problems, not least of which was crime, a preoccupation of the municipal authorities during the 1790s and 1800s. John Super argues that, although crime in the Bajío countryside had always preoccupied eighteenth-century officials, they saw conflicts as more identifiably racial or social by the end of the century, and blamed the numerous itinerant groups in the region.[27]

Given the economic expansion of the centre-north-west, profound differences continued to exist between those regions and the more heavily indigenous centre-south. Claude Morin makes a striking contrast between the type of labour relations obtaining in the centre-north-west and those in the eastern and southern zones. Morin compares conditions in Michoacán with those, for instance, in the Puebla-Tlaxcala region. In Michoacán, increased agricultural productivity resulted – as in the Bajío and Guadalajara – from greater irrigation and the extension of the cultivated surface. Such trends were usually accompanied by enclosures and disputes over water rights. In Puebla and Tlaxcala, estate owners, unable to adopt similar procedures through different ecological conditions and institutional practices, sought to raise production by increased pressure on the labour force. Morin argues that the result was a worsening of labour conditions on the land in Puebla–Tlaxcala in comparison with Michoacán. Resident estate workers in Tlaxcala and in Tepeaca, one of Puebla's principal maize districts, complained of long hours and of ill-treatment by hacienda owners or their managers. Morin suggests that the opening of new lands in the western zone enabled the work force there to 'escape the unbridled exploitation of their counterparts in eastern Mexico'.[28] James Riley's examination of labour relations in Tlaxcala draws attention to the generally small extent and perennially low yields of the Tlaxcala haciendas. Estate owners remained close to bankruptcy, a situation which led to pressure on the labour force and repeated litigation with the Indian villages.[29]

Puebla was the second most densely populated region after Guanajuato. However, in many Puebla districts the condition of the haciendas was little better than in Tlaxcala. By 1790, all such estates in the district of Cholula, near the provincial capital, were burdened with mortgages, nearly 70 per cent of which were in favour of some sort of religious foundation. Proprietors borrowed usually to supplement deficient incomes or to pay off past debts, rather than to make improvements. Eleven of the thirty-eight haciendas in Cholula were bankrupt. The *ranchos* seemed to have fared better, since only one of the sixteen was bankrupt. In Puebla's most populous district, San Juan de los Llanos in the north-east, which contained an estimated total of 41,928 predominantly Indian inhabitants in 1804, seven of the hacienda owners and ten lessees controlled the thirty-six estates. Of the sixty-two *ranchos*, half were under proprietors and the other half under tenants. Strikingly, only the Intendancy of Guadalajara, with 1,511 *ranchos*, exceeded Puebla, with 911, in the number of *ranchos* listed within its territory. Most of the Puebla *ranchos* were run as family enterprises. The haciendas tended to be market orientated, and, in contrast to the *ranchos*, required a substantial outlay of labour and capital, neither of which could be automatically counted upon. Such weaknesses constantly frustrated Pueblo *hacendados'* efforts to gain the upper hand in relation to the labour force.[30]

Both in Puebla–Tlaxcala and in Oaxaca, further to the south, Indian villages were reluctant to perform labour services on hacienda land. Often they resisted impressment, whenever attempted, during the planting and harvesting seasons. William Taylor points to the depressed condition of hacienda agriculture in Oaxaca and to the village retention there of subsistence lands, to which the present labour force understandably attached priority. Both in Tlaxcala and in Oaxaca, there was a rapid turnover in ownership of landed properties. Only in a few areas beyond the Valley of Oaxaca did the private estate acquire significance.[31] In the province of Oaxaca, the principal local figure was generally not the hacienda-owner, but the district administrator, the *alcalde mayor*, behind whom stood his merchant–creditor or *aviador*, usually a merchant of Mexico City or Antequera de Oaxaca, the provincial capital. By virtue of this financial connection, royal administrators, starved of proper salaries, became the commercial agents of monopoly suppliers to the Indian districts, who, in return, collected local products such as cotton textiles, cotton or the prized scarlet dye. Since the late colonial bureaucracy largely failed to eliminate such practices, the ensuing abuses continued. The conduct of district administrators and their lieutenants had been and remained a source of unrest throughout the Indian districts.[32]

The Indian element continued to predominate overwhelmingly in the south and on the central plateau, where, according to Cook and Borah, it constituted between 85 per cent and 90 per cent of the total. This component, however, became much smaller in the west-central region, at 60–65 per cent in New Galicia and Michoacán, and at 35–40 per cent in areas in which no major pre-Columbian settlement had been evident.[33] These regional variations correspond by and large to the proportions given by Taylor for the early nineteenth century: an Indian population of 88.3 per cent in Oaxaca, 75 per cent in Puebla, and 62.5 per cent in the Intendancy of Mexico. In Michoacán the Indian component fell to 42.5 per cent, a minority of the total population. In several areas of the central zone, Taylor points out that non-Indian elements predominated: in commercial mining and administrative centres, such as Actopan, Pachuca, Toluca and Taxco.[34] Evidence from eighteenth-century tributary counts shows an increase in the tributary population. In 110 districts of New Spain in 1714–19, Cook and Borah calculated 292,000 tributaries and 359,000 children aged between four and fifteen years; the figure for 1746–50 showed 338,000 adults and 464,000 children. Making allowance for changes in classification put into effect in the 1790s, the tribute assessment for 1804 for the whole of New Spain included 904,108 persons. From this figure Cook and Borah estimate a total Indian population of 3,265,720.[35] Within the province of Oaxaca, which contained the largest Indian population in New Spain, demographic recovery began during the course of the seventeenth century, and the process had been substantially completed by 1740. Population continued to grow until the 1810s, when a brief slowing down or even halt took place until the 1830s. Thereafter, the recovery resumed.[36]

Despite the protected juridical status of the Indian population under the Laws of the Indies, the exaction of tribute placed enormous burdens upon villagers. On many occasions, chiefly during times of food shortages, they could not sustain this obligation. Charles Gibson points out that 'by universally observed custom, any determined effort to collect tribute was accompanied by an exodus from the community'. Payment of tribute clearly differentiated the Indian element from the rest of the community.[37] Official records, at least until 1810, preserved the ethnic categories into which the population was divided, in order to distinguish the tribute-paying elements from those which did not pay tribute. This capitation tax marked out the conquered from the conquerors. Even so, the majority of the Mexican population was racially and culturally mixed (*mestizo*) by 1810. For the most part it was in the central and southern zones, where Indians had predominated in the Conquest period, that this component of the population preserved its distinct identity. Elsewhere, the three primary races, Europeans, Indians and Africans, merged with considerable rapidity to form a composite population by the end of the colonial period. Cook and Borah estimate that mixed racial types constituted half the total population at that time. The *mestizo* population did not pay the capitation tax required of the conquered race. Free negroes and mulattos were eligible to pay tribute, though slaves did not.[38] In practice, a large proportion had gained exemption through service in the militias of the Gulf and Pacific coasts.[39]

The preservation of these ethnic and caste distinctions exacerbated the social tensions of the late colonial period by adding a racial dimension. The Wars of Independence produced an explosion of such racial hatreds and fears. A great deal of bloodshed resulted. No other generation but that which lived through the experience of the 1810s had experienced such repeated horrors. The archival documentation abundantly reflects it. It is a major historical task, however, to account for the outburst of violence on such a scale. Central to any explanation of its occurrence is an understanding of the provocative power of social and racial disdain. No amount of meticulous quantitative methodology can elucidate such an intangible, yet all-pervasive factor. The disdain expressed very frequently by the dominant castes or *'gente de razón'* towards those described as *'los naturales'*, *'los indios'*, and *'los castas'*, was real enough. Disdain, of course, was implicit in the very term, 'Indian', a misnomer applied from the time of the Conquest to describe the American inhabitants encountered and subdued in stages by the Spaniards. Given the adoption of this term by the colonial judicial system and the persistent administrative use of the term 'Indies', it was not long before the subdued peoples began to refer to themselves by this combined term of abuse and legal classification. Indeed, it is difficult for historians to avoid using the term; it is so deeply ingrained in our entire historical thinking concerning the colonial and early national periods. Borah, Piel, Taylor and others have tried hard to rise above this perpetuation of the old pseudo-racial terminology by opting for the socio-economic description, peasant.[40] Yet this, also, presents difficulties in view of the complex social stratification within the 'Indian' caste, 'Indian' legal prerogatives under the *ancien régime* judicial system, and, not least of course, the distinct colonial and ethnic experience of the Mexican 'peasant', in relation, say, to the French or Italian peasant.

## Ideology and leadership

Racial and social resentments acquired a religious hue in the outbreak of the insurrection of September 1810 in the Bajío, led by the dissident American priest, Father Miguel Hidalgo. From 1803, Hidalgo, a former rector of the celebrated Valladolid College of San Nicolás Obispo, had been parish priest of Dolores on the fringes between the cereal plateau and the silver-mining communities of the Guanajuato sierra.

Hidalgo was a typical representative of the Mexican professional classes, a group we may conveniently refer to as the 'provincial bourgeoisie'. The bureaucratic revival of the Spanish absolutist state after c. 1770 and the increasing monopolisation of senior offices in Church and State by incoming *peninsulares* antagonised and frustrated the colonial professional classes. In the jobs trauma of late Bourbon Mexico lay the origin of the political dissidence of the 'provincial bourgeoisie' and, ultimately, of their readiness to inflame lower-class discontent against the Europeans. The leaders of the conspiracies of 1809–10 and of the insurrection of September 1810 all came from this social group. Hidalgo's intellectual interests were as broad-ranging as his social contacts. His ideas owed a great deal to the philosophical and educational reforms of the Mexican Enlightenment. In particular, he had been influenced by the Mexican Jesuit scholar, Francisco Javier Clavijero, like whom he was to acquire a knowledge of such Indian languages as Otomí and Nahuatl. Although a 'modernist' in his reaction to the neo-scholastic tradition in Mexico, inherited from the Spanish Counter-Reformation, Clavijero had become interested in the history of the apparition of the Virgin of Guadalupe. In 1532, the Virgin Mary had appeared to an Indian on the hill of Tepayac, the site of an Aztec shrine to Tonantzin, the moon goddess. The fact of the apparition demonstrated that the inhabitants of the Americas did not depend exclusively upon the Spanish Conquerors for their relationship to the divine. The tradition of Guadalupe, as it developed in the later seventeenth and eighteenth centuries, contributed subtly to the undermining of the moral basis of Spanish rule. Clavijero, furthermore, derived many of his ideas from the early Franciscan friars, who in the 1520s had brought to Mexico the ascetic ideals of the late medieval Observants, heirs of the Spirituals. To them, the conquest of the Americas had provided an opportunity to found an American version of the Apostolic Church. This ideal of a purified American Church, freed from the corruptions of Europe, appealed greatly to the clerical leadership of the 1810 rebellion.[41]

The Franciscans, however, had always viewed the Aztec associations of the cult of Guadalupe with suspicion. Nevertheless, they had propagated other Marian cults in Mexico by taking the image of the *Purísima Concepción* to Zapopan, near Guadalajara, and to San Juan de los Lagos, which became the poles of attraction for the cult of the Immaculate Conception. They had also sponsored the cult of Our Lady of Ocotlán, venerated at a hill-top basilica outside Tlaxcala. There were, in other words, several important cults of the Virgin in New Spain. The Peruvian Jesuit historian, Rubén Vargas Ugarte, in fact, described Mexico as '*tierra mariana*', and cities such as Querétaro, Celaya, Lagos, Guanajuato, Guadalajara, San Luis Potosí and Zacatecas – all centres of upheavals in 1810–11 – had profound Marian associations. They were, it should be stressed, the cultural heartlands of *mestizo* Mexico.[42] It was the seventeenth-century savant, Carlos Sigüenza y Góngora, who developed the neo-Aztec features of the Guadalupe cult. Clavijero, among others, took these ideas further. He not only regarded Indian civilisation as the 'classical antiquity' of Mexico, but argued that the Spanish Conquest had debased it. Such neo-Aztec tendencies were, however, confined to no more than a small group of Mexican intellectuals, who, since there was no social danger of an Indian revanche, chose to identify themselves with the pre-Hispanic past. This, they regarded, nevertheless, as an authentic American experience, to which they contrasted the European colonial imposition. The cult of Guadalupe came to epitomise the continuity of this experience through the colonial period.[43]

The educational developments in eighteenth-century Mexico, which are well known, were significant in that they expressed changing cultural attitudes among the élites. Their political importance, however, remains unclear. Bernabé Navarro regards the period, 1750–90, as 'the beginnings of a national and specifically Mexican consciousness, both in philosophy and in the arts, a development which soon prepared the ground for social and political consequences'.[44] It is difficult, however, to determine at what points such social and political elements became articulated. Conceivably, the literary polemic concerning the relative merits of America and Europe helped to raise consciousness. We lack, however, individual statements that can help us to transpose these cultural positions to the political plane. In the meantime, it is important to draw attention to two major objections to any assumption that American intellectual development automatically led to hostility to Spanish rule. In the first place, the 'modernising' of Mexican intellectual life took place, in general, with the enthusiastic co-operation of the viceregal authorities. González Casanova has pointed out that, while 'modernism' operated independently of the Spanish colonial state, the authorities, nevertheless, actively fostered it through support for new educational foundations and chairs. The opening of the *Colegio de Minería* in 1792 was a case in point. Since a parallel reform was going on at the same time in Spain itself, it is difficult to portray educational reform as necessarily revolutionary in content or intent. One of the insurgent leaders of 1810, for instance, studied philosophy in San Miguel from the texts prepared by the Oratorian, Benito Díaz de Gamarra. This fact demonstrated neither that the latter's works led to revolution, nor that Juan de Aldama became a revolutionary because he studied them.[45]

It is difficult, moreover, to portray the cult of Guadalupe as heterodox or subversive in itself. This cult had full papal sanction: Pope Benedict XIV in 1754 had designated the Virgin of Guadalupe to be Patroness of New Spain. Too much has been made of the supposed rivalry between a *mestizo* cult of Guadalupe and a Spanish *Virgen de los Remedios*. It is true that Viceroy Francisco Venegas responded to the revolutionaries' adoption of the banner of Guadalupe in 1810 by placing the Virgin of the Remedies at the head of the Royalist cause. Nevertheless, Viceroy the Conde del Venadito, in September 1819, invoked the assistance of the Virgin of Guadalupe during the dangerous swelling of the waters of Lakes Texcoco and San Cristóbal. Rather than a political attempt to appropriate an insurgent symbol, this invocation of Guadalupe probably represented no more than the unbroken continuity of Marian appeals in times of imminent natural disaster. Victor and Edith Turner argue that a distinction did, however, exist between the two cults, though it was one of emphasis. *Remedios* reflected the devotional patterns of the institutional Church; Guadalupe those of the general body of faithful.[46]

Hidalgo's invocation of the Virgin Mary – Guadalupe, as it happened – occurred at the peak of a two-year dearth. This compounded in the short term the long-term effects of the deterioration of lower-class living standards, particularly in the Bajío. Whether Hidalgo consciously had the natural calamity in mind remains unclear. Even so, it is useful to bear in mind the profoundly ingrained responses to natural disasters in the form of appeals to supernatural agencies. In September 1810, when food shortages were extreme, the Marian appeal brought together a powerful combination of elements, both social and psychological. For Jacques Lafaye, the insurrection of 1810 becomes, in that light, 'a messianic movement of spiritual, political and social liberation', a dramatic response to the colonial situation.[47] Perhaps the most striking feature of the Hidalgo movement was its extraordinary capacity for mobilisation. In subsequent chapters of this present work, we shall examine this problem and draw attention to the elaborate network of recruitment developed by the early revolutionary leadership. The rapid appearance of large numbers in support of Hidalgo, a popular local figure, has tended to obscure these relationships. It seems, however, that once Hidalgo had taken the banner of Guadalupe from the Shrine of Atotonilco and placed it at the head of his forces, the dissident priest became transformed into a revolutionary–prophet in the leadership of a Marian crusade, the chosen person to whom the Mother of God communicated.

Hidalgo formed part of a small conspiratorial circle which met in Querétaro and included a number of junior militia officers, such as Captain Ignacio Allende, and none other than the district administrator himself, Miguel Domínguez. The object was the removal of Spanish peninsular rule and the creation of some form of American state. The conspirators, unsure of support from the armed forces, had decided to launch a revolutionary movement during the two weeks of the San Juan de los Lagos Fair, between 1 and 15 December. This was the town in which the Virgin of Candlemas had performed a celebrated miracle in

1623. Fervent devotion to the cult of *Candelaria*, accordingly, accompanied the fair, which normally attracted thousands of people. Hugh Hamill observes that 'the religious factor could have been called on to play a sanctifying, if not dominant, role in the initial stage of the insurrection. With the eloquent priest Hidalgo suddenly taking advantage of the aroused emotions of the worshippers before the image of the Virgin, it would have been an easy matter to incite them to seize the Spanish merchants and their goods. The revolutionary army could have been constituted on the spot and the campaign, with the aura of a religious crusade, might have proceeded to an overwhelming victory over the *gachupines*.' At the head of this movement, of course, would have been *Candelaria*, rather than Guadalupe. The discovery of the Querétaro conspiracy aborted this attempt, and Hidalgo took the decision to launch the revolution on the night of 16 September in his parish of Dolores. It was that precipitate action which led to the adoption of the banner of Guadalupe.[48]

According to the revolutionary leadership, the peninsular-born ecclesiastical hierarchy by its condemnation of the insurrection had deserted the Mexican Church. They saw no role for a hierarchy of foreign origin, an integral part of the colonial structure of control. By placing the cult of Guadalupe in the forefront of his movement, Hidalgo laid claim to the monopoly of legitimacy and orthodoxy previously held by the Bourbon régime.[49] Apart from a curious regional rebellion in the Tulancingo area in 1769, Guadalupe had not before proved to be a rallying cry of revolt.[50] Religious questions as such, however, had given rise to rebellions of limited duration in the provinces – and were to do so again, but until 1810, they had never led to movements that could be described as general or national. The popular rebellions in San Luis de la Paz and San Luis Potosí in 1767 in response to the Bourbon government's peremptory expulsion of the Mexican Jesuits had similarly not led to a generalised revolt. In this sense, the insurrection of 1810 represented a unique phenomenon.[51] Hidalgo struck within the Christian community at the Spanish peninsular conception of the Church in America. Although he condemned the episcopate, he did not attack episcopacy itself. His aim was to free the American Church from Spanish tutelage and, by doing so, to release the American peoples from bondage to European colonialism. Hidalgo's response to episcopal excommunication was to attack the *gachupín* worship of money, and early in December 1810, to defend, in Guadalajara, his own Catholic orthodoxy.[52]

Hidalgo's political aims, however, remained ill-defined in practical terms. Since the initial insurrection was defeated by the Royalist Army within six months of its outbreak, it is likely that in this short space of time, taken up by campaign, defeat and flight, the revolutionary leadership were unable to work out any clear political programme. As a result, much of the early criticism of the Hidalgo movement focussed on its religious symbolism and undisciplined character. Later historians also adopted this view. Lucas Alamán, for instance, focussed on the atrocious massacre of the Royalist defenders of the Guanajuato Granary on 24 September 1810, which caused many propertied Americans to oppose the insurrection. Lorenzo de Zavala, commenting on the lack of clear political aims, suggested that 'theocracy would have been more congenial to Hidalgo', than the regalism of the Bourbon state. Francisco Bulnes saw little in the Hidalgo revolt but the upsurge of religious fanaticism: the 'insurgent horde can be compared to the Mahdi's horde in the Sudan in 1881'.[53] The *Guadalupanismo* of 1810 continued in the forefront for several years, but it diminished in intensity, in proportion to the disintegration of the revolutionary movement into the warring bands of an insurgency, and, conversely, to the emergence of a civilian leadership of lawyers behind José María Morelos, the second clerical leader, during the period, 1812–14. Although Morelos frequently demonstrated his Marian fervour, the official leadership began to work out constitutional alternatives to viceregal absolutism for the first time. In his *Sentimientos a la nación*, on 21 November 1813, Morelos himself proposed a constitutional law to establish the date of the apparition, 12 December, as a national celebration in honour of 'the Patroness of our liberty, the Most Holy Mary of Guadalupe'. When the insurgent leaders began the formation of a political organisation of the remote areas under their control, Morelos bestowed upon the newly created Province of Tecpan the designation *Tecpan de Nuestra Señora de Guadalupe*. The official seal of the insurgent Congress of Chilpancingo, which opened in September 1813, bore the Guadalupe monogram.[54]

The religious aspect of the Hidalgo movement possibly provided a unifying ideology capable of attracting the large numbers of people drawn from disparate groups in society, each with its own grievances. Never before had fragmented local conflicts come together with an underlying motif. The legitimist claims of the priestly leadership, moreover, threatened the entire moral basis of colonial rule. The mobilisation of aggrieved social groups threatened the internal colonial structure as well, and, accordingly, contributed to a counter-mobilisation, a realignment behind the Royalist cause. While the religious element provided an initial momentum, it could not give the movement a lasting organisation. The rapid loss of momentum and the regional fragmentation of the revolutionary movement explained how the insurrection of 1810–11 became the insurgency of 1811–21.

## The breadth of discontent

Doris Ladd has argued that the Hidalgo rising split the movement for Mexican self-government, a view which derives from Alamán and Mora.[55] It is tempting to argue that the revolutionary attempt in 1810 delayed the attainment of Mexican independence until September 1821. Such a view, however, underestimates the impact of the *gachupín coup d'état* in September 1808, which abruptly extinguished the brief experiment in autonomy, that constituted the response of the Mexican élite to the collapse of Bourbon Spain before Napoleon's armies. Important as the Mexican revolutionary movement was, then, it formed, nevertheless, but one aspect of a broad-ranging pressure for self-government. This was, for the most part, conceived still within the Spanish imperial structure and under the Bourbon monarchy. The 'Mexican or resident élite' hoped to share power at the centre and did not under any circumstances look to either a political or social revolution as the means of achieving this end. Still less did members of this group at the apex of colonial society envisage cooperation with discontented lower class groups in any common nationalist movement. Given the intimate financial and family connections that resulted from the investment of mercantile capital in land and silver-mining, agrarian entrepreneurs had become scarcely distinguishable in terms of economic activities and social status from the merchant–investors themselves. Together they constituted one social group, which is best referred to as the 'Mexican or resident élite'. It was distinguishable from the other two groups in the senior positions in the Mexican social hierarchy, the 'bureaucratic élite' and the 'provincial bourgeoisie'. The resident élite was neither exclusively a nobility nor a bourgeoisie, but a hybrid of both. The term, moreover, does not signify geographical provenance: this group had always contained both resident Europeans and native-born Americans. The former were not transient nabobs but were deeply rooted in New Spain by virtue of their financial, professional and matrimonial commitments. We should, therefore, distinguish them from the peninsular civil servants, senior magistrates, bishops, senior army officers, and members of the viceregal entourage, who expected either to return to Spain or to be transferred to employment elsewhere in the empire. Members of the 'Mexican or resident élite' included such

prominent, ennobled families as the Fagoagas, who had made their
fortune in the silver mines of Zacatecas, the Gándara family of San Luis
Potosí, who owned the Hacienda de Bledos and who derived their
wealth from mining operations at Catorce, the Marqueses de Aguayo,
who possessed enormous livestock estates in Coahuila, and the Condes
de la Valenciana, who had enriched themselves through the Guanajuato
mines. From this resident élite came the principal challenge to
absolutist government during the period from c. 1770 which culminated in its abortive bid for autonomy in July–September 1808.
Americans throughout the Empire had argued that their territories were
not colonies of Spain, but were kingdoms in their own right, equal in
status to Castile and Aragon, and associated within them by virtue of
their common sovereign. Since New Spain, for instance, was an
authentic constitutional entity, it was no more legitimate for Spaniards
to monopolise political power in Mexico than it would have been for
Mexicans to have done likewise in Spain. The American élites' demands
for equality of employment in the bureaucratic organisms of New Spain
grew in proportion to the Spanish Bourbon government's attempts to
reassert full peninsular control in the Americas after the 1760s and
divert American wealth into the Spanish economy following what
amounted to more than a century of *de facto* American autonomy. The
irritation felt among the American élites at exclusion from the process of
decision-making came to a head in the 1800s at a time when Bourbon
Spain was at its weakest, in view of the European situation. The
Napoleonic invasion of Spain in 1808 disorientated peninsular government in the Americas and provided the opportunity for the American
élites to recover the political initiative. Spain, therefore, became
confronted with movements of various types on many fronts and in rapid
succession.[56]

An essential factor to appreciate is that any alteration in the
relationship of the American territories to the metropolis required a
constitutional change within these component kingdoms of the empire.
The pressure for autonomy implied a departure from absolutism in
favour of some kind of nobiliar or corporate constitutionalism which
would preserve the gains of the élites as a permanent feature of American
political life. Though there was nothing incompatible in this with the
survival of the peninsular position in economic life or at the political
centre as a component part of the new structure, autonomy did threaten
to deprive the colonial bureaucracy of its hegemony. Fear that home rule
amounted to the 'thin end of the wedge' of outright separatism led to
the swift *coup d'état* by senior magistrates and Mexico City merchants on

15–16 September 1808 to remove Viceroy José de Iturrigaray, who had shown sympathy to the autonomist position.[57] The coup, however, incensed the country against the *gachupines*, particularly the clique in Mexico City which had brutally kicked aside the experiment in home rule. The élites in Mexico City were deprived of the opportunity to guide the viceroyalty towards peaceful home rule. For a time they remained without direction. The conspiracies of 1809 and 1810 formed the response of the frustrated provincial professional classes to the *gachupín* coup. Out of the Querétaro conspiracy came, as we have seen, the insurrection of 1810. This revolutionary attempt obliged the American élites to decide whether to support it or not.[58] Most either temporised or tactically aligned with the viceregal government to form a Royalist coalition.[59] Nevertheless, a broad span of support stayed with the insurgents. This did not necessarily imply active participation in the armed conflict. Discontent affected most groups in regions affected by insurgency, from the American propertied élites across the social spectrum. High on the list of American grievances was the role of the Spanish peninsular merchant–investors and governing groups. Americans complained of haughty Spanish behaviour and opulent styles of life, the draining of American natural wealth, the shortage of specie and goods, high prices, profiteering and speculation.[60]

Central to any proper understanding of the question of self-government in the Americas is an appreciation that in the imperial context any movement in that direction within the viceroyalties required as the prerequisite a parallel change in the political system of Spain itself. The collapse of Bourbon absolutism in 1808 made such a change possible. When, however, the Spanish Imperial Cortes in Cádiz produced the Constitution of 1812, there was no concession whatever to the principle of American autonomy.[61] The élites, accordingly, found themselves caught between the rising militarism of the Royalist camp and the unruly insurgent bands. Once more they were unsure of their direction. Many individuals who had supported the autonomist position in 1808 co-operated in the establishment of Cádiz constitutionalism in Mexico between 1810 and 1814, in order to modify peninsular absolutism. Mexican representation in the Spanish Cortes enabled deputies to criticise the viceregal régime in Mexico City. To insurgent fury, Spain appeared to offer Americans political representation and a voice in the decision-making processes. This, however, while it may have contributed to élite aloofness from the separatist insurgency, nevertheless, depended largely upon viceregal and military consent for any practical efficacy it might have within the viceroyalty. Conspiracies in the

Royalist zone and the activities of the secret society of the *Guadalupes* sought to alter the complexion of the régime. Elections under the Constitution in 1812–14 produced creole victories and viceregal embarrassment. The American victory in Mexico City in 1812 led to Viceroy Venegas' annulment of the municipal elections and the reimposition of press censorship. Ferdinand VII's nullification of the Constitution in May 1814, the dissolution of the Cortes, and the confinement of leading constitutionalists, ended this brief experiment with liberal representative precepts. The American élites were once more thrust into the political wilderness – at a time when a fragmented and a degenerating insurgency offered little alternative prospect.[62]

In efect, the political initiative in Mexico had passed to the Royalist military commanders in the regions, who, under the drastic impact of insurgency, had been obliged to organise a counter-insurgency response, in order to survive. In this development, they anticipated, in one form or another, many of the forms of warfare that have subsequently become identified with characteristic counter-insurgency techniques.[63] The role of the Mexican military has come under recent scrutiny in the literature of the late colonial period.[64] Problems of imperial defence led the Bourbon government in the late 1760s to opt for a policy of stationing regular peninsular units in the empire and of raising militia forces within the colonies. Until the 1770s, colonial Spanish America had been decidedly unmilitary. The initial defence policies proved to be expensive failures. There were few, if any, promotion prospects in the American armies, and the absence of retirement and pension plans meant that elderly and infirm officers remained in position beyond their capacity to serve effectively. Such a situation undermined discipline. The armed forces of New Spain, moreover, contained many idlers and malcontents. Accordingly, the Bourbon government hoped to remedy the problem by recruiting more Americans. This revived the old antagonism between creoles and *peninsulares*, which involved not only racial slurs by the latter against the former, but the usual Spanish desire to monopolise the senior positions. Christon Archer describes how such rivalries threatened to paralyse whole regiments, and, indeed, to compromise political control of provinces at the highest levels.[65]

Viceroy the Marqués de Branciforte (1794–8) made a point of courting the Mexican élites, and encouraged the exchange of donations for provincial militia commissions and privileges. By such procedures, he managed to produce enough officers to command the expanded militia. The new American officers saw active service for the first time in the cantonment of Veracruz in 1796–8, during the war against Great Britain. Such officers, however, were also businessmen with families, and departed from time to time, in order to attend to these other commitments. A second cantonment in the Jalapa region in 1804–8 filled them with little enthusiasm, and they avoided active duty whenever they could. This did not bode well for the general condition of the royal armed forces in New Spain on the eve of the events of 1808–10.[66]

Although some army officers chafed at civilian administrative intervention in military affairs, even before 1810, the army was contained within a civil framework in the period before the outbreak of the Hidalgo insurrection.[67]

The colonial military had anticipated neither the insurrection of 1810, nor the insurgency that grew from it. The armed forces had been brought into existence, in order to combat a supposed British invasion, and they were unprepared for an internal uprising on the fertile, centre-north plateau. At the moment of insurrection, the central government in Mexico City was in disarray; most of the field marshals and brigadiers had reached an advanced age, and experienced officers remained in short supply. The usual American–European tensions were henceforth compounded by a popular insurrection directed primarily against the Europeans. Such disorganisation thwarted any possibility of a rapid and coherent response by the military to the Hidalgo rising. As a result, support for the insurrection spread with alarming speed, leaving European merchant–investors, property-owners, and civil servants isolated from immediate prospect of assistance.[68]

# 1

## Social tensions in the provinces

A profounder meaning of events lies perhaps beneath the ideological superstructure of a movement of Independence. To discover this meaning we must examine attitudes and alignments at the provincial level. The provinces of Puebla, Guadalajara, Michoacán and Guanajuato clearly illustrate the uneven development of Mexico in the late colonial and early national period. With their regional and sub-regional variations, these provinces provide a feasible basis for comparison and contrast. Furthermore, each of them, at one stage or another, became a major theatre of operations during the War of Independence between 1810 and 1821. When it becomes appropriate to do so, in order to develop the themes that are central to the book, case instances from a number of other, usually contiguous, provinces, namely San Luis Potosí, Zacatecas, Veracruz and Oaxaca, will be given. In view of this strictly provincial approach to the late colonial and independence period, attention will not focus here upon the national level of policial economic life.[1] The intention is to examine certain specific themes, which are essential for a proper comprehension of the Independence movement as an expression of regional social tensions. Where documentary evidence permits, the discussion will move beyond the 'Mexican or resident' élite of merchant–investors, mine-operators, municipal councillors and landowners and the 'provincial bourgeoisie' of lawyers, clerics, intellectuals, writers, doctors, to the social strata beneath them. These were by no means homogeneous and in terms of social stratification are often difficult to place. Where exactly we place shopkeepers in the social structure is a virtually irresolvable problem, since this frequently neglected occupational group contained a broad spectrum all of its own. Shopkeepers at the top level were directly connected in terms of finance and management with the great merchants of the region. At their lower levels, they spanned such distinct categories as the recently arrived Basque trader or the small town dealer with his predominantly

24

poor clientele. Debt is the key to any comprehension of the general odium reserved for shopkeepers of all descriptions. In the countryside rural middle sectors also existed beneath or connected with the principal estate owners. Such groups would be the *rancheros* or smaller proprietors, hacienda-lessees, hacienda-administrators, peasant proprietors, and so on. Certain groups, which played an important role in the events of this period, have received little comment to date in the historical literature – artisans, urban workers, are cases in point. With regard to economic class, any attempt to categorise artisans presents innumerable difficulties. They did not constitute a proletariat: still less, did they consider themselves to be such. Nor can we describe mine-workers as a proletariat. They considered themselves to be, in effect, participants in the ownership of the mines they operated, and regarded the share-out (*partido*) of ore among them, as evidence of this special status. Efforts to reduce or abolish this privilege as in 1766, the 1790s, 1800s or, later, in 1827 produced conflict in the mining zones.[2] Similarly, the muleteer is difficult to place in any scheme of social structure based exclusively on economic position, in view of the considerable stratification that existed within this group. Many muleteers played a major role in the insurgency of the 1810s. Sometimes entire villages specialised in the mule-transit trade, and evidence exists in some of them – such as Justlahuaca (Oaxaca) and Huichapan (Hidalgo) – for collective participation in the revolt. The role of the lesser insurgent leaders, the muleteer-commander, the local caciques, bandit groups, and so on, is still a subject in its infancy.

In the era before the modernisation of the infrastructure, a significant medium of inter-provincial contact was the muletrain. In Ramón Serrera's study of late colonial Guadalajara, muletrain routes are seen as the vertebrae of communications and transportation within the viceroyalty. During the second half of the eighteenth century they extended over much of New Spain, in response to the expansion of commercial activities. The mule routes were particularly important in view of the absence of any internal river network of navigation. Not only professional muleteers, but also peasant and artisan traders, and seasonally employed farm workers travelled these routes in pursuit of their livelihood. Serrera estimates that in the Guadalajara region in the early nineteenth century some 10–11,000 individuals earned their living on the roads as muleteers or carters. Those of Aguascalientes and Lagos supplied the Zacatecas mining zone.[3] Morin points out that in Michoacán muleteers sometimes worked on behalf of a merchant-supplier. Spanish merchants, for instance, owned the eighty or so mulepacks that Victorino Jaso operated from Tangancícuaro in the northern trade. Mule proprietors of Zamora purchased sugar and transported it for sale in Guanajuato, Guadalajara and Zacatecas. The muleteers of Uruapan collected the cotton crop from the Pacific coast direct from the producers in return for basic essentials, on behalf of a few merchant–investors.[4] Such mercantile activities and muleteer contacts provided the links which brought the component territories of the viceroyalty more closely together.

## Merchant–investors and shopkeepers

In the cotton zones of Michoacán, in those of Veracruz, and in the districts of Puebla and Oaxaca local administrators operated *repartimientos de comercio*, with advance financing supplied by the merchants, to whom the crop was mortgaged. These practices bound the cultivators to the merchant–investor, and, in this way, incorporated them into the market economy. A profoundly important issue that forms a connecting thread right throughout this book, then, is the role of the merchant–investor. The expansion of mercantile connections and interests, coupled with the impact of mercantile finance in the localities beyond the provincial capital cities, is a striking phenomenon, perhaps the most significant of all, in eighteenth and early nineteenth-century Mexico. The connection between credit and personal relationships appears at virtually every juncture. In the Puebla district of Zacatlán, for instance, outside finance continued to be a major means by which travelling salesmen conducted their trades. One such merchant, Manuel González de la Sierra, claimed in 1804, to have paid the sum of 6,000 pesos to one sole individual in credits owing as a result of such practices. This person was probably a merchant–investor of Puebla, Mexico City, or Veracruz. Recession in the local trades, however, threatened to oblige González to renege, since, unable either to sell his products or to collect his debts, he was faced with bankruptcy. Although his financial backers knew of his circumstances, one of them, a merchant from Tulancingo, had already tried to levy interest. Since González' current debts totalled 4,050 pesos, he was requesting a moratorium.[5]

Both merchants and shopkeepers supplied credit in one form or another, and, accordingly, each group had its network of indebted dependents. The orbit of credit oscillated outwards from the capital cities in an ever increasing spatial dimension.[6] Merchants not only supplied credit to their fellows, but also to mine operators. They soon became partners in mining companies themselves, purchased landed estates and founded noble houses. They financed the cultivation and supply of raw materials, such as cotton on the Pacific or Gulf coasts, and the scarlet cochineal dye of the Mixteca villages of Oaxaca. Their method of operation was through the mediation of the local district administrators, the *alcaldes mayores*, who, thereby, entered their circle of credit and mutual interest. Merchants similarly intervened in the supply of raw materials and distribution of finished products of the textile industries, be they *obraje* or artisan in organisation of production. By virtue of this intermediate function they were described as *rescatadores* in the mining industry and *regatones* in the textile sector: in the latter particularly they were often hated middlemen. The role of the merchants and their dependents became a central issue in late colonial Mexico. It is perhaps the issue that caused the most social unrest, a symptom of the dislocation that resulted from this developing capitalism of the period up to the mid-1800s. It is important to study local reactions to the encroachments of profit-conscious investors, whether they invested in land, the mines or the textile trades in this period. Such an examination will help us to understand why the merchant–investor, and, of course, his lesser shadow, the shopkeeper, were the focus of such intense hostility by 1810. At its outset, the insurgency of September 1810 signified first and foremost an assault upon the merchant–investor and the shopkeeper at the popular level. The loss of investments and the withdrawal of considerable capital that resulted from this violent attack during the 1810s contributed seriously to Mexico's economic problems as a sovereign state during the 1820s and 1830s. Although this did not occur throughout Mexico, the blow inflicted upon the investors, followed as it was by political independence in 1821, the Spanish blockade of Veracruz from the fortress of San Juan de Ulúa, and, finally by the effort of Vicente Guerrero's administration to expel remaining Spaniards in 1829, took a drastic toll of business confidence. Foreign competition, particularly in the textile trades, material damage, interrupted communication and transit routes, government and private indebtedness, severely hampered economic recovery after the 1820s.

The violent assault on the merchants and shopkeepers can be seen readily in almost all the regions in which the popular insurgency of the 1810s became important. This was clearly evident in many localities in the Guadalajara region and in the city itself. Important and populous towns existed throughout the Guadalajara region, particularly in the lake basins of Chapala, Zacoalco and Sayula, and in the Altos. In the former zone agricultural, livestock and craft towns such as Sayula, the leading town, Zacoalco, Zapotlán el Grande, Chapala, Tonalá,

Jocotepec, Zapotiltic and La Barca, expanded in the course of the eighteenth century. Before the Spanish Conquest most such towns had participated in the broad and diverse *Confederación Chimalhuacana*, a conglomeration of monarchies, lordships and chieftaincies, with a variety of languages, such as Otomí, Huichol, Tarascan and Nahuátl, which extended from the western Pacific coast northwards into Zacatecas and Aguascalientes. Sayula and Zapotlán, for instance, had been two feudatory states of the powerful Coliman monarchy further to the south.[7] By the later eighteenth century Sayula was renowned for its leatherwork and for its textile production in which it was exceeded only by Guadalajara itself, while Zacoalco had become celebrated for its shoe-making.[8] During the course of 1796 the Consulado of Guadalajara established a deputation in Sayula, a reflection of the town's hegemony over the southern sub-region as industrial, commercial and administrative centre. Twelve shops there distributed not only Mexican but also Castilian and Chinese products.[9] Olveda highlights the changing relationship between the towns of Sayula and Zapotlán from the late eighteenth to the mid nineteenth century, by which time the latter superseded the former in importance. Sayula derived its wealth primarily from industry and trade, while Zapotlán, primarily an agricultural area, supplied Guadalajara and the mining centres of Zacatecas and Bolaños with maize and sugar-cane. A fundamental problem in Sayula lay in the saltiness of the lakeside soil, which left large tracts of land uncultivable.[10] Zapotlán and other districts with 'Indian' majorities produced predominantly maize. They did not, however, specialise in wheat cultivation for the rapidly growing urban market of Guadalajara. Van Young draws attention to the pressure of urban demand for wheat upon the rural maize economy. In view of the growth of population in the countryside, there were already land shortages in the southern villages after the 1780s and no longer a maize surplus in many of them.[11] The lake basin towns played a major role in the insurgency of 1810–13 in the central zone of Guadalajara. Insurgent depredations combined with the flight of capital to produce the long depression of Sayula's trades.

Perhaps the most significant development in the later eighteenth century was the penetration of mercantile capital and personnel into the district towns. Shops and warehouses in the lake basin towns and in mining centres such as Etzatlán were connected with the Guadalajara city houses. District administrators often tended to co-operate with local and urban mercantile interests. A number of Guadalajara merchants owned shops both in the city itself, in the plateau towns, and in the mining districts of Bolaños, Rosario and Etzatlán. Manuel de Olmos, for instance, while not one of the greater merchants of Guadalajara, was, nevertheless, sufficiently well known to appear in the notarial documentation. Olmos owned a shop in Guadalajara's Calle de San Agustín during the 1790s. In partnership with Pascual Fernández Rubio, two other city merchants and a merchant of Zapotlán, Mateo de Garibi, Olmos between 1791 and 1794 ran another shop in the city trading in Mexican, Spanish and Chinese goods. Stock-taking revealed total assets to the value of 9,453 pesos. Garibi himself resided partly in Zapotlán and partly in Guadalajara, even though his personal interests lay in the former. In 1782 he had married Doña María Antonia López de Lara, a Zapotlán resident. In the town he operated in company with Gaspar Fernández de la Madrid. Their total capital, including the family house and personal valuables, came to 23,637 pesos.[12]

Several merchants had become heavily involved in mining districts. Mateo de la Torre, who had come from Cádiz, owned a shop in Etzatlán in the mid-1790s.[13] Salvador de Escobedo y Daza, born in Spain in 1738, was the brother of the hereditary city councillor of Guadalajara, Captain Francisco de Escobedo. The former's property assets totalled 23,600 pesos, part of which derived from his trading activities in Etzatlán, where he had been Administrator of the Tobacco Revenue since 1770 and Subdelegate during the 1790s. When Hidalgo's insurgent forces entered Guadalajara in December 1810 and were hunting for Spanish merchants in order to kill them, Escobedo begged the rebel leader to spare his life, on the grounds that he was a widower with two sons and fifteen grandchildren to maintain. His life was spared.[14] Like Escobedo, another Spanish merchant, Josef Sánchez Hidalgo, who originated from the Rioja region, lost everything invested in his shop in the same district when insurgent forces arrived there.[15] Similar cases of mercantile penetration of the districts could be seen in Sayula,[16] Rosario,[17] and elsewhere. Morin points equally to the importance of shopkeepers in Michoacán and to the controversy surrounding their activities. Particularly irksome was their practice of offering credit. The shortage of fractional currency, moreover, had led to the issue by shopkeepers of their own substitute copper, wood or soap currency, called *tlacos*, which they distributed to customers for sole use in their own particular shops. In this way many people fell into debt to the local merchant-shopkeeper, especially the poor in the small shops or *pulperías*, where *tlacos* would usually be employed. Many shopkeepers cheated on weight and size of their products, notably bread. The activities of merchant–shopkeepers aroused hostility in the localities and provided a major source of social tension. It seems likely that such factors provide explanations of insurgent support in the districts affected. Nevertheless, they were constant sources of popular grievance and continued after the insurgency had subsided. On 12 December 1828, for instance, a Puebla mob sacked the greater part of the trading firms' properties in the city with cries of '*Viva la Virgen de Guadalupe y mueran los españoles!*'[18]

### Landowners and villagers

Furthermore, landownership and land utilisation provided equally deep sources of friction in the Guadalajara localities, primarily as a result of the penetration of city-based private capital into the properties across the Valley of Atemajac and through the lake-basin zones of relatively dense population. Cereal-producing land commanded high values. In the district of Zapotlán, for instance, the value of the Haciendas of Contla, San Lázaro and Santa Gertrúdis came to more than 80,000 pesos. One of the town's wealthiest residents had even been prepared to pay 90,000 pesos for Contla alone.[19] Archival evidence reveals many cases of land disputes, occupations and evictions, but at the same time shows that conditions differed according to locality. In consequence, it was likely that responses to insurgency after 1810 would also differ, though it is difficult to determine in what way or for what reasons. Understandably, local tensions antedated the conflicts of the 1810s and outlived them, too. As a result, we should not see local tensions over land, water, or customary rights uniquely and exclusively in terms of causes of the insurgency. Insurgent action, it may be concluded, was one of several popular responses to local problems.

As we shall see in chapter three, one of the most long-lasting of the land disputes proved to be the case of Zacoalco and its associated villages. The origin of these disputes could be traced to the late seventeenth century, but population growth during the following century intensified the struggle for food-producing lands. These villages, moreover, showed a marked tendency towards insurgency support during the 1810s, a position which may well have derived from the tense situation in these localities during the previous decades. The land disputes originated from the expansion of the surrounding properties, which were owned by three of the most powerful families of Guadalajara – the Porres Baranda, Vizcarra, and Echaurri. These families possessed entailed estates of major importance in or alongside the principal wheat-producing zone of the central district. The *mayorazgo* (noble entail) of the Porres Baranda had been founded in 1692 and was based on the Hacienda de Mazatepec, situated to the north of the Zacoalco lands. The Vizcarra family had received the noble title of Marqueses de Pánuco from Charles III in 1772, the consequence of their fortune made in the silver mines of Rosario and Pánuco. The Pánuco entail consisted of the Hacienda de Estipac, situated north-west of Zacoalco, and the Hacienda de la Sauceda, purchased in 1781. The Echaurris had entailed their lands as a *vínculo* based upon the Hacienda de San Josef de Gracia, also situated near the Indian villages. The other Echaurri properties lay generally between the city of Guadalajara and the town of Cajititlán, a few miles north of Lake Chapala. They included the Haciendas de la Concepción, San Francisco Javier and San Juan Bautista, and the Hacienda del Cuatro in the Toluquilla Valley. Members of this family held municipal office in Guadalajara, and supplied the city with cereals.[20] The Echaurri family survived the insurgency to prosper once again in the later 1810s and during the 1820s as maize suppliers to the city's public granary. Captain José María de Echaurri of the urban militia sat on the city council in 1822 and 1823, along with José María Vizcarra and another cereal *hacendado*, Rafael Villaseñor. All three supported the Jalisco federalist movement during the summer of 1823.[21] The *mayorazgo* of the Porres Baranda, in default of a male succession, passed on the death of Bernardo María Porres Baranda Núñez de Villavicencio to Doña María Francisca, wife of Captain Luis Luyando, militia officer of the Provincial Regiment of Mexico City, a municipal councillor there, and himself the possessor of an entailed estate, the *mayorazgo* de Luyando. The Zacoalco land dispute at the end of the eighteenth century was principally with Doña María Francisca. Substantially, the Audiencia of New Galicia decided in the years before 1810 in favour of the Porres Baranda interest throughout the land case.[22]

Social relations between the villagers, private proprietors, district administrators, merchants, shopkeepers, and even priests had in notable instances turned sour by the end of the eighteenth century. In other land disputes besides those of Zacoalco, villagers received little satisfaction from the magistracy. Those of Jocotepec, for instance, received an unfavourable decision from the Audiencia on 22 November 1800 in their suit with the local proprietor, Manuel de Ibarra.[23] Villagers of Zapotlán complained in 1800 of the conduct of the district subdelegate with regard to alleged appropriations of tribute revenue and lands rented from the community.[24] In Ocotlán in the district of La Barca villagers protested in 1804 that the parish priest had administered corporal punishment to several of their number.[25] Competition for land

and resistance to fiscal pressures, moreover, led to frequent litigation between villages, a factor which may have influenced attitudes to insurgency after September 1810. Local hostilities over such issues among villagers themselves may have determined why some villages opted for insurgency and others for royalism, or for non-participation.[26]

The insurgent passage through the Guadalajara districts and the rising of several of the principal towns took a serious toll upon the Europeans who traded there. Merchants and shopkeepers who were caught in what, after November 1810, became the dangerous exposed outlying districts of Tepic, La Barca, Zapotlán el Grande, Sayula and Etzatlán, faced a hideous death at the hands of vengeful rebels. Many of the latter were local people who resented the social and economic effects of the penetration of mercantile capital into their localities. We shall discuss the insurgency in the region more fully in chapter seven, since our focus at present remains upon the merchants themselves. Ramírez Flores has compiled a long list of forty-eight names of Europeans who perished in these districts at insurgent hands during the winter of 1810–11. Some of them, such as José Zaval from Guipúzcoa, a shop employee in a Tepic business owned by the Guadalajara merchant, Ramón de Murua, were dependents of more important men. Others owned their own shops or worked together in partnerships. Fernando Fernandez, for instance, ran a shop in Sayula in company with Isidoro de la Fuente. He died in the unsuccessful attempt to keep the insurgent forces out of Zacoalco. His other partner, Toribio de la Torre, died there too, along with a further number of Sayula's peninsular merchants. Antonio Yanguas, from the Rioja province, managed a shop in Sayula owned by Bartolomé de la Fuente. The insurgents killed him as he tried to flee from the town with various items and sums of cash taken from his employer's shop. An Asturian, José Sendís, who traded in Mascota, was murdered by the insurgents on the road to the coast. A fellow Asturian, José de Mestas, who came from Llanos, resided and traded in Tepic, where the insurgents caught and killed him. They killed the Burgos immigrant, Santiago González, in Ahualulco, where he lived and traded. The Subdelegate of La Barca, Gabriel de Peón Valdés, another Spaniard, was killed while in flight to Guadalajara with his cash. They similarly killed the revenue-collector of Tepic, a native of Gijón, and the sales-tax administrator of Sayula, who came from Liébana in the Spanish province of León.[27] The brothers, Pedro and Narcisco Romero, who worked the silver mines in Etzatlán, escaped a savage death, but found themselves facing difficulties when the insurgent commander, the priest Mercado, seized 240 marks of their silver. Fortunately for them, the

Royalists recovered this amount when they reduced Mercado's position in San Blas. As the rebels advanced, the de la Fuentes of Sayula suffered badly. Isidoro de la Fuente, the aforementioned Spanish merchant of Guadalajara, deeply involved in the district's textile trade, survived the insurgency. However his nephew, José Isidoro, who worked in his uncle's Sayula shop and had come out from Liébana, was killed at the age of seventeen in the fateful struggle to prevent the main rebel force from seizing Zacoalco. Melchor de la Fuente, another Sayula merchant, had his throat cut by the insurgents.[28]

The high level of capital investment throughout the most significant sectors of the economy including the agricultural, affected almost all social groups. The impact, however, differed according to region, since the nature of economic activities was not uniform in terms of structure or stage of development. In many respects, the eighteenth-century expansion of New Spain further exacerbated these regional distinctions, since the dynamic regions, such as Guadalajara or Guanajuato, grew faster than the relatively backward areas, such as Puebla, Oaxaca or Tlaxcala. Puebla's performance had been impressive earlier in the century. A transition had taken place in the textile industry of the provincial capital from woollens to cottons after the 1740s. This process had been linked to mercantile capitalisation of the Pacific and Gulf coast cotton-producing zones.[29] The textile industry, however, appeared by the 1790s and 1800s to have lost its earlier momentum and passed into recession. The flour trade to the Caribbean also fell into decay, in face of increasing U.S. competition. Atlixco estate owners were complaining of the losses from the 1780s onwards.[30] Perhaps only the sugar economy in the southern districts of Izúcar (now generally known as Matamoros) and Cuautla remained buoyant.[31] The dye sector of Oaxaca had already begun to lose its earlier expansiveness after the 1780s, while the agrarian economy of the region remained largely stagnant throughout the nineteenth century.[32] The impact of the insurgency affected each region differently. In the Guanajuato mining zone, it combined with long term technological problems and short term weather hazards to produce a long recession that lasted at least until the 1840s. The Zacatecas zone, in contrast, experienced a renewed expansion in the 1820s and 1830s, in spite of insurgent depredations and the flight of Europeans in 1810–11.[33]

While it is certainly possible to speak of a developing capitalism in the period up to the mid-1800s, it would be unwise to assume that labour relations were uniformly transformed into those of patron–employee, or landowner–tenant, landlord–wage-labourer. No agricultural revolution and no industrial revolution took place in eighteenth or early nineteenth-century Mexico, such as was taking place at the parallel time in the British Isles. In Mexico no revolution took place in either agrarian or industrial labour relations. Nevertheless, important changes did take place, which resulted from the expansion of capital and credit, such as we have outlined. These were sufficient to produce vital reactions at the local level, depending, of course, upon their social context and the intensity of the social change induced. Perhaps the decisive element of tension in several regions was not primarily land but the pressures of indebtedness. In other areas, such as the central district of Guadalajara, land disputes abound in the archival documentation. The Zacoalco conflict is a case in point. In many instances across New Spain, argument over labour conditions, wage regulation and water rights complemented disputes over land-ownership. In this period, furthermore, we clearly encounter the social problem of incorporation into the market economy, albeit through the medium of the still primitive methods of credit. Debt as a means of social control and forcible economic integration into a colonial society dominated by merchant–investors presents itself as a predominant issue here.

In this sense a vital ambivalence exists right at the heart of the role of the merchant–investor. On the one hand, he is the archetypal representative of the Spanish colonial system with its characteristic corporative organisation, but, on the other hand, he is the arch-destroyer of the very customs and privileges upon which the *ancien régime*, of which he is an integral part, subsists. It would be correct to regard him as both reactionary and revolutionary at the same time. Much of the so-called 'Revolution' of Independence is, in any case, reacting precisely against his revolutionary impact.

## Artisans

The relationship between the merchant–investor and the artisan appears to have altered in the course of the eighteenth century. The predominant role of the former became increasingly evident, and it affected not only artisans located in towns and cities, but also those resident in rural areas as well. Both were subject to considerable commercial pressures, and the latter seem likely to have been in closer touch with urban influences than the peasants or estate labourers around them. A major issue that divided artisans in the cities continued to be their relationship to the traditional guild organisation that, in New Spain, dated frequently from the sixteenth century. The large number of artisans in many urban areas and their poor condition generally precluded membership of the often exclusive guilds. It seems clear that the merchant–investor of the later eighteenth century preferred, in any case, to operate outside the context of the guild structure. The guilds, moreover, scarcely affected the rural artisan, especially where cotton spinning and weaving remained largely the preserve of women in peasant villages. There, a common identity and attitude of peasant and artisan might be found. In larger country towns, peasants would come into contact with artisans whose services they might need. This interdependence between the two groups suggests the possibility of a common front to defend the rural community against outside influences, particularly those which threatened to disrupt the traditional way of life. The structure of manufacturing in the textile trades helped to explain the grouping of artisans in specific rural districts. Nevertheless, the growth of the cotton textile industry in the city of Puebla from the 1740s – a time of transatlantic warfare – encouraged a greater concentration of spinners and weavers in the urban area itself. The rise of Querétaro as a centre of woollen production in *obrajes* probably helped to explain the decline of Puebla and Tlaxcala as woollen producers. Mercantile capital, supplied by Mexico City or Veracruz importers frustrated by long delays and interruptions in the European trade, helped to build up the Puebla cotton textile industry from the start.[34]

We still know remarkably little concerning the artisans of colonial and nineteenth-century Mexico. Occasionally notarial and municipal archives reveal something of the mental outlook of the artisans. Although notarial archives deal primarily with the legal arrangements of patricians, a few prominent artisans did, on occasions, record their proceedings before a public notary. This in itself, suggests a broad stratification throughout the social group described as artisans and indicates that at its higher levels, the artisan approached the shopkeeper and the lesser merchant. Municipal archives deal extensively with guild examinations and ordinances, a reflection of the intimate relationship between city councils and guild organisations. From such sources we are able to glean information concerning the relationship between the guilds and those artisans conducting their business outside the ordinances. Later eighteenth and early nineteenth-century documentation consistently suggests that the latter practice had become a growing tendency. Equally important, is the fundamental issue of mercantile penetration of the artisan trades. This phenomenon, contemporaneous with similar examples of mercantile influence, has already occasioned comment in the sparse literature on the subject. Manuel Carrera Stampa has pointed to the increasing importance of merchant-suppliers and distributors in the guild trades from the later seventeenth century. Increasingly, the artisan and the workshop master, he argued, ceased to sell directly to the public. Producers began to hand over their merchandise to distributors, who, already engaged in other forms of commerce with the areas of consumption, employed agents to sell the textiles thus acquired to mining communities or to hacienda shops (*tiendas de raya*). Parallel to this process, merchant-monopolists tapped the areas of cotton production, chiefly through the mediation of royal district administrators. Monopoly of the supply of raw material gave the merchant a prevailing influence over producers by means of credit. Nevertheless, this restriction of the producers' freedom did not transform them into the salaried employees of a patron-employer. It contributed to the diminution of artisans' economic status, but it did not depress them into a proletariat.[35] Resentment of mercantile intervention seems to have raised political consciousness among artisans. The merchants' own view of their interests in the textile trade tended to become the determining factor. Reinhard Liehr argues for a general decay of the guilds in Puebla in the early nineteenth century and for the existence of much production outside them.[36] Merchants might supply the capital, but they did not employ the weavers. Potash has put forward the view that, although guild ordinances forbade possession of looms by anyone not a qualified weaver, proof exists that merchants would provide financial assistance to weavers operating in their own homes beyond the vigilance of master weavers. According to Potash, some twenty-eight cloth warehouses existed in the city of Puebla, into which went the greater part of the produce of the 1,200 looms of Puebla and those of Cholula, Tlaxcala and Huejotzingo, their cloth handed over by the weavers to the merchants' commissioners.[37] The role of the merchant–investor appears in most, if not all, the textile and raw material zones. These evident capitalist elements, as we have said, had not advanced to the stage of entrepreneurial employment of labour. The woollen *obraje* or workshop, moreover, frequently contained impressed or criminal labour, which could not be described as employee labour. Modes of production, then, were not universally identifiable as capitalist. On the contrary, the social relations of production for the most part continued to be pre-capitalist.[38]

The municipal councils provided ordinances for the guilds and oversaw their observance, subject on both accounts to the superior authority of the audiencia. The city of Puebla began to do so from 1548.

Entry into guilds remained restricted, in order to limit competition, a practice that simply encouraged production and sale outside the guild system. 'Purity of blood' qualifications, though still required in theory, tended to be ignored in practice. The silk weavers of Mexico City received their guild ordinances in October 1583, stipulating the nature and quality of the product. Fresh ordinances appeared in February 1584, which established that no one could pursue the trade without first serving a two-year apprenticeship followed by a further year as an operative in the work place of a matriculated guild master. Only after this could an artisan examined by the guild inspectors be granted, if found to be satisfactory, permission to practise. Puebla cloth weavers received guild ordinances in 1676, and Oaxaca cotton weavers in 1757.[39] City councils repeatedly re-examined guild ordinances and investigated the condition of operatives. These latter fell among the tasks of the *fieles ejecutores*, first established in Puebla in 1543, who also inspected bakeries and markets, and fixed prices for foodstuffs. The *fieles* were supposed to see whether artisans observed guild ordinances. In the later eighteenth century, charges alleged by them against offenders were brought before their tribunal by the municipal syndic (*síndico personero del común*). Liehr argues that in the late colonial period the *fieles* remained impotent in face of the general decay of the guilds.[40] The Puebla municipality, for instance, discussed reports made by guild inspectors in 1742 with a view to prohibiting the mixture of silk and cotton fabric by weavers in cloth manufacture, but seems to have had little success.[41]

Roughly the same number of guilds existed in Puebla in the early 1740s and in the early nineteenth century – saddlers, milliners, blacksmiths or ironmongers, dyers, shoemakers, tailors, carpenters, tanners, chandlers and confectioners, white or coloured porcelain manufacturers, weavers of broad or narrow cloth, silk-mercers, cotton-weavers, bakers, cutlers and so on.[42] The existence – and, implicitly, the activities beyond their confines – illustrated the broad range of economic life in the city and the differentiated social structures that reflected this. A few woollen workshops (*obrajes de lanas*) still survived in Puebla at the beginning of the nineteenth century. Mariano Alatriste, one of the owners, was chosen in 1807 to exercise the office of inspector of the woollen-weavers' guild.[43] The city syndic, Juan Antonio Reyes, reported on the condition of woollen weaving in August of the same year. He presented the council with a heavy list of woollen manufac-turers' grievances. They complained that *obraje* workers robbed cloth from the owners and sold their illegally worked woollens from clandes-tine establishments. According to these mistrustful manufacturers, the

workmen would then 'apply the proceeds to the pursuit of their vices'.
This customary drunkenness cost the owners, they went on, the first two
or three days of every week in defective workmanship. The guild, as
always, pressed for prohibition of all production outside its own system
of supervision, and blamed poor sales on 'free purchase and acquisition
of woollen cloth'. The Puebla city council heard many such requests
from guilds for a tightening of regulations. In the above case, as in
others, the municipality ignored them through fear of the social
consequences of provoking the large number of small 'illegal' traders in
the city. The syndic, in 1807, argued that a total ban issued in the
interests of manufacturers threatened the many poor artisans who,
'worthy as they are, cannot afford to sustain the cost of officially
authorized operations'.[44] The ordinary working people of Puebla
consisted in the main of precisely such struggling artisan producers. The
economic uncertainties of the 1790s and 1800s kept the city authorities
wary of the potential trouble for them that could result from artisan
distress or sense of grievance.[45] Furthermore, the city *barrios*, suburbs,
subordinate districts, and areas within the Tax District of Amozoc
contained a large number of Indian or 'caste'-worked looms which
produced local mantles and popular garments. The Puebla weavers'
guild had little precise information concerning their number. This, too,
was clear indication of the extent of textile production, woollen or
cotton, outside formal guild sanction.[46]

The cotton-spinners' and weavers' guild was described in 1803 as in
'total disarray', with open violations of the ordinances and extortionate
practices that harmed the spinners. Accordingly, the city *fieles* conducted an investigation, from which it transpired that many weavers,
unmatriculated with the guild, produced poor quality cloth from
shoddy material. The guild inspectors argued that the situation resulted
from mercantile financing of guild masters, a virtually generalised
practice. Once again, the guild's answer was full subjection to the
ordinances, and once again, the threat was greeted by cries of protest
from poor artisans who pleaded that their livelihood and that of their
families depended upon their trade. They could never afford the cost of
proper guild examination. Other artisans replied that, since they did
not work on their own behalf, they simply could not subject themselves
to guild regulations. Yet others, explained that they operated not
through their own funds, but from those provided by merchants. The
guild officials, however, had no sympathy for what they regarded as
mere excuses. They warned the weavers to comply with the ordinances,
on pain of closure of their places of work. Although the weavers were

nominally conceded a month within which to present themselves for examination before qualified masters, little, if anything, could, in practice, be done.[47]

A similar story of guild decadence came from Tlaxcala. Competition from Querétaro and other districts had contributed to recession in the woollen trades by the middle of the eighteenth century. Similarly, city cotton weavers described in 1744 the urban economy's depressed condition, which had obliged 'patricians' to emigrate elsewhere in search of work. The decay in woollens had encouraged the transfer to cottons, which alone sustained the textile producers. Viceroy Fuenclara supported the cotton weavers' request for guild ordinances on the Puebla model in May 1744.[48] The Tlaxcala weavers' guild, which received its ordinances in November 1745, never succeeded in exercising control over the urban textile trade. Instead, shopkeepers and freelance weavers bought thread directly from the spinners. Many weavers' looms had never been examined by the guild. Furthermore, Indian producers continued to trade freely in the city. From 1759 the Tlaxcala weavers' guild ceased to function. Several individuals rose to prominence in the textile trade. One of them, José Pineda, described as a 'usurer', supervised the operation of some fifty looms in the village of Santa Inés Zacatelco. Other individuals did likewise. Such persons had risen through their position as intermediaries (*regatones*), who purchased raw cotton, distributed it to spinners and weavers, and then sold the finished product.[49] Weaver hostility to the *regatones* led to allegations that the city *fieles* had been protecting them. Accordingly, the Tlaxcala weavers pressed in 1790 for re-establishment of the guild, as a way of squeezing out their rivals. They accused the *regatones* of undermining their livelihood, forcing unemployed artisans to leave the province and their families in search of work, and of exploiting Indian traders with indebtedness and low wholesale prices. As *gente de razón*, the *regatones* rarely lost an opportunity to express their disdain for the Indians, as if to give the impression that the latter had no rational faculties at all. The weavers went on to describe how they provided the Indians with strong drink or with foodstuffs, taken on account, in return for their spun thread, whereas the weavers said that they themselves always paid in cash. The Superior Government reconstituted the Tlaxcala weavers' guild in April 1790 on the basis of the 1745 ordinances, as a means of hopefully restoring prosperity to the depressed city. When the Spanish government in February 1800 ordered reform of all guild ordinances in New Spain, Tlaxcala's Governor reported in 1806, that only the weavers' guild existed in the city.[50]

Tlaxcala's neighbouring district of Santa Ana Chiautempan was a major woollen textile centre, where at the beginning of the nineteenth century, two *obrajes* functioned.[51] One of the owners, José Ignacio de los Reyes, had complained in 1794 of the flight of thirteen indebted weavers from his workshop.[52] It appears that social relations between Chiautempan natives and incoming Spaniards remained tense. In 1793, residents complained that 'Spaniards' had opened four disorderly drinking houses (*pulquerías*) there, and requested their closure. Local 'Indians' protested that outsiders operated a '*taverna*' near the Chapel of Jesús Nazareno, where the Holy Image was customarily venerated. They wanted it closed down. The Governor of Tlaxcala agreed to these requests.[53] Uneasiness in the Tlaxcala districts and continued recession in the city itself may have contributed to insurgency recruitment in the region after 1810. Certainly, as we shall see in chapter 6, rebel activity was intense throughout the area.

Perhaps Morelos' thrust towards the city of Puebla had as part of its goal the provocation of artisan discontent therein, or, the provision of an opportunity for such to combine with peasant action and insurgent pressure outside. Whatever the case, no rising based upon the artisan took place within the city in the dangerous winter months of 1811–12. In 1813 the great epidemic would have, in any case, frustrated such an attempt. Even so, as the Puebla authorities became aware of the danger posed to them by the insurgency from the autumn of 1811 onwards, they remained equally aware of the potential internal danger to their position. They repeatedly expressed fear of collusion between the rebels in the country districts and 'unruly elements' in the city. Members of guilds – a privileged minority among the mass of artisans and small traders, whom they disparaged and sought to coerce – contributed as best they could to the maintenance of the Royalist régime in Puebla. Rebel presence in the countryside aggravated conditions in the city, as a result of migration from the rural to the urban environment.[54] The conjunction between the urban artisan and the country farm-worker or peasant, which the insurgent commanders might have hoped for, did not materialise in Puebla. It could be said, then, that the turning point of the revolutionary struggle occurred when events in Puebla failed to take the course that they might have.

Guadalajara's long relationship to the livestock trade explained the existence of tanneries in the city, along with tanners', saddlers', shoemakers' and blacksmiths' guilds. Cotton production in the southern districts gave rise to spinning, weaving and tailoring, and wheat production to bakery. Guilds provided recruits into the urban militia forces of the counter-insurgency period, and, in this way, sustained the Royalist cause. An array of guilds continued to exist well into the late colonial period – carpenters, hat-makers, barbers, chandlers, as well as those already mentioned.[55] More than 3,000 individuals appear to have worked in some form of textile production in the city in the 1790s, and further large numbers in towns connected to the Zacatecas mining districts or the San Juan de Lagos fairs. Although the region imported woollens from Bajío towns such as Querétaro and San Miguel, it produced its own cottons, to a total value of nearly 1.4 million pesos by 1804. According to Abascal, some 20,000 persons were involved throughout the province in all stages of cotton industrial production from cleaning the raw materials to cloth manufacture. These occupations, however, were not their only ones, since many supposedly industrial workers also continued to engage at other times in agricultural activity.[56]

Official guild examination continued to be the practice for permission to pursue a craft, although Guadalajara guilds like those of Puebla, could not uniformly enforce the provisions of their ordinances. Only those who could afford to pay the fees for matriculation, as well as the government *media anata* tax, ever contemplated applying for guild examination. Nevertheless, a few of the more privileged artisans successfully did so. In July and August 1807, for instance, José Teodoro Berdín and José Diego Estanislao, were admitted to the shoemakers' guild and were each duly authorised to open a shop wherever in the city it suited them to do so, and to take in apprentices. They undertook to observe the guild ordinances and to defend, as part of the guild's tradition, the mystery of the Immaculate Conception of Our Lady.[57] Guild religious traditions imposed obligations upon members, but the latter did not always choose to observe them. The municipal *Junta de Policía* in April 1807 agreed to the request by the *alcalde* of the tailors' guild for fines to be levied upon eleven masters who had failed to assist in person and in proper livery in the procession of the Holy Angel on Good Friday.[58]

In effect, few guild regulations corresponded to economic realities as they appeared by the end of the colonial period. The city bakers, for example, had received the regulations governing their sliding scale of prices in relation to wheat supply, as far back as 1674. They understandably complained of rising costs by 1808. Little appears to have been done by the municipal council to accommodate their interests, which were naturally not those of the consumer, since further complaints about the rising price of flour arose in 1810 and again in 1819.[59]

Guild attempts to subordinate workmen to their regulations or drive them out of business aroused hostility, but usually failed. An Indian tributary of Tonalá, José Guadalupe García, resented attempts by guild authorities in 1799 to oblige him to pay full membership charges, which he argued he did not owe by virtue of his tributary status. A resident of the city's outer *barrio* of San Juan de Dios since 1785, García worked in his rented house as an iron-craftsman making spurs, bridles and hangings. He sold his produce in the public square like other Indians of Tonalá, and from this trade he maintained his family and paid tribute and other dues required of him in Tonalá. The Guild Inspector had visited his home to demand payment of *media anata*. In his defence, García cited parallel instances of Indian exemption from all contributions to artisan guilds. The *fiscal protector de indios* upheld his case.[60]

Small producers could not afford to pay the cost of guild examination. The shoemakers' guild in 1817 and 1818 attempted unsuccessfully to curb the many small producers who worked in their own homes and sold their shoes in the public squares, in order to provide their families with a livelihood. The poor greatly benefited from such a low cost alternative source of supply to the guild, which charged double or treble the price. Twenty of these competing, smaller producers put their names to a request that the municipality should not permit the examined masters to throw them out of business, in order to enforce the guild monopoly. They were sceptical to the utmost of guild-master offers of employment, since they maintained that experience had shown that shop-keepers were as poor as they were themselves, and either could not afford to pay proper wages or held them back in order to maximise their own profits. The Guild Inspectors had recently toured the places of sale where poor producers traded and 'had issued threats and insults to them, trying to impose fines and confiscating their shoes, with the utmost provocation'. One trader, Juan el Escobetero, had been hurled to the ground and beaten for refusing to hand over his shoes.[61]

Shoemakers served in the militia forces of the city during the counter-insurgency. A group of four of them, corporals in the Fourth Company of the Guadalajara Urban Battalion of Loyalists of Ferdinand VII, stressed in 1818 that they had volunteered for active service despite their slender means, and that several of their fellows had lost their lives in defence of the Royalist cause. Their families, however, suffered for every day sacrificed from their work, which took place in their homes. In view of the cheapness of their product and the scant possibility of accumulating capital as a result of their labours, the shoemaker militiamen saw no prospect whatever of saving enough to cover the cost of guild examination and matriculation. As a result, they saw themselves pushed out of their crafts by prosperous guild producers who owned their own shops, on the pretext that all production should conform to the guild ordinances. 'These examined masters claim to be offering us work in their shops as workmen, but in reality, there are so many of us that they cannot possibly hope to employ us all, and, even in the case of the few who are so employed, they pay them such puny wages that no one can afford to meet his obligations.' These four petitioners refused to believe, they said, that the king's intention was to preside over the ruin of his own subjects, least of all of loyalists who had sacrificed so much.[62]

Such protestations received no sympathy whatever from the Guild Inspector, who portrayed such small producers as thieves and drunks, who sought to undercut the 'legitimate' producers by shoddy workmanship and surrender themselves to their vices with the proceeds. Nevertheless, one of the Inspectors, Luciano Arias, was himself sergeant of the same battalion as the petitioners, and, accordingly, experienced divided loyalties. He disclaimed any suggestion of wanting to harm his own militiamen and pointed out that he himself had officially licensed their work so that they could maintain themselves.[63] The city syndics similarly described the ordinary shoemakers as 'rough and ready, many of them drunks, incapable of saving money to cover the cost of guild examination. They either sold their wares from their homes or hawked them in public: if not they died of starvation – unless they could win at gambling or succeed in theft.' However, they declined to sustain the guild's demand for strict adherence to the ordinances, in order not to deprive genuinely poor producers of their means of livelihood. Instead, they recommended that the tariff for matriculation should be lowered, in order to accommodate the worthy poor. The syndics saw this as a means of preserving the integrity for the guild, which faced extinction if any producer was allowed to sell, and of differentiating the needy poor from the profligate.[64]

Master hat-makers, most of whom were serving as soldiers in the urban militia regiment, protested that they had never seen the ordinances to which their craft was supposed to be subject. The prospect of enforcement of the decree of 28 January 1818 binding them to observe guild regulations within six months on pain of the destruction of their workshops, filled them with abhorrence.[65] It was vital in cities such as Puebla and Guadalajara that the military and municipal authorities should not provoke the multifarious artisan population into outright opposition, since it was precisely from such groups that they recruited

manpower for the militia. The Royalist militia corps, in effect, held the
rear behind the main troops operating in the field.

## Localised grievances and national movements

Peasant and lower-class grievances had not received the support of any
élite group in the years, or even centuries, before 1810. Certainly
individual priests, civil administrators, bishops, or senior magistrates
had upheld and sympathised with specific cases of injustice. There had
been, however, no multi-class alignments which had focussed around
the grievances of the rural population. Political dissent in New Spain
did not, as a rule, encompass peasant grievances, still less did it seek to
encapsulate them. The autonomists of 1808 and the conspirators of
1809–10 had political, rather than social, objectives, and their support
came from within the élites. Not until the original conspiracy failed in
its prime objective – the subversion of the armed forces – did rural
grievances come to play any part in revolutionary thinking. Even then,
it was secondary rather than primary.

Although sometimes of long duration and of broad territorial extent,
social tensions, whether in town or country, rarely showed uniform
characteristics. The broad geographical and economic distinctions
within New Spain alone accounted for that. Such grievances did not
lend themselves easily to expansion into revolutionary movements,
whether spontaneously or systematically. Even if the dislocation that
resulted from dearth and recession is taken into account, localised unrest
could not of itself bring down the official powers, no matter how much
it weakened or disorientated them. While after September 1810, a
segment of the Mexican professional bourgeoisie was prepared to align
itself with popular opposition to *gachupín* dominance, the most powerful sector of the bourgeoisie, the entrepreneurial group, remained either
aloof or distinctly hostile. The analysis of the entrepreneurial bourgeoisie of the pre-1820 era presents certain difficulties, not least of which is
the issue of its national or non-national character. With regard to the
Revolution of 1910, in contrast, it has become customary to focus upon
the decisive support given by the national bourgeoisie, which was
prepared to align with sectors of the popular opposition, chiefly urban
labour. In 1810, the situation was different, because a large number of
entrepreneurs were of direct Spanish origin. In fact, it was they
themselves who took the brunt of the popular opposition. In 1810,
among the principal group of investors and innovators were often
precisely those *gachupines*, against which the rebellion of both the creole

professional classes and the popular classes was directed. The close participation of the Spanish immigrant merchant–investor in Mexican enterprises and his frequent marriage into Mexican families transformed the complexion of the upper classes into a hybrid of Spanish immigrants and Mexican descendants. While the economic interests of such Spaniards were Mexican-orientated, their social origins and political alignments were peninsula-orientated. These internal divisions meant that, in any direct confrontation between Mexicans and Spaniards on the question of independence, the entrepreneurial bourgeoisie would be unable to take the leadership of a nationalist movement within New Spain. It further implied that the bourgeoisie of New Spain would be divided between its entrepreneurial and its professional component elements. These divisions weakened the revolutionary potential of the Mexican bourgeoisie and ultimately aborted its challenge to the *ancien régime* and to the colonial structure that went with it. The entrepreneurial segment of the bourgeoisie failed to identify with a national struggle for liberation from colonial rule. This was not surprising in view of its ambiguous relation to the colonial power and in view of its constant and successful pursuit of noble titles and privileges, which were grants from the Spanish Crown. This failure resulted in its tactical alignment with the bureaucratic and military structures of the *ancien régime*. A formidable anti-revolutionary coalition took shape and was able to resist and reverse the insurrectionary onslaught of 1810–11. The events of the 1810s revealed that, neither by themselves, nor together, were the professional bourgeoisie and the popular classes capable of successfully challenging the alliance between the entrepreneurial élite and the colonial power. As a result, the external colonial situation continued for a decade following the execution of Hidalgo, and the internal colonial structure for a good deal longer.

In this discussion of the roots of insurgency, I propose to regard the regional theatre as the primary one. This is to argue that in many instances – though not all – the insurrection of 1810 magnified the pre-existing local conflicts, which, understandably, continued to manifest themselves after the War of Independence proper had finished in 1821. In short, the achievement of political independence neither resolved nor eradicated these tensions – nor should one expect it to have done so. These local realities, rather than the superimposed nationalist rhetoric of the official leadership represented the essential *leitmotiv* of Mexican social and political history. We should regard, then, the complicated struggles of the 1810s and early 1820s as broader expressions of previous and subsequent tensions. Unless we strip the

'Independence Period' of its nationalist framework, we shall not expose the continuing threads which run through both the colonial and early national experience of Mexico. We shall never, for instance, understand the nineteenth century, comprehension of which is, perhaps, the key to many contemporary mysteries.

# 2

## Insurgency – characteristics and responses

### The historical theme

A considerable literature developed in the 1960s and 1970s on the subject of insurgency, peasant wars and national liberation struggles. The contemporary importance of a wide range of movements from the Malayan insurgency and the Algerian War of Independence to the war in Indo-China and the Cuban Revolution has accounted for this interest. It has joined the existing and continuing body of literature on the subject of the historical conditions of revolution and methods of waging a revolutionary struggle. We have now a number of studies that attempt to explain what insurgency implied and to compare it with the more familiar types of rebellion or revolution.

Rebellions are not revolutions: they result from specific, often limited localised grievances, though they are certainly capable of generating an intensity of feeling that can spread over a wide area and last for a long time. This, perhaps, distinguishes them from riots, which are usually spontaneous protests against a single action. In spite of their frequent social conflict characteristics, rebellions generally do not constitute movements for structural change. Their strategic objective rarely tends to be the capture of political power at the centre of decision making. On the contrary, their aims are usually tactical, in that, by a demonstration of force, they seek to push the established power from the course of action which had given rise to the discontent in the first place. As such, rebellions represent a form of armed protest, which, in themselves, constitute only a limited challenge to authority. They either peter out, are deflected by persuasion or promises, or are subjected to equally sporadic demonstrations of armed force by the official power.[1] Rebellions only tend to present a fundamental threat to government, when they are accompanied by other factors, such as recession, foreign threat, war, dearth, natural disasters, a combination of internal movements of

47

armed dissent, or a crisis of authority within the governing regime. We shall examine many of these issues in chapters three and four. Revolution – a term used here in the contemporary sense, rather than in accordance with Early Modern usage – involves not just a change in the personnel of government, but of the political system itself. This can only be achieved ultimately by the capture of power at the centre. Such a political revolution often precedes, accompanies, or results in a change in the organisation of society, and in the structure and purpose of the economy.[2] In New Spain, for example, a military victory by the revolutionary movement, led in September 1810, by Padre Miguel Hidalgo, to overthrow Spanish colonial rule would presumably have been followed by the capture of Mexico City and the formation of a revolutionary government. This new regime would have brought into effect a political revolution on two levels: the internal – designed to remove the colonial élite; and the external – to replace the sovereignty of the Spanish Crown by that of the Mexican nation. This transformation would have brought the professional bourgeoisie into the centre of government, pushed out the Spanish bureaucratic élite, replaced Bourbon absolutism with some form of republican constitutionalism, and presaged an alteration in the legal basis of society in accordance with the principle of equality before the law. Such readjustments within the educated and propertied classes could scarcely have amounted to a social revolution in the sense that either wealth or power would have been redistributed to the popular classes. That type of transformation was not implicit in the bid for power by the professional bourgeoisie.

Insurgency is more closely related to revolution than to rebellion, and emerges often alongside the main revolutionary attempt to capture power at the centre. Its causes are similar: in many respects it reflects the broad, social dimension of a revolutionary movement, those aspects which operate at the local levels of political perception, rather than at the level of the insurrectionary leadership. Revolution tends to carry insurgency with it, but in such a way that, should a revolutionary attempt to capture power fail, insurgency can continue for a long period of time, entrenched at the local level. In this sense, insurgency, rather than an attempted revolutionary putsch, could result from a potential revolutionary situation, rather than the type of insurrection usually associated with revolution. According to one American commentator, David Galula, 'an insurgency is a protracted struggle conducted methodically, step by step, in order to attain specific intermediate objectives leading finally to the overthrow of the existing order . . . ; its beginnings are so vague that to determine exactly when an insurgency starts is a difficult legal, political and historical problem . . . ; though it cannot be predicted, an insurgency is usually slow to develop and is not an accident, for in an insurgency leaders appear and the masses are made to move'.[3] The principal illustrations in recent studies are usually taken from the mid-twentieth century examples of insurgency warfare: China, 1927–45; Greece, 1943–4, 1946–50; Indo-China, 1946–54; Vietnam 1964–75; Malaya, 1948–60; and Algeria, 1954–62. This is understandable since 'the years, 1945–65, saw the most important developments in the history of Mao Tse-tung's rural pattern of guerrilla warfare, and of the techniques for opposing it. It had some classic successes, notably by General Giap against the French from 1946 to 1954, and against the American-supported South Vietnamese from 1959 to 1964; also some classic failures, as in the Philippines from 1950 to 1953, and in Malaya from 1948 to 1960.'[4] Such case studies provide information on how and why insurgency develops, upon what social groups it is based, how issues come into being, how leadership emerges, what tactics are adopted, and what techniques the existing order has applied for the purpose of combating it.

Few of the contemporary commentators, however, have concerned themselves with the eighteenth or nineteenth centuries.[5] In view of this preoccupation with the impact of Marxist ideology and revolutionary tactics, this is understandable. Nevertheless, the phenomenon of insurgency is by no means a new one; its characteristics do not derive exclusively from the socio-political consequences of the Second World War and the loss of empire. With the impact of the Cuban Revolutionary struggle of 1956–9, and subsequently the success of the Nicaraguan Revolution of 1979, Latin America began to take a place in contemporary discussion of insurgency. In the aftermath of the Sandinista capture of power in Managua in July 1979, the subject of insurgency and counter-insurgency has regained its former vigour, notably with regard to the conflicts of the 1980s in Guatemala and El Salvador and the attention given in United States' government and military circles to Central America.[6] Insurgency in Latin America has a long tradition; the Latin American experience of insurgency considerably predates current events. There, too, rebellions or attempted revolutions frequently led to protracted and deeply rooted insurgencies, which required full-scale military responses. In the course of these, counter-insurgency techniques were developed, that provided antecedents for those applied in more recent times. The colonial situation of Latin America provided such rebellions and insurgencies with their impetus, and, in their anti-imperial and popular aspects, they anticipated the type of national

liberation struggles that contributed to the demise of colonial empires in
the twentieth century. The movements which centred around the personalities of Juan Santos Atahualpa (1742–56) and Tupac Amaru II
(1780–3) in Peru provided the first large scale examples of rebellions
against colonial abuses; they required a serious military response from the
official power. Although localised conflicts had been relatively frequent
phenomena throughout the Andean regions in the later seventeenth and
eighteenth centuries, the leadership provided by these two claimants to
Inca divinity enabled the scattered discontent to coalesce into long-
lasting or widespread rebellions.[7] In the type of insurgency with which
we are dealing here, the colonial situation is the paramount factor.

The conflicts of the Wars of Independence (1809–26) gave rise to a
number of guerrilla movements, risings by peasant bands and rebellions
that originated in the countryside, or contained a predominantly
popular element. Such risings, whether directed against the Spanish
colonial power or the internal colonial situation, frequently exercised a
powerful influence on the turn of events, since both the Royalist
authorities and the creole leaderships of the independence movements
were obliged to respond to them. A broad variety of popular rebellions
took place: the Murillo rising in La Paz in May 1809,[8] the Hidalgo
Revolt in New Spain in 1810,[9] the rebellion of the Venezuelan *llaneros*
under Boves in 1814,[10] the Cuzco rising by the Angulo brothers in
August 1814 and the adherence of the Indian *cacique*, Pumacahua,[11] and
guerrilla warfare in Upper Peru between 1814–16 and in some regions
until 1825,[12] the guerrilla bands in New Granada between 1816 and
1819,[13] and the *montoneros* of the Central Andes of Lower Peru between
1821 and 1823.[14] With the notable exception of the Mexican case
between 1810 and 1821, few of the above movements developed into a
protracted and costly insurgency. In Mexico, in mid-century, moreover,
further instances of the warfare of guerrilla bands recurred during the
Civil War of the Reform (1858–61) and in the War of the Intervention
(1862–7). In these conflicts, which were also struggles between regular
armies, guerrilla bands and bandit groups, often only nominally Liberal
or Conservative, operated on both sides. Counter-insurgency techniques
were devised to deal with them.[15] Porfirio Díaz in 1910–11 attempted,
ultimately without political success, to employ counter-insurgency
techniques against the insurgents of Chihuahua and Morelos.[16]

## Characteristics

It has been argued that insurgency results from the breakdown of
consensus. When the governed no longer consent to be governed by the

official power is difficult to determine, since a long process of alienation is usually involved. Insurgency movements strive to break up entirely the surviving remnants of popular consent or passivity towards the authorities. In this sense, insurgency is primarily a political problem and secondarily a military one. Galula's discussion stresses the primacy of the political dimension. He argues that, no matter how great the military impact of insurgency, the civil power ultimately needs to gain the upper hand in the counter-revolution, which, as a result, should only temporarily remain predominantly under the direction of army officers. The later would often be ill-equipped to deal with the difficult process of political reconstruction. Furthermore, continued military control of the civil organs would strengthen insurgent charges that legitimate government had broken down. This, in turn, would lend credence to the insurgent claim to represent the legitimate government within national territory.[17]

Always important in any study of rebellion, revolution or insurgency is the spatial dimension of dissent, which posed both a physical and a political problem for the authorities. In New Spain, government forces, throughout the War of Independence, retained control of the capital city, Veracruz, the chief port of exit and entrance from Europe, the second city Puebla, and the strategically located industrial city of Querétaro, located north of the Valley of Mexico. If they had lost any one of these, the Royalist cause would probably have been doomed. At specific periods, government defenders remained marooned within these redoubts. Widespread insurgent support across the Bajío led to the early encirclement of Querétaro in October 1810. A major explanation for the revolutionaries' failure to take the city may be the absence of a movement within Querétaro capable of challenging Royalist control. It does not appear that a conjunction of artisan and worker discontent inside the city with the insurgent movement outside its walls actually took place. A comparable situation arose in the case of the industrial city of Puebla, which insurgent bands surrounded, and Morelos' main rebel army threatened, in December 1811 and January 1812, as we shall see in chapter six. It is conceivable that Morelos hoped for a rising of artisans and urban workers or urban unemployed within the city, when his army reached its defensive perimeter. Neither in 1811–12, nor in 1812–13, however, did such a coalescence of revolutionary forces materialise. For this, perhaps, and for other reasons, too, the Royalists narrowly managed to hold on to this key city. Royalist recovery of Guanajuato, San Luis Potosí, Valladolid, Guadalajara and Zacatecas by early 1811 enabled the government to build up, in difficult stages, a counter-revolutionary position in these major regional capital cities.

Although, as we shall see in chapter seven, both Guanajuato and particularly Valladolid, continued to be exposed to insurgent attack until 1814, none of these cities was ever lost again by government forces. The counter-insurgency, then, often seemed to take the form at first of an urban holding operation, followed by cautious, not always successful, concentric probing movements into the countryside. This increasingly strong government position in the main cities reinforced the earlier urban–rural dichotomies that characterised the insurgency.

Distribution of settlement has a major bearing on the mobilising capacity of insurgency and on the type of techniques employed in counter-insurgency. Four key areas were among the most densely populated in New Spain: the Bajío and Guanajuato–Querétaro; the central districts of Michoacán between Lakes Cuitzeo and Chapala; the central districts of Guadalajara – the Valley of Atemajac and the lakes basin zone as far south as Zapotlán and Zapotiltic; and the central cereal valleys of Puebla between Huejotzingo and Tehuacán. All were focal points of insurgency, and all were in close economic and cultural contact with the principal cities of New Spain beyond the administrative capital itself. In each of these cities – Guanajuato, Querétaro, Guadalajara, Valladolid and Puebla – there existed an active regional élite of complex stratification, members of which often expressed views different to those of the central governing élite in Mexico City. Areas of entrenched and long-lasting insurgency tended to be those of remoter geographical location or difficulty of access, though strategically located adjacent to densely populated zones of intense economic activity, broader social stratification, and, in all, at a different stage of cultural development. Along these lines, one might contrast the Llanos de Apan with the Valley of Mexico, the north and south perimeters of Puebla with cereal valleys, the Mixtecas Alta and Baja with the Puebla and Oaxaca Valleys, the southern sierras and dispersed coastal settlements of Michoacán, Jalisco and Colima with the central plateau of Guadalajara, the Sierra de Comanja with the plains of León, the Altos de Jalisco and the Chapala zone, and so on.

An insurgency, of course, need not be revolutionary in its political goals; it could also be counter-revolutionary. Nevertheless, similar characteristics apply to both types of movement. The French risings of 1793 in the Vendée and the Norman *Chouannerie* were popular rebellions of a counter-revolutionary nature, which exhibited the characteristics of a regionalised insurgency of long duration. Charles Tilly's study of the Vendée describes how 'a number of separate counterrevolutionary movements' coalesced into 'one great rebellion' in the first three weeks of

March 1793, and draws attention to their 'combination of common themes and deep localism'. [18] As we shall see in the case of the Mexican insurgency of the 1810s, this intense localism remained a prime feature of the movement as a whole. On rare occasions, and generally for only a short time, local rebels perceived a broader national dimension. In localised insurrections, they sought to settle old scores with their enemies at hand, rather than primarily with any national foe. Their vision of the events in which they participated seemed limited to the grievances of the communities out of which they came. As a result, it would prove difficult, if not impossible to link this narrow ideological perception to the broader movement for revolutionary change at the national political level. [19] In western France, a major cause of rebellion was local opposition to conscription, and it accounted for the early predominance of young hired hands, day labourers, and artisans in the first outbreaks. A cross-section of the rural population became involved – more than half of it accounted for by peasants and more than two-fifths by rural artisans. Participation cut across class lines: the rebellion could not be explained in terms of the actions of one single social group. Tilly's model provides a useful comparison with the Mexican insurgency, which also had a marked popular and rural character, but could not, equally, be described as a one class movement. [20]

Most insurgencies require large deployment of troops, regular and irregular, to bring them under control. Even if an initial rebellion or attempted revolutionary seizure of power fails, an ensuing insurgency often produces a civil war situation. This, however, would not be equivalent to a civil war in which both sides were belligerents, with roughly equal armed forces, engaged in a conventional struggle. In many, though not all instances, insurgent forces begin to operate from an unequal position in relation to the regular army, but benefit from subversion of the official armed force and the defection of troops along with their weapons. Since insurgency rarely resembles a conventional war with its pitched battles and recognisable fronts, there is no front and no rear – other than the rebel base area, from which often distant operations can be launched. As a result, insurgents pass through local populations often with impunity and are hard to distinguish from the ordinary labouring inhabitants. For the counter-insurgency, this inter-mingling facility poses the problem of separation. Its essential task is to separate insurgents from the rest of the population; though frequently insuperable, it is the prerequisite of final success. [21]

In a non-insurgency situation, it is possible for only a small number of troops and militiamen to hold down the country, providing the

political edifice of control remains intact.[22] Such had been the case in
New Spain before the insurrection of 1810. A relatively small and
widely distributed armed force had been sufficient to maintain Spanish
political authority and the internal colonial situation. The explanation
lay in the absence both of any major and co-ordinated challenge and of
any breakdown of central political control from either Madrid or Mexico
City. In 1784, for instance, the army of New Spain consisted of only
4,196 men, and even this was a nominal figure. Given the shortage and
inefficiency of peninsular garrison troops, inevitably the defence of New
Spain came to depend upon the militia, raised in Mexico itself and with a
manpower of potentially dubious loyalty. When Viceroy Flores inspected the army in 1787, he found it in a thoroughly deplorable condition.
By 1794, the total force available, both regular and militia, amounted
to only 4,767 troops, and nearly half of these were required for the
defence of Veracruz and the Gulf coast, where, nevertheless, they
encountered the obstacle of tropical diseases.[23] With the danger of a
British invasion, Viceroy Iturrigaray assembled a force of 11,000 troops
at Jalapa and other Veracruz upland towns by the end of August 1806.
The cantonment force increased to a total of 15,516 men by the end of
October 1807, and to 17,000 in the following year, if the garrison of
Veracruz is included. After 1800, the viceregal administration finally
embarked upon the task of forming ten militia brigades for the defence
of New Spain, often with Intendants, who also happened to be army
officers, as their commanders. Only the Tenth Militia Brigade under
Colonel Félix Calleja in San Luis Potosí came into active existence. It
would play a major part in defeating the rebellion of 1810. The smallest
of these brigades, in Acapulco, consisted of only 377 men: this zone
would become a major insurgent base area from the winter of 1810–11.
The total enlisted forces in the ten brigades, which included veteran
troops, came to 24,462 men, in the period before 1810. In Guanajuato,
which was to be the initial centre of the insurrection, Colonel Antonio
Pérez Gálvez, a representative of one of the leading local silver-mining
families, disputed the right of the Intendant, José Antonio Riaño, to
exercise military command of the Provincial Infantry Battalion, which
formed part of the Eighth Brigade with its headquarters at Querétaro. As
late as 1809, this issue remained alive. Civilian-military disputes in
Oaxaca made the city 'a hotbed of unrest and discord' by the end of
1807.[24]

Although defence considerations remained paramount in New Spain
until the reversal of alliances in 1808, the armed forces had, on
occasions, been used to control internal unrest, both within major

provincial capitals such as Guanajuato and San Luis Potosí in 1766–7 and in Mexico City itself. Similarly, militia forces, often with only limited success, had been used to contain localised rebellions such as those of 1781 in Izúcar (Puebla) and 1787 in Papantla and Acayucan (Veracruz).[25] Apart from the agents of the *Tribunal de la Acordada*, there were no official police forces capable of operating over broad areas of countryside. The senior bureaucratic agencies found few solutions to the outstanding problems of lawlessness. The *Acordada*, which was established in 1722, since 'neither justice nor order could adequately be served by existing judicial organizations', did not concern itself primarily with rebellion, but with crime, two quite different phenomena.[26] The localised type of rebellion presented very little danger in itself to the structure of colonial rule, even though the task of suppression might prove too much for the militia. A generalised revolt, however, threatened to expose the limited manpower and broad distribution of the armed forces as a whole. Until 1810, no such generalised rebellion had ever taken place in New Spain. As we shall see, the initial shock of rebellion prevented the official power from retaining control of such key regions as Guanajuato, Michoacán and Guadalajara, and contributed to the loss of major cities such as San Luis Potosí and Zacatecas.

Furthermore, large areas of territory, even as late as the end of the eighteenth century, still remained beyond the effective control of the royal administration. Where the authority of the state did not, in practice, reach, powerful individuals and interest groups frequently managed to entrench themselves. Diffused private power remained the bugbear of the reforming ministers of late Bourbon absolutism. In effect, local *caciques* became brokers who mediated between the government and the people they controlled.[27] *Caciquismo* existed as a recognisable phenomenon within the colonial period; it did not need the War of Independence to create it. Nevertheless, the decades of turmoil after 1810 magnified the importance of *caciques* and extended the sphere of their operations.[28] As we shall see, leaders of the insurgent movement often depended upon their co-operation; *caciques* themselves provided the leadership of many rebel bands, as the careers of the Villagráns of Huichapan or the Galeanas of the Pacific coast would show. Such networks lent themselves readily to transformation into insurgent bands. For this reason, the armed forces of the official power, once they had regrouped after the shock of insurrection, found it necessary to penetrate areas of remote geographical location or difficult terrain. Their success in these territories, which provided the lairs of the *caciques* and the base areas of rebel bands, proved to be only limited.[29]

Examination of the conditions that contributed to the revolutionary capture and retention of political power in France in 1789 suggests that the disintegration of the regular army played a decisive part.[30] The Mexican conspirators of 1809 and 1810 were urban-based members of the professional classes. They hoped to subvert a large section of the armed forces, which would, thereby, become their instrument for the seizure of power. They were prepared to accept the possibility of some kind of spontaneous popular revolt accompanying this action. Nevertheless, their *principal* instrument was to be the armed forces of the viceregal state. In their efforts at subversion, however, they were only partially successful. As a result, the army command was able, not without great effort, to reassert its control. The conspirators' inability to count upon the armed forces meant that their attempt to seize power had either to be abandoned altogether or made *primarily* dependent upon a popular revolt. Few, if any of them, had worked out any concrete plans concerning such a revolt, though it seems likely that some locally dissident individuals and chieftains were being contacted at the time the authorities uncovered the Querétaro conspiracy in mid-September 1810. However, failure to deprive the government of the use of its armed forces ultimately signified that the rebel leaders had to rely on a combination of spontaneous revolt and the mobilisation by *caciques* of their clientele. This unleashing of popular violence, pregnant with social dangers, could only be tactically justified, if it delivered such a shock to the existing order, that it made the political position of the viceregal government untenable. Perhaps this was what Hidalgo urged upon the conspirators. Perhaps that is why he was prepared to take the risk of advancing the date of the projected rising from December to September. If this shock should prove to be insufficient, then the rebels would face the prospect of a direct confrontation with the armed forces of the state. Whatever his colleagues may have felt on the subject, Hidalgo appears to have believed that a popular uprising was not so much a desperate gamble but more a calculated risk.[31] Even so, the failure of the Mexican separatists to gain control of the armed forces deprived them of the possibility of a Buenos Aires-type solution. There, in May 1810, the commander of the creole militia, Cornelio Saavedra, acting in concert with civilian pressure in the capital city, was able to remove the peninsular regime without recourse to a popular insurrection.[32]

In consequence, the Mexican revolutionary struggle moved away from the main urban areas into the smaller towns and the countryside. If the Saavedra example represented an urban model of revolutionary capture of power, then the composition of the Hidalgo movement reflected a rural model, with its attendant social and political implications.[33] A rural struggle ensured that the battle between rebel and government forces would centre on control of the peasant, rural worker and small town population. Whatever the initial political goals of the revolutionary leadership, this type of struggle in the countryside would sooner or later focus upon the social and economic grievances of the rural populace, which, for the most part, given its geographical isolation and lack of intellectual opportunities, could have little appreciation of the constitutional arguments of aspiring lawyer–politicians. The development of a revolutionary campaign based in the countryside would require not only a broadening of ideology but also a more complex structure of leadership. If the original leaders sought to retain control of the movement which they had precipitated into armed conflict, they would have to organise support in the villages on the basis of long-term co-ordination with political objectives.[34] The crucial requirement of retaining peasant support would have to be sedulously observed. Oppression of the peasantry by rebel forces threatened to destroy any chance of co-operation, undermine the entire basis of the revolt and play into the hands of counter-revolutionary forces astute enough to abandon terror policies in favour of overtures to the country populace. The Mexican insurgents faced all these problems, once the implications of popular revolt became clear. Furthermore, failure to assert and retain official leadership control over the whole movement would result in the autonomous operation of local rebel bands, the pursuit of limited and often personal interests, the rapid abandonment of any pretensions to social and political transformation at the national level, a generalised oppression of the rural population, the spread of banditry, and a readiness to trade or deal with the local forces or interests sustaining the official power. In the Mexican insurgency the early destruction of the official leadership in 1811, the failure of Lic. Ignacio López Rayón to consolidate his claim to unchallenged succession, and of Morelos to establish his full military and political control over the increasingly diverse movement, ensured that precisely those latter options took root during the period, 1814–21. They were, in any case, always present as possibilities. They co-existed, as it were, alongside the more exalted goals of the political leadership of the insurrection at the national level.[35]

Contemporary commentators have argued that a major prerequisite for the success of insurgency is the breakdown or near breakdown of the administrative system within national territory. Usually the impact of war and enemy invasion, as in Indo-China, Malaya and Indonesia during and after the Japanese occupation, has been sufficient cause.[36] Where enemy action might not operate as a contributory factor to either general or regional administrative breakdown, internal factors such as the impact of repeated subsistence crisis might cause sufficient dislocation of the food supply, employment and normal transit to produce an intolerable strain on an administrative system, particularly where, as in New Spain, local officials were traditionally weak and underpaid. We shall examine such factors in chapter four. In Mexico, the internal breakdown of the administration within certain provincial capital cities, notably Guadalajara, Zacatecas and San Luis Potosí, contributed to early insurgent control. Rapidly, these urban positions were lost by the rebels. Control of rural areas in Guanajuato, Michoacán and Guadalajara remained, however, of long duration. Before the official army could regroup after early failures, and launch its counter-offensive, the established power had already lost control of a large amount of national territory. The principal zone was the rich agricultural Bajío, through which passed the main communication routes between Mexico City and the north. It took nearly ten years for full government control to be re-established there.[37]

In spite of their impact, guerrilla struggles have only rarely by themselves resulted in the overthrow of governments. Generally, insurgent bands, if they are to attain their objectives, need to act in concert with some form of regular military force, whether surviving segments of the old army or a new type of revolutionary army. Guerrilla activity can harass the rival army, pin it down, or even force sections of it to capitulate, but final victory frequently has depended upon the regular fighting force of the revolutionary side.[38] In the Spanish peninsular struggle of 1808–14, a two-fold warfare took place, with the remaining core of the regular army operating in concert with local guerrilla bands, sometimes led by serving officers. It was the former which decided the final outcome of the war in 1813–14. In Spain in 1821–3 and again in 1827, irregular bands rose against the Madrid government: this time they could not count on the co-operation of the regular army, which itself engaged in counter-insurgency warfare.[39] Similarly, in the Greek insurrections of the 1820s, the klepht or brigand bands could not inflict the decisive blow in the period, 1821–7, even though they deprived the Ottomans of control of most of the peninsula.[40] In New Spain, after the defeat of Morelos at Puruarán in January 1814, scarcely any revolutionary army existed at all as a regular force capable of challenging government forces in a pitched battle. It became inconceivable for the Mexican insurgents to fight the Royalist army on its own ground. The war of the rebel bands became the norm. The disintegration of the leadership loosened what ties there had been between the political and military objectives of the insurrection. Without effective direction by a co-ordinated political leadership and without constraint by a regular army force, the guerrilla war rapidly degenerated into little more than brigandage, a plague on the country-side. The Mexican insurgency lacked direction: it was not an on-going concern, it could not win a strategic victory. As a result, it had already lost the political battle for regional supremacy, legitimacy, and ultimately control of the state. Failure to establish lasting control of either a major region or an important city frustrated insurgent attempts to construct a parallel hierarchy to that of the central government.[41] No revolutionary political structure existed that could undercut the official regime and challenge its legitimacy.[42] It would only be a matter of time before military actions caught up with political realities.

## Criminality and banditry

Government propaganda branded insurgents as brigands or bandits: in this way it denied them a political existence and reduced them to the level of common criminals. Although criminality and banditry undoubtedly posed problems to the authorities before the outbreak of rebellion of 1810, they were conceptually distinct from insurgency. Even so, banditry also posed a challenge to authority itself in matters of social control. For such a reason, rural communities could be tempted to group around bandits as a protection from outside powers. The persistence of banditry placed a continued strain upon the official forces of law and order. Bandit groups contributed manpower and leaders to insurgency when it developed during the late summer and autumn of 1810. In many respects, insurgency recruited in similar conditions. As a result, the transition back from insurgent band to bandit group was an easy one to make, if, in many cases, there had ever really been a distinction in the first place. The existence of widespread rural unrest, especially among farmhands and day labourers, or among village communities opposed to enclosures and other losses of customary right, contributed to the emergence of brigand groups, in which the dispossessed or disaffected of the countryside formed a representative part. Such groups, in many different instances, provided fuel to insurgency, not only in terms of escalating disorder but also with regard to tactical co-operation.[43]

The *Acordada* combated banditry from the first instance. Its early trial areas had included the densely populated district of Querétaro, with its woollen textile concentration, and the vicinity of Valladolid, a zone of endemic banditry. The armed bands of the *Acordada* were empowered to carry out sentences on the spot. Notable successes in the 1730s included the breaking of the power exercised in Zacatecas by the bandit chieftain, Pedro Razo, and the crushing of a group in the district of Celaya in the Bajío. Free of subordination to the audiencia or to territorial governors, the *Acordada* exercised unlimited jurisdiction in rural areas, responsible directly to the viceroy himself. McLachlan shows that agents of the *Acordada* often served local interest groups. After 1756 this jurisdiction extended into urban areas. The *Acordada*'s principal function consisted in reassuring Spaniards that the viceregal government was acting to uphold law and order. In effect, this amounted to a political demonstration of royal authority, rather than to the functioning of an all-embracing police force. Nevertheless, the *Acordada* did show force now and then to bandit groups and highway robbers, especially after 1747, with the merging of the *guardia mayor de caminos*.[44]

The *Acordada* could not and did not eliminate crime. Several cities, among them Oaxaca and Guadalajara, had a reputation for unruliness. In the 1770s Viceroy Bucareli (1771–9) sent two regular companies to preserve law and order in Guadalajara. In 1789 the Audiencia of New Galicia urged Viceroy Revillagigedo (1789–94) to send troops once again to help defeat the plague of crime. The city could not afford to hire any additional police constables to patrol the streets. Since the Viceroy could spare no troops, the city continued to be unsafe throughout the 1790s. Furthermore, highway robbery and banditry hampered travellers throughout the Intendancies of Guadalajara and Michoacán. In anticipation, as it were, of the type of action that characterised the insurgency of the 1810s, gangs of thieves raided royal tax offices or robbed treasury funds in transit. Similar daring attacks occurred in Puebla and even in the vicinity of Mexico City. Archer draws attention to the efforts of Viceroy Branciforte (1794–7) to extirpate banditry, lest it should prove to be the prelude to a general insurrection.[45]

The Intendant Manuel de Flon complained that the city of Puebla was beset by 'many vagrants, unruly drunks, quarrelsome elements, and other perpetrators of crime'. He referred interestingly to the 'wars between the barrios of the city, in which members of the popular classes would slaughter each other like wild beasts'. We have little documentary information on this; the disorganised judicial archives of Puebla may one day reveal the secrets they may contain. Flon regretted that his predecessors had failed to prevent such conflicts. He proposed to consign offenders to hard labour in road construction and hoped that popular terror at the sight of chain-gangs would provide a deterrent to crime. The Intendant successfully requested the introduction of 'this type of correction' into the city as a means of 'maintaining public order'.[46]

The tighter administrative control provided, particularly at the fiscal level, by the Intendant system, seems to have had little effect on law and order in the localities. The Intendant of Michoacán complained repeatedly in 1792 of thefts of livestock and grain seeds, highway robbery and banditry. The Intendant appeared to believe that local administrators, hacienda owners and *rancheros* were not exhibiting sufficient zeal in the pursuit of thieves. It is difficult to ascertain whether this reflected simply apathy or, more seriously, the complicity of rural élites in the protection of bandit groups. Following a highway robbery on the Pátzcuaro road, he imposed a $100 fine upon any person who failed to assist the local lieutenant of the *Acordada* in his duties. A particularly alarming feature of the Intendant's correspondence is the attention it draws to government failure to apprehend a band of thieves lodged in the Salamanca and Valle de Santiago districts across the Guanajuato border, which became an area of entrenched insurgent activity into 1821.[47] In a comparable exposed border region, between Guadalajara and Michoacán, bandit groups also operated, among them the group led by Martín Toscana and Francisco Gil in the Jiquílpan zone during the 1800s. This band specialised in robbing Spaniards, on the grounds that they had plundered Mexico.[48]

The Intendant of San Luis Potosí feared the consequences of criminality. In the growth of settlements on hacienda lands, he saw a potential source of crime and unrest. Population, furthermore, had increased significantly in the silver-mining district of Catorce and in the town of Matehuala. The economy of San Luis Potosí, however, could not absorb the surplus labour available, especially in view of the rudimentary conditions of industry. Unemployment remained high and the scale of poverty deplorable. The Intendant had appealed in vain to wealthy citizens to invest in employment-creating enterprises that could reduce the level of vagrancy. The haciendas faced similar problems, since many villagers had abandoned their homes in pursuit of a livelihood on the private estates. These 'attached' families ('*arrimados*') lived with neither a regular food supply ('*ración*') from the haciendas nor a regular wage. They depended upon occasional labour or overtime. Whatever they earned came at planting or at the harvest, or in small jobs, such as weeding, or in cattle roundups, when the proprietor or his admini-

strator chose to have them. Their recompense was the right to cut wood
and consume what victuals they could find without actually cultivating
the land themselves. Evidently the landlords feared colonisation of their
own properties by the impoverished marginal groups. Such families
remained idle for much of the year, without a means of livelihood. As a
result, they were driven to theft. The Intendant regarded them as a great
potential danger, and pressed for the formal incorporation of such
groups into villages with a sufficient amount of subsistence lands.[49] The
case of San Luis Potosí will require considerable archival investigation in
the future if we are to understand the connection, if any, between such
factors of underemployment and the origins of social dissidence during
the 1810s.

The assumed connection between unemployment and crime also
appeared in the Bishop of Guadalajara's instructions to his parish priests
in 1797. The Guadalajara region experienced major economic changes
in the late colonial period, which had profound social repercussions.
Yet, despite the evidence of growth, particularly in the expansion of
cotton textile production – valued by 1803–4 at $1.38 million – the
region's economic activities were still not sufficient to absorb the
available labour. The bishop in 1805 suggested the possibility of
tobacco cultivation in the hot coastal zone near Compostela, but the
Royal Tobacco Monopoly had restricted this crop to certain districts in
the Intendancy of Veracruz. Similarly, he urged the crown to protect
industrial workshops and mills in Guadalajara, in order to create further
employment opportunities. This request, however, ran counter to
metropolitan Spain's efforts to stimulate its own textile production at
the expense of American, as a means of Spanish economic revival.[50] Van
Young points to an increasing incidence of rural violence and vaga-
bondage in the decade before 1810. He suggests that the explanation
may lie in 'an ever-increasing impoverishment among the mass of rural
inhabitants during the last century of Spanish domination', since
population pressure in the countryside lessened the amount of land
available to small cultivators.[51] The possibilities of connection between
such conditions and the roots of local insurgency are certainly tantalising. For a brief period in December 1810 and January 1811, Guadalajara became the insurgent capital.

The authorities in Puebla and the landowners of the cereal belt of
Atlixco attributed the high incidence of crime to the agricultural
recession there, which U.S. competition in the Havana flour market had
precipitated. The Intendant saw the 'castes' as the principal offenders,
though he did not elaborate. Within the provincial capital he saw the

lawless element predominant out of a total population of 80,000.52 The estate owners at Atlixco shared this view. They presented a view of 'all kinds of miscreancy' disturbing the peace of their district, caused by high unemployment throughout the central zone. Farm labourers remained idle, unable to pay either tribute or tithe. Vagrancy had become the prevailing pastime.53 In view of the high incidence of insurgent activity in the Intendancy of Puebla and the adjacent region of Tlaxcala, particularly in the period 1811–13, we shall need to examine local conditions more closely if we are to understand the bearing such arguments might possibly have for the 1810s. The marked regional divergences that separated Puebla-Tlaxcala from the centre-north-west help perhaps to explain the different timing of insurgent activity in the former and suggest also a wide variance of social support. The vital Atlixco zone became a key area of dispute. Insurgent activity gave rise to constant and varied problems of public order, which exacerbated those already serious before the rebellion. Disruption in the countryside led to migration into the towns and cities. The records of municipal councils – those of Puebla, Valladolid and Guadalajara, for instance – amply testify to that. Not only questions of order but also of public morality arose. The Military Governor of Puebla, Ramón Díaz de Ortega, for instance, expressed his worry concerning the large number of unattached women that had come into the city during 'the present calamitous circumstances' of the insurgency. Their disproportion in relation to the number of men presented, in his judgement, a cause of moral corruption. In consequence, he proposed to the municipality the establishment of a house of correction, into which such women could be gathered, and put to 'work befitting their sex', under the direction of 'women of well-known virtue'. From their wages, they could thereby earn a living.54 Law and order continued to pose problems in Puebla even after the insurgency had died down. In March 1823, the Civil and Military Governor, the Marqués de Vivanco, supported the payment of a nightwatch which had patrolled the streets when the city had been without military garrison. Vivanco argued that these patrols had banished the 'multitude of thieves, which in the darkness of night used to attack Puebla citizens'.55 Later in the same year, the acting Civil Governor, Lic. Morón, urged the municipality to take action to drive vagrant thieves from the territory under its jurisdiction, since they threatened travellers.56

Landless labourers, dispossessed peasants, the underemployed and the unemployed provided likely recruits to criminal bands. While no inevitable connection should be assumed, crime, nevertheless, offered a means of access to wealth or even status, when legitimate avenues of

ascent proved too competitive or too restrictive. Banditry provided a
major source of income, infinitely preferable to burdensome toils in the
fields or in artisan crafts. Much dispute surrounds the origins and nature
of banditry: it is important to separate it, for instance from vaga-
bondage, which usually resulted from economic stagnation or recession.
Banditry may well reflect conditions of economic growth and, in fact,
represent a by-product of it, particularly where it affected small town
and village communities hitherto remote from the impact of the market
economy.[57] Even so, it has been argued that banditry did not flourish in
colonial New Spain, to anything like the degree that it did in the
nineteenth century. Although the Wars of Independence provided a
stimulus, it was not until after 1857 that brigands commanded regional
control. This state of affairs acquired decisive significance in the 1860s.
Banditry, however, was a common enough phenomenon during the half
century following independence.[58] If banditry did not prove to be the
major preoccupation of government in the colonial period, the activities
of bandit groups certainly took a major toll on life and trade. The
tendency, moreover, for the incidents of banditry to increase as a result
of the unsettling conditions of the 1790s and 1800s appears to be likely.
No peculiarly lower class propensity for crime should be assumed. All
ranks of society, including those at the top, produced recruits and even
leaders of bandit groups. Landlords sometimes entered into arrangements with bandit chieftains to mutual benefit. In such ways an
extra-legal network of relationships permeated the countryside.[59]

Although bandit groups and contrabandists operated outside the law,
they did not function beyond the confines of society. In many cases they
were closely related to the processes of economic life. They dealt with
property-owners, merchants in transit and local villages, and, indeed,
with public officials. In some cases they offered protection; in others
they themselves were protected. Whole families, if not whole clans and
entire villages, earned their livelihood from such clandestine operations.
The profession of muleteer, in great demand since mule-trains formed
the principal means of commercial transit, proved to be but a hair's
breadth from that of contrabandist. Notorious clans, like the
Villagráns, oscillated between the profession of muleteers and that of
bandits. The Osorno clan in the Llanos de Apan was little different.
Such clans merged easily into the freer-flowing violence of the insurrection of 1810, through which they sought to improve their prospects.
Anton Blok argues that the success of the bandit remained contingent
upon protection by local interests. Taking Sicily as his model, Blok
argues that the key to understanding banditry lies in the bandit's

contact with established power-holders.[60] E. J. Hobsbawm sees in banditry a type of primitive social protest. Where bandit groups emerge in response to the deterioration of peasant living standards, their plunder of the rich amounts to a kind of proto-revolutionary action, which Hobsbawm classified as 'social banditry'. In this sense a class conflict element has entered into this characteristic form of rural anarchy.[61] Such an interpretation, while it has the merit of drawing attention to the phenomenon of banditry focusses too singlemindedly upon the concept of social protest. Wider social objectives seem often to be a far cry from the limited and localised self-interest of most such bands. Nevertheless, certain targets were usually regarded as legitimate – itinerant merchants, particularly *gachupín*, landowners who had not come to arrangements with local bandits, and possibly peasants who had not. Geographical and territorial rivalries probably entered into the picture as well. Banditry did not, in any case, recruit uniquely from lower-class sources. It represented not so much a class protest, but the dispossession, resentment and consequent ingenuity of whole regional groupings in a vertical rather than horizontal, fashion. Blok has argued that banditry defused rural protest, rather than acted as a focus for it. It diverted social tensions into a search for quick material rewards at the expense of all groups in society, not merely rich merchants or large landlords. In consequence, Blok sees banditry as 'essentially conservative'.[62] The frequent merging of bandit groups into the local insurgencies of Mexico during the 1810s in no way detracts from such a conclusion, since the autonomous actions of their chieftains in no sense contributed to the realisation of the political goals of the official leadership. They proved to be a constant frustration. Because of its Janus-like quality, banditry is an elusive subject to analyse. In certain cases, it was socially cohesive, in other cases, divisive.

Bandit groups repeatedly changed sides, with the result that a constant overlap existed between the forces of order and disorder. Frequently, it was impossible to distinguish which was which. Both groups contributed to an escalation of anarchy. Royalist authorities developed the process, later continued under Juárez and Díaz, of turning bandits into policemen, who, in turn, adopted bandit methods against their quarry.[63] Rebel bands and bandit groups in the Mexican insurgency did not hesitate to terrorise the rural population, whether for allegedly political objectives, or through naked greed. Archer stresses the impact of violence from both Royalist and insurgent bands upon the country populace. Rebel and bandit incursions inflicted a terror comparable to that incurred from the Royalist forces: each sought to terrorise the village population into severing all contact with the opposing side. For the inhabitants of the countryside, one terror was the same as another.[64] It is difficult to see in Mexican bands any kind of empathy with peasant sufferings. Villages frequently turned against guerrilla bandits, even to the extent of fully co-operating with government authorities. However, peasant co-operation depended strictly upon the government forces' capacity to provide effective protection from marauders.[65]

As insurgency became deeply rooted, illicit trading between merchants and rebel captains became frequent. Central government, which regarded such practices as obstacles to its concept of pacification, failed lamentably to extirpate them. Merchants and entrepreneurs were prepared to pay protection money to armed bands, in return for security of passage through insurgent-occupied areas. In 1811, for instance, the Marqués de Aguayo agreed to pay Rayón $20,000 in goods and cash in order to secure passage for his flocks to market. Guadalupe Victoria in 1815 maintained his band in Veracruz from the sum of $5,400 contributed by local *hacendados*.[66] After rebel bands imposed a blockade upon Veracruz from July 1812, merchants engaged frequently in the payment of protection money, in order to see their convoys through rebel territory. Juan Bautista Lobo, one of the wealthiest Veracruz merchants, paid $60,000 for transit rights.[67] Heavy taxes on trade between the port and the uplands sustained the rebel bands: from such sums, they were able to pay and equip their fighting men. Even strong regular troop formations found it almost impossible to pass fortified rebel positions, such as the Cerro Zapilote, above the Royal Highway to Veracruz. Not only security of transit, but also the termination of irregular trading practices lay behind viceregal efforts to clear the highway from rebel interception. Every social group took part in this illicit commerce.[68] In 1814 rebel-bandit leaders such as Osorno engaged in similar practices with Mexico City from his redoubt in the Puebla sierra.[69] Pedro Moreno in the Altos de Jalisco and P. Torres in Guanajuato, were veritable merchant–chieftains. Such activities signified an alteration in the type and scale of operations pursued by band commanders.[70]

Insurgency frequently subsumed banditry and other expressions of criminality. It is possible that banditry did represent a form of class conflict or of anti-authority protest, at times and in places where political insurgency flourished. Once the political colouring of the revolutionary movement had faded, however, brigands and common criminals reverted to their more characteristic pursuits. In an area of former insurgent activity, banditry continued as if insurgency had never happened. The tithe collector for San Andrés Chalchicomula, for instance, reported to the Cathedral Receivers (*jueces hacedores*) of Puebla that on 29 January 1824, highwaymen had robbed him of $1,000 in tithe receipts.[71] In that sense, the experience of insurgency proved to be for them nothing but a passing phase. In the history of Mexican criminality, the year, 1821, is not a date of significance.

## Responses – counter-insurgency

If an insurgency breaks out within national territory, what should a government do, in order to contain and eventually defeat it? What should be the political response of the established power? Such questions persisted throughout the initial stages of insurgency warfare, largely because government forces, in whatever context, rapidly discovered that punitive measures did not resolve the problem, but, on the contrary, frequently served to keep insurgency alive. The political shock of insurgency exposed, however, the lack of military effectiveness in a number of key provinces, the virtual absence of government armed power in the remoter regions, and the weakness of official authority in areas where long-standing social tensions had already manifested themselves. Counter-insurgency, which develops several stages later in any semblance of coherent form, takes its shape from insurgency. Nevertheless, counter-insurgency need not remain on the defensive. It stands to gain little by accepting a protracted war, which can only benefit insurgents by wearing down the government and expending funds, material and men. The principal objective of insurgency has been to remove population and territory from government control; as a result, insurgent bands would then be able to receive supplies, recruits and intelligence from the areas under their control. The response of counter-insurgency has been to separate insurgent bands from the population, usually by a process of transfer of inhabitants from contested or fringe areas, to places under the surveillance of government forces. The object of such a policy has been to create a military zone, in which those apprehended would be regarded as hostile. In this way, government forces sought to cut off the insurgents from their food supplies, manpower and sources of information. The ultimate goal would be to proceed stage by stage to the elimination of the insurgent-held zones, culminating finally in a concentration of forces upon the usually geographically remote rebel base areas by a process of strategic encirclement. These objectives, however, could require enormous supplies of

material and manpower, in order to gain the military superiority
required to deliver this decisive blow. The marginalisation and military
defeat of insurgency would destroy the political credibility of the
revolutionary movement.[72] If, however, government forces should fail
to clear one major area of insurgent activity and then move away to deal
with another, the likelihood would be that the military and political
challenge of insurgency would rapidly reappear in the first locality,
while the official forces were operating elsewhere in the country.
According to McCuen, the conclusion to be drawn is that 'the first
object of the government authorities must therefore be to establish firm
control of one or more strategic bases from which to operate'. Such a base
has to be not only territorial but also political. Within it, counter-
organisation and the formation of self-defence forces should immediately follow.[73]

Counter-insurgency needs, then, to re-establish control of population. This could not, of course, be done, if government forces were to
remain perpetually confined only to towns and cities that they themselves could more or less defend. The campaign had to be taken from
these urban strongholds into the countryside itself. Sporadic sweeping
of the countryside, no matter how formidable or how frequent, could
not in the long run re-establish government control, unless an effective
presence were first to be established there. As a result, clearing
operations had to be accompanied by the gradual establishment of
strong, defensible positions, first at the perimeter, and then, stage by
stage, deeper into the countryside, until it became possible to advance
the lines of government-held territory further into rebel-held zones.
Within these newly occupied government-protected zones, a new type
of defence force had to be created from among army veterans, militiamen, reservists, property-owners, and sympathetic local populace.
These self-defence forces could then take over from the army in the
regions within and continue the task of counter-insurgency there, while
the armed forces operated in the vanguard and concentrated upon the
extension of the government line of advance. From these lines, probing
expeditions into rebel areas could take place in swift thrusts. The key to
the defeat of the rebel bands would be to turn the insurgent technique of
armed infiltration against them, and to accompany this with territorial
offensives. Patrol of highways and a defensive strategy based on the
cities would not be enough.[74] The tenability of the government-held
zone depended ultimately upon the capacity of the official armed forces
and the self-defence arm to protect villagers within its perimeter from
rebel incursions and reprisals. If villagers could not be adequately

protected, nothing existed to prevent them — generally for their own good — from co-operating once more with rebel infiltrators or armed bands.[75]

The concept of counter-organisation recurs repeatedly throughout the Mexican documentation of the insurgency period. The full implications of this aspect of counter-insurgency policy were explored and applied in New Spain in the 1810s. The phenomenon of the defended village or estate, however, was nothing new in Mexico, since it had already become normal practice in the north as protection against Indian raiding parties, which the soldiery were unable to defeat. The classic strategy of defence — the holding position — had led to the line of fortresses across the exposed north known as *presidios*. From these positions, an offensive strategy could also be applied. From the later sixteenth century, such internal fortifications were no longer necessary in the settled and pacified central regions. In the north, however, especially with the worsening Indian incursions after the mid eighteenth century, hacienda-owners fortified their properties and armed their work force. Several of the military commanders who took part in the counter-insurgency of the 1810s had had experience of the turbulent northern frontier.[76] Royalist commanders frequently referred to their 'organisation' of villages, towns and estates. 'Organization' required earthworks to defend perimeters and the garrison of volunteer forces, sometimes under army command, but usually raised by local towns and proprietors, in areas that had once been prime centres of insurgent activity. The object, outlined by Viceroy Venegas in 1811 and Viceroy Calleja in 1813, was to involve prominent citizens in the defence of their own interests. The application of these policies coincided with the degeneration of the Mexican insurgency into marauding bands, and strove to combat their depredations.[77]

To give effect to re-organisation, Mexican Royalist commanders began to apply resettlement policies. These were designed to overcome the obstacle presented by rebel control of the countryside, which prevented government-held positions from receiving food supplies. Resettlement involved clearance of disputed areas or remote localities and concentration of population in protected localities. Iturbide, then military commander in Guanajuato, explained this policy in June 1816,

The military commanders shall delineate, after proper reflection, the places and estates to which all the districts' inhabitants are to be concentrated. Our troops will abandon those small villages which they cannot patrol. The immense number of scattered settlements throughout the hills and mountains are to be destroyed without exception. Anyone discovered beyond the loyalist demarcations established in each province will be pronounced hostile and subjected to capital punishment.[78]

Such actions proved in many instances to be counter-productive. They either obliged peasants to flee into the towns and cities, or drove them to seek refuge with the rebel bands. Nevertheless, concentration policies proved to be a classic expression of counter-insurgency techniques.[79] Rebel fortification of strong positions, combined with strikes at government positions, frustrated the organisation and resettlement policies, especially since insurgent forces threatened reprisals against those villages which co-operated with counter-insurgency strategy.[80] The survival of strong rebel redoubts in mountainous or remote areas obliged Royalist commanders to adopt a style of mobile warfare similar to that waged by the irregular insurgent bands: Anastasio Bustamante and others developed the sweeping unit strategy, the *destacamentos volantes*. Bustamante was already practising it in the northern districts of the Valley of Mexico and across the Llanos de Apan in 1813–15, and developed it in the Bajío and the adjacent mountainous perimeter between 1817 and 1820.[81]

Combating insurgency fell to the military. During the period, 1811–16, the military dimension clearly predominated in New Spain. Civilian authority receded before the extension of military power. In many instances where civilian local administration had broken down, army officers took over civilian authority as well as their military command.[82] Within the insurgent zones, as well, civil–military relations frequently became tense. Rebel chieftains superseded the previous civilian administration and, accordingly, collected taxes and tithes. The blurring of civil and military roles at many different levels impeded not only the political goals of insurgency but also those of the counter-insurgency as well. The evident superiority of the military arm over the civil administration in government-held zones served to reduce the credibility of the official power as the effective and legitimate authority. Military rule in the provinces threatened to compromise government claims to be able to control the insurgency.[83]

However, the greatest problem for the counter-insurgency seems to have been that of numbers. There were simply not enough troops. Royalist commanders frequently complained not only of the unreliability of their men, but also of the inadequacy of their numbers. The latter complaint, not uncharacteristic among generals, was exacerbated by the insurgent style of warfare. French Revolutionary and Napoleonic armies, for instance, had been pinned down and on occasions severely defeated by irregular bands in central and southern Italy in the later

1790s and 1800s, and in Spain between 1808 and 1814.[84] At the height of the peninsula insurgency, 250,000 French army effectives in 1810–12, still failed to eradicate the guerrilla bands. In New Spain, the defection of militiamen to the rebels in the early months of the insurrection revealed the extent of subversion and rebel support. The continued struggle in the peninsula prevented the arrival of Spanish regiments until early 1812, when the Third Regiment of Asturias, the First Battalion of Lovera and the First Battalion of the American Regiment, commanded by the Mariscal del Campo, the Conde de Castro Terreño and Brigadier Juan José Olazábal arrived in Veracruz.[85]

As the official armed forces recovered control of the main provincial cities, lost after September 1810, self-defence forces were needed to defend positions won and to hold ground in the rear of the advancing army. The cost of such forces to municipal councils and private proprietors raised further the question of civil-military relations. This was especially the case, when *hacendados* expressed resentment at the cost involved or delayed in fitting out the self-defence force on their estates. Insurgent depredations, moreover, further reduced their willingness or capacity to raise and equip such a body. Such conflicts formed the background to the allegations made by private proprietors against a number of army commanders, chief among whom was Iturbide in the Bajío.[86] Nevertheless, local defence forces were formed by many private proprietors. In San Luis Potosí, for instance, the administrator of the Hacienda de Bocas supplied 180 employees and dependents of the estates in the region as an auxiliary force to fight with the Royalists. From the colour of their jackets, they became known as '*los tamarindos*'.[87] The formation of private defence forces was not a new phenomenon in the Mexican north. Chevalier cites the example of a henchman of the Conde de San Mateo Valparaíso who became a Royalist colonel between 1810–18 and maintained for one year a force of 800 men, to whom he paid one peso per day, along the northern frontier. This body, however, was formed more to combat marauding Indians than insurgent bands.[88] Royalist militia commanders, often themselves local proprietors, in many central and centre-northern regions attempted, with varying degrees of success, to mobilise their rural labour force for the purpose of combating the rebel bands. Sometimes, these efforts were not successful. Sugar-estate proprietors in the districts of Cuautla, Cuernavaca and Yautepec, when faced with the advance of Morelos' forces in 1810–11, attempted to raise a fighting force among their workers to resist the insurgents. In Cuautla, for instance, the local Royalist commanders, pointed out late in November 1810, that it was the Indian villagers who had risen. At Tlaltizapán, for instance, he commented that it had taken only one insurgent to raise the entire village. In response, he called for the arming of the hacienda work force. There were nine haciendas in the district. He wanted a force of ten men, armed and mounted, from each, and ten men each from the villages which had not risen.[89] On the dangerously exposed eastern edges of the Valley of Mexico, Ciriaco de Llano, at that time operating with government forces out of Texcoco, urged estate-owners to arm their work forces – 'if the hacienda-owners who suffer so greatly would only get together and, at the cost of very little sacrifice, defend, as they certainly should, their own interests, which are the same as the holy and just cause that we ourselves defend, then this accursed plague will be finished in a few days'. Llano wanted to form a Patriot Company from hacienda owners and leading citizens. Similarly, he convened a meeting of residents, *hacendados*, *rancheros* and village governors from the districts of Apam and Otumba, areas of recurrent guerrilla activity, to see whether they were willing to maintain two veteran dragoon companies from their own resources. Full support was promised for all the above, with the exception of, perhaps the decisive group, the *hacendados* of Otumba and Zempoala, whose replies had not been received.[90] Rebels continued to recruit support from rural workers in the Llanos de Apan and adjacent areas, and from Indian villagers. Early in February 1812, rebel contingents, raised by associates of Morelos and Rayón, occupied the Hacienda de San Bartolomé del Monte, near Calpulalpan, and threatened not only that town itself, but also Otumba and Texcoco.[91]

The formation of self-defence forces among hacienda workers and dependents suggests that hacienda owners could count on the loyalty of their employees and peons. Obviously this varied from property to property in accordance with labour conditions and patron-client relationships. Nevertheless, the recurrence of this phenomenon throughout the archival documentation and the clear readiness of both royalist commanders and proprietors to attempt their creation, indicates that it was regarded as a feasible proposition. Although there is evidence of hacienda worker fraternisation with insurgent bands, it cannot have been such a generalised phenomenon that proprietors identified it as the principal source of insurgent support. As we shall see subsequently, there were many disputes on private estates concerning payment and labour conditions. Occasionally there was a strike or a minor rebellion. It was usually the grievances of the resident labourer, the *gañán*, that lay at the root. Yet, the resident workers, the *peones acasillados*, were a relatively privileged group, with their secure labour, their wage and maize ration, their housing and integration into the structure of hacienda patronage. They had much to lose if they joined itinerant rebel bands. Perhaps it would take only exceptional circumstances, such as the breakdown of the food supply, to throw into jeopardy the security they had gained. Even then, there was no guarantee that life outside the hacienda would be any better than within. Furthermore, a subsistence crisis, no matter how momentarily severe, did not alter the long term trends that weakened the rural workers' position – population growth, rising prices, competition for land. Only when the resident work force was confronted with the realities of insurgent incursions and the flight of owners to the cities would the issue of changed allegiances become uppermost. Such arguments suggest that the problem for the hacienda was not as a rule the dissidence of the internal labour force. Most probably, the prime source of insurgent support in areas in which haciendas and *pueblos* existed side by side, derived from aggrieved and hard pressed village communities, particularly where peasants were short of subsistence lands or deprived of their traditional pasture, cultivation or water rights. Village resentment at private proprietors' pressure on the labour force added further fuel to the fire. The threat presented by the hacienda may well have been the decisive factor in revolutionising the peasant. Within the hacienda, it is probable that in many cases the patriarchal bonds remained intact. There would, of course, be many exceptions. Once insurgency had died down, these bonds would, however, last for another century.[92]

# 3

## Conflict, protest and rebellion

Localised rebellions of limited duration were not infrequent occurrences in the colonial and early national periods. Most such occurrences stemmed from administrative abuses, fiscal impositions, altered labour practices, violated customary rights, or injured religious sentiment. In predominantly rural communities, the demands of the agricultural cycle alone restricted the possible duration of these types of rebellion. Many of them, in any case, were little more than extended demonstrations or protests. In Spanish America, the infrequency of large-scale revolt generally resulted from the colonial system's apparent capacity to absorb grievances, to provide some prospect of legal redress, and above all to ensure the survival of peasant communities that often derived from the pre-Columbian era. In regions distant from the central administrative core of New Spain, geographical remoteness often contributed to this survival. Paul Friedrich, for instance, has drawn attention to the survival of Tarascan lands in central Michoacán, where 'the ruling castes of *mestizos* and Spaniards were mostly content to collect taxes from the local caciques and village elders without interfering in other matters'.[1] William Taylor's examination of peasant society in Oaxaca reveals a very substantial survival of indigenous landownership.[2]

While documentary evidence shows readily enough the sources of local tension, the causes of rebellions are difficult to uncover. The former did not inevitably lead to the latter. The search for the roots of insurrection leads in many directions. Yet, wherever we look, further causes appear, and the complexity and diversity of motivation multiplies. Rebellion could result from exploitation of local grievances by ambitious power-seekers, or from power struggles among local personalities. Both such agencies were capable of linking local events to a wider scene and to broader social and political forces, in an effort to further their own positions. Since grievances existed with a frequency not difficult to identify, exploitation and escalation lay inherent as

74

possibilities – potential, though rarely, as it turned out, actual. Potentiality for extension lay, not merely in common sources of conflict across a broad geographical area, but more especially in confluence with other, generally more pressing elements. These might consist of a crisis at the viceregal government level, a conflict of legitimacy at the highest levels, a loss of religious harmony, an alteration in the nature of the relationship between the Mexico City administration and the regions, dislocation as a result of unemployment and food shortages. We shall discuss the confluence of such factors in the subsequent chapters. At present, though, we need to examine in depth the roots of conflict in the locality.

These roots lay more often than not in local variations in land-ownership, labour services, water rights or customary practices. Ecological conditions and abrupt weather changes could exacerbate the impact of such conflicts, and intensify them to the pitch of a rebellious outbreak. A combination of changing pressures from without and subsistence crisis within the villages was capable of inflaming local sentiments to a dangerous extent. Breaches of traditional practice by landowners or public officials at a time of intensified search for subsistence could well produce the shock that drove a sedentary community to rebel. It seems that frequently the origins of rebellion lay in the erosion of rights and status formerly enjoyed but subsequently thrown into jeopardy. The erosion of traditional modes of life would undermine the entire basis of a community's existence, and thrust it to the brink of despair. Even so, fear of the consequences of armed rebellion, not least of which was the likelihood of punishment, often acted as a powerful deterrent to action. Only rarely, and certainly not in New Spain until September 1810, did a broad enough spectrum of rural and urban discontent provide sufficient manpower for a generalised insurrection.[3] Even in such instances, rebel forces would tend to return to their lands at planting and harvest times, and, thereby, call off any offensive action that might be contemplated. Government forces, in contrast, faced no comparable restraints. Similarly, rebel leaders frequently encountered difficulties in persuading peasant groups to fight beyond their own localities and in defence of their immediate families.[4] J. C. Scott's conclusions could well apply to colonial New Spain: 'to speak of rebellion is to focus on those extraordinary moments when peasants seek to restore or remake their world by force. It is to forget both how rare these moments are and how historically exceptional it is for them to lead to a successful revolution'.[5]

We should perhaps make a conceptual distinction between urban riot and rural rebellion, while at the same time bearing in mind that most urban areas were closely related in social and economic terms to their agricultural hinterland. Though few riots lasted long, they did on occasions threaten government control of major cities. In the main, however, urban riots tended to have localised causes, such as the riot in Puebla in August 1744 and the disturbances resulting from food shortages in Querétaro in November 1749. Nevertheless, there were some dramatic exceptions. The most notable was the Quito 'riot' of 1765, during the course of which the audiencia virtually lost control of the city for nearly a year. In New Spain, the eruptions of 1766–7 throughout the cities of the centre-north-west had profound consequences and in their detailed local outcome anticipated later events in the 1810s. Yet, at the time they never ceased to be disunified, incoherent, and short-lived. The root cause of the riots of the years 1765–7 lay in popular opposition to renewed fiscal pressures by the Bourbon state. Motivated primarily by metropolitan rather than by specifically American interests, these policies reflected a largely unwelcome reassertion of peninsular control in an American Empire that had been traditionally left to its own devices. The significance of these earlier riots lay in two aspects. They revealed a broad hostility to government policy that cut across social groups and for a time aligned non-élite and élite members of colonial society. They tended, furthermore, to extend beyond anti-fiscal protest to encompass a range of grievances, and thereby became for a brief period movements of a threateningly political nature. The memory of such activities tended to influence the perspectives of subsequent generations. In the later phase of protests, between 1779 and 1783, urban riot and rural rebellion tended to coincide in a manner deeply menacing to the survival of metropolitan authority in two viceroyalties, New Granada and Peru. The Arequipa riot of 1780, initially against fiscal innovations, was a case in point. The early stages of the Tupac Amaru rebellion after November 1780 revealed not only a similar propensity to collaboration among varying social groups in southern Peru, but also the role of local traders and muleteers in providing the means of cohesion over broad geographical areas. In the Socorro province of the north-eastern highlands of New Granada, the *Comunero* revolt began as a protest against the fiscal impositions of the Visitor-General, Juan Francisco Gutiérrez de Piñeres, and extended to complaints of peninsular monopolisation of offices. This revolt, equally, cut across social groups. A series of localised rebellions and riots generally in opposition to fiscal measures broke out across the territories of New Granada and Quito from the late 1770s into the 1800s. Few were of more than local significance in themselves. In contrast, the major rebellions such as those in Lower and Upper Peru in the early 1780s showed how the Spanish imperial state could lose control of large areas of territory for relatively long periods of time. Rebellion and temporary loss of territory resulted from the Madrid government's apparent abandonment of its traditional methods of rule by consent and collusion, practices which had enabled a weak Spanish metropolis to maintain its position in the Americas for so long. The actions of over-zealous Visitors-General after 1765 initiated a process of break-down of consent, which threatened to endanger the balance which previous metropolitan governments had managed to hold intact. This, then, was the historical context within which localised riots and rebellions in that period took place, though in themselves they were rarely connected to this wider projection. Nevertheless, as factors capable of influencing popular mobilisation, these lesser issues, often unresolved over decades, enabled bridges to be built between the dissident élite and non-élite social groups. This, in turn, recreated in the 1810s on a larger scale the dangers already foreseen in the mid-1760s and the early 1780s, especially since the general imperial crisis after 1808 magnified their potentiality.[6]

During the colonial and early national period four types of conflict appear most frequently. The first type resulted from administrative abuses or fiscal pressures. It involved confrontation between subjects and state employees or their merchant-investors. The second type derived from conditions on the land, and involved day labourers, resident workers, tenants, estate-managers and landlords. In the third category changes in customary rights or mining practices provided the source of discord. Fourthly, pressure on the food supply, following harvest failures, dislocated many peasant communities and generated varying degrees of unrest in town and country. We shall examine this fourth type in chapter four. At present we shall consider the first three types of conflict. None of them posed any serious challenge either to the viceregal government or to the dominant groups in the locality. Their causes varied and the districts in which they took place differed widely. In consequence, though certain common features are distinguishable, conditions did not exist for their development into broadly-based regional rebellions capable of challenging the colonial régime. Such a political vision, in any case, would have advanced well beyond the limited context of the village or district protest movement. The three categories of rebellion we shall now consider contained within them-selves their own idiosyncrasies and unique characteristics.

## Conflict resulting from administrative abuses or fiscal pressures

These were the most common types of conflict in the colonial period; often little more than demonstrations or protests. While such rebellions cannot under any circumstances be regarded as precursors for the rising of 1810, they, nevertheless, drew attention to persistent, unresolved problems, and to areas in which grievances had become pronounced. The existence of such problems and the failure to secure redress may explain the deep-rooted nature of the insurgency in such localities during the 1810s. The insurrection subsumed many of these pre-existing tensions and gave them wider range on a broader scale of conflict. Even so, few, if any, such conflicts ceased to exist either after a locally successful counter-insurgency policy or after the achievement of Mexican Independence in 1821. On the contrary, the origins of many nineteenth-century rebellions lay precisely in these colonial roots.

Administrative abuses provoked opposition: where redress failed through legitimate channels, recourse to violence followed. Such often proved to be the rule. A well-documented source of conflict was the *repartimiento*.[7] In contravention of the law local administrators (*alcaldes mayores*) enforced trade monopolies on behalf of their merchant backers (*habilitadores*) in the districts entrusted to them by a metropolitan government that could not afford to pay their salaries. The abuses that frequently arose at the hands of the *alcaldes mayores* or their lieutenants provided the mainspring of grievances. In its sporadic struggle for reform, the viceregal government often found itself reduced to impotence or simply outpaced by events. The *repartimiento* helped to explain the origins of the rebellions which spread across Oaxaca during the middle of the seventeenth century. Beginning in the district of Tehuantepec in March 1660, villagers, seeing no legitimate means of redress available to them, killed the *alcalde mayor* and burned down his official residence. Similar outbreaks followed in Nejapa, Ixtepejí and some twenty towns altogether. In Tlaxcala and Michoacán, regions with comparable problems, rebellions also occurred in the same period. That is not to argue that they had become generalised, since conditions in each district remained distinct and distances great. Nevertheless, in Oaxaca, at any rate, the news had spread. No overall unifying factors existed which could have resulted in a broadly based or, still less, co-ordinated insurrection. In consequence, the Oaxaca rebellions did not constitute a threat to the viceregal government from a popular movement in the regions. Instead, these revolts simmered down within a few months. A demonstration of authority by an *oidor* (magistrate) of the Audiencia of Mexico and by the Bishop of Oaxaca managed without much difficulty to secure the return of peace during the course of 1661. Justice for the ringleaders; mercy for the beguiled; these were the maxims followed in the punishment of the rebels. Little, if any, evidence exists of severe government repression of these aggrieved villagers. On the contrary, the political skill and strength of personality exhibited by the *oidor* and the bishop would have rendered such a violent government response wholly redundant. In any case, the miscreants of Oaxaca, as so many others elsewhere, had constantly affirmed their loyalty to the crown, in which in ideal terms they saw the source of justice and revindication.[8]

Similarly, more than a century later the rebellions in Papantla and Acayucan in August and October 1787, respectively, showed no hostility whatever towards the idealised symbol of the crown. In both cases hostility towards the *alcaldes mayores* proved to be a cause, as in Oaxaca in 1660. Indian resentment towards officers of the royal tobacco monopoly further complicated matters and led to seizure of the town. When the local militia proved incapable of putting down the revolt, the Governor of Veracruz sent in regular troops to do the job. Indians also took possession of Acayucan for a few weeks, and the town had likewise to be recovered by force. It is worth examining the case of Papantla, since the experience of the insurgency of the 1810s should be set within the context of a series of earlier and subsequent rebellions. Previous revolts had taken place in Papantla in 1743 and 1768. In the latter year, the issue had been the *alcalde mayor*'s proposal to cut down trees.[9] When the rebellion of 1787 broke out, the 100 or so men of the Mixed Company of Militia, in theory stationed there, were nowhere to be seen. They lived in remote *ranchos* in the Tuxpan district. It took a whole month to put together one company. Papantla was a district in which considerable mercantile capital was invested in the vanilla trade, an important Mexican export to Europe. In 1804, its population came to 26,028. Like so many other districts in the gulf coastal zone and in the warm uplands, clandestine tobacco plantings were detected in Papantla by the authorities, which in the mid-1790s embarked upon sporadic campaigns to uproot them, in face of local opposition. During the nineteenth century, the district continued to be a scene of conflict. In the 1810s, it remained for long an insurgent stronghold in the Huasteca of Veracruz, in close association with the rebel base areas of Misantla and Nautla.[10] The Spanish Vidal de Villamil family controlled the town administration and militia, until they were expelled in the insurrection of June 1812, when all the Papantla troops and a large part of the inhabitants went over to the insurgents, who by then had gained a powerful position in the Veracruz interior. The Vidals left behind assets calculated at $100,000, which fell into the hands of the 'bandits'. The small ruling clique of 'good Spaniards' or 'honourable' citizens, however, managed to recapture the town for a few days in a 'counter-revolution', launched with the assistance of the parish priest. Lack of assistance from Tuxpan and the imminent convergence of rebel bands on Papantla, however, forced the counter-revolutionary group to abandon their position and flee to Royalist-held Zacapoaxtla in the north Puebla sierra.[11] Papantla became the scene of further rebellions which covered a vast area from the gulf coast into eastern Hidalgo and the north Puebla sierra in 1836–8 under the leadership of Mariano Olarte. In 1845-8 rebellion spread across the Huasteca. Further revolts occurred in 1891, 1896 and 1906.[12]

A similar history of turbulence could be seen in the case of Acayucan. This cotton-producing district had, like the dye or textile-producing districts of Oaxaca, experience of the *repartimiento*. The men worked on the plantations, while the women spun and wove at home. There and in the districts of Tlalixcoyán, Medellín and Tuxtla (Cotaxtla) merchants of Puebla with interests in textile production traditionally capitalised the processes of cotton production through the agency of the local *alcaldes mayores*. During the 1780s and 1790s the latter had on occasions sought to preserve trade monopolies and keep out interlopers. The districts of Acayucan, Tlalixcoyán and Cosamaloapan became centres of insurgent activity after 1812.[13] One of the causes may have been the general economic decline and social dislocation of the Gulf coast hinterland zones. Quirós certainly suggests such an explanation in his report of 1814, where he attributes the reasons for decline to the squeezing out of tenants (*colonos*) and *rancheros* by large proprietors from c. 1790 onwards and to the recruitment of militia lancers from among the local farming population. The testimony of Quirós points to the impoverishment of the *colono* and *ranchero* element of the rural population in the two decades before 1810. As a result the dispossessed farming population had resorted to crime as a means of earning a livelihood. They had rustled the cattle of the estate owners and stolen their horses as a better means of rounding up the cattle, which they slaughtered and sold as jerked beef in the upland towns of Córdoba, Orizaba and Jalapa.[14] Acayucan remained a centre of discontent after the War of Independence. Reina refers to the revolt of 1840 as a 'caste war'. A further revolt in 1881–4 broke out against hacienda-owners.[15]

A similar trouble spot of long duration proved to be the southern border zone of the Intendancies of Puebla and Mexico, where quite different cultural and ecological conditions prevailed. This was the region that included the districts of Tlapa and Chilapa, where the Indian population spoke several different languages, among them Nahuatl, Tlapaneco and Mixtec. Given the wide range of climatic zones in this region, a diversity of products were grown, that ranged from the normal maize, beans and chile to cotton, sugar-cane, cochineal dye, medicinal sage (*chía*) and gourds for sale in Puebla.[16] Villagers in Tlapa had since 1716 been engaged in conflict with the Moctezuma family over disputed communal lands. From the mid-1760s the audiencia had investigated the question of Chilapa's alleged dispossession by the same family, though it had ultimately decided in favour of the latter.[17] This region had remained unsettled – and certainly not well known by the authorities – throughout the period up to the Hidalgo rising. The appearance of Morelos on the Pacific coast in November 1810 spread rumours throughout the hinterland and further sierras. The chief Indian of Tlapa, a former governor by the name of Agustín Mariano Vázquez, was arrested by the subdelegate as a suspect, on the grounds that he had expressed a willingness to co-operate with the insurgents. The incoming governor, Diego Dolores, and his colleagues, were prevented from taking office for the same reason. Between them the subdelegate and the parish priest sought to nip in the bud any dissidence that manifested itself. Even so, the *asesor ordinario* of Puebla feared that such hasty action could precipitate an insurrection throughout the entire district.[18]

Chilapa became Morelos' destination at the end of his first campaign on 17 August 1811. This town for a time became the southern insurgent base. Its inhabitants – as in a number of other cases of towns with strong insurgent affiliations – earned their livelihood as muleteers, specifically in the cotton trade, from the Pacific zones of production to the textile cities of Puebla and Mexico City. Chilapa and Tlapa became Morelos' bases for the offensive of November 1811 into Puebla.[19] The same region became the focus of widespread insurrection in 1842–4 and to a lesser degree in 1849 – partly in response to the collapse of the cotton economy through imported fibres, and partly in opposition to recent government fiscal pressures. Moreover, in 1842 the Tlapa Indians complained that in 129 years no judicial recourse had resulted in the return of their lands.[20]

The regions to the north-east and south-east of the Valley of Mexico contained some of the most turbulent communities in the viceroyalty, a situation not mitigated by the presence of the silver-mining zone of Real del Monte in the immediate vicinity of Pachuca. These areas would become centres of deeply rooted insurgency for much of the 1810s. Taylor refers to the Actopan revolt of 1756 in opposition to a labour draft for the drainage of mines precisely at the time of the crop harvest. In response to a projected draft of 2,000 individuals, an alliance of villagers with lower-class townspeople led to a three day riot and eight deaths or injuries among the Spanish element of the population. In the Tulancingo district in 1769 several thousand villagers from places as distant as Mextitlán and Tenango took part in a millenarian upsurge fired by the cult of Guadalupe.[21]

These were the zones of maguey cultivation, lands yielding poor cereal crops, hard pressed through their ecological vulnerability. Here the huge estates of the Condes de Jala and Regla were concentrated. Regla, of course, had risen to prosperity as a result of timely investments in the Real del Monte mines. We shall shortly examine his relationship with the mine labour force. The districts of Zempoala and Otumba had become centres of unrest from at least 1780. Several villages claimed exemption from *pulque* tax on alcohol used for their own consumption. In consequence, the Royal Customs Administrator in Apan complained in February 1802 that the Indians of Zempoala district had always been unruly and disobedient when it came to *pulque* tax payment. They had not even shrunk from violence in their resistance to it. In Tulancingo the subdelegate put the Indian governor and officials in prison in 1807 after refusal to pay an extra tax for the repair of the parish church. Almost from the first these regions became areas of entrenched insurgent support.[22] Late in 1813 the Royalist commander in Pachuca, Lieutenant Colonel Francisco de Villaldea, felt that he could not count upon the loyalty of the urban militia forces that garrisoned the town and Real del Monte. Furthermore certain citizens of Pachuca maintained close contact with the insurgents in the countryside. By April 1814 Villaldea concluded that the situation throughout the entire region was 'critical'. Until Zempoala which he identified as the focus of rebellion in 1814–15 had been reduced, he saw no hope for the pacification of the Llanos de Apan, without which the silver supply, the *pulque* estates and the transit routes to Mexico City would continue to be endangered. Pressure from hacienda owners continued to provide causes of rebellion in Otumba and Pachuca in 1847–8.[23]

In all the above categories of unrest – and in those in the Sierra Gorda of Querétaro–Guanajuato–San Luis Potosí, which we shall examine shortly – a striking feature is their prevalence throughout the eighteenth century and their recurrence during the nineteenth century. Many districts, then, remained trouble spots of long duration, in which outstanding tensions became for a time subsumed into the broader insurrection of 1810–21, conveniently described as the War of Independence. In this sense the latter represented merely another stage – albeit a more consciousness-raising affair – in a protracted series of conflicts, that appeared to have neither a beginning nor an end. Tutino draws attention to the anomalous position of the communities of the Sierra Gorda, the mountain zone which ranged across north-eastern Querétaro and eastern Guanajuato and San Luis Potosí. There, Indian cultivators remained largely unaffected by Hispanic influences until the delayed military, religious and economic penetration of the area. Indeed, as late as the mid eighteenth century, Gómez Canedo shows that the Sierra Gorda still continued to be to a large measure a pagan redout of '*Indios mecos*' or *Chichimecos*, who frequently robbed or attacked haciendas in the vicinity. Expeditions of punishment had achieved little success. During the 1740s and 1750s, however, the Franciscans embarked upon a programme of evangelisation and mission construction. At the same time, in 1742 the crown placed the Sierra Gorda under the military authority of Colonel José de Escandón, as a special 'frontier' region. The Sierra Gorda, the cordillera borderland zone of three distinct regions, had already in the eighteenth century become an area of sporadic unrest over scant maize lands, inadequate water supplies, pressure of taxation and disputed customary rights. These were areas of extreme ecological vulnerability. We shall examine shortly the impact of such pressures upon the villages of Toliman and Xichú, two cases in point. The maize crisis of 1785–7, which we shall discuss in chapter four, took a severe toll in such regions, as it did likewise in the Pachuca-Tulancingo-Zempoala zone and its neighbouring districts of Tula, Cadereita, Ixmiquílpan and Zimapan which requested substantial tribute relief.[24] Many such regions, like similar trouble spots in Mexico, were remote or undesirable for settlement. As such they frequently lay beyond the effective political control of the central government. They had never been centres of sedentary agricultural exploitation, and, as such, had not provided governments with the prospect of a firm tax base.

Local rebellion and village unrest could not and did not of themselves challenge either the colonial élites or the republican state that emerged after 1823. Such regions as those mentioned above, moreover, were quite distinct from those from which, for very different reasons, the insurrection of September 1810 arose. Nevertheless, they help to account for the long duration of the local insurgency which resulted from it. Taylor has argued for the absence of any general insurrections against colonial rule, or in the form of class war: 'nearly all were spontaneous, short-lived armed outbursts by members of a single community in reaction to threats from outside; they were 'popular' uprisings in which virtually the entire community acted collectively and usually with identifiable leadership'.[25] Those we have examined so far certainly correspond to this model. Mexican revolts tended to focus upon hated symbols of outside authority or upon agents of alien power – the official royal residences in towns, the district administrators, the *repartidores*. In this respect, then, Mexican rebellions differed little from those of medieval Europe in their limited features – opposition to impositions, to foreign domination, or to expansion of city dominance. Such instinctive reactions did not presuppose political objectives on a wider scale. Dispute rarely focussed around the role of the crown or the person of the king: rebellion occurred in default of redress and in protest at the actions of the king's servants, or, indeed, those of the Church, or the *seigneurie*.[26] Most times the Spanish colonial system was capable of absorbing the shocks thus meted out to it. Limited rebellion did not presage collapse.

## Protests resulting from abuse of the labour force or from alterations in customary rights and tenure

Labour or land disputes rarely give rise to outright rebellions. Similarly their easy appearance in the archival documentation should not lead us to assume a frequent breakdown of social relations among rural communities. We should not conclude from the evidence of disputes that a constant tension between employers or administrators and day labourers or resident workers characterised rural life. On the contrary, evidence also exists – more by the lack of it than by its abundance – of harmonious relationships among the multifarious groups living and working together in the locality. It is certainly true that isolated rebellions, themselves little more than incidents, occurred on the land, but the countryside was not seething with discontent. They originated from working conditions, physical or verbal abuse of the labour force, from changes in recognised practices, disputes over land or water rights, from peasant incursion into hacienda lands, or from invasions of peasant cereal lands by landlords' livestock. Riley's study of labour relations in Tlaxcala shows that in 1741 estate-owners of the provinces were complaining that shortage of labour was pushing up wages. They wanted to enlist government support to enforce labour residence on their properties and to forbid increases in wages. Such requests, of necessity, involved the whole issue of whether the Spanish colonial régime was prepared to tolerate the enserfment of rural labour in the interests of the private proprietor. That policy was never adopted, since the colonial authorities, whatever their limitations and failings, consistently opposed the idea of serfdom. The contrast between Spanish America and Eastern Europe was, therefore, striking. In effect, the viceregal government acted as mediator between employer and labour force.[27]

A series of disputes resulting from abuse of labour occurred throughout the province of Puebla from the 1770s involving in particular the districts of Atlixco, Huejotzingo and San Juan de los Llanos. The resident labour force (*gañanes*) secured the support of the viceroy and audiencia for a series of official statements to the effect that *gañanes* were free men possessed of the right to take their labour where they chose. Option to exercise this right occasioned a series of appeals by landowners based upon the argument that workers were naturally 'idle' and 'drunken'. Evidence exists of their failure to retain resident labourers on their lands in some cases. *Gañanes*, moreover, would not tolerate verbal abuse or physical ill-treatment without protest. They frequently successfully resisted it or collectively demonstrated their indignation when it occurred. Between 1776 and 1778 the *alcalde mayor* of Tepeaca registered nine cases of ill-treatment of workers by proprietors, administrators or their dependents. One frequent cause of worker complaint was employer indebtedness to the labour force. Failure to pay wages, often through economic difficulties of proprietorship, encouraged *gañanes* to assert their right to take their labour elsewhere. In 1777, for instance, a group of *indios gañanes* from a Tepeaca estate, the Hacienda de San Marcos in Acatzingo, appeared in the city of Puebla in order to press their claim for unpaid wages on behalf of themselves and of their companions. Although the long lawsuit which they had pursued in Puebla was finally decided in their favour, a new dispute arose when it was revealed that the hacienda account books had been lost in the Tepeaca civil court. The Puebla authorities continued to uphold the labourers' position, and accordingly, the creditors agreed to a private agreement with their workers. However, nothing was paid. Accordingly, the *gañanes* returned to Puebla to plead their case once more and to protest that litigation was proving too costly for them. 'We cannot spend several days in a row in Puebla. It is necessary to have knowledge of the law, which we do not have, since we are uneducated *gañanes*, and we need to go back to work on our estates.' They duly appointed a priest to negotiate with their creditors and collect the amount owing. Before the public notary, they explained that 'we

ourselves do not know how to read and we cannot sign our names'.[28]
*Gañanes* on the Hacienda de San Sebastián Puchingo in San Juan de los
Llanos appealed in 1782 for the finalising of accounts. Their spokesman,
Melchor Nicolás, described as their '*capitán*', complained to the *alcalde
mayor* of their discontent and impoverishment, as a result of failure to
pay them whether in cash or kind anything more than a derisory amount
of maize with which to feed their families. The estate owner's wife,
however, when they protested to her, denounced them as '*unos perros
cuenteros*', who should clear off hacienda land. The labourers blamed the
hacienda administrator for their current condition and drew attention to
the flight of thirteen of their number already. Although instructed by
the district administrator to pay up, the owners dragged their feet, and,
instead, threatened to burn down the labourers' homes and prevent
further maize sowings, if they did not quit hacienda land. It seems,
however, that a settlement of obligations was actually made in the long
run.[29]

On the other hand, counter-charges of Indian 'drunkenness and
idleness' came from the district administrators of Atlixco and Huejotzingo. They blamed Viceroy Bucareli's *bando* of 14 July 1773, which
regulated conditions of labour on hacienda lands. The resident labourers
of Tepeaca appealed to the viceroy to confirm their status as free
workmen; this he did in the *bando* of 21 August 1779, which the
viceregal decree of 28 March 1784 confirmed. In a further *bando* on 23
March 1785 the viceregal government upheld the rights of workers as
free men and reiterated the prohibition set in 1687 that no more than $5
was to be lent to individual labourers. The crown sought to prevent the
reduction of the hacienda labour force to serfdom through indebtedness.
The principle of a cash wage and the prohibition of corporal punishment
were also repeated. At the same time, however, the viceregal government instructed district administrators, in consort with the parish
clergy, to curb 'idleness'.[30]

Government legislation did not, of course, prevent the recurrence of
abuses. In 1779 resident labourers in the district of San Juan de los
Llanos took matters into their own hands. An employee on the Hacienda
de Virreyes, the property of Juan García, had beaten a workman. A body
of labourers thereupon marched in protest to the owner's residence. The
*alcalde mayor* responded by hastily forming a body of men and arresting
twenty-five of the demonstrators, whom he escorted to the district jail.
No severe punishments, however, followed. On the contrary, the owner
expressed his willingness to take the workers back after a mild
chastisement for their lack of 'due subordination'. Since at that time he

was not short of labour, he offered them the opportunity to liquidate their accounts with him and leave his employment. In these dealings the Indian governor and *alcaldes* (village officials) acted as intermediaries between García and his recalcitrant labourers. The latter chose to go their own way.[31]

Landowners continued to protest that freedom of movement by *gañanes* thwarted their efforts to maintain a ready labour force for the cereal agriculture. In Atlixco, Huejotzingo, San Juan de los Llanos, in Tlaxcala, and in the Veracruz districts of Otumba, Córdoba and Orizaba landowners blamed their difficulties on government measures, and requested the audiencia to intervene. Attempts at constraint led to protests from workers of ill-treatment, such as the case of the estate labourers of Otumba in 1781, who appealed to the Intendant of Veracruz. Workers complained elsewhere of wage differentials.[32] Labour relations in the Puebla district of Izúcar actually degenerated to the point of rebellion in 1781, when resistance to forced labour led to violence. As a result the local *alcalde mayor* remained wary of further recurrence throughout the decade. Even so, the estates still required extra labour during the harvest season and appealed to him to put pressure on the villagers. When the administrator approached the Indian governor of the district head-town, the reply he received indicated complete indifference to the expressed needs of the private farmers. In view of the violence of 1781, the *alcalde* feared to exert pressure, and, instead, confined himself to complaining of the 'laziness' of the working population, to which in 1787, he attributed the loss of hacienda maize and other crops. In Mexico City, distant from the local events, the civil fiscal, Alva, instructed the *alcalde* to put pressure on the governor to 'give' to the district *hacendados* the 'Indians' they required. If the governor were to refuse, he should be charged with 'disobedience'. We do not know exactly what resulted, but the dilemma of the *alcalde mayor* illustrates the difficulty of the local administration, whenever it sought to maintain a balance between worker rights and proprietor interests, and the danger to public order that could result from preference for the latter. Throughout the 1800s, moreover, a number of villages and *barrios* in Izúcar pressed lawsuits against one of the wealthiest proprietors in the district, Mateo Musiti, owner of the hacienda and refinery of San Juan Bautista Ravoso. Villagers complained that Musiti's cattle encroached on their lands. Such disputes had a long history, since in the case of suits with previous landowners, the Audiencia of Mexico had already decided in favour of the villages in 1743 and 1747. Clearly, there were several causes of social tension in

Izúcar. Little, however, is known as yet concerning the position of the many tribute-paying negroes and mulattos in the district, many of them sugar plantation and mill-workers, of whom there were even more than in Cuautla. When insurgent forces arrived in the vicinity in December 1811, they may well have encountered a district receptive to revolutionary appeals. It proved to be Musiti who vainly tried to rally resistance to insurgent forces when they appeared in the district, from the direction of Chiautla. Musiti was obliged to flee, leaving his properties at the mercy of the insurgents.[33]

The viceregal government referred the entire question of abuse and free status to the Council of the Indies, which in April 1788 upheld the spirit of the *bandos*, but warned that Indians should not be permitted to relapse into idleness. In reaching its decision, the metropolitan government sought to balance the interests of the parties involved – 'this matter is among the gravest that could arise in New Spain. To favour hacienda owners would diminish the liberty of the Indians, which the law sustains. To favour the Indians, however, would damage the agricultural sector by encouraging idleness. Therefore, it is necessary to proceed in such a way as to reconcile the one with the other. They are both equally important.' The crown upheld the principle of voluntary labour, paid in cash.[34]

The gradual recovery of village population levels in the course of the eighteenth century added a further dimension to the sources of local conflict. Many villages engaged in law suits with one another, or with adjacent haciendas and *ranchos*, concerning possession of disputed borderlands. Sometimes, lack of past incentives had left such lands uncultivated. On the other occasions, Indian communities had rented land not utilised by their own farmers to the owners of private estates. They had often in this way lost them as the decades passed. In general, the norm in New Spain continued to be an appeal to the law, rather than to force. Village authorities would produce their land titles, which dated back to the sixteenth century or beyond: landowners would take their stand on rival documented claims. To the audiencia fell the task of deliberation. During the latter part of the eighteenth century many land disputes involved requests by hacienda labourers for formal incorporation as a legally recognised *república de indios*, with the official endowment of the minimum land circumference, the 600 *varas* of the *fundo legal*. Many such petitions argued that existing land resources could no longer sustain the increased number to feed. The response of the viceregal government to such Indian petitions proved in many instances to be favourable. Viceroy Azanza and the audiencia, for instance, upheld the request from the *gañanes* of the Hacienda de San Miguel Villanueva (Tepeaca) in 1799 for formal constitution as a village. The parish priest of Acatzingo testified to their good character. The estate owner, however, fearing reduction of his properties, opposed the request, under pretext that the hacienda's water resources would be insufficient to provide for the needs of a village of increasing numbers. Requests for municipal status implied redistribution of segments of hacienda land in favour of the petitioners. The *fiscal protector de indios* proposed compensation for proprietors from the royal patrimony. The viceregal government, then, sought to override the opposition of the proprietor. The Indians had already built a church and appointed a sacristan to look after it. The *fiscal* duly warned the proprietor not to expel the labourers from his lands on pain of a 1,000 peso fine.[35] The *gañanes* of the Hacienda de San Pablo in the same district similarly requested municipal status between 1792 and 1805.[36] Elsewhere in New Spain the tenants of the Hacienda de Tequisquiapa in Dolores at the northern edge of Bajío argued in 1806 that population pressure obliged them to request formal constitution as a village with the requisite 600 *varas de fundo legal*. The owners and those of the Haciendas de La Petaca, La Venta and San Gabriel opposed the tenants, on the grounds that they would lose their lands and their water resources. They proposed the establishment of the village on *tierras realengas* or *baldías*.[37]

Indian villagers in the Puebla district of Cholula took matters into their own hands in 1809. When years of litigation failed, the Indians of Chalchoapan invaded lands possessed at that time by the Hacienda del Portezuelo. Two neighbouring subdelegates had been attempting to determine the issue. Litigation and arbitration were the traditional methods of resolving disputes, rather than violent action. Indeed, the contentious instinct of the Indian villages aroused the hostile criticism of the Intendant of Puebla, Manuel de Flon, who during the 1780s and 1790s had championed their positions on such issues as the *repartimiento*. Flon, a man whose patience was easily lost, scathingly commented on the villagers' aptitude for litigation – 'it is well known and a constant occurrence that the Indians with a blind passion and tenacity pursue in the law courts of this realm their claims to the land'. According to Flon, Chalchoapan, frustrated by failure of redress, had already resorted to 'several noisy demonstrations', designed to further its claims by direct methods. The Intendant in 1809, aware of the weakness of the district subdelegates in their localities, feared an escalation of violence. The source of obstruction was the Provincial Junta of Consolidation in Puebla, which had taken control of the estate under the Consolidation procedure of 1805. Portezuelo owed 20,000 pesos to Pious Foundations and a further 24,000 pesos of unpaid interest. For this reason the Junta was anxious to find a buyer as quickly as possible. The villagers' claims threatened not only to deter any prospective purchaser, but also to reduce the extent of the estate by one-half. A motivation for the Indians' land invasion in September–October 1809 may well have been the urgency of access to further maize lands, in view of the mounting food shortages of those months. The Viceroy, however, pledged his support for methods the Intendant chose to adopt to contain the villagers' 'insubordination'.[38]

In north-eastern Guanajuato the Indians of Xichú adopted a similar course of direct action by occupying the lands they claimed. The village was situated in the Sierra Gorda on extremely arid, rocky soil, which produced only cactus, prickly pear and thistle. The villagers regularly imported their foodstuffs from outlying areas such as San Luis de la Paz and Celaya, and the Hacienda Casas Viejas. Xichú and, indeed, the whole of the Sierra Gorda, had, in consequence, suffered particularly severely during the subsistence crisis of 1785–6. The year, 1786, had become known locally as 'the year of hunger'. Then the maize price had risen to 24 reales ($6 per carga) after the loss of two harvests. During the subsistence crisis of 1809–10, which resulted from similarly extensive harvest failures in the cereal-producing districts, the maize price in Xichú had risen to an unprecedented peak of 48 reales ($12 per carga) by late October 1809. The Intendant of Guanajuato believed that this situation would worsen by April–May 1810, especially in view of the activities of grain monopolists and money lenders.[39]

In the eyes of local estate-owners and administrators, the Indians of Xichú had always had a history of rebellious conduct. One of the explanations lay in the tension between the Indian *república* and the nearby mining settlement and with the mulatto soldiers of the Sierra Gorda Militia. The latter made a point of causing trouble, whenever they appeared at village festivals, such as Holy Week. Fighting had broken out during Holy Friday in 1791.[40] A more serious source of conflict, however, resulted from changing practices on the part of the nearby estate-owners. Villagers bitterly resented hacienda efforts to curb their customary practices of chopping wood, burning charcoal, tapping maguey, picking prickly pear, gathering wild lettuce, or grazing their few animals on lands hitherto utilised by estate owners. Xichú, then, proved to be a case in point, with respect to the general trend of terminating customary rights, that Brading sees elsewhere in Guanajuato, and attributes to rising land values and a surplus of manpower.[41]

At the turn of the century the Haciendas of Salitre, Charcas and Palmillas had begun to remove such rights. Beatings could be expected by any villager discovered reverting to previous practices. As a result, the conflict over rights began in earnest in 1803, when villagers threw down the maguey boundary fences erected by the estate-owners, invaded the disputed lands, and began to plant. The proprietors could count upon the support of the subdelegate of the district of San Luis de la Paz, José Manuel de Septién y Primo, owner of the Hacienda de Casas Viejas and member of one of the most powerful families of Guanajuato. The estate owners protested at the 'terror' inflicted upon them by armed bodies of villagers ripping out their fences, and appealed for a show of military force to clear them from the disputed lands. The villagers' lawyer appealed to the audiencia and warned that he would lay the case directly before the viceroy and the *Juzgado General de Naturales*. The owner of the Hacienda de Charcas, Francisco Antonio de Alday, alleged that the governor and village council in Xichú had not only sanctioned the land seizure in 1808 by a 'multitude' of Indians armed with stones, but had also distributed lands among the occupiers with a view to permanent possession. The villagers' lawyer countered by arguing that these land seizures resulted from the failure of the law to guarantee his clients' rightful possession to lands recognised as theirs for the previous fifty years.[42]

The Xichú case made no mention of population pressure in the villages. Although the Mezquitic case in San Luis Potosí in 1807 mentioned that the population had risen, the central issue was once again loss of customary rights. The Indians' own statement that their village did not require more land provided adequate evidence that pressure of population was not the mainspring of action. The community had rented village lands assigned by the audiencia in 1591, and had not needed them subsequently through the general decline of population. The type of arrangement had been a virtually permanent *censo* or emphyteusis. As a result the surrounding Haciendas of Cerro Prieto, Peñasco, Bocas, Canoas and La Parada had come to regard the lands as their own. A more resilient community began to challenge their assumption at the end of the 1790s, since the tightening control by the *hacendados* had deprived the villagers of maize lands sown in response to the recovery of population during the course of the eighteenth century. The Indians appealed to the audiencia, because they suspected the partiality of the attorney of the Intendancy of San Luis Potosí. The village, however, could not give undivided attention to the case, since internal conflict over elections to its council had divided the community into factions.[43] This dispute, as in so many other instances, was overtaken by the insurrection of September 1810. The insurgents captured the city of San Luis Potosí on 14 November. The presence of rebel forces in the district encouraged some 2,000 of its inhabitants to join their bands. Marching off to campaign with them, they never returned. When the Royalists recovered the provincial capital on 3 March 1811, the pro-insurgent element became the 'perverse' sector of the population, while the 10,000 who had stayed at home became the 'innocent', the 'wretched', deserving not punishment but protection. The villagers petitioned the audiencia to save them from retribution for the sins of their departed brethren. Viceroy Calleja in May 1814 ratified the audiencia's favourable verdict, in spite of complaints from the administrator of the Hacienda de La Parada, a dragoon captain with the Royalist force, that they had invaded his lands and planted their maize.[44]

Landowners' efforts to define their property rights led to enclosures. The Conde de San Mateo Valparaíso, who had also inherited the title, Marqués de Jaral, invested large sums in fencing. Boundary markers and fences, however, challenged customary rights. The Conde became involved in the dispute over lands and rights with the Villa de San Felipe in northern Guanajuato. A group of tributaries worked a section of the commons (*ejidos*), which had come to be known as the Rancho de Bravo. They claimed grazing and water rights and had also sown maize. In 1809 a legal decision awarded these lands to the Hacienda de Jaral, which put its cattle on the property. The Indians argued that they were rightful tenants. They also alleged that the majordomo of the Hacienda de Huisache, adjacent to the *rancho*, had insulted them and had been trying to charge them 2 reales for the recovery of stray livestock. The majordomo had begun to protect his boundaries with a band of cowhands. The Indians appealed to the authorities in Mexico City to oblige the hacienda owners, particularly the Marqués de Jaral, to produce their title deeds. Deprived of grazing lands and water, especially serious during a drought, their livestock were dying. The Marqués defended his enclosure by arguing that they encroached in no way at all upon the town's *ejidos*. He maintained that the disputed rancho was his property and that the Indians were nothing but squatters. The Marqués' lawyer denounced the 'bold opposition' of the Indians. Although Archbishop-Viceroy Lizana, apparently sympathetic to the Indians' case, had ordered the enclosures to cease, the audiencia on 1 June 1810 upheld the Marqués' position. The insurrection of September, which originated precisely in northern Guanajuato, prevented any attempts by the Marqués to remove the Indians. Such local issues as the case of the Rancho de Bravo could well have fuelled insurgent support in such towns as San Felipe.[45]

The long-lasting conflicts in the central zone of Guadalajara have already been alluded to in chapter one. They arose from hacienda pressures on peasant subsistence lands. The recovery of the Indian population by the latter half of the eighteenth century made the problem of village land shortage an urgent one. The end result was peasant direct action during the 1780s and again during the insurgency of the 1810s, periods, moreover, in which the impact of severe food shortages in 1784–6 and 1808–10 may well have contributed to the desperate search for further subsistence lands. In this sense, it is likely that peasant militancy during the early 1810s would have occurred, irrespective of whether P. Miguel Hidalgo had appeared in the central district of Guadalajara or not. These land disputes involved a chain of villages situated beyond the western shore of Lake Chapala as far south as Lake Zacoalco: they included Zacoalco itself and the villages of Santa Ana Acatlán, Tizapán, Tizapanito and Atotonilco. Population recovery within these peasant communities had placed renewed demands on diminishing subsistence lands, often of poor quality, at a time of significant growth in the urban market and consequent hacienda response to its cereal requirements. The villages struggled to preserve their identity and protect their lands from encroachment by the private estates that surrounded their communities. The territorial expansion of the haciendas owned by the Porres Baranda, the Vizcarra and the Echaurri had made it impossible for the Indian villages to break out of their confinement.[46] Initially, Indian resistance to hacienda encroachment did not signify either opposition to the private estate as such or to the Spanish colonial authorities. On the contrary, villagers in Guadalajara as elsewhere appealed to Spanish colonial law and sought redress through the legitimate channels. It is difficult to discover, however, whether Indian perceptions altered and their aims radicalised under the impact of insurgency. Rebel control of the countryside would have presented villagers with the opportunity to take back what they believed to be their own properties and to cultivate the lands as they saw fit.

The conflict between the five villages and the private estate owners took the form of a confrontation between the hacienda, with its urban market orientation and its own internal structure of tenants, *rancheros* and employees, on the one hand, and the maize-producing peasant village, often with pre-Columbian traditions, on the other hand. Vigorous litigation took place during the 1770s and 1780s between the village of Zacoalco and the Echaurri brothers, resident in Guadalajara. The issue at that time centred on the villagers' alleged encroachments on hacienda lands. During the 1780s, peasant resistance to hacienda expansion led to direct action: villagers occupied disputed lands, maintaining that they had always been theirs, and planted subsistence crops. In 1791, for instance, Joaquín Ignacio de Echaurri, owner of the Hacienda de San José de Gracia, complained that peasant direct action had been taking its course over the previous eight years. He protested to the audiencia that villagers' land incursions had dispossessed his 'poor, but long-standing tenants and their families, who had been obliged to abandon their homes and ranches, or at least, have been prevented from planting in the current year'.[47] Similar actions accompanied the Zacoalco dispute with the Porres Baranda and Vizcarra estates. The villagers of Tizapán and Tizapanito maintained in the early 1780s that they possessed insufficient good quality lands to feed themselves or to graze their livestock. They appealed to the audiencia to award them definitive rights to the disputed lands. The legal representative of the *mayorazgo* protested at unrestrained Indian encroachment upon hacienda lands. Vizcarra's representative protested in 1783 that land invasions by the villagers of Tizapán and Atotonilco had dispossessed the hacienda tenants.[48] At this time the *fiscal protector de indios*, the audiencia's attorney entrusted with the legal defence of Indian interests, attempted to mediate between the interests of the private proprietors and those of the villagers, acknowledging the latters' genuine difficulties. In spite of its deep involvement with the provincial élites, the royal administration sought as best it could to assist the Indians in their search for alternative sources of food, particularly during the years of shortage in the mid-1780s.[49] Nevertheless, the audiencia decided in Echaurri's favour on 26 March 1791 and increasingly in favour of the other proprietors thereafter. As a result, the villagers reopened the law suit in 1793.[50] Renewed litigation, however, involved delay and expense. For such reasons, it is not unreasonable to suppose that law suits constituted a last resort, the symptom of failure to reach a working arrangement with the private proprietors at the local level. This implied, in turn, that social relations in the central district of Guadalajara had entered a seriously adverse phase from the 1780s. Hérmes Tovar suggests the possibility of a type of *hacendados*' counter-offensive during the 1790s, with the aggressive use of estate employees of San José de Gracia, Sauceda and Estipac against the villagers. *Hacendados* armed their own settled population of tenants and resident peons for the promotion of hacienda interests.[51]

The formation of virtual hacienda self-defence forces suggests an early anticipation of the type of forces created both spontaneously and under official military supervision during the counter-insurgency of the 1810s. It points significantly to the implicit connection between the land disputes of the pre-insurgency and rebel affiliation during the 1810s. Not only do we see how the hacienda was capable of creating its own defence mechanism, virtually independent of the colonial state, but also we can catch a glimpse of how the aggrieved peasant might have become transformed into the insurgent participant of the 1810s. Furthermore, the hacienda's capacity for self-protection through reliance upon its internal structure of wealth and power divided the rural working population into those who derived security and position from their membership of the patron-client network and those who remained outside it, the dispossessed but dissident villagers.

The above instances do not necessarily indicate a general trend. They are discussed as local incidents in their own right, and their relevance is primarily to their own localities. It is, however, precisely in such localised conflicts that the roots of insurgency lay. Wider issues capable of linking one theatre of conflict to another remained absent until the coalescence of factors in 1808–10. We shall discuss this process in two subsequent chapters. Conflicts such as the above did not foreshadow a general insurrection. Nevertheless, their frequently long duration, the frustration of redress through litigation, and the resort to unilateral action by either of the contending parties helped to keep alive bitter memories in the locality. Such conflicts helped to explain why individuals or whole communities became susceptible to recruitment into insurgency movements after September 1810. In chapter eight we shall discuss the impact of the subsistence crisis of 1808–10 as a far-ranging factor of dislocation.

## Riots and strikes resulting from alteration in mining practices

In comparison with hacienda workers, miners enjoyed a relatively high standard of living. This, however, began to deteriorate during the period c.1760–1810. Diminishing living standards among mine workers, moreover, took place at the same time that mine-operators and investors were acquiring greater and more conspicuous wealth. Social tensions between rich and poor in the principal mining centres helped to fuel revolutionary potential and provide an eager response to insurrection in 1810. Although mineworkers' salaries stood at between $5 and $8 per month at the beginning of the nineteenth century, pay had scarcely improved since at least 1600.[52] Furthermore, such workers were subject to repeated periods of unemployment, the result of recession in the mining industry brought on either by mercury shortages, as in 1780, or by general failure of the food supply, as in the great dearths of 1785–6 and 1809–10. Even so, a problem constantly identified by investors continued to be the high cost of labour, which accounted for 75 per cent of all costs in the mining industry. Mineworkers, moreover, enjoyed the customary right of part payment in cash and part in a share of the ore, the *partido*. Any attempt on the part of mine-operators to economise on labour costs by interfering with the *partido* usually provoked riots throughout the mining camps. Greater emphasis on profitability, chiefly as a result of the infusion of mercantile capital, led precisely to such conflicts. The mining zones of Real del Monte and Guanajuato had a reputation for unruliness. Pressure on the work force made things worse. In 1766 disturbances broke out in both centres. In the latter, unrest continued into the following year, when on 1–3 July mining disputes merged with the popular indignation provoked by the metropolitan government's summary expulsion of the Jesuits, the majority of them Mexicans. At Real del Monte the riots of 15 August 1766 resulted from efforts to abolish the *partido*. Miners stoned to death the *alcalde mayor*, and threatened to set fire to the jails in Real del Monte and nearby Pachuca. Some 4,000 workers downed tools and made off for the surrounding hills. The mine-operators responded by bringing in blackleg labour. Mine-operators regarded the *partido* as an expensive nuisance, the principal obstacle to cutting costs. In view of the overheads needed for blasting, drainage and innovation mining costs were prohibitive, and broke many an investor. The miners regarded any attempt to remove the *partido* as fraud, since they argued that a 4 reales per day wage was not enough to keep their families. Indeed, the Conde de Regla, leading operator in Real del Monte, had, in some instances, already reduced wages to 3 reales. With good quality metal, mineworkers argued that in the past the *partido* could yield as much as 4 pesos, though recently the normal yield had fallen to scarcely 4–6 reales. The common practice was to sell the *partido* ore to middlemen known as *rescatadores*, as a means of supplementing wages, an extra bonus that on occasions reached as much as 15 per cent. The Conde complained that by such a practice the silver from his own mines went for refinement to other plants. He proposed to retain in his own hands all the profits of his mines. The dispute, however, involved the question of the dignity of labour. The miners regarded themselves not as employees but as joint exploiters in company with the mine-operator. The *partido* reflected this shared enterprise. Abolition of the share-out resulted in a loss of status. Historically, the *partido* originated from the operators' need to attract voluntary labour to the mines.

Viceroys Cruillas (1760–6) and Croix (1766–71) inclined in favour of the mineworkers and upheld the practice of *partido* as the guarantee of a willing labour force for the mines. Indeed given the general unrest in New Spain in 1766–7 over fiscal pressures, hostility to the imposition of a state tobacco monopoly, and the controversy over the expulsion of the Jesuits, the viceroys could not afford to provoke a further conflict with the mineworkers of Real del Monte. During the last months of Croix's viceregency, however, the Visitor General, José de Gálvez, took the opportunity presented by the return to calm, to order the outright abolition of the *partido*. The incoming Viceroy, Bucareli (1771–9), strenuously opposed this policy and protested to the crown on 24 December 1771. Regla, in the meantime, proposed to take advantage of Gálvez's order by substituting only one half real daily for the *partido*. The crown finally upheld the traditional practice in the Mining Ordinances of 22 May 1783.[53] Even so, the mineworkers' position generally deteriorated as a result of the Gálvez policies. The *tienda de raya* or company store became ever present, and indebted workers were forbidden to leave their place of work.[54]

No savage reprisals followed the Real del Monte protests of 1766. The viceregal administration gave the matter its prompt attention by sending the much respected *alcalde del crimen*, Francisco Javier de Gamboa, the leading Mexican magistrate of the audiencia, to resolve the conflict, and sending the men back to work. Gamboa took with him a Grenadier Company of sixty men, with a thirty dragoons and twenty-four riflemen. When he arrived in September, he dismissed the auxiliary forces sent in by the neighbouring administrators from Tulancingo, Zempoala, Atotonilco and Tetepango to prevent striking miners from setting fire to the timbers of the mines. Gamboa began to interview members of the workforce on 27 September. Forty or so ringleaders were punished with whippings (200 strokes) and then sent to Pachuca under militia escort. The regular infantry remained in Real del Monte to guarantee law and order. The mines eventually reopened in 1775.[55]

Gálvez dealt in person with the rebellions and demonstrations that had broken out in the centre-north-west in 1766–7. A lasting bitterness resulted from his unprecedented severity. Some 3,000 persons were brought to trial, of whom 674 were sentenced to life banishment or long imprisonment, sometimes in the presidios, 117 sent away from their homes, 73 subjected to whippings, and 35 executed. The discontent in those regions encompassed all social groups, and had been crystallised by the peremptory expulsion of the Jesuits, which Gálvez himself with military support accomplished with little delicacy. Fiscal pressures, such as a tightening up of tribute collection and the collection of an excise duty on locally produced liquors, combined with mine-operators' efforts to phase out the *partido*, particularly in Guanajuato, to inflame opposition to the Visitor's policies.

The popular riot of 1 July 1767 directed its hostility towards the *alcalde mayor* at a time of difficulties in the mining sector, which affected all classes of the population in the city of Guanajuato. The immediate cause proved to be the fiscal implications of a new census to be taken late in June, which unfortunately followed the recent establishment of the Tobacco Monopoly, one of Gálvez's most notorious revenue-raising devices. The city councillors, in effect, warned the viceroy on 9 July that law and order could only be guaranteed in the city, if a militia force were in residence.[56] In San Luis Potosí, the disorders originated from attempts to clear vagabonds from the mining areas. Violence spread through the city barrios and nearby villages, to the Indian towns of El Venado and La Hedionda, and to the mining town of Guadalcázar. Popular hostility focussed upon the *alcalde mayores* or their lieutenants, or the urban *alcaldes ordinarios*. A mob in San Luis Potosí broke into the city jail and stoned the city chambers. Indians from the sierras joined with the urban populace to seize control of the city briefly on 8 July 1767. The Spaniards in the city, fearing a general massacre, had already fled to the refuge of convents by the time of Gálvez's arrival on 24 July. Such upheavals anticipated similar events in the autumn of 1810 throughout the cities of the centre-north-west. A local proprietor, Francisco Mora, who in 1768 received as a reward the title of Conde de Santa María de Guadalupe del Peñasco, organised a permanent militia to control the city. Gálvez had found himself obliged to leave the militia company, paid for from taxes levied on the town, in control of San Luis de la Paz, where riots had broken out in response to the *alcalde mayor*'s attempts to expel the local Jesuits from the college. Similarly Gálvez placed a cordon of 8,000 militiamen around Guanajuato for three-and-a-half months, in order to trap fleeing rioters and to keep the miners at work. A government force remained stationed in the surrounding hills until the insurrection of 1810.[57]

Perhaps feeling a sense of security with the proximity of government forces, Guanajuato mine-operators in the early 1790s sought once more to replace the *partido* by a daily wage of up to 10 reales. Again such measures proved to be unpopular and greatly contributed to the unsettled condition of labour relations in the mining zones.[58] In the Zacatecas zone, only a few mineworkers still received the *partido* by the 1800s. Even so, continued efforts to phase it out still aroused hostility, especially in view of the general deterioration of workers' living standards in face of mine-operators' conspicuous wealth. Although some 60 per cent of the active population in Zacatecas was employed in the various processes of the mining industry, wealth by the 1800s was increasingly concentrated in the hands of a few individual investors, merchants, and estate-owners. Richard Garner has described this situation as the formation of the Zacatecas 'oligopoly'. Just a few individuals, in fact, controlled up to four-fifths of the production and refining of silver. Prominent among them were the eleven proprietors of the richest Zacatecas mine, Quebradilla, where the principal investor was the controversial Basque immigrant, Fermín Azpechea (or Apezachea). The Quebradilla mine produced three million pesos of silver in 1809, a time of severe food shortages throughout the mining zones and little prospect of relief. As food prices in Zacatecas doubled in the period, 1807–10, social tensions began to reach a crescendo. An anonymous letter sent to the Viceroy in the spring of 1810 demanded a government inquiry into the allegedly scandalous profiteering of such mine-operators, denounced generally as '*gachupines*'. The latter were accused of preying off their 'creole' workers, reducing the *partido* and paying not in wages but in merchandise.[59] This denunciation was followed shortly afterwards by warnings of bitter popular hatred of the Europeans in the city.[60] The long term deterioration of living standards in mining communities which had long been centres of unrest combined with the impact of the great dearth of 1809–10 to escalate popular discontent, especially in face of the evident wealth of the investor plutocracy. Such conditions made the mining zones a receptive area for recruitment into the insurgency movement of the 1810s.

It is difficult to see a common purpose among the participating social groups in New Spain, especially in view of the wide disparities of motivation. Moreover, none of the riots and demonstrations of 1766–7 produced a general insurrection. In short, inflammatory though the combined pressures of tax increases and efforts to abolish the *partido* were, especially when combined, in some instances, with a religious grievance such as the expulsion of the Jesuits, they could not mobilise opinion sufficiently broadly or strongly to produce a revolutionary movement against Spanish rule. Even so, they foreshadowed what was to come later.

Most rebellions, riots, protests and demonstrations, originated from local situations, and tended to remain in them[61]. Particular instances of administrative abuse, fiscal pressure, removal of customary rights, land and water disputes, land encroachments, or alterations in mining practice remained of their nature localised, and unlikely to become generalised. The elements needed for galvanising a common action throughout the localities, and producing, thereby, a powerful regional, if not national movement, remained absent. Not even the limited *prise de conscience* of 1766–7 produced a unified, widespread insurrection. Indeed, the attention given to unrest places us in danger of forgetting how exceptional large-scale violent protest was during the colonial period. Long-lasting trouble spots certainly posed problems for local and regional authorities, but the fact was that they were exceptions, rather than the rule. The frequency of land and water disputes between villages, or between them and private estates, helps to account for the abundance of archival documentation concerning contention. It also reinforces the contemporary view that villagers engaged naturally in litigation in their own defence. The recovery of population during the eighteenth century and the expansion of the organs of government may well account for the accessibility of these case instances. Nevertheless, such issues do not make for a common sense of grievance. None of the above cases led to revolutions, still less to a revolution of independence. Even so, they provided in many cases long-lasting conflicts, especially where frustration had led to the use of force by either or each of the contending parties. These examples of lasting bitterness may have contributed to insurgent sympathies during the 1810s. Many of the late colonial trouble spots became theatres of persistent insurgency, sometimes into the 1820s, and even into the 1840s and beyond. These conflicts similarly did not in themselves involve the attainment of political goals at the national level. The outbreak of generalised insurrection in New Spain required a broad coincidence of factors. In ordinary circumstances the relatively highly paid mineworkers could scarcely find an identity of interest with the hacienda workers. Nevertheless, the question of the survival of the *partido* continued to result in unsettled conditions throughout the mining zones. Tense labour relations during the decades before 1810 probably contributed to the expansion of insurgent support from the cereal and textile zones of the Bajío to the mining communities of the sierra.[62]

It would take the impact of the subsistence crisis of 1808–10 to provide common conditions of hunger and unemployment. Even so, unemployment and hunger were regular occurrences in New Spain; but they did not contribute to revolutionary uprisings in the centuries prior to 1810. None of the other subsistence crises coincided with a national insurrection. Given its uniqueness, the insurrection of 1810 requires a broader explanation than the impact of subsistence crisis alone. Many problems remain, not the least of which is the precise significance of the type of isolated conflict and localised rebellion we have examined in the present chapter. To what extent should we view them as part of a pattern? It will not be possible at this stage to argue unequivocally for the existence of subtle connections between them, though, of course, such may well have been the case. While it is correct to argue, that incoherent, individual cases demonstrated no underlying progression or direction in the tensions evident from time to time during the colonial period, we can, nevertheless, also point to certain identifiable roots of conflict that recur. But do they recur with sufficient frequency – if not predictability – for us to regard them as parts of a pattern or process? Perhaps, our guide should be the evidence of local continuities of long duration. It would be risky indeed to regard the ample evidence of late colonial tensions as evidence of a deepening crisis of Spanish rule. Many of the conflicts of the 1770s, 1780s or 1790s reappeared in the 1820s, 1830s or 1840s and for a long time after. Instead of regarding late colonial disputes as preludes to general insurrection – or to a 'War of Independence' – we should place the struggles of the Independence period within the context of the on-going local disputes that linked the late colonial and early national periods in unbroken continuity.

# 4

## Dearth and dislocation

Dearth was not an exceptional occurrence, but part of the pattern of life in town as well as country in the era before the development of mechanised industry and the modernisation of the infrastructure. Appeals to the supernatural personalities to intervene, in order to stave off or bring to an end the disasters of the natural world recurred at frequent intervals. The predominance of agriculture in the economy did not provide the sole explanation for this unavoidable exposure to the vagaries of daily life. Meteorological fluctuations affected a variety of activities besides farming, since commerce and industry remained heavily dependent upon animal transportation and animal power. Altitude ensured that these uncertainties affected different regions, if not localities, in different ways. Primitive conditions of transportation and communication frustrated what efforts were made to bring relief supplies to the zones worst affected by shortage. In general, a rise in cereal prices would be transferred to all other foodstuffs, a factor which under famine conditions, prevented the substitution of one cereal for another, or of non-cereal foodstuffs for cereals. The most serious dearths followed the loss of two harvests, as in 1739–40, 1785–6 and 1808–09, and produced a 'subsistence crisis'. This latter term may be convincingly used to describe the phenomena we are about to discuss, providing we appreciate beforehand that dearth did not of itself give rise to structural transformation in society or the economy. The 'crisis' concept is useful, then, to describe the very real and repeated struggle for existence on the part of ordinary people faced with the prospect of starvation. The late colonial dearths, moreover, should be understood within the context of a general rise of prices, at least, after c.1760. Dearth, like disease, did not alter the general trend of population growth from c.1660 to the 1790s. This growth, as we have already seen, stabilised late in the eighteenth century and seems to have halted altogether between 1800 and the 1840s. Although dearth did not alter long term trends, it did form part of a discernible, though imprecise pattern that exposed the vulnerability of an agrarian-based economy. Agriculture passed in cycles from one food shortage to another, with the ensuing social strain and tension.

Passivity before crisis did not necessarily characterise the reactions of public authorities. The municipalities constantly strove to hold back the worst excesses of dearth, and to employ what powers of coercion and persuasion they possessed to release fresh supplies of food on to the market. The mechanism for this was the *pósito* and *alhóndiga* system, the public storage and provision of cereals, practices dating from 1580. The *pósito* was a municipal granary designed to combat maize shortages and counteract food speculation. The *alhóndiga* was a public repository for grain, from which maize and wheat could be sold at fixed prices to the lower classes. The efficacy of these municipal-administered institutions bore direct relation to the condition of public order. As a result, instances of inefficient administration, notorious corruption and evident partiality, tended to have both social and political consequences. The public supply at the *pósito* was designed to supply urban consumers when private sources of supply were scarce, generally after the harvest had been consumed, but it did not attempt to undercut private producers. Municipal practice established that private grains could be sold uniquely at the *alhóndiga* and nowhere else, though many cases of illicit sales, resale, and speculation did take place, as the Puebla municipality, for instance, repeatedly complained.[1]

## Types of cereal

Mexican cereal agriculture reflected not only the distinct topography and ecology of the regions, but also the cultural patterns superimposed upon them. Altitude affected climate and rainfall patterns, and from the earliest times influenced the distribution of the population. Settlement patterns established in the pre-Columbian era frequently conditioned the type of land utilisation still practised during the colonial era. The Hispanic presence considerably modified the traditional structures of landownership, but here again, regional differentiation prevailed. A new structure of private proprietorship – and the territorial hierarchy that followed from it – grew up alongside the older community agriculture. European crops further influenced the method of cultivation and determined the amount of capital and labour to be employed. As we have seen in the previous chapter, the eighteenth century witnessed considerable tension between village cultivators and private estates concerning the exploitations of land and water, livestock encroachments on arable, customary practices, and labour conditions.

Maize continued to be the staple crop in New Spain just as it had been during the pre-Columbian era, but it was, of course, by no means the sole grain consumed. Recent studies have drawn attention to the increasing importance of wheat consumption in several regions, and have pointed to the possibilities of substitute grains, such as barley and rye. The most striking point that should be made at the outset is that the cultivation of maize took place at a different time of year to that of wheat, and depended upon entirely different conditions. As a result the two grains were not necessarily susceptible to the same dangers. It proved to be frequently the case that in times of maize shortages, wheat remained available, or, indeed, flourished. In regions where the possibility was feasible, wheat or other grains might be used as a replacement grain for lost maize. A basic relationship tended to exist between the maize price and those for other cereals. Maize did not require irrigation and could be cultivated on poor soils. The planting season took place between March and May before the beginning of the rainy season early in June. The plant germinated and grew during the rainy months, June to September, and, unlike wheat, was resilient to the damp and pests brought by the rains. On the temperate plateaux maize ripened during the autumn months following the cessation of the rains. The maize harvest took place during the early winter months, November and December, which would be the months of the lowest price levels. Maize would be stored throughout the winter, but as the crops were consumed, prices would rise. The highest price levels tended to occur during the late spring and in the summer, between May and October. If the harvest had failed in the previous November and December, those months would see the beginnings of a subsistence crisis, which could intensify throughout the following year, if no relief was available, until the subsequent harvest had been gathered. With shallow roots maize did not require much soil preparation. As a result, village communities and small cultivators, operating on low capital outlays, could grow it. Such groups tended to provide the largest numerical category of maize producers. In many areas of maize production, however, use of primitive tools and the results of overplanting had led to serious ecological consequences, such as deforestation and soil erosion. Such conditions magnified the impact of subsistence crises.[2]

Wheat could not be grown during the rainy season, because of the excessive humidity: it had to be cultivated during the dry season with the aid of irrigation. The latter required heavy capital investment and a clear technological commitment. Small farmers could not meet these conditions of wheat production. Hacienda owners within range of large populated areas, such as those of Puebla and Guadalajara, or Valladolid and the Bajío, for instance, tended to cultivate wheat, barley and rye, rather than maize, encouraged by the higher profits that demand provided. Humboldt refers to the irrigation channels, water-wheels and dams of the Bajío, and of the serious attention given by major wheat producers to the advice of hydraulic engineers.[3] The Bajío plains and the Puebla valleys became principal zones of wheat-cultivation in the eighteenth century. Tehuacán, for instance, exported various types of wheat into Oaxaca.[4] Van Young and John Super, respectively, have drawn attention to the many bakeries in the cities of Guadalajara and Querétaro, while Liehr points to the number of flour mills in the city of Puebla.[5] The meticulous attention devoted to cereal supply into the cities may be traced from study of municipal archives. Those of Guadalajara and Puebla, for instance, provide considerable illumination concerning food supply and the personalities and properties involved. As we have seen, members of the city councils, frequently local estate owners, were heavily involved in grain movement. Wheat supplies to Guadalajara came not only from the lake basin haciendas, but also from the Altos and from the Bajío.[6]

Given Mexico's topography, climatic conditions, and with them maize prices, varied widely from locality to locality. Valleys in the *tierra caliente* at the edges of the central plateaux sometimes yielded two maize crops in one year, due to their higher rainfall and richer soil. Such regions could at times of shortage provide relief supplies to the zones of the *tierra templada* within range of transit. The mining zones of the centre-north and north tended to be beyond this range, with the result that in times of shortage prices could rise to three or five times the level in the central zones. Such a state of affairs indicated that reliance on one basic staple could be totally disastrous, and that the essential problem beyond that was one of transportation and marketing.[7]

In the case of food supply many conflicting interests came into play. Guadalajara's maize came not only from the haciendas but also from the villages. The city required annually some 60,000 fanegas of maize. Much of the supply proceeded from such villages as Zapotlán. In view of the tense situation throughout the lake basin area, the city council encountered difficulties at times in securing its supplies. During the spring of 1808, for instance, the municipality found itself faced with local resistance to carting. The city had purchased 13,000 fanegas, and a further 8,000 fanegas was owing to the ecclesiastical tithe agency. The villagers resisted the transportation of these cargoes to Guadalajara, on the grounds that they needed their cart-oxen for the planting season. The municipality was prepared to employ mule-trains despite the higher cost, in order to prevent shortages in the public granaries. It seemed that, in view of successful harvests in 1807 in La Barca, Cocula and Ameca, the villagers of Zapotlán were trying to hold back their own supplies, in expectation of subsequent price rises.[8] By late October 1810 the arrival of insurgent forces in the lake basin, particularly in Zacoalco and Zapotlán, further exacerbated the problem of maize supply to the city, despite the evidence received by the municipality of abundant cereal crops at that time.[9]

## Subsistence crisis and popular unrest

There is no easy solution to the problem concerning the relationship between dearth and popular unrest. Still less is it easy to understand what relationship, if any, existed between the subsistence crisis of 1808–09 and the revolutionary outbreaks of September and October 1810. We have already seen that loss of the maize crop generated serious repercussions throughout the entire economy, and that cereal crises took a serious social toll. The absence of any general uprisings in earlier periods of dearth testifies to the absence of factors uniquely present in 1810 – imperial and dynastic crisis, political breakdown at the centre of viceregal government, loss of control in several key provinces. The dearth of 1808–09 accompanied a pluri-dimensional crisis of profound repercussions. Even taking into account the long-term social and economic changes in the centre-north-west of New Spain during the eighteenth century, the factors present in the crisis of 1808–10 were primarily of a political nature. It was these latter which gave to the dearth of those years its unique potentiality. Dearth produced dislocation: perhaps, in fact, dislocation was more important in social and political terms than dearth itself. Without widespread dislocation, the political factors present in 1808–10 could not have had their peculiar efficacy. They could not have contributed to the emergence of a revolutionary situation. They could not have transformed the long-term social consequences of economic change into insurgency. While the impact of dearth and the impulse of change were certainly present in 1785–7, the broader political factors were absent. Hence, there was no pluri-dimensional crisis in 1785–7 or 1739–40. The uniqueness of 1810 lay in the conjunction of external and local factors, of conditions within the provinces with those in the empire as a whole. The widespread insurrection and ensuing insurgency resulted from this coming together of disparate agencies. Without this conjunction, the characteristic responses to food shortages continued to be riots, protests or demonstrations – or nothing at all. With the arrival of a new harvest, crisis conditions would recede and the charged situations simmer down.

It is useful to place this problem of the relationship of food shortages to popular unrest within its wider historical context, and, for a while, to examine it accordingly. I have argued above that food shortages and indigence did not generally produce revolutions. Nevertheless, attitudes to dearth and famine were key elements in popular behaviour. R. C. Cobb, referring to the background of the French Revolution in 1789, stresses that no other subject but the problem of food-supply inspired greater passions and fears. Such attitudes conditioned popular responses to wider issues such as relationships with government. Even so, of the three famine situations experienced in late eighteenth-century France, only the dearth of 1788–9 formed the context of the Revolution. The explanation lay in the prevalence of profoundly important political factors.[10] To pose the problem in this way is not to minimise the conjunction of social and economic factors, which served to exacerbate the impact of dearth and which provided mainsprings of popular action. Such action became widespread and particularly efficacious precisely because of the political malaise at the centre of government. The general ineffectiveness of the armed forces in France at that decisive moment helped to explain why the government could not protect itself and stave off a revolutionary seizure of power. The parallels with New Spain on the eve of 1810 are remarkable, though the differences, which we shall identify, are equally significant, and help to explain the varying outcome of events. Georges Lefèbvre draws attention to a number of pressures that existed in eighteenth-century France, which similarly applied in Mexico: fiscal pressures by the agencies of the bureaucratic state, shortage of work except at harvest time, industry incapable of absorbing surplus labour, the erosion of customary rights of pasture and fallow, the wage lag behind inflated prices.[11] Nevertheless, it is still not sufficient to outline the objective pressures that exacerbated prevailing poverty, since alone they do not explain the outbreak of revolution. Further factors always need to be present. The really decisive elements are (1) the existence of political crisis at the centre, and the relationship of the locality to the political centre, (2) how local issues are exploited, by whom, and for what political purpose, and (3) the condition and distribution of the armed forces.

Famine conditions produced the French riots of the spring of 1789, but other issues of broader implications kept the discontent alive. The authorities, already frightened, branded the rioting mobs as 'brigands'. The high price of bread sparked off further riots in June and July, and anarchy posed a real threat in many parts of France. Repression of 'brigands', however, depended upon the efficacy of the police and armed forces. The former were too badly organised to cope. With regard to the latter, little sympathy existed between the soldier, usually drawn from the lower classes, and the authorities. Non-noble officers, moreover, felt ill-inclined to make efforts to save the nobility. Furthermore, the widespread nature of the disturbances of the army, scattered as it was across the country, left it powerless in face of them. This inability to control the vast geographical extent of national territory was probably the most important element in the military loss of control over events.[12] Ultimately the capitulation of the army officer corps and the disintegration of authority in the army opened the way for a revolutionary capture and retention of power at the political centre in France.[13] This did not happen in New Spain in 1810. The two most salient differences were the recovery of the political initiative at the centre by the viceregal government under Viceroy Francisco Venegas, and the retention of control over the armed forces by the officer corps, albeit at a hair's breadth. Decisive factors such as these explained the failure of the Mexican revolutionary movement to capture political power at the centre.

In New Spain the high price of maize affected the price of all other types of cereal, and would lead to a general rise in the cost of living. This, in turn, reduced purchasing power for textiles and tools. High cereal prices forced up the meat price. A maize shortage affected mining operations, since the mules, which provided the main source of power for drainage and in the refineries, also had to be fed. Humboldt suggested a total of 14,000 mules involved in the amalgamation process at the Guanajuato mines at the beginning of the nineteenth century, and drew attention to the enormous quantity of maize required to feed them.[14] A subsistence crisis could lead to a virtual suspension of operations at the mines, and to large-scale unemployment throughout the mining and textile sectors. Famine and unemployment produced social dislocation, with sometimes whole communities uprooted in search of food. Rural banditry and urban crime multiplied. Torcuato di Tella, for instance, has argued that the Hidalgo revolt originated in the textile-producing centres of Querétaro and San Miguel el Grande, and that the labour force in the mining zones joined the movement shortly afterwards.[15]

## Mexican subsistence crises

We should now turn to examine the three principal food crises of eighteenth-century New Spain: 1713–14, 1749–50, and 1785–6. The great shortage of rain during the two previous years produced the dearth of 1714. In Guanajuato and throughout virtually the entire viceroyalty food shortages resulted, which Lucio Marmolejo, at any rate, described as of unprecedented dimensions. Already in 1713 the country had witnessed the death of livestock and the withering of crops through lack of water. In the following year meat shortages, an unabated hunger exploited by greedy shopkeepers, and the outbreak of sickness combined with a sharp curtailment of economic activities. Many individuals found themselves driven to crime or prostitution, in order to earn a livelihood. The streets abounded with begging children and starving bands of people that resembled groups of living skeletons. Those who could manage to do so survived through a diet of herbs or strips of cactus. Marmolejo vividly described how the general hunger drove even wild animals from the mountains into the towns and villages only to be driven off with sticks and stones by their human competitors for whatever scraps of food remained.[16]

Brading and Wu in their study of Silao and León in the north-western Bajío point to the existence of four great peaks of maize price rises: 1695–6, when the price in Silao reached 22–30 reales, and in León 24.9–32 reales; in 1713, when the León peak rose to 30.5 reales; in 1749–50, when the price in León reached 36.3 reales and then fell to 16 reales, and in Silao rose to 34.5 reales only to fall subsequently to 14 reales; 1785–6, when the Silao peak reached a record of 48 reales. In these four periods of crop failure production dropped to one-fifth or one-tenth of the normal yield. Uncertainty of rainfall always remained a factor in determining the prosperity or failure of a harvest. Only in these four periods, however, did meteorological fluctuations result in catastrophe. Death by starvation became a widespread occurrence. The burial rate accelerated notably in 1749–50, 1784–5 and in 1809–14.[17]

Drought caused the great shortages of September 1749, followed in October by daily frosts. Villagers migrated in search of food: tribute was not paid; livestock perished through lack of pasture. In this subsistence crisis we can see clearly the chain reaction, visible again in 1785–7 and 1808–10. The city council of Guanajuato complained of shortages and the high price of maize. Work at the mines slowed down, and even in some cases stopped altogether. Regional differences, moreover, remained remarkably potent factors, where distribution was concerned.

Although the drought had not been as severe in the Valley of Mexico as elsewhere, food prices had risen alarmingly and Viceroy Revillagigedo the elder had tried to prevent speculators from hoarding grains. The crop had succeeded in the *tierra caliente*, but the problem for the deprived areas lay in the distribution of supply. In these former zones the producers were small cultivators who rented strips of land from sugar-mills. They differed widely in their yield and supply could not be collected on a regular basis, as it could from the upland hacienda producers. A special consultative session of the audiencia (*real acuerdo*) advised the viceroy to appoint a committee to supervise extra purchases of maize, particularly with a view to increasing receipts from the *tierra caliente*.[18]

In Querétaro food shortages early in November 1749 led to riots when the maize prices reached the unheard of levels of 48 and 52 reales per fanega. The city council could not control the price, and on 16 November a mob rampaged through the streets and attacked the granary. Colonel Joseph Escandón, a prominent citizen, immediately took forty mounted troops to the scene and after four hours dispersed the crowd by force, though without the need to fire on it. This action cost him five wounded soldiers and left an officer with a contusion. Some Indians and mulattos were also badly hurt. The mob had consisted of *obraje* workers, forced back to their benches after the riot. The Audiencia of Mexico, particularly concerned at the potential violence of such workers, congratulated Escandón for his vigilance.[19]

The chain reaction foreshadowed in 1749 reappeared strikingly in 1785–6, particularly in the mining zones.[20] In Pachuca, for instance, 'a large body of working men and women presented themselves before the administrative buildings late in September 1785, and clamoured for maize to buy, complaining that they were dying of hunger'. The local authorities feared a riot against the tithe administration, which was refusing to sell its grains. Only when these supplies came on to the market, as a result of official order, did the people quieten down.[21] In the Zacatecas mining district of Sombrerete, the small amount of maize available for purchase from growers cost 10 pesos per carga (or 40 reales per fanega), and wheat 30 pesos per carga, early in December 1785. These supplies, brought in from the Valle del Maíz and the district of Taltenango, were evidently inadequate, since the municipality des- patched one of its councillors and a private merchant to Guadalajara in search of grains. The Superior Government went some way to assisting the hard-pressed mine labour force in Guanajuato, Zacatecas, and Sombrerete, by granting remission of tribute and sales-tax on foodstuffs for 1785 and 1786.[22] Zacatecas had experienced the great shortages of 1749–50, but recovered with a good harvest in the autumn of 1751. Since the region's cereal supply largely depended upon the Bajío, itself hard hit, the subsistence crisis of 1785–6 took a drastic toll. Silver production fell and royal revenues duly dropped. Although lower prices returned in 1787, Zacatecas was hit by another food crisis in 1789–90. The public granary could not provide sufficient relief on any of these occasions.[23] The district of Aguascalientes, like the Bajío, customarily exported its grain surpluses to Zacatecas. As the food shortage of 1789–90 began to take effect, the Intendant, late in December 1789, expressed his concern at the lack of maize in the city, where weekly consumption ranged between 1,400 fanegas and 2,000 fanegas. The current dry season made cartage in short supply, which consequently delayed receipt of relief supplies from Aguascalientes or Guadalajara. Since none of the local estates could sustain the food requirements of the city, the viceroy instructed the subdelegate of Aguascalientes not to hold back supplies.[24] The city of San Luis Potosí was similarly badly hit in 1785–6, in view of the nearly generalised drought in the urban environs and in the mining zone of Catorce. The city council sought to prevent extraction of maize from the province and to curb, albeit unsuccessfully, the activities of speculators. The council established a relief committee from among its membership to purchase maize in the vicinity. Within one month the committee had put 20,000 fanegas on the market. These supplies, however, attracted outsiders into the city, in search of food. This and continued private speculation had forced prices to rise from 5 pesos to 5.5 pesos, and presented the city with 'terrifying circumstances'.[25] San Luis Potosí, however, recovered fairly rapidly from the dearth of 1785–6. By 1792, the Intendant commented that agriculture had reached a height of prosperity. After some further shortages in 1788, sterility in 1789, and an average crop in 1790, an abundant harvest had resulted in 1791. Although irregular and scant rainfall produced an average crop for 1792, sowings had proceeded so rapidly that proprietors had begun to construct larger storage barns in anticipation of a bumper crop. The price in December 1792 had dropped to between 2 and 6 reales.[26]

The shortages of 1785–6 were much greater in the mining areas than in the central valleys. The early frosts of August 1785 took a drastic toll in the Bajío, a situation particularly serious in some districts in view of the very poor harvest of 1784, when, in Silao, at any rate, the maize price at 21.2 reales had already reached the highest level since the crisis year of 1749. In 1785 the peak price reached 48 reales, as a result of the

near failure of the harvest. The impact of such a rise could be understood
from the average annual fluctuation in Silao and León between 2–4 reales
and 12–15 reales during the latter half of the eighteenth century.
Nevertheless, it does not appear that in 1785–7 the drop in silver
production was either extreme or of long duration. Early in 1788 the
Guanajuato mines seem to have regained former levels, after a fall in
production of less than one-fifth.[27] Marmolejo compared the great
hunger of 1785–6 to that of 1714, particularly with regard to
Guanajuato. According to his information, 'the most distressing scenes'
occurred in that city. When prices began to escalate, mobs invaded the
public granaries, with the result that local guards were on many
occasions obliged to resort to force of arms to hold them back. Starvation
and disease took a heavy toll on lives. Perhaps some 8,000 persons died
in the city during the dearth. Marmolejo, himself a member of one of
the principal landowning families of the province, praised the relief
efforts of his peers, such as the Otero family and the Conde de la
Valenciana. The latter fed queues of starving poor. Their actions and
those of the municipality prevented, in his view, the local catastrophe
from being worse.[28] In the Michoacán mining district of Tlalpujahua,
the miners' committee feared a popular commotion, if private growers
refused to put their maize on the market. The *alcalde mayor*, moreover,
had already warned that not even two weeks' supply was left in the
*alhóndiga*. The chief offender identified was Ignacio Retana, Tlalpujahua's principal landowner. In 1809 the Retana family still controlled
three of the district's four haciendas, and one of them, Manuel Retana,
was deputy for the administrator of justice there. Another offender was
Andrés Rayón, who had not released quantities of maize pertaining to
the tithe-farmer of the district, and appeared, like Retana, to be waiting
for the price to rise further when the *alhóndiga* exhausted its supplies.
The miners' committee drew attention to the public scandal if the tithe
administration should be seen to profit at the expense of public
misery.[29]

In Guadalajara the maize failure affected a population already
weakened by the impact of disease since the previous year. In view of the
harvest failure of 1785 in the maize-producing zones of the Guadalajara
plateau, villagers began to migrate from the countryside into the city.
Van Young suggests a total of 12,000 by February 1786. Two factors
combined, however, to relieve some of the hardship. In the first place,
the city drew upon maize supplies from warmer districts south of Lake
Chapala or from the coast, where the harvest was normal. The latter

were regions normally beyond the city's orbit of supply.[30] The city council feared that by mid-May 1786 there would be no grain left in the *alhóndiga*. The year, 1785–6, was a 'calamitous year' for the Guadalajara region. The city tried to collect maize from the villages, in order to supplement urban supplies, only to encounter hostility. Supplies in the district of Ameca, Cocula and Ahualulco were scant. In the villages of Ahualulco and Etzatlán riots resulted from absolute shortage of maize. Crowds of women went on the street to prevent by force the transfer of maize to the city by its specially appointed commissioner. It seemed likely that, if they failed or received some injury, the menfolk would take up their cause.[31] The city council made purchases of wheat, as a substitute grain for maize, though the current price stood at 18 pesos per carga, since all types of foodstuffs were in short supply in the city, not least because of the immigration from the outlying areas.[32] Many proprietors, it turned out, had already disposed of their wheat crop or sought to use the remainder as their resident workers' maize ration. Yet, in a number of districts, such as Zamora, Lagos and Irapuato, the wheat harvest in 1785 was normal.[33]

In most subsistence crises the regional impact varied widely. Areas of ecological vulnerability usually suffered worst. The district of Zempoala, east of the Valley of Mexico, lay, as we have seen, in a region of arid soil without irrigation. In this maguey-producing zone, maize cultivation was strictly for subsistence. During the subsistence crisis of 1785–6, many inhabitants migrated in search of food. A committee of local property-owners and estate-managers met on 2 March 1787 to assess the situation, and reported a virtually total crop failure in 1786. On the Hacienda de San Josef Gazabe, a property owned by the Conde de Jala, rain had actually fallen precisely on those fields growing maize, but the crop had been used to feed a hungry labour force. The shortages on Gazabe were exacerbated by the local tax administrator's attempts to exact *alcabala* on the estate-manager's relief supply. Popular indignation, however, had forced him to back down. However, the work force had moved elsewhere in search of food, with the result that production remained at a standstill.[34] A terrible situation obtained in the Guadalajara–Zacatecas border zones, such as Colotlán, San Andrés Teúl and Mezquitic. These were areas of the poorest Indian communities, with no village revenues and only a few confraternity funds. The drought had finished off their scant maize sowings, and the price by mid-November 1785 rose to 7 pesos per carga. The population had already begun to migrate in search of food. The frontier military command, accordingly, pressed for permission to contract for purchases in the Guadalajara plateau and lakeside districts, themselves, as we have seen, hard-pressed.[35]

In Puebla, maize suffered greatly, though not uniformly, though the wheat crop appears to have been abundant. From March 1786 until the end of July, maize supplies from the Valley of Tepeaca relieved districts faced with shortage until itself faced with difficulties. As a result, the local administrator halted further extraction. From the warmer valleys of Orizaba and Córdoba, abundant surpluses would have been sent up to the plateau region for sale.[36] Early frost had ruined half the expected maize harvest in the Tehuacán district late in 1785. In mid-November, the *alcalde mayor* went in person to the areas of his own district, such as Zoquitlán, Mazateopam, and Tlacotepec, located within the *tierra caliente*, in the expectation of persuading villagers there to grow extra maize for the relief of the uplands. He encountered a favourable response, but we do not know the result. Moreover, it appeared that no other district administrator had ventured through these regions, through which the only transit was on foot. The *alcalde* described how the terrain dropped towards the lands of great humidity as if by steps. He gained viceregal approval for his scheme, and permission to levy 50 pesos each from the funds of village community treasuries for the purchase of maize.[37] Throughout the *tierra caliente* the maize crop seems to have been unaffected by the disasters on the plateau and in the sierras. The city of Puebla itself continued to count on maize supplies from such sources into 1786. However, continual excessive rains throughout the month of June 1786, which particularly affected areas of sandy soil, pushed up the city maize price to 40 and 44 reales per fanega, though by October the price had dropped again to 20 reales.[38] Repeated maize shortages in both the districts of Texcoco, in the Valley of Mexico and Huejotzingo, in Puebla, in March 1786, were reported by José Heredia, a proprietor with estates in both. He had found that the maize ration and wages which he paid to his workers were so inadequate in proportion to currently inflated prices, that the latter had left his land and transferred their labour to other estates, *where there was not a shortage of maize*, irrespective of the debts they owed him. As a result, Heredia remained without labourers at the critical approach of the planting and harvest seasons for both maize and wheat. Both crops, he anticipated, promised to be abundant.[39]

As in the case of the *alcalde mayor* of Tehuacán, the Mexico City municipality's committee of prominent citizens proposed, in mid-July 1786, methods of securing relief maize supplies from the *tierra caliente*, chiefly from villages in the districts of Cuernavaca, Yautepec, Masatepec and Cuautla, which had produced successful harvests. At the same time, they stressed the need, as they saw it, to 'compel the workshy *"naturales"* to labour in the fields'. Mistaken indulgence towards them, they warned, could only lead to general starvation. The Superior Government agreed, but stressed the proviso of good treatment contained in its instructions of 23 March 1785 and 28 March 1786.[40]

In Michoacán, comparable discrepancies separated the experience of the plateau from that of the coast. In Valladolid, for instance, the maize price reached a peak of 48 reales per fanega during November 1785. The price on the Pacific coast, however, stood at only 3–4 reales in the parishes of Atoyac, Teipan, Petatlán and Coahuayutla. The problem, of course, lay in supply, as we have seen in similar cases. In the light of recommendations from two Spanish priests working in Urecho and Teipan, the Bishop of Michoacán discussed possible methods of transporting relief supplies from the coast to the upland regions where the price was at its ceiling.[41]

In most areas prices fell during 1787 because of successful harvests. In the city of Puebla, however, shortages of foodstuffs recurred during the summer, not as a result of harvest failures, but on the contrary, due to retention of supplies. One priest complained to Viceroy Flores in mid-August, that the *alhóndiga* itself was the culprit. There were 8,000 cargas of maize stored there and not put on the market, with the result that the price per carga had risen to 5 pesos at the lowest. He accused the city councillors who controlled the administration of the *alhóndiga*, of trying to profit out of rising prices at the expense of the consumer, who faced a peak of 7 pesos per *carga*. The councillors, moreover, prevented private suppliers from sending their cargoes into the city, precisely in order to prevent the price from falling. In such a way the poor could not take advantage of the successful harvests. This priest described Puebla's councillors as not 'city fathers, but city pirates, as anyone, particularly the poor, would testify'. Intendant Flon, in response, promised the viceroy to ascertain which estate owners in Tepeaca and Tlaxcala were holding back maize supplies and how much they had in their possession.[42]

Local authorities were reluctant to permit maize extraction from their zones in times of shortage. Manuel Antonio de Otero, a senior member of the Guanajuato Mining Community, experienced this problem during the shortage of 1789. Otero operated six *haciendas de beneficio*, eight mines in Guanajuato and mines in the Catorce region of San Luis Potosí, with investments exceeding $600,000. Despite his high hopes, he had secured no profit to date. Moreover, he kept in employment a workforce of some 10,000 men. Together with his enormous over-heads went the cost of feeding his labour force and work animals. He had requested relief supplies from Guadalajara, but had encountered the obstacle of an order from the audiencia forbidding extraction. Otero had already contracted for relief supply from La Barca. He warned that without it, he would not be able to keep his workforce in active employment, still less feed their families. Lack of food supply would disperse the labour force to the villages in search of subsistence. A mass of unoccupied labourers threatened to increase crime. The viceroy undertook to exert pressure in Guadalajara to release these surpluses.[43]

## The subsistence crisis of 1808–10

Florescano argues that the prolonged drought of 1808, 1809 and 1810 produced an even greater mortality among cattle than in 1785–7, despite the higher peak maize price in the latter crisis. The central zones of cattle agriculture – Lerma, Cuautitlán, Zumpango and Temascal-tepec – were badly affected in 1808–10. In Guanajuato, Querétaro, Guadalajara and San Luis Potosí the death of livestock aggravated the impact of the cereal crisis by reducing the number of oxen available for work in the fields. Rain again failed in June, July and August 1809, the planting season. In the northern mining zone from San Luis Potosí to Zacatecas, the maize price rose, for instance, to a peak of 40 reales at Mazapil in San Luis Potosí by September, the decisive month of shortage between the consumption of the past year's crop and the harvesting of the new. In both Mazapil and Sombrerete all the maize crop was lost: only poor yields were expected in Nieves, Jerez, Fresnillo and Aguasca-lientes. The zones experienced higher prices than the capital city in the same period. By August 1809 half the maize crop in Guanajuato had been lost. The price already stood at 20 reales and would rise.[44] In the mining zones, remoter regions on the upland fringes, the maize shortage coincided with a shortage in the supply of mercury used in the amalgamation process of silver extraction. This situation had not occurred in 1785–6, and accounted for the particular severity of the crisis of 1808–10 in these regions of the centre-north. Irregularity of the mercury supply from Europe had proved to be a perennial obstacle to profitable silver production in New Spain. In war years the mine labour force faced the prospect of unemployment, if mercury could not be imported in sufficient quantities and stored in reserve. These problems of supply rose to a climax by 1808. Riaño, who had experienced the previous subsistence crisis in 1785–6, compared the two shortages, and concluded that by August 1809 the latter extended beyond foodstuffs throughout all sectors of the economy. He particularly stressed the shortage of mercury in the silver-mining zones in 1809, and argued that lack of circulating medium had paralysed trade. The Intendant warned that a further sharp rise in the price of maize would endanger the livelihood of thousands of families whose daily wage went solely in the provision of subsistence commodities.[45] The seriousness of the subsistence crisis on the eve of the insurrection of September 1810 resulted from the impact of not one, but two harvest failures. Cobb points out that most eighteenth-century French dearths extended over two harvests, which was certainly the case in 1787–8.[46] Maize failures during the summer of 1808 led to Indian inability to pay tributes to royal officials. In the case of the district of León the ministers of the royal treasury complained to the subdelegate at the delays in collection. The latter could not produce the $3,696 due for the period from the last third of the year, 1807, to the end of September 1808. By December the debt stood at $5,000 as a result of the maize loss. By February 1809 this debt had risen to $6,183. Although the Intendant removed the subdelegate, the latter's successor fared no better, and complained that he encountered enough difficulties in his attempts to collect the current tribute, let alone that outstanding from past years.[47]

Shortage of rain had already led to the loss of half the maize crop in Guanajuato and to a conspicuous absence of livestock in the fields. If the meat price ascended to a prohibitive level, then the shortage of cash prevented the further rise of the maize price to heights known only in the dearth of 1785–6.[48] In Querétaro the situation was equally grave. The Corregidor, Lic. Miguel Domínguez, drew attention early in September 1809 to the scant rainfall, and to irregular crops, even within the bounds of the same estate. In his estimation one-third of the expected crop of maize, beans and barley had been lost. The poorer and remoter regions of the Sierra Gorda and the Mezquital, moreover, depended for their livelihood upon importation of cereals from the fertile plains of the district. Already the maize price had risen from 11–12 reales in July to 18–20 reales per carga. Continued shortage of rainfall presaged further increases. Like Riaño, Domínguez, also, compared the current situation to those before and concluded that the crisis was of the same proportion as those of the 'calamitous years, 1750 and 1786'. The disaster, moreover, afflicted not merely the Bajío, but the entire kingdom. Domínguez similarly drew attention to the damage done in 1786.[49] In November 1809 the district lieutenant in Tolimán

at the edge of the Sierra Gorda informed Domínguez of Indian resistance
to tribute-payment. There the price of maize and beans had risen to 48
reales per fanega. Already the shortages had obliged many families to
abandon their homes and wander in search of food. A local merchant
estimated that the worst shortage would occur in and after March 1810.
As Domínguez had foreseen earlier, the brunt of the shortage had fallen
precisely on the areas of ecological vulnerability, such as the villages at
the foot of the Sierra Gorda, which subsisted through the manufacture of
sail-cloth. The depression in the mining industry had cut off demand.[50]

The expected maize harvest in Zacatecas could only be half the
quantity of favourable periods, since the rains had ceased on 28–9
August. In view of the death of livestock in 1808, animals continued to
be in short supply during the following year. By September 1809 the
price of flour had risen to $10–$12 per carga in the provincial capital, in
Aguascalientes, Fresnillo, Jerez and Juchipila, and to $15 in Nieves,
Mazapil and Sombrerete. In most regions rain had fallen abundantly in
May, when some scant maize sowings had already been attempted,
though the short supply of team oxen prevented much success. Only in
Valparaíso Taltenango and some villages in Juquila would a reasonable
harvest be expected. The maize price in Zacatecas, Aguascalientes,
Jerez, Fresnillo, Juchipila and Taltenango stood at between 24 and 28
reales, and between 32 and 40 reales in Mazapil.[51]

The agrarian crisis adversely affected the manufacturing workshops
and interrupted supplies of raw material to domestic producers. Super
has pointed out that, due to the conditions already referred to in the
northern livestock areas, the price of wool had been increasing
throughout the latter part of the eighteenth century. Both in 1785–7
and 1809–10 producers in Puebla, Mexico City, Texcoco, Querétaro,
León and Guadalajara cut back production. Smaller producers, such as
the inhabitants of the town of Temascaltepec in the Intendancy of
Mexico, were ruined by the high price of primary materials combined
with general shortages. According to Super, unemployment in the
eastern Bajío in 1809–10 may well have provided a cause for insurgent
support.[52] By the end of 1809 troops were needed in Querétaro and
Celaya to escort maize to the granaries, through fear of assault upon the
muletrains. The Querétaro authorities remained apprehensive about
food distribution for the following year. Riaño in Guanajuato considered employing troops to requisition maize.[53]

The situation in the central areas presents a contrasting picture.
Mexico City's normal supplies from Chalco were diminished, not least
through the actions of district subdelegates and local parish priests in

the more temperate areas of Chietla, Tepeacuilco, Yautepec, Cuautla, Cuernavaca, who had prohibited extraction, in order to guarantee home supplies. In Cuernavaca maize sowings had been so extensive that, despite the loss of one-quarter of the crop, a surplus for extraction was expected. Usually merchants had brought surpluses from these districts for sale in the Chalco maize market. Estate owners in the Valley of Mexico, moreover, were holding back supplies until the months of greatest demand, between June and October 1810. The government preferred not to adopt too dramatic measures to release these quantities, through fear of inflaming an already volatile situation. The relief of the capital city depended upon supplies from the *tierra caliente*, where the harvest by November 1809 had already been brought in. Stocks there could not be conserved as they were in the stone barns of the haciendas of the *tierra templada*. In any case, producers were small proprietors, generally poor peasant farmers, who depended upon rapid sale of their grains in Chalco. Some parish priests were already warning of existing unrest or potential trouble as a result of food shortages in such districts as Tacuba, Toluca and Apan, all within easy reach of the capital city. The authorities in Mexico City did not expect famine conditions in the capital city, since they estimated maize supplies to reach 38,760 cargas, a figure considerably higher than urban consumption, which was estimated at 28,888 cargas. Even so, the audiencia doubted the accuracy and completeness of these figures, and had no clear knowledge of whether the harvest had failed or not in the *tierra caliente* and in those other nearer districts which customarily supplied the city.[54]

Thirty out of forty-one districts of the Intendancy of Mexico had experienced drought and crop losses, in spite of two or three sowings. Scarcely eight districts had experienced good weather. Although the maize price in the districts of Actopan, Tepepango and Cuautitlán had already reached 32 reales per fanega by September 1809, the authorities in Mexico City did not expect a repetition of the calamities of 1785 and 1786. Despite maize and wheat losses in Chalco, the Valley of Toluca had yielded a good crop, with the result that the capital city could be supplied, though many other regions could not. In such areas two harvest failures had taken their toll. In Zempoala a middling crop in 1808 had been followed by a complete loss of maize, barley and beans, as a result of the night frost of 26 July 1809. The maize price reached 28 reales early in September, when it was freezing, instead of raining. In the mining zone of Zimapán, where abundant rain fell in the last days of August, a two-month drought had ruined more than three-quarters of the expected harvest. No other grain but maize had any significance there. In the Pachuca mining zones the maize price had risen sharply: in Pachuca itself the price stood at 28 reales, but in the two areas of greatest shortage, Real del Monte and Atotonilco el Chico the price had already reached 34 reales and 36 reales per fanega, respectively. Much of the barley crop had also been lost, and the price at 21–4 reales per carga, was expected to rise, in view of the shortages and the needs of the work animals in the mining zones. Supplies of wheat, chick-pea, chile and rice, in any case, normally came from outside. The erratic nature of cultivation and supply was amply illustrated by the district of Huichapan, the district where, as is well known, the celebrated Villagrán clan came to hold sway. In the second half of 1808 abundant rains had led to an abundant maize and barley crop, though worms had attacked the bean crops. Early rains had in 1809 given way to drought, and only a scant crop had resulted. This drought continued through August, and, even if rain fell, the maize crop would be almost entirely lost. Although the local maize price reached 24 reales per fanega, supplies still arrived from the haciendas of San Juan del Río, south of Querétaro, where the harvest had been abundant. Barley, nevertheless, stood at the peak price of $3 per carga. In Huichapan the fields were so stripped of pasture that several haciendas had removed their livestock elsewhere. If the rains held off, the livestock would suffer drastically.[55] The peak price rise in Mexico City, nevertheless, between August 1810 and November 1811 came to 36 reales per fanega, considerably less than the peak of 48 reales in 1786.[56]

In Michoacán, the price of maize had not yet begun to rise, despite the lack of rain, by the end of June 1809. The highest price at 14 reales was to be found precisely in the mining district of Tlalpujahua. This was similarly the case with wheat and chile. Furthermore, the range of variation among the Michoacán districts is also striking, and suggests that not only were the obvious topographical and ecological factors evident, but also the quite unpredictable meteorological uncertainties. The general situation in Michoacán altered as the summer advanced into autumn and winter. The burden of tribute payment, as in 1785–6, once more became an issue. Late in December 1809, the Intendant, José Alonso de Terán, wrote to the subdelegate of Zinapécuaro, that he had received notice that some individuals had been trying to stir up village inhabitants into a state of revolt by promise of relief from tribute-payment and other community fiscal obligations. Terán instructed the subdelegate to keep close surveillance over the district, in order to root out any suspicious activity, evidence of lack of respect for the crown, or intimations of rebellion. Reports taken, however, concluded that no such stirrings were in evidence, nor were there any signs of reluctance to pay the tribute quota due by the end of the month.[57] A few months later, nevertheless, the villagers of Tancícuaro in the mountainous and infertile district of Huaniqueo, requested tribute exemption for the year, 1810, in view of the general loss of maize not only in the province, but also, as they put it, throughout the entire kingdom. Since maize was their prime necessity, they could not pay tributes due for April.[58] The 'naturales' of the village of San Francisco Angamacútiro had reported maize shortages in 1807 and 1808, and, accordingly, had hoped for improvements in 1809, only to be sadly disappointed. In view of these past failures, they could not pay tribute without jeopardising their own livelihood. The situation in their locality, they argued, was particularly bad, since the price of dirty, rotten, and bad quality maize had already risen to 28 reales by April and May 1810. They feared to think of the price by August, and described how they would then have to cook and eat wild herbs. At such a time 'we can expect nothing else but to die'. Not a few families, moreover, had witnessed the death of their own members, since dearth and disease had struck the village.[59]

The diocese of Puebla had suffered poor maize harvests in 1805 and 1806. By May 1807 the price had risen to between 32 and 40 reales, but subsequently fell sharply to 20 reales, a state of affairs which ruined local speculators. One of the principal explanations of this collapse of prices was, according to Bishop Campillo, the necessity on the part of hacienda owners to put the supplies they hoarded in their storage buildings on to the market, in order to raise funds with which to pay the instalments required of them by the Consolidation Commission.[60] The city itself experienced food shortages in 1809–11. The municipality, for instance, reported a shortage of meat in mid-October 1809.[61] By mid-June 1810 rain had still not fallen in the vicinity. The city syndic warned that 'we have no cause to delude ourselves that the city will be sufficiently fed in the near future in maize and the other grains consumed here, especially in the case of the former, which is the basic subsistence grain for all the city poor'. Frost and drought together presaged a negligible crop and threatened the death of livestock through lack of pasture and water. Already faced with such extremities, farmers had been obliged, if they could, to transfer their animals to other areas at great expense. The excessive heat had brought on fever in the city, and the physicians of the Royal Hospital of San Pedro could scarcely cope. The syndic saw calamity on the horizon and, to ward it off, he saw only supernatural recourse, and urged the municipality to provide for the celebration of a nine-day cycle of prayer to invoke the protection of the Almighty, so that rain might fall.[62]

Food shortages, exacerbated by the problem of supply, continued in Puebla into 1811. Still without any effective *pósito*, the municipality in April 1810 had tried in vain to endow a permanent fund to sustain one. The public had suffered miserably throughout that year, and prices at the *alhóndiga* had remained high. Relief supplies had been urgently sought from the Tepeaca haciendas. The city council had hoped for a lower maize price in 1811, but its predictions at the beginning of that year foretold even worse conditions than in 1810, especially given the impact of the insurrection in the areas of Mexico City, which had taken its general toll on food supplies and impeded communication. Only anticipated purchase of grains could prevent a serious dearth in 1811, the city fathers warned. For this purchase, they successfully secured viceregal authorities for the transfer of $50,000 to municipal funds from the provincial treasury's sugar-cane brandy tax.[63] By March 1811, however, the meat shortage in the city was critical. Since Puebla normally consumed 36,500 cattle annually, current supplies were expected to run out by early April at the latest. The war in the interior prevented relief supplies from the north.[64]

The impact of two harvest losses differed from region to region. Accordingly, events followed different courses. In areas of poor soil, lack of irrigation, and imported foodstuffs, such as the Llanos de Apan, the Pachuca–Real del Monte–Actopan zone, the Sierra Gorda and the Mezquital, the dislocation of village society combined with the impact of recession in the mining industry to create conditions in which banditry and insurgency could thrive. The striking difference, when viewing the subsistence crises across New Spain, lay between the centre core and the centre-north-west. In the former, notably the Valleys of Mexico and Toluca, the crises did not take as drastic a toll as in the Bajío and the mining zones. Moreover, the former regions were not directly connected to adjacent or dependent mining zones. As a result, the far-reaching chain reaction in those areas had less extreme consequences. In some districts, notably San Juan del Río and Toluca, good harvests had been recorded even in 1809. Prices in many regions never reached the peak levels of 1785 and 1786; the highest recorded in the public granary of Mexico City in 1810–11 came to 36 reales per fanega. The centre core zone, furthermore, stood to benefit from the possibility of the release of surpluses from the warmer regions around its fringes, such as Cuernavaca, Yautepec and Cuautla, or from the *tierra caliente*, where frost did not threaten crops. Guadalajara, similarly, could take relief supplies from the Colima coastal zone. In contrast, maize prices in most of the northern mining districts, notably Zacatecas, exceeded central zone levels, and scaled upwards to the heights reached in 1785–6. In Zacatecas, San Luis Potosí and Guanajuato the full impact of the recession in the mining sector, coupled with the shortage of mercury, compounded the effects of dearth and were, in turn, exacerbated by it. Pachuca–Real del Monte shared this experience with the northern districts. The chain reaction observed in 1749–50 recurred on a broader scale in 1785–6 and again in 1808–10, and disrupted all sectors of the economy, agrarian, industrial and commercial, throughout the centre-north-west. The central valleys passed through this crisis less damaged than the regions north of San Juan del Río.

## A crisis at many levels

Recession, dearth, dislocation, and momentary government loss of control combined in a uniquely dramatic way in 1810. Dearth produced dislocation, which exacerbated the problem of control of territory. Political divisions in several major provincial capitals exposed central government weakness in several geographical areas at a decisive moment. Provincial authorities were left to their own devices, and suddenly cities and major towns seemed to be perilously isolated pockets within an unpredictable countryside. It is probable that dispossessed manpower provided insurgent leaders with an available resource to tap at a time of political crisis not only in Mexico City but in Spain as well. This potential for recruitment becomes apparent when we take into consideration the long-term deterioration of lower-class living standards in town, country and mining community in key areas during the fifty or sixty years prior to the insurrection of 1810. The potential danger of an appeal to the lower classes by the leaders of the Querétaro conspiracy at the peak of a long dearth is self-evident. The events between August and November 1810, moreover, revealed the extent to which the viceregal government had lost control over large areas of territory. Reports of conspiratorial activity in Querétaro in August passed unheeded. To the contrary, Archbishop-Viceroy Lizana's obsession with the prospect of a French invasion had led to troop withdrawals from the interior precisely at the time of increasing dislocation as a result of dearth. Warnings from Querétaro, Guadalajara and Zacatecas that local authorities would be hard pressed to maintain public order, resulted in no positive response from the central government.[65] The army did not possess sufficient manpower in any one zone affected by insurrection to prevent the initial loss of most of the major towns and provincial capital cities of the centre-north-west, but it did recover from the shock of the rising in time to hold the strategically situated city of Querétaro and to push back the insurgents from the Valley of Mexico, where the capital was defended by only 2,500 men. Cadena, who had rushed from Puebla to take command of the defence of Querétaro with only 1,194 troops, saw no ideology or political platform in the rising, but only the results of widespread dislocation produced by dearth. Pillage and plebeian violence became his bugbear and he threatened to stamp them out with exemplary bloodshed. Throughout the Sierra Gorda, Europeans went in fear of their lives, according to Royalist informants. The villagers of San Pedro Tolimán and Tierra Blanca, severely hit by dearth, co-operated with the insurgents through the medium of their governors. The subdelegate of San Juan del Río, on the road southwards to the Valley of Mexico, feared an imminent uprising in the district, but Cadena warned him to expect no relief from a beleaguered Querétaro. Not even Calleja felt that he could trust the loyalty of his own troops, since the areas from which they had been recruited had already fallen under insurgent control. Viceroy Venegas could do little more than threaten to spread 'blood and fire' through the villages.[66]

# 5

## Insurrection – recruitment and extension

The Mexican insurgency spread through contact between the leadership and local dissident groups. Through the mediation of special emissaries the original leaders brought into their movement a wide range of groups. Hidalgo extended the revolution through contact with those most intimately involved in the management of men: hacienda majordomos, work force overseers, miners' spokesmen, village headmen and councillors, small town lawyers, and parish priests. From them came many of the military leaders, irregular commanders and political ideologists of the insurrectionary movement. The task fell to Hidalgo and later, Morelos, to bring these disparate, often mutually contradictory elements, together. The spontaneous nature of Hidalgo's call for insurrection on the night of 15–16 September 1810 obscures the network of relationships which permeated the insurgency from the start. Concentration upon the official leadership had left in abeyance, as it were, the problem of how, in practical terms, the movement spread. The precedent, often forgotten, had been set during the abortive Valladolid conspiracy of 1809. The Michoacán conspirators, reacting to the coup of 1808, had first raised the question of popular support. Themselves isolated, they set the process of recruitment in motion by sending out agents to outlying districts. Contact was made, therefore, with powerful local figures, such as the *cacique*, Rosales, reputed to exercise an ascendancy over the Indian villages of Michoacán. Despite the betrayal of this conspiracy, the task of mobilising support still continued.[1]

Both Hidalgo and Morelos worked to spread the insurrection of 1810, either through specially commissioned agents or through contact with local networks of power. Rayón's position depended precisely upon the support of the latter. Morelos himself began his revolutionary career as Hidalgo's commissioner to the Pacific coastal zone. An examination of the role of these commissioners reveals a wide-ranging series of connections between the urban bourgeoisie and the rural middle sectors. Leaving aside the two failed missions to Veracruz and Oaxaca, Hidalgo despatched nine commissioners to the regions that lay beyond the heartland of the insurrection.[2] The role of parish priests, hacienda majordomos and ranch-operators appeared graphically in the cases of Zacatecas, San Luis Potosí, Guadalajara and Tepic. The links between these groups emerged in the events which led to the brief insurgent captures of Zacatecas on 8–9 October and San Luis Potosí on 10–11 November 1810. Rebel support, there is no doubt, came from both urban and rural sources.

## The situation in Zacatecas

News of the insurrection in the Bajío provoked similar risings north-wards and westwards. On 7 October 'lower elements' rampaged through Aguascalientes, though little real danger seems to have existed. very shortly the few frightened Europeans who had left returned. In the city of Zacatecas, however, the political situation was more precarious, in view of the predominant position of the small group of wealthy Spanish merchant investors involved in the silver-mining industry, among them Fermín de Azpechea. This group was generally hated for its arrogance and ostentation. Azpechea originated from the Spanish province of Navarra. As a leading Zacatecas financier, he lent to merchants in Guadalajara. Well before the Hidalgo revolt, Dr José María Cos, a local parish priest, later to become one of the most celebrated insurgent propagandists, had already warned of a 'seething hatred of Europeans' in the city. According to Cos, they were regarded as 'foreign thieves who came here to plunder what is ours'. Only the appearance of the clergy had prevented a serious incident in the streets on 29 May 1810.[3] In view of such antecedents, the alarm among the Europeans was understand-able. Upon the approach of a rebel band early in October, European residents gathered what they could and prepared to flee for their lives. This panic precipitated the popular insurrection in the city. On 7 October the populace seized control of the streets, in order to prevent the extraction of merchants' funds. Mine-workers demanded immediate payment of salary arrears. The Intendant, Francisco Rendón, who had a distinguished military career in the 1780s, lost control of the situation. Power fell not to the people, however, but to the leading representative of the American nobility, the Conde de Santiago de la Laguna. Politically ambitious and anxious to exploit the disturbances to the full, Laguna, who commanded 200 mounted and partially armed followers, presented himself as the only conceivable representative of law and order upon the collapse of the European administration. Rendón suspected him of collusion with the rebels. Even so, Laguna's intervention prevented the massacre of the departing Europeans. The merchant, Avella, with his wife and children, was caught in his coach, as it tried to press a way through the crowded main square. A deputation from the crowd went to Laguna, as if he alone represented legitimate authority in the city, to request permission to murder Avella. This extraordinary deferential gesture cost the mob the bloody scene for which it might have wished. The Avella family left the city, terrified but unscathed. Azpechea, for his part, reached Mexico City, where he was listed in 1811 as a member of the Mining Tribunal. Three years later, he received official permission to return with his family to Navarra. Laguna's intention was not to preside over the killing of the fellow members of the upper caste, but to frighten Europeans into departing and abandoning the city, with its mining revenues, to his charge. Since no possibility existed of defending Zacatecas against the insurgents, Laguna evidently intended to co-operate with them. Defections from the New Galicia cavalry regiment of *escuadrones*, and warnings from the Bajío, persuaded Rendón, encouraged by Laguna, to depart on 8 October. The latter, thereupon, reconstituted the city council, which pronounced him to be interim Intendant of Zacatecas. In effect, Laguna had painted such a horrifying picture of plebeian vengeance, that Rendón surrendered power to him without a struggle.[4]

Laguna sent Cos to Aguascalientes to treat with the insurgents under Rafael Iriarte, who was Hidalgo's commissioner there. On 25 October, Hidalgo, acting in his capacity as 'Generalissimo of America', formally invested Laguna with the Intendancy and bestowed upon him the rank of *Teniente General* of the American Armies. The latter accepted this appointment on 5 November.[5]

A Royalist force under another American nobleman, the Conde de Pérez Gálvez, operating on the borders of Zacatecas, encountered European refugees from the city. They included the plutocrat, Fermín de Azpechea, the object of intense loathing in Zacatecas. Azpechea, a heavy investor in the mining industry, had managed to take 400,000 pesos of funds with him. Among the forty or so European refugees were Bernardo de Yriarte and Dr Manuel Retegui, with their families and funds, prominent Basques of the city. Pérez Gálvez appeared to be favourably disposed towards Laguna, and reported that, with the assistance of the municipality, he had the city under control. For the American nobility, then, the chief preoccupation seemed to be containment of popular hatreds. On the road from Zacatecas an insurgent force, however, had seized Rendón and his family at dawn on 29 October, and stripped them of their possessions. The insurgents held them captive for thirty-three days, before placing them before Hidalgo in Guadalajara, which had fallen in December. In the meantime, the militia companies of Colotlán, formed for the defence of the northern frontiers of Zacatecas, had risen against their officers and joined the rebel priest, Calvillo, in Aguascalientes.[6]

Laguna's position in Zacatecas, nevertheless, was by no means secure. His continued efforts to protect Europeans led to his arrest on Hidalgo's orders on 11 January 1811. Removed from office, he was conducted to Guadalajara, though he escaped in the confusion following the insurgent defeat at Puente de Calderón. His story reflected the dilemma of many others like him, who could not initially decide clearly which side served their interests better. Laguna was recaptured by the rebel chieftain, Toribio Huidobro, on 27 November, but he again escaped, this time to seek pardon from Calleja in Guadalajara. There, however, some vengeful Spaniards denounced him as a collaborator and he was duly arrested, but escaped during a rebel attack, while under escort near León. He returned to Guadalajara and handed himself over to the Royalist authorities. Repenting of his earlier collusion with the insurgents, whose cause, after Puente de Calderón he believed to be lost, Laguna was freed a year later and died in Zacatecas at the end of 1814.[7]

The case of Zacatecas illustrates the local dimension of the breakdown of governmental authority in New Spain during the late summer and autumn of 1810. In this mining region, which was seriously affected both by recession and food shortages, the political situation proved to be particularly precarious. Laguna's capture of power in the city enabled brief insurgent control, though rebel power did not extend to capture of the other major mining centres in the Intendancy. Yet, the case of Laguna highlighted the ambiguous position of the American nobility towards lower-class unrest and insurgent violence. For upper class Americans it must have seemed a daunting prospect to have to decide which way to turn. Rendón's case illustrated how a prominent soldier with administrative experience could lose control of an entire province under threat of extreme violence and under a sense of total isolation from the political centre.

## The situation in San Luis Potosí

Iriarte became for a time the predominant insurgent figure in Zacatecas. He himself originated from San Luis Potosí, which he had not dared to approach as long as Calleja's principal force remained there. Iriarte had once been an employee on the Gándara family estate, the Hacienda de Bledos. For a time he had worked as a clerk under Calleja's orders when the latter had commanded the Tenth Brigade in San Luis Potosí. He had held a low military rank and amongst his subalterns he became known as *'el cabo Leytón'* a nickname which stuck with him into the insurgency. Iriarte, who may possibly have been in contact with the Querétaro conspirators, was one of the first to receive military rank from Hidalgo, and immediately began raising men in León and Lagos. After receiving control of Zacatecas from Laguna, Iriarte thence proceeded to San Luis Potosí where, as we shall see, local conspirators had in expectation already seized control of the city.[8]

Alamán described San Luis Potosí as the centre of a 'revolutionary vortex', beyond which the insurgency flourished throughout the Serranía de la Huasteca and the whole region from the Río de Tampico to the coast. Bands in northern Guanajuato, particularly from the Dolores area, were in communication with those across the border in San Luis Potosí.[9] Hidalgo's commissioner, Fray Luis de Herrera, became the principal rebel commander in the zone stretching across San Luis Potosí and Zacatecas. Herrera, originally from the Convent of San Juan de Dios, had first joined Hidalgo in Celaya, but had been captured at the Hacienda del Jaral, and taken under arrest to San Luis Potosí. From jail he had then been transferred to a convent in the city under the surveillance of the Prior. While in the convent he contacted Joaquín Sevilla y Olmedo, a local officer in the Lancers' Regiment of San Carlos and together they conspired to seize control of the city once Calleja's main Royalist army had departed on campaign, and, thereby, hand it over to the insurgent forces. In the same convent, moreover, was Hidalgo's agent in the city, Fray Juan Villerías. The conspirators were greatly assisted by the absence of effective royal authority in the provincial capital, since the Intendant, on his sick bed, remained in no position to take control of events. On 10–11 November, the conspirators, unopposed by the estimated 4,000 militiamen in the city, captured power, and appointed a sympathetic American, Miguel Flores, to assume the office of Intendant. Five days later, Iriarte's forces entered San Luis Potosí from Zacatecas. They drew support from the surrounding villages and from the *'indiada'* of San Miguel Mezquitic.[10]

The Royalists recovered San Luis Potosí on 5 March 1811. Calleja appointed a sympathetic municipal council at the head of which was his father-in-law, Manuel de la Gándara. Arredondo's forces captured Herrera and executed him on 17 April. Villerías was killed in action against Matehuala on 13 May 1811.[11] Iriarte perished late in March

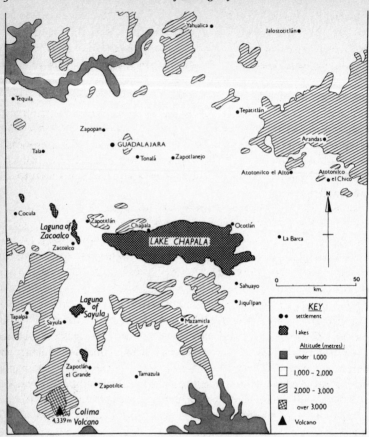

Map 2  The Guadalajara region

1811. He was one of the most unruly of the rebel chieftains, and put the
city of San Luis Potosí to the sack. He quarrelled with other chieftains
and earned the particular hostility of Allende, whose order to assist in
the defence of Guadalajara in January 1811 he disobeyed. Absent from
the field of Puente de Calderón, only the arrival of the retreating rebel
army at Zacatecas prevented his defection. Allende placed Iriarte under
surveillance, but in Saltillo he escaped. Iriarte was the only rebel leader
to escape the betrayal at the oasis of Baján, which threw further
suspicion upon him. Allende instructed his successor, Ignacio López
Rayón, to have Iriarte shot. This Rayón did, late in March 1811, when
Iriarte fatally presented himself in Rayón's camp.[12]

## The situation in Guadalajara

Royalist resistance in the region simply disintegrated. The military campaign carried little conviction, in view of the political collapse within the city during the months preceding the outbreak of the rebellion of Dolores. Guadalajara fell to the insurgents without a siege and without a revolutionary capture from within. The city dropped into their hands, an unexpected prize. Royalist administration broke up after the failure to hold the rebels at La Barca and Zacoalco. The Europeans, who could, fled for their lives, leaving American members of the city council, led by José Ignacio Cañedo and Rafael Villaseñor, to treat with insurgent leaders.

The complex situation in Guadalajara originated in the audiencia's conflict with the Captain General of New Galicia, Colonel Roque Abarca, who, of course, was also Intendant of Guadalajara and president of the audiencia. Abarca had distinguished himself in the Roussillon campaign of 1793–5 against the French revolutionary forces which had invaded Catalonia. In Guadalajara, he had earned a reputation for favourable disposition towards Mexicans. Moreover, Abarca was a friend of Viceroy Iturrigaray, who himself had gained the sympathy of senior Mexican noblemen early in his viceregency. It was thought that Abarca shared Iturrigaray's views on the constitutional question during the summer of 1808. A struggle followed between the European magistrates of the Audiencia of Guadalajara and the Intendant. The former, strongly opposing Iturrigaray's concessions to the autonomists in Mexico City, sought to bypass the Intendant and undermine his position, as if he were himself politically suspect. At the same time the audiencia began to browbeat the municipal council. The coup of 15–16 September in Mexico City accordingly left Abarca dangerously exposed. Frightened of suffering the same fate as Iturrigaray, the Intendant lost his nerve, and effectively abandoned power to the magistrates. The latter pressed the municipality in September and early October to pronounce the deposed Viceroy a traitor. This the councillors duly did on 15 October by declaring that he had been an enemy of king and religion.[13]

In spite of the uneasy political situation within the city, Abarca tried to attend to his military duties, in case of a French invasion. Viceroy Marshall Garibay, Iturrigaray's successor, appeared to have retained confidence in him, since he appointed him to command the Ninth Brigade, still in the process of formation since its initial foundation in 1796. The insurrection in Guanajuato overtook this state of affairs in

Guadalajara. Late in September 1810 two rebel forces crossed into the Intendancy, the first under Toribio Huidobro by way of La Barca, and the other under José Antonio Torres by way of Sahuayo and thence towards Zacoalco, where considerable support could be expected. The European magistrates, backed by some of the merchants, took advantage of the rebel threat to strip Abarca of his military powers, and reduced the political leader of their region to impotence. This group on 29 September effectively replaced him by a 'Governing Committee for Security and Defence', which reflected its views. Defence of the city, as a result, lay not in the hands of the legitimate military commander but at the disposition of a handful of magistrates and merchants, several of whom sported militia titles but possessed no military experience. The *oidor* Juan José Recacho, bitter enemy of Abarca, took command of city militia forces, promoted from captain to colonel for the purpose. The committee tried to form mercantile companies under two city councillors and to persuade hacienda owners to arm their farm-workers, a risky expedient, but unlikely to materialise in view of the shortage of funds. In vain expectation of their continued loyalty, the committee summoned to the city the militia forces on the Colotlán and Tepic frontiers. Bishop Cabañas appealed for loyalty from the pulpit and on 24 October excommunicated insurgent supporters. Recacho failed to hold La Barca and Royalist resistance east of the city disintegrated.[14] The insurgents resumed their advance on Guadalajara and the defence of the city itself began to collapse. Conflict had already broken out between the city council and the governing committee concerning the best means to hold the city. On 20 October, the municipality complained that the latter merely impeded decision-making, and urged Abarca to take command once again in face of desertions amongst defence forces. Abarca duly led 500 men the short distance to Tonalá, despite the menacing insurgent presence in Zacoalco, but they, too, deserted. The cereal farmer, Tomás Ignacio Villaseñor, *Mayorazgo* proprietor of Huajotitlán, led 1,200 militia men against Torres only to be severely defeated at Zacoalco on 4 November, even though only 50 of the insurgent force of 2,000 men had firearms. The bulk of the Royalist dead in the government defeat there and in the murder of prisoners afterwards were merchants of Sayula.[15]

Hidalgo's chieftain, Torres, knew the Guadalajara region well and had himself lived for a time in Zacoalco. A *mestizo*, born in 1760 in San Pedro Piedragorda over the Guanajuato border, he had worked as a muleteer and as an hacienda administrator in the district of Irapuato, where he had acquired the popular title, '*el amo Torres*'. Torres knew the merchants operating in the main cities and was familiar with the principal trade routes. In Irapuato he had joined the revolt during the early days. With his sons, José Antonio and Manuel, known as '*el niño Don Manuelito*', he had raised a formidable band from among the farming population of Guanajuato and Michoacán. With the rank of colonel bestowed upon him by Hidalgo, Torres had appeared in New Galicia by way of Mazamitla into the region of the lakeside towns. The insurgent cause derived major support from the lakes basin. Alamán, for instance, identified the chief rebel positions early in 1811 as Zacoalco, Sayula and Zapotlán.[16] These were, as we have seen, relatively large and prosperous towns of considerable significance in the regional economy. According to the Subdelegate of Zapotlán, the 'Indians' there had wanted to rise since 1808, without the examples of Dolores and Guanajuato to follow.[17] Once Torres had entered these regions, local land disputes and tensions with merchant–investors may well have become for a time subsumed within the broader insurrection. To the former problem, Hidalgo's celebrated Guadalajara decree of 5 December 1810 addressed itself, when it sought to legislate the restoration of lost community lands.[18]

As the Royalist defences finally collapsed with the failure to hold back the insurgents at Zacoalco and La Barca, panic set in among the city's Europeans, who began to fear for their lives. Abarca raised another force, but it deserted to the rebels. The Europeans refused either to stay and defend the city or to contribute the funds required for others to do so. Authority disintegrated within the city, and Bishop Cabañas, the *oidor* Recacho, and some 200 Europeans began their arduous flight on 9 November to the supposed safety of the small Pacific port of San Blas, whence they hoped to sail to refuge. Abarca tried to hold his position in face of this defection, but his personal force of 110 soldiers likewise deserted, and the Intendant, in consequence, went into hiding. Many Europeans, including merchants and businessmen, who had decided not to leave the city, took refuge in convents or in sympathetic private houses. In such a way, without a prior revolutionary putsch within the city, Guadalajara presented itself as an easy prize to the insurgents. Torres, in association with local bands under Alatorre, Huidobro and Godines and the dissident militia of Colotlán, took over control in the capital of New Galicia on 11 November.[19]

Guadalajara's principal militia commanders were among those who fled to San Blas. The appearance of a rebel force of 2,500 men under the priest, José María Mercado, further worsened the weak Royalist position on the coast. It meant, in effect, that a struggle to embark on ships bound for Acapulco would ensue: Recacho and other audiencia members managed to get on board. Mercado, who until the insurrection had been parish priest of Ahualulco, west of Guadalajara, originated from the district of El Teúl on the Zacatecas border, an area which had been the scene of the long land dispute between the 'indios' of San Andrés del Teúl and the Condesa de San Mateo de Valparaíso.[20] Under Torres' instructions, Mercado took Tepic with a few *rancheros* and 600 Indians armed with sticks and *garrotes*, once the town militia had defected. When the majority of the San Blas garrison of 800 well-armed men with 12 cannons deserted also, the remaining Europeans caught there voted to capitulate, and Mercado entered on 1 December without a fight. The collapse of San Blas' defence became the subject of a subsequent official inquiry. In the meantime, Torres' commissioners had already taken Colima on 8 November, whereupon the insurgents there began to send the district's Europeans under escort to Guadalajara. Those taken in San Blas were similarly sent back.[21]

Hidalgo entered Guadalajara in person on 26 November and reconstituted the audiencia in a manner acceptable to the insurgents. Accordingly, the civil court reopened under his presidency on 3 December. Among its ten magistrates were three insurgent lawyers, José María Chico, José María Izazaga, and Ignacio López Rayón. The senior magistrate was the *regente* Antonio de Villaurrutia, brother of Jácobo, who had argued in favour of autonomy during the summer of 1808 in Mexico City. The brothers were the sons of the Mexico City born (b. 1712) magistrate, Antonio Bernardino Villaurrutia.[22] The insurgent occupation of Guadalajara between 11 November 1810 and 17 January 1811 was sullied by evidence of the systematic massacre of Europeans. Early in the occupation Torres began the embargo of European properties and the confiscation of merchandise found in the shops. The murder of Europeans held in Guadalajara began on 12 December, the feast of the Virgin of Guadalupe. Groups of twenty to thirty were taken out of the city at night and done to death on the outskirts. According to Ramírez Flores, they were killed with the full authority of Hidalgo, but under the supervision of his subordinate commanders, generally with machetes and knives. One of these band commanders was 'colonel' Manuel Muñiz from Tacámbaro in Michoacán, who would play a major role in the continuing struggle in that region. These murders continued over a thirty-day period. Some of the prisoners brought from Colima, Aguascalientes, and other areas were also killed in this way. Few authorities agree on the total number of victims; estimates generally vary between 200 and Calleja's figure of 500–600. These massacres further tarnished the reputation of Hidalgo, already compromisd by the slaughter of the defenders of the Guanajuato granary and the execution of some 60 Spanish prisoners at Valladolid.[23]

The issue of the massacres proved to be so sensitive that captured insurgent leaders found it necessary to stress their ignorance of them or their non-participation. One such instance was that of the parish priest of Jilotlán, José Antonio Díaz, one of Torres' subalterns. His revolutionary career, moreover, illustrates the type of support that went into the movement in the Guadalajara region. Díaz, born in Zapotlán in 1753, had been a college companion of Hidalgo in Valladolid, a fellow professor, and eventually Vice-Rector of the College of San Nicolás Obispo. He had heard of the insurrection late in October 1810, when in Colima. His first position with the insurgents had been as chaplain to José Antonio Torres, son of '*el amo*', whom he accompanied through the southern towns where he raised funds for the insurgent attacks on Guadalajara, Zapotlán and Sayula. Hidalgo, after his arrival, had entrusted Díaz with the conduct from San Blas of the cannons captured there from the Royalists. As a result, Díaz stressed that he had nothing to do with the massacre of Europeans in Guadalajara, and pointed out that he had even pleaded for the life of a captured Spaniard.[24]

The insurgent presence in the Guadalajara region posed as many problems of loyalty as in the city itself. Incidents that took place in the town of La Barca may well have been typical. When the insurgent chieftain, García Ramos, appeared in the district, the Indian Francisco Mungía was a leading influence in inciting the town to rebel. He was opposed by another Indian, Martín Gutiérrez, a *cacique* from Zacoalco, who had been living in La Barca for nearly a quarter of a century. Gutiérrez, along with his cousin, Agustín Juan, at that time Governor of Zacoalco, had on the news of the rebellion, visited villages, *ranchos* and haciendas in the district, appealing for loyalty to the Crown. The *cacique*, a member of the Third Order of St Francis and well considered among the 'better class of inhabitants', had earned, he stressed, the dislike of the 'riff-raff' through his role as criminal prosecutor. Upon the rebel advance, Mungía had managed to remove the Royalist *alcalde* in the town and take over that office himself. He approved the removal of the church bell in order to melt it down for the production of artillery. Furthermore, Mungía had taken part in the arrest of Gutiérrez when the insurgents entered La Barca, and, according to testimonies, had been one of those calling for his death. According to Gutiérrez, the rebels had put him in irons and in court martial sentenced him to death, with the '*plebe*' calling for his head. He survived, nevertheless, to testify in

October 1811 to his own loyal conduct during the insurgent occupation of La Barca. Mungía, however, was apprehended by the Royalists, and on 8 May 1812 sentenced to death by hanging by the Committee of Public Order in Guadalajara. The jailor of Royalist prisoners in La Barca, José María Jiménez, known as 'Jondaso', was sentenced to 200 lashes, to be followed by seven years in presidio. Luis Ramos, the insurgent who had arrested a religious who had denounced the rebellion, received a similar sentence.[25]

The insurgent defeat at Puente de Calderón on 17 January 1811 broke up the rebel army, estimated at between 80,000 and 100,000 men, scattered the leadership, and led to a war of rebel bands and Royalist detachments. In no sense, did the insurrection cease: it became a long insurgency, difficult to eradicate. Calleja entered the city on 21 January to decorated balconies and the ringing of bells, and to the same professions of loyalty, which had greeted Hidalgo. Trusting no one, Calleja two days later expressed his surprise at the extent of Hidalgo's support in the city, especially among the 'lower classes'. Many citizens had accepted employment under the insurgent regime. Yet, at the same time, he gained the impression that the chief figures there were glad to see the insurgents go. As a result, he adopted a policy of conciliation, rather than of retribution, which he justified by his belief that, though a large measure of support, even among Europeans, existed for the separatist cause, the excesses of the insurgents and the terrible impression given by their army, had alienated many pro-separatists from the Hidalgo rebellion.[26]

Rebel control of the countryside remained entrenched, and for years posed major problems of counter-insurgency. The Royalists faced the prospect of a bitter war of attrition. Calleja compared the type of warfare to that waged by the insurgent Spanish provinces against the French generals in the peninsula. Only a carefully conceived series of campaigns throughout the countryside could undermine the rebel position there. Commodity speculation, by which merchants and food producers sought to boost incomes at a time of high prices and shortages, continued to provoke resentment in the villages and to fuel insurgent support.[27] Although citizens of Guadalajara celebrated the defeat at Calderón, rebel strength in the lake basin region grew. In Zapotlán, for instance, Indians attacked the subdelegate's house on 3 February and forced him to take refuge in the city. The lives of non-Indian residents once more lay in peril. The situation rapidly deteriorated, as Indians seized hold of anyone who refused to cry '¡ *Viva Hidalgo!*' or '¡ *Muera Calleja!*'. Several other villages, notably Zacoalco and San Gabriel, joined the movement, and the authorities in Sayula appealed for assistance.[28] Leading inhabitants of Zacoalco sought to persuade neighbouring villages to revolt against what, with evident local feeling, they described as 'the Mexico City government'. The Audiencia of Guadalajara heard that eight such places had already risen, including Zapotlán and Sayula. This rebellious stance, however, was by no means universal: responses varied according to locality. The parish priest of Jocotepec, for instance, found that the inhabitants of the villages of San Antonio, Ajijíc, San Juan and Jocotepec itself, were not disposed to revolt at all.[29]

After Calleja's departure for San Luis Potosí, where the situation also continued to be serious, Brigadier José de la Cruz in February 1811 took office as Commandant General of New Galicia, a position he retained until the summer of 1821. Just as Calleja had done, Cruz adopted a policy of conciliation, issuing amnesties in all the villages through which he passed on his campaign to destroy Mercado. Hundreds responded. A counter-revolution in San Blas overthrew Mercado, who encountered a sudden death at the foot of a precipice. Another counter-revolution took place in Tepic.[30]

Cruz responded to insurgent control of the country towns and villages by despatching a series of offensive campaigns through the localities. Colonel Rosendo Porlier passed through the villages of the Lake Chapala zone and moved towards the Michoacán border. In February 1811 Porlier put down unrest in the three main insurgent strongholds, Zacoalco, Sayula and Zapotlán, and from Zapotiltic and La Barca, pressed across the Michoacán border into Zamora and Jiquílpan. Porlier acted promptly, but without undue severity. Four Indians of Zapotlán were to be executed, their bodies strung up as a warning. Most dissidents received only a few lashes for their alleged complicity with the insurgents. Porlier finally swung southwards, and entered Colima on 21 August.[31] Indian sympathies for the insurgent cause remained strong in Zacoalco, despite the periodic strong Royalist presence. In October 1812 the village welcomed the rebel chieftain, Juan Bautista Cárdenas, when he appeared in the district and killed 78 of his opponents. Villagers armed with slings assisted Cárdenas' attack on Sayula.[32] A special brigade under Lieutenant-Colonel Pedro Celestino Negrete operated into Zacatecas against insurgent-held positions – Juchipila, Taltenango and Colotlán – located between Guadalajara and the city of Zacatecas, which the Royalist Captain José Manuel Ochoa entered on 17 February. Colotlán fell to Negrete on 7 April. Thereafter, the latter concentrated upon the exposed Michoacán border zone, with a view to establishing control, as Porlier had sought to do, over Jiquílpan and Los

Reyes. Although these brigades operated relatively successfully against insurgent positions in major towns and villages, the Royalists had little success in remoter or inaccessible regions.[33]

## Huichapan and the Villagráns

Hidalgo sent another hacienda majordomo, Miguel Sánchez, one of the original Querétaro conspirators, to contact the Villagráns, local *caciques* of the Huichapan district. Sánchez, already personally known to them, secured the support of Julián Villagrán and his son, Francisco, known as 'El Chito'. Christon Archer has drawn attention to the importance of this town, strategically located above the main Querétaro to Mexico City route, in the carrying trade. Once more, we can point to the role of the muleteers: the menfolk of Huichapan worked as mule-drivers in good times, but applied their intimate knowledge of the countryside to banditry in hard times.[34] The Villagráns were not unique in seeing in the insurgency a means to improve their prospects. Julián Villagrán, born some time in the middle of the eighteenth century, had become Captain of the Tula militia regiment resident in Huichapan. Well before their decision to align with Hidalgo, the Villagráns had gained local prominence. In the list of thirty owners of looms prepared in 1785, for instance, the name of Doña Francisca Villagrán, described as an '*española*', appeared at the head. There were no *obrajes* in the district, but 102 individual looms existed, not subject to another person. Eighty-one of them were owned by 'Indians' and the rest by a handful of 'Spaniards'. According to a report of 1793, the cloth trade of Huichapan had fallen under the control of Spanish merchants who brought in the cotton and collected the cloth, leaving no opening for the local weavers to trade directly with the market. What implications, if any, this may have had for the Villagráns is not as yet known, though if the clan's weavers found themselves within a network of mercantile control by outsiders, resentment may have resulted, with long-term political consequences.[35] The Villagrán clan, as *vecinos de razón* did not shrink from uniting with the Indian inhabitants of the district in a common defence of traditional rights. The water dispute of 1786 illustrated this local hostility to certain innovating private proprietors. Julián, Antonio, José and José Antonio Villagrán took the leadership of the town opposition. The case originated from the financing of a dam and pool for public use in this arid zone by the town's benefactor, the late Manuel González, who had died in 1782. A private proprietor, Manuel de la Paz, seized control of all the water at the beginning of 1786 for his sole use, with the assistance of his two sons, who stood on armed guard to prevent anyone else taking it. The Paz clan did not even allow the townswomen to do their washing. Paz used the water to irrigate his wheat. Another proprietor, Antonio García, diverted the course of the streams that led into the pond, with the result that it dried up. García had even tried to cut channels through the streets and across town lands for the conduct of water to irrigate the vegetable and fruit gardens he was in the process of farming. In view of the grave maize shortages of 1785–6 this was a serious moment for the local food growers. The Indians of Huichapan accordingly protested against these innovations by private owners and maintained that 'since we are Indians, we are deprived of everything that is our own'. When the *alcalde mayor* defended the protestors, the proprietors denounced him. The town's legal representatives countered that its livestock transit trade, especially the mule trade, suffered through the shortage of water. In April 1787 the Mexico City government came down in favour of the townspeople, but we do not know as yet what actually transpired in practice. Whatever the final result of the case, the Villagráns showed themselves ready to form bridges to the non-Hispanic population in a common opposition to whatever conflicted with their interests.[36] By 1812–13, we shall see Julián Villagrán and his son Francisco, who was already a fugitive from justice in 1810, lords of the Serranía de Ixmiquílpan and the mining zone of Zimapan. The criminal violence of the Villagráns would become legendary.[37]

Insurgent support in Huichapan fell into the context of repeated unrest in the region. The relative proximity to the Pachuca–Real del Monte mining complex greatly assisted insurgent efforts to divert the silver supply from the Royalist treasuries. In December 1810 the rebel chieftain, José Vicente del Moral, operated from San Agustín Metztitlán with a large band of men. In the Real de Atotonilco el Chico, near Real del Monte, 'the village folk, armed, crown the hill tops', preventing recruitment into the Pachuca Royalist battalion.[38] Rebel forces in the Cardonal formed part of the network of bands under the command of the Villagráns; they gained adherents from Actopan itself and from the mineworkers of Atotonilco el Grande and el Chico.[39]

## The Osorno clan – the Llanos de Apan and the northern Puebla sierra

Hidalgo sent the 25-year-old dragoon officer, Mariano Aldama, a nephew of Allende's companion, Juan Aldama, to raise support in the

Llanos de Apan. Aldama gained the assistance of José Francisco Osorno, with whom he secured the adherence of the town of Zacatlán in northern Puebla on 30 August 1811 apparently with little difficulty. This town, too, had been a centre of unrest before 1810. A disturbance had broken out in 1802, led by a certain Ignacio Aguilar, who in 1806 had been condemned to perpetual banishment from there. Shortly after the outbreak of the Hidalgo revolt in the Bajío, Aguilar was arrested, on 27 October 1810, in Texcalac in Tlaxcala. The authorities probably feared that he might become once more the focal point of insurrection, in view of his alleged ascendancy over the Indians.[40] The Osorno clan exercised a predominant influence across the Llanos de Apan and the northern Puebla sierra. This *ranchero* clan held Zacatlán as their operational base until August 1813. Members of the family either owned or leased *ranchos* or haciendas in these areas: they commanded a wide clientele of relatives and associates, who supplied them with horses, food and other requirements. They were, like the Villagráns of Huichapan, criminals of long-standing, who saw in the insurrection a chance to extend their operations. Osorno's parents and sisters lived on the Rancho de Laureles: his brother lived on the Rancho de Gregorio Calderón: both properties were rented from the Hacienda de Tecoyuca. Osorno's *compadre*, José Latiri, an insurgent who had previously been arrested, supplied the rebel band from his Hacienda de Atlamaxac. The head of the Rancho de las Trompetas, Eugenio Vega, was Osorno's father-in-law: all its inhabitants were Vega's relatives or relatives of the Guarnero brothers, his apparent associates. According to Royalist information, they were generally supposed to have taken part in the burning of the Hacienda de Tecoyuca. The inhabitants of these *ranchos*, it was said, had always been thieves: in 1810 and 1811 they became insurgents as well. The insurrection enabled those who had been *rancheros* to become masters of entire haciendas. Not all the villages, however, followed their leadership: many found themselves caught between two fires, obliged to play off one side against the other as best they could by a general attitude of dissimulation. José Francisco and three others formed a group of *rancheros* into a well-mounted, well-armed band in the district of Zacatlán, and operated throughout the Llanos de Apan and northern Puebla in August 1811. After breaking into this town, Osorno released prisoners from jail, who thereupon joined his forces. Aldama adopted the title '*Mariscal*', while Osorno took the rank of '*Teniente General*': their total manpower appeared to reach some 700 men.[41]

The Royalist government sent Ciriaco de Llano, a naval captain recently arrived from Havana, to counter the movements of Aldama and

Osorno. Llano began operations out of Calpulalpan in September, frustrated Aldama's designs on Tulancingo, and occupied Apan. Aldama and Osorno apparently quarrelled and divided their forces, which Llano estimated at about 400 men. Aldama was brutally murdered on a Royalist rancho in Hueyotlipan. Although Osorno exacted a cruel vengeance upon the perpetrators, the removal of Aldama opened the way for a reunited command under the *cacique* of Zacatlán. Llano regarded the possible fusion of the rebel bands operating north-east of the Valley of Mexico, in the Puebla sierra, and into Tlaxcala as a potential danger to the viceregal capital.[42]

Royalist counter-insurgency measures drove many villagers into the rebel bands. The beginnings may be discerned at this stage of an effort on the part of some commanders to work out a response to the type of insurgency they were encountering in the field. From this experience emerged the first attempts to implement a resettlement policy, such as would later be implemented in several theatres of conflict, both in New Spain and in other parts of the world at different intervals when comparable types of insurgency developed. Llano in 1811 sought to undermine the rebel support in the countryside by burning scattered *rancherías* throughout his zone of operations. In this way he hoped to oblige their inhabitants to take refuge in villages under Royalist control. Measures of this nature were designed to deprive rebel bands of contact with the country population, from whom they derived their information and their food. The cleared areas would become war zones, in which rebel bands would be relentlessly hounded. Llano's methods proved to be counter-productive: they served, instead, to increase the available recruitment to Osorno's band. During this period Osorno gathered support from hacienda workers, *rancheros*, shepherds and peons in these regions. Miguel Serrano, for instance, brought him fifty such individuals from the Conde de Santiago's Hacienda de San Nicolás el Grande. Within the city of Puebla, Vicente Beristáin y Sousa, brother of the celebrated Royalist cleric, Mariano Beristáin, became Osorno's contact. Beristáin, an artillery expert, represented the liaison between the rebel leaders in the field and the professional bourgeoisie of the city. To his mediation was attributed an agreement between Osorno and the *pulque* hacienda owners to send cash at regular intervals as protection money to rebel bands.[43]

After the insurgent attack on Zempoala on 25 September 1811, no bands presented any serious threat in that district. In the Apan region a Royalist presence ensured that only small bands of some fifty men remained active. Llano believed that for a time peace had returned to the

Llanos. Villagers, he reported, had already taken an aversion to the rebel bands and saw no difference between them and bandit groups. Although the insurgents still occupied the Hacienda de Nopalapan between Tulancingo and Pachuca, Llano believed villagers had the capacity to hold off marauding bands, if they so chose. He urged hacienda owners to follow suit, and to grumble less about the cost of self-defence.[44] Even so, few areas remained entirely free of danger. A large band attacked estates in the district of Calpulalpan, and 'thieves' were reported to be infesting the San Juan Teotihuacan area only a short distance east of the capital city. Llano moved north from Texcoco to deal with them. Not until 30 May 1813, moreover, after holding the town for seventeen months, did the insurgents lose control of Zimapan, north of Tula. As late as July 1813 rebel bands still controlled the district of Metztitlan, and the Royalists had only then commenced the pacification of Huichapan.[45] Osorno, with the assistance of Ignacio López Rayón, held on to his personal stronghold of Zacatlán until 23 August 1813. Even then he continued in the field, took Texcoco briefly in 1815, and attacked Apan at the end of the year. During the course of 1816, however, many of his fellow chieftains, tiring of a futile insurgency and anxious for greater rewards on the other side, applied for government amnesty. Osorno, instead was captured and not finally released until the Spanish Liberal régime issued a general amnesty in 1820.[46]

## Morelos in the south – the Galeana and Bravo clans

Morelos' campaigns intially originated from the *tierra caliente*. The explanation lay not only in the strategic opportunity afforded by these remote, underpopulated regions, but also in the fact that the drought and frost, which had brought about the subsistence crisis of 1808–10, had minimal effect, if at all, in the scattered, cereal-producing valleys of these vast zones. Moreover, relief food supplies could, in any case, be found in tropical produce and in fish, where proximity to the coast made such a recourse feasible.

Hidalgo commissioned Morelos, the parish priest of Carácuaro to take the insurrection to the *tierra caliente* of the Pacific south. Between 25 October 1810 and 5 January 1814 Morelos' five campaigns clung for the most part to these regions and to the intervening territory between the coast and the central valleys. Morelos, who until the age of twenty-five had worked in the vicinity of Apatzingán in the *tierra caliente* of Michoacán, had gained a familiarity with the region from an early age. His subsequent experience as a muleteer in the trade between

Mexico City and Acapulco reinforced this knowledge. In effect, Morelos' campaigns represented an insurgent southern strategy. Furthermore, the method adopted differed markedly from the haphazard approach of the Hidalgo period with its massive forces of undisciplined men, women and children on the central plateau. A difference of geographical location, military techniques and strategy separated the Morelos phase of the insurrection from its predecessor. Morelos trained a smaller force and resisted massive peasant enrolment. The south became his base of operations in the struggle to control the central valleys of Puebla and Mexico. This affinity for the south, however, had its disadvantages, as we shall see. Morelos twice forfeited the chance of taking the city of Puebla. In the first instance, Morelos in February 1812 opted for a stand in Cuautla, where Calleja was able to surround his forces, instead of making for a weakly defended Atlixco at the end of 1811. In the second instance, Morelos withdrew into Oaxaca, where he took the provincial capital in November 1812, but, instead of striking back into Puebla, he took the decision to invest the fortress of San Diego in Acapulco early in the following year. The long siege cost Morelos his last chance of securing a permanent foothold on the plateau, where the outcome of the war would be decided. Finally, with Iturbide's victory at Puruarán on 5 January 1814, Morelos' attempt to seize the city of Valladolid petered out in disarray.[47]

At the height of his power between 1811 and 1813 Morelos controlled a vast area of land that stretched from Apatzingán in the west to the valley of Orizaba in the east, and from the valley of Guayangareo in the north-west to the Isthmus of Tehuantepec in the south-east. The Sierra Madre del Sur and the Río Balsas–Mezcala formed the centres of operations, the points of refuge and the lines of communication during the Morelos phase of the war. Chilpancingo, which lay at the heart of this geographical zone, became for a time the insurgent seat of government in 1813. Morelos' first campaign between 25 October 1810 and 16 August 1811 brought him within striking distance of the southern perimeter of the Intendancy of Puebla. Inability to capture the strongly held position of Acapulco and its fortress of San Diego in November and December 1810 obliged Morelos to turn northwards from the tropical coast into the uplands, in order to establish rebel control over the valley towns of Chilpancingo, Tixtla and Chilapa. During May and June 1811 the first two positions fell, and on 17 August the insurgent leader entered Chilapa and terminated his first campaign. This campaign, however, had singularly failed to attain its prime objective, which had been the reduction of Acapulco. Hidalgo's

initial intention in despatching Morelos to the south had been precisely
that. Nevertheless, Morelos had, in perspective, achieved a more
important gain than that: within ten months he had taken the insurgent
movement from the north-centre plateau to the Pacific coast and its
upper altitude hinterland. From Chilapa he could advance into Puebla,
which the Royalists had had little need or, indeed, opportunity to
defend. Though by no means unchallenged leader of the insurrectionary
movement, Morelos by August 1811 offered the only real possibility of
success for the cause that Hidalgo had brought into being.[48]

A campaign through the region between Acapulco and Cuernavaca
seemed propitious during the winter of 1810–11. Already in November
1810 seven of the villages in the district of Taxco had risen. Despite
local Royalist efforts to recruit forces, rebel sympathisers formed the
majority of the district of Iguala, which rapidly fell under insurgent
control. These were areas of scant white settlement, and local Indian
villagers formed the overwhelming body of rebel support.[49]

On the coast Morelos issued a decree from Aguacatillo on 17
November 1810, which abolished slavery and caste distinctions, a
measure clearly designed to mobilise support in a region with a
relatively large negro and caste population.[50] Morelos' successes on the
heights above the port of Acapulco won him the support of the principal
family of the coastal region, effectively the *caciques* of the whole zone,
the Galeanas. Very marginal to the life of the viceroyalty, though
dominant in their locality, the Galeana family possessed a substantial
amount of land in the form of a series of *ranchos* with negro workers
engaged in cotton production. The *costa grande* of what is now the State
of Guerrero, along with the *costa chica* further along the coast in the
direction of Oaxaca, provided examples of two of the least governed and
most turbulent areas of the viceroyalty. In the former the Galeanas held
sway and the authority of the viceroy and the influence of Mexico City
counted for little. Morelos entered Galeana territory and worked
through this local structure of power to advance the cause of his
movement. Without Galeana support, it is doubtful that he could have
achieved anything in that region. Certainly Morelos did not arrive in the
Acapulco hinterland with the object of confronting and removing the
power of such local interests. On the contrary, they provided excellent
recruits to his cause, both in terms of what they represented in political
power and in view of the important contributions they would make in
the military campaigns. Hermenegildo Galeana, for instance, would
become one of Morelos' best commanders.[51] One explanation for the
Galeana family's political dissidence may be in the trading activities in

which they engaged from the cotton-producing lands in the Acapulco region. Juan José Galeana owned the cotton Hacienda del Zanjón, where his younger brother, Hermenegildo worked. This estate formed part of the Galeana patrimony which extended through the region between the Pacific Ocean and the Río Balsas.[52] The question why the Galeanas were prepared to join Morelos in a campaign ultimately designed to expel the Europeans from Mexico, and with the central valleys of Puebla as the strategic objective, does not appear to have been posed, still less answered. Morelos' campaign, in effect, required the Galeanas to operate far beyond their native, political base. That conditions for their so doing may well have been already operative is a proposition worth advancing. External factors may have contributed to a weakening of this base. The cotton zone of the Pacific *tierra caliente*, which streched from an area north of Acapulco through Ometepec to the district of Jicayán in Oaxaca was traditionally linked to the cotton textile industry of the city of Puebla. This region and the Gulf *tierra caliente* formed the two sources of Puebla's raw material.[53] The Spanish peninsular merchants and their network of dependents formed the intermediary elements in the capitalisation of cotton production and in the distribution of the finished product from the domestic sources of manufacture. Throughout the cotton, textile or dye-producing zones, where such arrangements applied, notably in the Mixteca and on the Pacific coast, local villagers, be they Indian dye-producers or negroid cotton workers, resented the *repartimientos* conducted on the merchant–investor's behalf by the local *alcalde mayor*, subdelegate or other type of dependent. These *repartimientos* usually amounted to an attempt by the investor and distributor to enforce a monopoly in the locality, with the resulting indebtedness, coercion and low prices for raw materials or local textiles. It is possible, though no evidence of corroboration has as yet come to light, that the Galeanas, local landowners with scant ready capital, fell into a similar pattern of resentment towards the Spanish peninsular merchant–investors and the local agents. If this was in fact the case, then it is possible to understand how a formidable chain of alliances came into being which included creole *caciques* of the Pacific coast, such as the Galeana family, the negroid work population, and the Indian villages of very diverse social composition in the Mixteca Alta and Baja. This opposition alliance remained only a potentiality during the late colonial period. It needed the catalyst of the Hidalgo insurrection and, more directly, the politicisation and recruitment by Morelos, to render it active. This alliance resulted from the final interconnection of all the local and diffused disputes and hostilities concerning the expansion and abuse of mercantile power, with its obligatory incorporation of marginal groups into the wider economy. These groups after 1810 now sought to exact their revenge for the wrongs they believed had been done to them. Incorporated, often against their will into the wider economy, the groups now sought to displace the *gachupines* precisely on that wider stage. The expansion of mercantile power had severely dislocated local activities, structures and relationships. Support in these areas for Morelos was the local reaction to these powers beyond the locality. This alliance, then, formed a southern parallel to the pressures on land and labour in the expanding centre-north-west.

Political and economic factors probably combined to determine the insurgent allegiance of the Galeana family in opposition to the predominant structure of power in the centre core region.

Hermenegildo Galeana, known affectionately to his peons as 'Tata Gildo', brought to the Morelos movement a wide series of relatives, dependents, neighbours and compadres, as well as a great number of their negro and mulatto workers. Moreover, his two brothers, Juan José and José Antonio, had already served as militia officers of the Pacific Coast battalions. Fermín Galeana brought a further fifty men each armed with rifles. As a result, in addition to the militia forces of Zacatula and Petatlán, which had earlier joined Morelos, a force of c.2,000 men assembled above the government-held part of Acapulco in December 1810.[54]

The Bravo family, predominant in Chilpancingo, occupied an outstanding position as much through great accumulation of land, as through the relationships and contacts, which they had with a wide range of influential persons in the region. In effect, the family occupied a crucial strategic position in geographical terms south of the sugar-producing zones of Cuernavaca-Yautepec-Jojutla-Cuautla and on the flank of the Taxco silver mines. The viceregal authorities had already tried to woo them with promises of militia office. Morelos contacted them on their Hacienda de Chichihualco through the mediation of Hermenegildo Galeana. A sudden ambush by Royalist forces, which suspected the Bravos' loyalty, determined their adherence to the Morelos movement, along with the peons of their hacienda. Morelos duly entered the Bravo stronghold of Chilpancingo on 24 May 1811.[55] Along with the Galeana brothers, the Bravos formed part of Morelos' military command. In Tixtla Morelos secured the support of another figure who would assume great significance in the movement, Vicente Guerrero.[56]

With the adherence of the Galeanas and Bravos, Morelos gained the allegiance of their wide clientele of relations, compadres and dependents, hacienda or ranch workers, and available manpower. In short, in order to 'revolutionise' the south, Morelos had to work through the local élite and the descending chain of command beneath them. That Morelos could bring together *caciques* such as the Galeanas and Bravos was a testament to his political aptitude. Similarly, as Morelos advanced northwards in the direction of southern Puebla, away, that is, from the negroid coastal zones, he found it both necessary and desirable to work through the existing Indian structure of government in the villages. In this sense two parallel chains of support came into existence, that of the creole or *mestizo* local élite and that of the Indian *caciques* and governors. In turn, Indian villages expected insurgent commanders to comply with their own particular objectives, such as the removal of unpopular subdelegates. The Indian villagers of the district of Jojutla, for instance, requested Nicolás Bravo, the rebel commander in their locality, to remove the district lieutenant, Miguel de Figueroa, and appoint Juan de Oliván, a native and resident of the town of Jojutla, on the grounds that he understood the 'Mexican language', essential for communication with the Indian communities. The Indians described Figueroa as haughty and disdainful towards them.[57]

Morelos' readiness to work through the existing structure of relationships in the locality gave his movement a conservative hue. In effect, Morelos received the support of a representative segment of society in the south. This region's already endemic social and ethnic tensions became, as a result, subsumed into the insurgent movement. From the outset Morelos struggled to prevent these tensions from breaking up the vertical coalition of social elements that he laboured to construct. In view of the central goal of the insurrection, which was to remove the '*gapuchines*' from the government of New Spain, Morelos strove to prevent the degeneration of the movement into race and class war. Such an unfortunate outcome would have played into the hands of Royalist propagandists, who, from the outset, had portrayed the insurrection exactly as that kind of conflict. Morelos' instructions from Tecpan on 13 October 1811 warning against caste war revealed the extent of the problem and the principal commander's own fears of the political consequences of its escalation. Morelos stressed that the formation of a government by Americans, that is, segments of the white élites, was the objective of the movement. Class or racial attacks on whites simply justified Royalist Americans in their option for continued co-operation with the Europeans.[58]

Morelos, then, despite his own mixed racial origins, remained a representative figure within the mainstream of creole politics. For precisely such a reason other representative figures, such as Andrés Quintana Roo and Carlos María Bustamante, felt able to join him in 1812 in his southern sanctuaries. While the insurgent leadership, virtually unanimously white in ethnic origin, sought to dispel racial hatred directed towards the white race, hatred of the Europeans was by no means confined to Indians, negroes and mixed-bloods. José María Liceaga, a member of the insurgent Junta of Zitácuaro, expressed a violent hatred of the *gapuchines*, in such terms as the following, 'experience has told us that only once they are dead, do the Europeans cease to be our enemies. For our part we are resolved to finish off anyone who falls in battle, since this is the only way to secure our position.'[59]

Viewed from the lower social echelons of society, a real difficulty often existed in distinguishing between white Americans, especially when they were of Royalist allegiance, and white Europeans. Nevertheless, the insurgent leaders strove to retain a respectable image for their cause. They were careful to avoid where possible the alienation of the creole upper segment in the towns and villages that fell under their control. When, for instance, the rebel commander, Valerio Trujano, well known for his brusque and impolitic behaviour, placed an unknown individual in charge of the district of Acatlán, Miguel Bravo reacted indignantly. In Bravo's view Trujano's appointee was a 'cowhand or who knows what sort of uncouth fellow'. The appointment had alarmed the local residents, that is to say, the handful of whites and *mestizos* in this predominantly Indian town. This 'cowhand' had proceeded to leave the Indian governor in charge of the entire Subdelegation in face of 'general public indignation'. Bravo wrote to the parish priest of Acatlán, instructing him to summon together the citizenry and Indian inhabitants, in order to set the district government in order by choosing a 'respectable American' as subdelegate. Bravo had similarly written to a reliable supporter in Huajuapan, Nicolás Berdejo, since in that town Trujano had demonstrated the same 'stupidity'. Berdejo would take over the administration of the district until 'a person of note could be appointed'.[60]

Many of these southern regions through which the insurgent commanders passed had long histories of social tension, with the result that the Royalist authorities in Puebla felt little confidence that they would remain for long under their control. Such proved to be the case with respect to Chilapa and Tlapa. When insurgent forces appeared in the vicinity of Chilapa, the Indian authorities in Tlapa had tried to contact them. Fully aware of such sympathies, the subdelegate and parish priest tried as best they could to stave off an Indian rising throughout the district.[61] When Chilapa fell, the rebel occupation force of some 2,000 men expropriated the movable property of émigré personnel and transported it to the Bravos' Hacienda de Chichihualco and thence into the sierra for security, on the grounds that it was 'American by right'.[62] From the Acapulco zone and its hinterland support for the insurgents extended through the Mixteca Baja and the Mixteca Alta. In February 1811 the inhabitants of the cotton-producing district of Jamiltepec in southern Oaxaca welcomed rebel forces, although later in the year local Royalist troops managed to hold out in Tututepec. Far to the north in Chazumba and Tepejí de la Seda villagers adhered to the insurgent cause, while the governor of the village of Acatepec in the district of Tehuacán equally pledged his support. In the main sugar-producing region of Oaxaca, both creoles and Indians of Tlaxiaco received Morelos' commissioners with an enthusiastic welcome. A specific explanation for rebel support lay in long-standing grievances against the *repartimientos* supposedly made illegal in 1786.[63]

While the main thrust into Puebla would come from Morelos' forces, other insurgent bands operated on the perimeters of the Intendancy in 1811. Their activities contributed not only to the general disruption of trade and communications, but also to the growing sense of encirclement experienced in the central, cereal-producing valleys. Nevertheless, little co-ordination could be discerned in these operations. Most bands pursued their own limited objectives. Already during the summer of 1811, as he advanced northwards to the Puebla perimeter, Morelos heard of the confusion of commands among many rebel chieftains. Combined action seemed impossible: mutual assistance proved rarely, if ever, forthcoming. Furthermore, rebel bands tended to seize whatever they could carry off without difficulty. It was the poor who suffered most. Miguel Bravo singled out for especial opprobrium the alleged excesses of Trujano and another chieftain, Manuel Antonio de Loya, in the villages they had taken. According to Bravo, the villagers' resentment against rebel bands had only with difficulty been contained.[64]

# 6

## The struggle for Puebla, 1811–13

The insurrection of September 1810 had not originated in the province of Puebla: no leaders of the early movement originated from that region. Nevertheless, by 1811 and 1812 the Intendancy of Puebla had become the 'principal theatre of war'.[1] This striking turn of events has received little comment or explanation. Its significance has largely been misread. As a result, we have a distorted view of this turning-point in the war in New Spain. From the secondary literature we have a disjointed narrative, a series of set pieces, such as the sieges of Cuautla, Huajuapan and Acapulco, the capture of Oaxaca, and the deliberations of the Congress of Chilpancingo. From these fragments we cannot piece together the image at the centre of the picture. What we lack, then, is the centre piece, the explanation to the broken picture. This key lies not in an examination of these peripheral incidents, so often reiterated in the literature, but in a direct confrontation with the archival materials concerning the long neglected battle for Puebla in the years, 1811 and 1812. Without such a study the set pieces around the perimeter of the main theatres of action lose their significance, which lay in their relation to the struggle for control of the central cereal-producing valleys.

### Early insurgent activity in the Puebla region

Long-standing grievances in several localities provided a fertile recruiting ground for insurgent bands. Osorno and Aldama, as we have seen, operated across the Llanos de Apan and into the sierras of northern Puebla. Insurgent bands in this latter region entered the villages of Zacatlán and Chinahuapan on 31 August 1811, and indiscriminately sacked shops, irrespective of whether they were European or American-owned, and looted the royal administrative buildings. Such actions revealed the traditional resentments at debts incurred to shopkeepers and private traders, and demonstrated once more the hostility towards

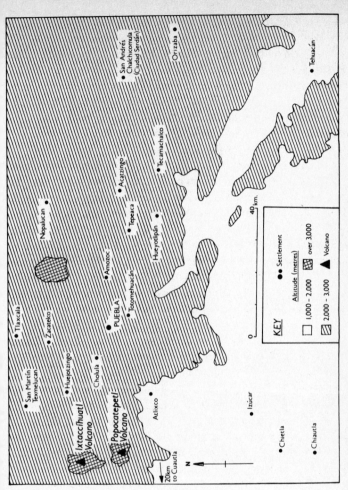

Map 3  Central Puebla

symbols of authority that we have already noted in many local instances
of rebellion. It seems probable that the survival of *repartimientos* in the
Puebla villages accounted for readiness to join rebel bands. The
continued shortage of food in the sierra explained why rebel bands
encountered little resistance. Most of the villagers had already abandoned their homes in search of food. Those who remained, however,
were not prepared to see marauding bands make off with their food. As a
result, the experience of rebel pressure on the food supply proved
enough to drive them into the Royalist camp.[2]

During the course of September 1811 the rebel chieftains, Osorno
and Aldama, operated in the direction of Tetela with some 400 men, of
whom the greater part were described as 'Indians'. Further to the south
in the province of Tlaxcala, which separated the northern from the
central region of Puebla, Royalist commanders reported that a band of
thirty or forty men under a leader called Fragoso stood watch over the
pro-insurgent village of Tlaxco.[3] The vulnerability of Tetela led to the
fortification of the village of Zacapoaxtla, which the local commander
proposed to defend with a Patriot Corps which he had recently formed.[4]

Effective control of operations within the Intendancy of Puebla fell to
Brigadier Ciriaco de Llano, who had been appointed second-in-
command in the province on 1 November 1811. The activities of Llano
between 1811 and 1821 have received little comment in the literature of
the 'War of Independence', though both Alamán and Bustamante and
later writers have alluded to them. One possible explanation for this
neglect may lie in Iturbide's efforts to portray Llano in 1814 and 1815 as
an incompetent military commander, as a result of disagreements
concerning tactics when the two officers conducted operations together
against insurgent positions in Michoacán. Furthermore, Llano remained
among the small group of senior officers who remained loyal to the
metropolitan government and refused to adhere to the Plan of Iguala in
1821 and, instead, prepared to defend Puebla against the Army of the
Three Guarantees. In consequence, Llano's name did not appear among
the founders of the Mexican sovereign state. Llano had paid for having
chosen the losing side at a decisive moment. In 1811–13, however, it
was largely due to his efforts that the insurgents failed to secure control
of the province of Puebla. He is, therefore, a military figure of major
significance, because this insurgent failure ultimately affected the course
of the war. It certainly frustrated insurgent attempts to co-ordinate
political strategy and form a credible provisional government.[5]

Llano sought to prevent any co-ordination of activities between the
bands operating in the regions to the north-east of the Valley of Mexico

and those active in the sierras of northern Puebla and across Tlaxcala. In view of Osorno's strong position in Zacatlán, the Puebla Royalists could not afford to permit the formation of a vast block of territory under rebel control across their northern flank. Llano believed that Osorno intended to spread the insurrection throughout the sierra.[6]

During the course of September, rebel bands began to move inwards from the perimeter and threaten the central plains of Puebla. In the district of Huejotzingo, only a few miles north-west of the provincial capital, rebel bands robbed the cattle of the Hacienda de Zavala, an estate belonging to Captain Joaquín de Haro y Portillo, a Spanish merchant, who had become one of the richest citizens of Puebla.[7] At the opposite end of the plains another band entered San Juan de los Llanos on 11 September, a village within striking distance of the fortress town of Perote over the Veracruz border. The fortress commander, fearing imminent danger to Perote itself, took prompt remedial action, in order to forestall more widespread depredations to the estates of the district. The sack of San Juan de los Llanos spread terror among the property-owners of the Veracruz uplands. The town council of Jalapa had already become alarmed at the activities of Villagrán and Osorno. The town councils of Orizaba and Córdoba dreaded the prospect of an insurgent arrival in the region, in view of the large number of negro slaves employed in the sugar and tobacco plantations there.[8]

During the autumn of 1811, then, a number of rebel bands, including the principal groups under Osorno, operated across northern Puebla and had begun to threaten the Veracruz borderlands. From their northern positions they had already begun to threaten the cereal-producing valleys. The main insurgent force under Morelos had by this time secured its position to the south of the Puebla border with the capture of Chilapa in August. Morelos a few months later opened a fresh campaign designed to establish a foothold on the plateau.

### The insurgent campaign on the Puebla plateau: December 1811 to February 1812

Morelos began his second campaign in November. Three divisions took part in a simultaneous offensive. Moving to the south-east, Miguel Bravo entered the Mixteca Baja and threatened Oaxaca. Galeana pushed north-westwards to assist Rayón in Zitácuaro, seat of the insurgent junta. Morelos himself advanced north-eastwards into the province of Puebla. The struggle for control of Puebla opened early in the winter of 1811. Advancing from their base in Chilapa, Morelos and Bravo parted company at Tlapa. The former followed the course of the Rio Tlapaneca northwards into the Intendancy of Puebla, and on 3 December entered Chiautla with 1,000 men. The local militia companies of this tactically important town situated well in the south of the province passed over to Morelos. In Chiautla, the priest, Dr José Manuel Herrera, joined the insurgent movement, and during 1812 acted as vicar general of Morelos' forces.[9]

Izúcar, the important southern valley town, taken on 10 December, proved to be Morelos' first major gain in fourteen months of activity. More than 2,000 mixed infantry and cavalry troops with six or seven cannons followed the initial assault force of 600 well-armed cavalrymen, and together provided a formidable insurgent force. Izúcar, thereupon, became Morelos' forward base of operations on the Puebla plateau. His declared objective was the city of Puebla. The Royalist command in the provincial capital well understood this. The arrival of the principal insurgent *caudillo* on the plateau was awesome enough, but to compound the dilemma, Llano considered that the city's defences were utterly useless. Only basic fortifications, inadequate to cover such a large urban area, had been completed. Evidently no one thought that Morelos would ever be in a position to threaten the city. Instead, the insurgent commander had arrived in greater strength than Llano had believed possible. Much of this apparent prowess resulted from widespread support given to him from the villages of the districts through which he had passed. Izúcar had greeted him enthusiastically. That district had, in any case, a long history of unrest. The struggle for land among the villagers had led to expensive lawsuits and conflicts of long duration with adjacent sugar plantations and mills. The arrival of Morelos may well have provided the opportunity for villagers, frustrated at delays and failure of recourse, to take the law into their own hands.[10] In the town of Izúcar, Morelos gained the adherence of another local cleric, Mariano Matamoros, who since 1807 had been parish priest of Jantetelco. Matamoros would shortly emerge as one of Morelos' most gifted military commanders. Izúcar's strategic position at the southwestern end of the cereal zone opened the way to the dangerously exposed town of Atlixco. As we have seen, Atlixco lay at the heart of Puebla's major wheat-producing region. Control of this district not only threatened the city's food supply, but also opened the way to the capture of Puebla itself. Panic spread throughout the provincial capital.[11]

We should, then, examine conditions within the city itself, where the need for defence arose as an appalling reality. At first, in the early days of the imperial crisis, enthusiasm for military service had been evident. In late July 1808, for instance, some 2,000 individuals from both the wealthy and the popular classes had volunteered for service in an infantry regiment of Volunteers of Ferdinand VII, but, then, the likelihood that they would actually have to fight was minimal. A more exclusive group of prominent Americans and Spaniards had at the same time asked Flon to form a special squadron of Noble Patrician Volunteers of Ferdinand VII with a special uniform.[12] Flon, however, left the city in October 1810 to combat the Hidalgo revolt, and never returned. For a time, the municipality, composed of civilians, took charge of defence, and proposed the creation of further militia reserve battalions composed of wealthy volunteers who could cover their own costs. At the same time councillors saw the need to recruit more broadly, and fit out artisan volunteers.[13] The municipality also attended to the problems of internal order and control of movement by establishing a Committee of Police and Public Security on 7 November 1810, under the presidency of a city councillor, José Ignacio Bravo, a prominent merchant. This body lasted until 25 June 1813, when it lapsed under the constitutional system. Its authority, however, did not extend over either muleteers or Indians proceeding to market, both of which groups might well have provided sources of information for insurgent bands operating in the countryside.[14] Viceroy Venegas sanctioned the transformation of the region's tobacco guards into a 45-man cavalry company under Puebla's military commander.[15] Enthusiasm for militia service had cooled off by the winter of 1810, especially in view of the prospect that such volunteers might actually be called upon to participate in military action. In December, the city syndic complained of lack of public response to the municipality's appeals for contributions, despite the release of 10,000 pesos by the bishop and cathedral chapter for the purpose of defence. A body of some 1,300 men had been formed from volunteers, but still had not been fully equipped with uniforms and armaments. The syndic warned that the insurgents had much to gain from the capture of Puebla.[16] In March 1811, the veteran militia officer, Captain Gabriel Bringas, took command of the Urban Corps of Distinguished Patriots of Ferdinand VII.[17]

The Superior Government in Mexico City appointed Mariscal del Campo, García José Dávila, to take charge of the civil and military administration of Puebla early in February 1811.[18] Almost immediately Dávila and the city council came into conflict over the question of finance for defence. The municipality complained to the viceroy of Dávila's high-handed measures: the latter similarly complained of the council's recalcitrance. Such a conflict alarmed the viceroy, who rebuked the city authorities for allowing a dangerous state of tension to prevail at a time of mounting insurgent threat.[19] Late in April, Dávila drew attention once more to the poor condition of the city's defence, as government authority began to disintegrate in the countryside, many areas of which had fallen under the control of insurgent bands or were prey to gangs of thieves. He had little confidence in the Patriot Corps enlisted by the city council, since many of its members had already begged to be discharged of their obligations.[20] The city council was well aware of such problems but found it could do little to improve the situation. Councillors had already warned that the prospect of an insurgent strike at the city made their present circumstances critical. Although effective defensive measures were an urgent priority, they found that volunteer forces were still poorly manned and inadequately funded. Without proper uniforms and with insufficient rifles, the urban defence forces remained in a sorry state.[21] Dávila warned the council that daily news from the subdelegates of Zacatlán, San Juan de los Llanos, and Huejotzingo, and despatches from the military commander in Huamantla, led him to believe that the insurgents' objective was the city of Puebla. Accordingly, he urged the municipality, in association with the bishop, to levy a contribution from wealthy citizens to pay for defence costs.[22] By the end of May, 112 merchants and 28 farmers had contributed more than 6,000 pesos towards the upkeep of the 300 men of the Urban Volunteer Regiment of Ferdinand VII, only 100 of which had rifles. Further tiny contributions came from 39 members of the legal profession and various members of the guilds.[23]

By early October, the situation in the city was described as urgent in the extreme, due to the shortage of arms.[24] In response, the viceroy appointed Colonel Ciriaco de Llano to act as Dávila's second in command on 1 November 1811.[25] At the end of the month, the city council voted 4,000 pesos from its municipal funds (*propios*) for the purpose of financing the construction of defence works already begun by Dávila and Llano. This sum was soon consumed. Early in January 1812, estimates put the cost up towards a further 7,000 pesos, which Dávila pressed the council to raise without delay. With viceregal approval, the municipality transferred this sum from its fund for paving the city streets.[26]

It seemed difficult to imagine that Puebla could escape the closing of the vice. Rebel bands already surrounded Tehuacán at the south-eastern extremity of the valleys below the mountains that separated the province from Oaxaca. Detachments of Morelos' forces occupied the routes from

Tehuacán to Orizaba in the Veracruz uplands.[27] Within the central valley another band had been sighted above the Hacienda de San Francisco in the district of Tepeaca. Very little stood in Morelos' path between Izúcar and Atlixco. The town residents, chief of whom were the estate owners of the district, took pains to resist the expected insurgent assault by raising, at their own expense, an infantry company of a hundred men and a cavalry force of sixty, and covered the cost of their equipment, armaments and mounts. The expense, which exceeded 15,000 pesos, testified to the continued wealth of the Atlixco proprietors, in spite of recession and insurgent raids. Llano, for his part, took the decision to make a stand in Atlixco, and, in anticipation of an insurgent advance from Izúcar, despatched a division of 500 of the best infantry and cavalry from Puebla to defend the town.[28]

This attack, however, did not come. Morelos' failure to strike promptly at Atlixco with his superior force in December 1811, and thereby force the Royalists out of Puebla, may certainly be regarded as a turning point in the second phase of the rebellion. With some surprise Llano learned that Morelos had decided not to attack Atlixco, but to turn away from the city of Puebla altogether and move in the direction of Cuautla, outside the cereal valleys. Even so, Atlixco still remained potentially in danger, and Royalist commanders believed that an insurgent attack on Puebla would come sooner or later. Indeed, the likely explanation for Morelos' diversion from Atlixco appeared to be that he had moved in the direction of Cuautla, in order to rendezvous with other rebel leaders proceeding from the south, chiefly from the district of Taxco.[29] Whatever the case, the opportunity for a swift, decisive capture of the provincial capital had been lost. Morelos forfeited his opportunity to gain the most significant insurgent objective since Hidalgo's entry into Guadalajara in December 1810. This failure gave Llano the time he needed to fortify the city and train his forces. Already at the end of November Llano had been investigating the state of defence and exercising his men daily: early in December he expected the prompt completion of the surrounding ditchworks.[30] Morelos by that time was already turning westwards to Cuautla, which he entered on 26 December. Immediately he ordered the fortification of the town, but departed himself in search of Galeana, who had advanced from Chilapa through Tepecuacuilco and Iguala to Taxco, which he had taken two days previously. Morelos and Galeana joined forces there – well to the south-west of Puebla – on 1 January 1812. As yet Morelos had still not encountered any major Royalist force, still less the army of Calleja, which had broken the Hidalgo insurrection on the north-centre plateau.

Late in 1811, however, Calleja resumed the offensive in pursuit of
Rayón, and with 5,000 men took Zitácuaro on 2 January, putting the
insurgent political leadership to flight in the direction of Sultepec. On 5
January Calleja razed Zitácuaro to the ground.[31]

The dimension of Morelos' miscalculation in not striking without loss
of time at Puebla could now be perceived, as Calleja's army began to
move in his direction. The realisation that the main Royalist force was
approaching brought forth a confusion of responses in the rebel
command. At first Morelos and Galeana advanced northwards from
Taxco towards Tenancingo, where, however, they encountered vigorous
Royalist resistance from Colonel Rosendo Porlier, the military commander in the town, over a three-day period. Although the town fell on
23 January, Porlier managed to break through the rebel force and reach
Tenango at the edge of the Valley of Mexico. The capture of Tenancingo
took Morelos within striking distance of Cuernavaca, which he entered
on 4 February, and Toluca, which he did not manage to reach. Calleja's
advance around the perimeter of the Valley of Mexico removed any
immediate danger that a forceful insurgent appearance in the vicinity
presented to the viceregal capital. This Royalist activity forced Morelos
back upon Cuautla by 9 February, where Matamoros and Leonardo
Bravo had arrived two or three days previously, and where Galeana
would reach on 15–16 February.[32]

Calleja's entry into Toluca on 27 January had prevented any rebel
threat from Tenancingo with a view to seizing the passes into the Valley
of Mexico.[33] Even so, the activities of rebel bands within the Valley
obliged Calleja to move across from Toluca through the passes to
Cuajimalpa at the edge of the Valley above Mexico City on 3–4
February. These bands had approached perilously close to the city limits
during January and early February from the south-east, and had pushed
Royalist forces from the Valley towns en route for Cuautla, that is, from
Chalco, Ozumba and Amecameca. As a result, Calleja returned to the
capital on 5 February. This diversion enabled Morelos to strengthen the
fortification of Cuautla, though shortage of manpower prevented
utilisation of local haciendas' resources and left the strategically situated
Hacienda de Buenavista, to the south of the town, unfortified.[34] While
the main insurgent body hastened to prepare Cuautla for defence,
Morelos and Rayón from their respective bases of operations sent agents
into the Llanos de Apan, north-east of the Valley of Mexico, with a view
to recruiting support for the formation of a band throughout the estates
and villages of the region. Assembling together on the Hacienda de San
Bartolomé del Monte, near Calpulalpan, this band threatened not only

the village of Calpulalpan itself, but also Otumba and Texcoco to the east of the capital. This attempt to delay Calleja failed. In any case, the threat of Morelos' gathering of forces at Cuautla could not go unchecked, whatever the risks involved in leaving the capital city to its own devices. For that reason Calleja resumed his offensive on 13 February. In this way Morelos with the bulk of the rebel army came to be trapped in Cuautla by Calleja's undefeated Royalist army. Puebla, in the meantime, the city which might itself have faced a siege, had other decisions been taken, remained under Royalist control.[35]

With Morelos bottled up in Cuautla between 19 February and 2 May 1812, the other insurgent activity across the northern border of Puebla and into the central region failed to result in material advantages. In any case, the opportunity had been lost when Morelos turned away from Atlixco to rove, instead, through the vast territory between Izúcar and Taxco and thence to Cuernavaca. At precisely that time, other rebel bands held most of the province of Tlaxcala to the immediate north-east of the city of Puebla. Indeed, on 1 January insurgent bands seized control of the crucially-placed village of San Martín Texmelucan, which lay across the main route between Mexico City and Puebla. Llano could spare no forces to assist the Governor of Tlaxcala, since he had already despatched 500 of his best men to hold Atlixco, which logically he believed Morelos would attack. This inability to contribute to the removal of the threat from the north exposed the scant options in Llano's defensive calculations. Evidently, however, local Royalist forces managed to recover control of Texmelucan, since two weeks later on 14 January a rebel band of some 800 men under Serrano attacked the village. Insurgent cavalry broke into the main streets and reached the central square, until pushed out by troops. A subsequent attack had also failed, leaving thirty rebel dead strewn across the outskirts of the village. The local Royalist commander recounted how, so far from urging on his men, he had found it difficult to restrain their fury. Even so, his own small force of only seventy-two men, which included both dragoons and volunteers, needed reinforcements, since the '*canaille*' still surrounded the village. The main rebel force operated from Apisaco.[36] Already on 2 January an insurgent force of 2,000 men had attacked the city of Tlaxcala. After heavy fighting the rebels withdrew, suffering more than eighty losses, but leaving the houses on the outskirts and the Puebla gate lodge ablaze. The governor appealed to Puebla for reinforcements, 'since all this province is now in revolt'. The rebels had even killed the parish priest of Santa Ana Chiautempan just outside the city. Llano, sympathetic to these appeals from Tlaxcala, once more could offer no prospect of relief, and, instead, contacted the governor of the Royal Fort of Perote in the hope of securing munitions from that quarter for the beleaguered defenders of Tlaxcala and the more northerly town of Huamantla.[37] In the meantime, insurgent foundries at Apisaco forged cannons from church bells donated by the eighteen villages of the region which supported the rebel cause. No immediate prospect existed of dislodging the insurgents from their stronghold at Apisaco, since their cavalry forces already surpassed 1,000 men.[38]

With the danger from the north unabated, rebel bands struck at Tepeaca to the immediate south-east of the city of Puebla. Llano duly reinforced the village of Amozoc, located between the two positions, with a detachment of infantry and cavalry, since he expected a prompt attack on Tepeaca by the rebels operating jointly with the '*indiada* of the nearby villages'. During the nights of 28 and 29 January the rebels attacked, but were beaten off. Llano heard how rebel bands 'inundated' the district of Tepeaca and operated from their base on the Hacienda de San Jerónimo, which they had seized.[39] To the immediate north-west of the city of Puebla, the Subdelegate of Cholula reported the appearance of rebel bands in the vicinity, and expected an imminent attack. Llano sent forty dragoons and twenty grenadiers to hold the town. Further north in Huejotzingo rebel activity had also been in evidence.[40] This village fell to the rebels early in February 1812, and Royalist opposition there and throughout its district collapsed, leaving the haciendas at their mercy.[41] At the same time, the road to Mexico City was described as 'inundated by bandits', with the mail intercepted, and safe transit prevented.[42]

Vital as this insurgent activity might have been in closing the circle around the city of Puebla, it came to nothing in the long run, because Calleja kept the principal insurgent leader trapped in Cuautla. The Royalist siege of Cuautla enabled the viceregal authorities to seize the initiative in the battle for Puebla. Venegas instructed Llano to move without delay to Atlixco with the object of seizing Izúcar from Bravo, and thence to advance against Chietla or Chiautla, in the event of a collapse of resistance at Cuautla. Llano opened his offensive, but twice failed to take Izúcar on 23 and 24 February. Insurgent fortifications and a fierce defence by more than 1,500 men, with numerous '*indiada*' on the roof tops, armed with bows and slings as well as firearms, held back the Royalists' assault. Since the Royalists could not take the town, they subjected it to a heavy bombardment, until they finally ran out of ammunition. Llano reported to Calleja how Izúcar for the most part lay in smouldering ruins, fire still raging through its outlying quarters.[43] Despite Llano's failure to recover this town, the Royalists had been allowed, as a result of the siege of Cuautla, to take the offensive. For the insurgent cause this was a serious reversal of fortunes, since only a few weeks previously the main force had been in a position to seize the provincial capital. By the end of February, Llano and his fellow Royalist commanders had slowly become aware of the magnitude of Morelos' tactical error, and that, in consequence, they had thereafter a real chance of winning the struggle for control of the region.

### The Puebla perimeter and the Cuautla affair

Calleja's assault on 19 February 1812 opened, as is well known, one of the most dramatic episodes of the war. After an eighteen-hour bombardment, coupled with a combined infantry and cavalry attack, Calleja realised that he would have to subject Cuautla to a debilitating siege. The Royalists had hoped, of course, to finish off Morelos there and then. The tenacity of insurgent resistance shattered their illusions. Calleja summoned Llano from his own operations before Izúcar, in order to assist in the siege of Cuautla. This siege lasted until daybreak on 2 May, when Morelos' forces managed to break through the besiegers' lines. Both armies, however, were exhausted by the long struggle, their commanders and many men wracked by disease. It would be difficult to ascribe defeat or victory to either side. Morelos had allowed himself to be trapped in Cuautla, but had cost Calleja many months in reducing the place. Morelos had failed on the Puebla plateau, but had escaped from Calleja's trap. Even so, the Royalists had captured his second-in-command, Leonardo Bravo, whom they subsequently executed. With Matamoros replacing Bravo, Morelos sought refuge in his Chiautla base and brought his second campaign to an end.[44]

Despite the survival of the Royalist position in the city of Puebla and in Atlixco, insurgent bands remained strong throughout the Intendancy for most of the first half of 1812. New bands sprang up in many districts and could count upon widespread support. Indeed, it seemed to be the case that nearly half the total government revenue of the province had fallen under insurgent control. From sympathetic sources within the provincial capital rebel leaders gained valuable information concerning the disposition of Royalist forces. Particular hostility in the city was reserved for the peninsular troops newly arrived from Spain. They had reached Veracruz in January 1812 under the command of Mariscal del Campo, the Conde de Castro Terreño and Brigadier Juan José Olazábal. In spite of Bishop Campillo's welcoming Pastoral Letter, *poblanos* greeted these troops with surly indifference. Many soldiers were murdered in the city's *barrios*, some stoned to death, others knifed in the streets. Llano, when he returned from a brief campaign across the Vera-cruz border, found himself obliged to order Spanish soldiers to enter certain city districts only in groups of three for their own protection. As soon as he could, Llano transferred the Spanish *Batallón Americano* to the Mexico City garrison.[45] Even so, insurgent bands still operated within a menacing striking distance of the city, which remained short of defence forces. Militia commanders continued to urge the municipality to recruit further able-bodied citizens for the purpose of defending the inner city, should the rebels break into the outskirts. Similarly, such a force could provide a replacement garrison on a temporary basis, in the event that troops should be summoned to deliver a blow against the enemy. This inner city militia might also serve as a police force, in case of upheaval within, especially in view of immigration from country areas under insurgent occupation. Dávila, in the meantime, pressed for prompt completion of city defenceworks before the onset of the rainy season. The municipal council protested that it could not be expected to raise funds and have no control over their disposition.[46]

The dispersal of Morelos' forces enabled Llano to recover Tepeaca on 30 May 1812. The town had been crudely fortified by the peasant leader, José Antonio Arroyo, whom the Royalists held to be nothing but a bandit. Arroyo fled to Acatzingo, leaving behind six cannons that came into his possession. Llano found Tepeaca deserted. The inhabitants had fled apparently through fear of Royalist reprisals. Llano threatened to confiscate their property, if they failed to return, and vowed to run rivers of blood through the villages of the district, if the inhabitants failed to abandon the insurgent cause.[47]

Morelos' third campaign opened in June. Following so closely upon the ordeal at Cuautla, the renewed insurgent advance rapidly dispelled any notion that their forces had been annihilated. Galeana and Miguel Bravo began his campaign by first attempting to recover positions lost to the Royalists during and immediately after the siege of Cuautla. Never-theless, insurgent leaders soon discovered that any attempt to consoli-date a second offensive position in southern Puebla in any way compar-able to the strong potentiality of December 1811 would prove to be impossible. Furthermore, a major distraction diverted their attention across the Oaxaca border. Therefore, once Chilapa had been recovered on 4 June, Morelos, Bravo and Galeana went to the relief of Huajuapan. There, Oaxaca Royalists under Lieutenant Colonel José María Regules had trapped Trujano since 5 April. The siege of Huajuapan lasted 111 days until its final relief on 23 July.[48]

The recovery of Huajuapan gained no strategic advantages. While it removed a Royalist threat in western Oaxaca, it merely served to delay Morelos' second attempt to take the city of Puebla. This time, however, the Cuautla option was denied to Morelos by the activities of the Royalist commander in that area, Captain José Gabriel Armijo, an American from San Luis Potosí. Armijo, who had been a dragoon sergeant at the time of Calleja's formation of the San Luis Potosí militia, had joined the Calleja circle in the city and had fought at Puente de Calderón, Zitácuaro and Cuautla. At the time of Armijo's offensive through the Cuautla hinterland, rebel bands still controlled the villages of the Ozumba district, but upon the Royalists' approach they fled into the Cuautla district itself. Armijo began extensive mopping-up operations, and struck at the rebel position on the Hacienda de Temilpa, near Yautepec. On that estate the rebel commander, Colonel Francisco Ayala, had been forging cannons, and with the assistance of his 400 men proposed to make a stand beneath the security of nearby mountains. Despite the obstacle of a swollen river in the rainy season, Armijo reduced the position after heavy fighting, and executed Ayala and his two sons. This peremptory execution may have been occasioned by knowledge of Ayala's practice of sending Morelos the decapitated heads of his European captives. Morelos had discouraged this practice and had instructed Ayala instead to fix the heads in appropriate positions as a warning to other potential Royalist sympathisers. In retaliation Armijo ordered the bodies of the Ayalas to be strung up in Yautepec and Tlaltizapán. According to this Royalist commander, the defeat and death of the Ayalas had spread terror through rebel ranks, with the result that insurgent forces had scattered in all directions.[49]

Armijo's prime concern involved the rehabilitation of the formerly prosperous sugar estates of the Cuautla region. The insurgency had recruited from the work force. The Royalist commander saw his task in the guarantee of a ready labour force to the hacienda operators. This he proposed to do by means of personal visitation of the villages, in order to supervise at first hand the reorganisation of their government. Armijo made the Hacienda de Santa Clara in Yecapixtla his base for the reorganisation of the villages and haciendas of the region and for the formation of patrols to curb the resurgence of rebel activity. The scant extent of hacienda cultivation made it essential to ensure the forthcoming maize planting so that a threat of food shortages could be prevented. Armijo's method had been to assemble villagers together and offer them a government amnesty, if they had been found guilty of insurgent affiliations; he had despatched them to work on the haciendas.

Nevertheless, Armijo regarded his own efforts in the Cuautla region as merely a partial and incomplete contribution to the pacification of the areas through which Morelos had passed. Only the fall of Izúcar could guarantee that, since, according to Armijo's information, the bulk of rebel manpower in southern Puebla had been recruited from the Cuautla–Yautepec region. Armijo recommended in the meantime that a force of 50 Royalist Patriots should be stationed at the rebel point of reunion in Ozumba. Furthermore, he advised the placement of some 100 troops of the line along the radius of reorganised villages between Cuernavaca, Cuautla and Chalco. Already Royalist Patriots, based on the four haciendas of Santa Inés, Casasano, Calderón and San Carlos, had pushed out a rebel band of 80 men, drawn mainly from the local ranch population, and which Galeana had sent out from Chiautla to probe Royalist positions. Two Royalist companies of 40 and 50 men respectively already operated from the villages of Yecapixtla and Tlayacapa-Totolapa. The financial contributions of hacienda owners and village authorities maintained them. Local estate owners similarly paid for a Patriot Company in Yautepec.[50] Rebel control of the haciendas and sugar mills of southern Puebla led to a thriving trade in cattle, hides, sugar, honey and sugar spirits, which redounded to the benefit of the insurgent cause. These trading activities spread across the region from Acatlán to Izúcar, Chietla, Chiautla and Huaquichula during the course of 1812, a clear sign of the failures in Royalist pacification strategy across the region, in spite of parallel failure by the main insurgent force. Llano had already heard from the Subdelegate of Atlixco at the end of January that illicit trading in cacao from shops in the town probably involved insurgents, particularly in rebel villages, through the medium of Indians who came into Atlixco. Insurgent bands occupied the extensive properties of Captain Ignacio Ardit, a prominent member of the Puebla Infantry Regiment of Urban Patriots. From the Rancho de Tlapayuca, they had taken cow hides to Izúcar for tanning: some 4,000 hides appear to have been appropriated in all. According to Armijo, rebel bands had been intimidating the hacienda labour force throughout the region: in consequence, rural workers handed over to them whatever they requested. By securing control over estates in such a manner, the insurgent bands deprived property owners of their customary markets in the cities of Puebla and Mexico.[51] Village agriculture suffered as a result of constant fighting. The villagers of Tlayacapa, for instance, had become incensed at repeated insurgent depredations. In consequence, they had requested Armijo to give them arms, so that they could defend their village against marauding bands. Their parish priest had travelled to Mexico City with the object of bringing back arms.[52] Llano had reported similar village hostility to rebel bands in the case of Tepejí in late November 1812.[53]

## The second insurgent threat to Puebla: June–November 1812

From Huajuapan Morelos swung westwards across the mountain barriers between Oaxaca and Puebla, and entered Tehuacán with 3,500 men on 10 August. Arroyo had first seized this town in May amid an orgy of plunder. From Tehuacán and Tlacotepec another rebel band had already struck at the crucially located town of Orizaba and had managed to break in on 28 June. Vital as a transit town on the route from Puebla to the port of Veracruz, Orizaba was the place where the Royal Tobacco Monopoly assembled its produce for carriage to the capital city. The rebels had planned to burn down the tobacco warehouse, but, instead, they had made off with what they could carry, in view of the imminent arrival of Royalist forces. These troops intercepted the rebels on the heights of Aculcingo. Llano inflicted heavy losses upon them, and recovered 4,098 tercios of tobacco, which he took back to Puebla. On 9 and 11 July the rebels failed again to take Orizaba, and fell, instead, upon Córdoba, which resisted them, despite the burning of all the houses on the outskirts of the town. Llano pressed for the adequate arming of these two towns, so that they could withstand such attacks in the future. Although the Córdoba–Orizaba region had remained largely quiescent during the first period of the insurrection, the appearance of the insurgents in the summer of 1812 radically altered the situation.[54]

Tehuacán became the principal insurgent base of operations after August, the first stronghold of duration to have been established on the cereal-producing plateau. Tehuacán commanded the routes from Oaxaca to Puebla, and downwards through Orizaba and Córdoba to Veracruz and communication with Europe. In July, the Veracruz city council warned Llano that all the villages and hamlets of its hinterland had risen in rebellion, and that food supply into the port had been cut off. Rebel bands on the land side blockaded Veracruz and tension was mounting in the city at the prospect of food shortages.[55] Morelos' options were essentially three-fold: a thrust towards Veracruz through the four tobacco towns of Córdoba, Orizaba, Zongólica and Coscomatepec; a direct advance north-westwards along the Puebla valleys to threaten the provincial capital for a second time; or to withdraw southwards into Oaxaca, which the insurgent presence in Acatlán, Izúcar, Tehuacán and Huajuapan had cut off from Puebla. This latter move, however, seemed likely to remove the rebel forces considerably further from the central valleys of Puebla and Mexico. In the first instance Morelos took the decision to strike into the Veracruz perimeter of Puebla, perhaps with the object of linking up, if he could, with rebel bands operating in the Jalapa region and above Veracruz itself. Llano had hoped to catch the insurgents at San Andrés Chalchicomula, but the town had fallen, and on 27 October Morelos began his movements in the direction of Orizaba. Two days later Morelos appeared in the valley within which the town was situated. It was widely believed in Puebla that Orizaba had fallen, but, upon the approach of Royalist forces, Morelos had withdrawn, and, in fact, had been repulsed by Luis de Aguila on the heights of Aculcingo. This time the Royalists recovered 300 cargas of tobacco taken from Orizaba and acquired 200 prisoners. By 3 November Morelos was back in Tehuacán. The offensive into Veracruz had failed in two of its principal objectives: (a) to link up with rebel forces in the Jalapa-Gulf zone, and (b) to cut off the Puebla valleys from Veracruz along their north-eastern perimeter.[56]

In consequence the main insurgent force could not take advantage of the risings that had taken place in the regions between Perote and Jalapa during the summer. Llano learned of this failure to his great surprise while in Perote with the intention of proceeding through Jalapa, in order to assist newly arrived Spanish troops to break through the insurgent cordon around Veracruz. For more than ninety days neither travellers nor news had reached Jalapa from Veracruz. Moreover, these 2,600 Spanish troops remained bottled up in the steamy heat of the port city, since rebel bands had reached its very limits. As yet no attempt to dislodge them had succeeded. With a force from Jalapa Llano tried to cut his way through to Veracruz, and on 29 July reached the Hacienda de Santa Fé, within a few miles of the port, after five days. On the following day he broke into the city. Llano began the return journey on 4 August, taking with his forces 500 mules laden with government paper that Juan Bautista Lobo, the wealthy Veracruz merchant, had contracted to deliver, and whatever remaining cargos could be safely conducted. With Llano went 800 Spanish soldiers of the Castile Regiment. One-quarter of the peninsular force had already died in the unhealthy climate of Veracruz from the sickness which had swept through the port. By 10 August this convoy arrived without incident in Jalapa. After securing the defence of the town, Llano returned to Puebla for a few days rest.[57]

The failure of Morelos in the Veracruz uplands, the arrival of Spanish regulars in Jalapa, and the safe return of Llano to Puebla prevented the realisation of Morelos' first two original options. As a result, faced with the alternative of simply remaining where he was in Tehuacán, or taking his third option, Morelos utlimately decided to withdraw into Oaxaca. Llano, for his part, remained anxious for a prompt strike at Tehuacán, in order to remove the potential threat to Puebla and Orizaba. For this reason he opened an offensive without delay, in conjunction with Armijo, against the two rebel strongholds of Izúcar and Tehuacán. In view of the combined assault, the first major Royalist offensive since the siege of Cuautla, the insurgents evacuated the two positions. With the loss of Izúcar and Tehuacán, the insurgents forfeited their two key positions on the plateau. This evacuation, moreover, involved not merely the retreat of scattered bands, but of the main force under Morelos in Tehuacán and under Matamoros in Izúcar. The Royalist capture of the latter of 14 November and of the former six days later represented, then, two major gains, and a significant development in the course of the war. No rebel force of consideration remained on the Puebla plateau, which from the end of 1811 had been the region of contention. In effect, the insurgents had lost the battle for Puebla. The Royalist vanguard penetrated southwards to Chiautla and the old rebel heartlands of 1811. Llano reported that not only had fugitive workers from the haciendas and villages begun to return, but also that many former insurgent sympathisers and activists were requesting government amnesty. On 23 November the Royalists entered Chietla to the applause of the few inhabitants who had remained in the town, since the departing insurgents had spread terror among the majority of the local people by saying that the Royalists intended to massacre them.[58]

Morelos' main force, in the meantime, had crossed into Oaxaca. Although forced out of Puebla, Morelos did not seem unduly perturbed at the loss of Izúcar and Tehuacán. On the contrary, he held high expectations of success for his movement in Oaxaca. Indeed, the situation around Jalapa, where Nicolás Bravo had attacked the town itself, gave rise to similar hopes.[59] Nothing, however, materialised in that direction. Padre Sánchez, whom Morelos had left in control of Tehuacán immediately before its fall, had upon the approach of the Royalists taken the remaining rebel forces into Veracruz, where they had taken up position in the insurgent village of Zongólica. Even so, Aguila, who had taken Tehuacán, proposed to flush them out and keep open the route to Jalapa. At this stage, rebel bands moving upwards from the *tierra caliente* of the Gulf zone had attacked the town of Jalapa on 20 November, only to be beaten off. Nevertheless, Jalapa with its 138-man garrison remained surrounded, though the town still held out.

Although the insurgents never took the three main upland towns of Veracruz, their position along the coast continued to improve. From Papantla, Misantla and Nautla they continued to threaten the port of Veracruz and the lifeline from Mexico City to Europe.[60]

The Royalist position, however, continued to improve on the plateau. Morelos' main army removed itself further and further from Mexico City. Llano pressed for concerted action to drive the insurgents from their remaining areas in the *tierra templada*, while at the same time 1,500 acclimatised troops would push downwards into the *tierra caliente* in co-ordination with the other Royalist Division Commanders of the South. Llano in this way hoped to prevent any further grouping of rebel forces. At the same time on the plateau the recovery of rebel-held Tepeaca enabled the Royalists to patrol the villages of the district and the access routes to the Veracruz towns, in conjunction with the garrison from Perote, operating from the north. Llano envisaged a far-ranging series of operations, with a further division attemptiong to drive the remaining rebel bands from the hills of the Zongólica district. Another detachment in Huamantla would patrol the territory towards Nopalu-can and San Juan de los Llanos. In essence, Llano's aim was to maintain freedom of communication between Córdoba and Veracruz, and between Perote and Puebla. When the time was right, a joint operation from Jalapa and Perote would open the route to Veracruz. To the north Llano stationed some 200 men at Texmelucan, in order to protect Huejotzingo and clear the route from Puebla to Mexico City. In the south his objective was Chilapa, as a prelude to the final pacification of the insurgent base zone of 1811. With these measures, Llano gradually undid what Morelos had put together. The only seriously vulnerable point still continued to be the province of Tlaxcala in view of Osorno's presence at Fortín de San Miguel, near Zacatlán.[61] Although Llano believed that he could complete these mopping-up operations in Puebla and the perimeter within two or three months, Armijo suspected that Morelos would return from Oaxaca to threaten Puebla for a third time.[62]

## Oaxaca – a revolutionary nucleus in the south?

Morelos' main force of 5,000 men grouped in Etla in the Valley of Oaxaca late in November 1812. The defence of the city of Oaxaca, conducted by 2,000 men under the command of Lieutenant-General Antonio González Saravia, collapsed against the insurgents' first assault on 25 November.[63] Oaxaca, then, became the first provincial capital city to fall into rebel hands since Hidalgo's departure from Guadalajara in January 1811. Even so, it did not represent a major strategic gain: its remote location in no way strengthened Morelos' chances on the central plateau. The most he could hope for was that Oaxaca would provide him with sufficient time to prepare for another offensive north-westwards. It is true that Oaxaca commanded the trade route to Guatemala, but this did not constitute a life-line of the Mexican economy. Alamán's statement that, 'the occupation of Oaxaca and its rich province by Morelos entirely changed the character of the insurrection', is misleading. In the sense that the occupation of a provincial capital city, the seat of a bishopric and an Intendancy might have provided a base for the formation of a provisional government, this view carried some conviction. In practice, however, Morelos chose not to do this, in spite of pressure from Bustamante, himself a native of Oaxaca. The city of Oaxaca, in consequence, served only as a brief haven.[64]

Morelos' forces advanced across the Intendancy in the direction of the Isthmus of Tehuantepec, in order to secure their occupation of the province. Late in December Miguel and Victor Bravo left for Juquila in the south-east, but turned westwards along the coast in the direction of Jamiltepec, which they entered on 10 February 1813. In January, Morelos himself left Oaxaca after scarcely six weeks' presence there. It could not, then, have been his intention to transform Oaxaca into his permanent base of operations, still less, the seat of the insurgent provisional government. On the contrary, Morelos complained to Rayón that, 'this province resists government'.[65]

Although Matamoros had arrived in Oaxaca with a further 3,000 men and had employed part of that force in April to push back the Guatemalan Royalists from the Isthmus, Morelos attached greater priority to an objective quite distinct from the concentration of rebel manpower there. His aim was to capture the fortress of Acapulco. This strong position he had failed to take in November 1810. Morelos, then, preferred to invest the citadel of Acapulco than to push back in the direction of Tehuacán or Orizaba with a view to threatening Puebla or Veracruz once more. By January 1813 it is difficult to see what other alternative course of action Morelos could have chosen. An offensive north-westwards would have brought him into frontal conflict with the Puebla Royalist forces engaged in reducing insurgent positions in the southern zone of that Intendancy. Evidently a pitched battle, the outcome of which might have decided the war there and then, was still to be avoided. By choosing to avoid it and move ultimately south-westwards to the Pacific coast, Morelos, in the first place, exposed Oaxaca itself to the possibility of a Royalist recovery, and, in the second

place, took his forces back to the region from which they had first
emerged at the end of 1810. In every sense the campaign to reduce the
fortress of San Diego was a retrograde step. It is, of course, difficult to
ascertain whether Morelos, in face of a Royalist advance into Oaxaca,
could have sustained his position in the city. Nevertheless, a major
factor standing in his favour continued to be the support given to him in
the villages of the Mixteca Alta and Baja. Morelos passed through many
of these villages on his way from the Valley of Oaxaca across the sierra to
Nochistlán, Yanhuitlán and Teposcolula. These larger villages and the
smaller settlements between the highlands and the coast had long been
torn by social conflict. This region had suffered greatly from the
*repartimientos* enforced by their local administrators on behalf of merchant backers in the city of Oaxaca, in Puebla, Veracruz or Mexico. The
scarlet cochineal dye continued to be the main attraction for outsiders
and the principal cause of the pressures placed upon the villagers.[66]
Morelos sought to hold on to this country by leaving Matamoros in the
region. Finally, by way of Ometepec, Morelos appeared on the heights
of El Veladero, above Acapulco, early in April.[67] The siege of the citadel
occupied more than four months of Morelos' campaign. The assault on 6
April failed: the siege opened on 12 April: the fort did not capitulate
until 20 August. Insurgent propaganda exploited the victory. Even so,
the capture of the fortress proved to be of no strategic value to the rebel
cause, even though Lemoine Villicaña has described it as a 'climactic
moment . . . when the insurgents were nearer than ever to achieving a
definitive victory'.[68] The insurgents already possessed several ports on
the Pacific coast – through which no assistance could be expected from
any foreign source – and with the fall of the citadel of Acapulco they
merely gained another. Morelos reduced the fortress to rubble and
burned the town itself to the ground 'as a warning to the *gachupines*'. If
the victory at San Diego gained anything at all, it opened the possibility
of extending operations further westwards into the *tierra caliente* of
Michoacán, where Padre Torres' band had scored successes against
Iturbide's forces and had appeared in the vicinity of the highland town
of Pátzcuaro. Operations in this zone, however, would bring Morelos
back into the area from which he had first gained support in October
1810, as if the battle for Puebla had never occurred. In effect, the
abandonment of Puebla and Veracruz as feasible objectives, the evacuation and loss of Oaxaca, and the option for the *tierra caliente* of Mexico
and Michoacán presaged the opening of a further phase in Morelos'
peregrination. This phase represented not a triumphant new offensive,
but the symptoms of defeat. It pointed to the application against

Valladolid during the course of 1814 of the strategy that in 1811–13 had already failed before Puebla.[69] In March 1814 Brigadier Melchor Álvarez recovered Oaxaca for the Royalists. In Puebla Osorno, the rebel *caudillo* in the Zacatlán locality, failed to deflect the Royalist advance by an attempt to cut off the provincial capital.[70] By the time the official leadership of the insurgent cause had begun the long delayed attempt to establish a provisional government not in Oaxaca but in Chilpancingo, in Bravo country, time had already run out for Morelos and for the insurgents in New Spain.[71]

As a result of the insurgents' loss of the battle for Puebla, two political entities, two states, never co-existed in New Spain during the period of the 'War of Independence'. The official leadership of the insurgent movement never constituted an effective political challenge to the viceregal state. No revolutionary state challenged the viceregal government within the territory of New Spain. The military victory in 1812 and 1813 passed not to Morelos, but to his Royalist opponents. Not an encirclement strategy, but its opposite, the marginalisation of the insurgency, triumphed. By the end of 1812 the insurgents had lost their chance of controlling the Puebla valleys. The Royalists not only held their ground, but improved their position. Although the Puebla treasury continued to be short of funds throughout the decisive year, 1812, Llano managed to raise 16,000 pesos from city merchants as a loan to be repaid from first receipts.[72] By the time Brigadier Conde de Castro Terreño received appointment from Viceroy Calleja as General-in-Chief of the Puebla *División del Sur* on 9 March 1813, Royalist forces totalled 7,498 men.[73] During the course of 1814, Royalist garrisons held all the centres of cereal-production from Chalco to Atlixco and the border regions between the Valley of Mexico and Cuautla.[74] With the disintegration of any encirclement strategy, Royalist commanders, operating outwards from the provincial capitals, had the opportunity to advance in ever-widening circles through the countryside. In this way they would, in due course, take the counter-insurgency into the heartlands of the insurrection. Calleja specifically recommended such a strategy.[75]

## Counter-insurgency in Puebla

The strain of counter-insurgency took a serious toll on the leading citizens of Puebla. The municipality regularly conflicted with the Governor-Intendant over the question of raising funds. Early in August 1813, Dávila, after his return, denounced what he described as 'this culpable indifference on the part of many citizens to the prospect of Spanish defeat'. Since the government treasury in the province had already run out of money, Dávila believed that only by squeezing private citizens could the counter-insurgency be pressed forward. Reluctance on the part of merchants, farmers and other wealthy citizens to contribute to a patriotic loan imposed by the viceroy, led the governor to threaten to exact what sums he needed by executive action, a recourse which further infuriated the municipality. Similarly, Castro Terreño, anxious to see the fortification of the Cerro de Guadalupe above the city, persuaded the city council in October to draw up a list of citizens who might be able to pay for it.[76] Shortly after the Commander of the Army of the South, Ramón Díaz de Ortega, became Governor-Intendant of Puebla in January 1814, he imposed taxes on imported overseas products, barrels of sugar-cane brandy, and sales in bakeries and general stores. Conflict with the municipality encouraged Calleja to relieve Ortega on health grounds early in September.[77]

The conflicts over finances, bitter as they became, should not, however, obscure our appreciation of the developing awareness among Royalist commanders of the implications of counter-insurgency strategy. In May 1815, Saavedra, the commander of the militia Provincial Battalion of Ferdinand VII, showed a clear conception of the type of tactics needed to re-establish government control of the countryside. He proposed a force of 1,200 men drawn exclusively from the 'wealthiest classes', who by taking charge of the defence of the city in the rear of troops operating in the field, would be defending their own interests and could cover their own costs. By this means, two companies of *divisiones volantes*, or 'flying columns', would then be free to scour the countryside with no fixed headquarters at any point. In such a way the districts of Amozoc, Totomehuacán, Cholula, Huejotzingo and San Martín, the vital perimeter of the city, could be covered in both directions. Saavedra estimated the total cost at 78,000 pesos, an investment well worth the end result, which he argued would be the recovery of production on the private estates.[78]

Military commanders frequently offered amnesty to rebels willing to lay down their arms and return home. In many cases, however, amnesty policies proved to be counter-productive. A number of rebel chieftains received government pardon only to rejoin other bands or revive their own, once the immediate danger of military presence had receded. Osorno's continued activity provided a natural pole of attraction. In the troubled perimeter zone to the east of the Valley of Mexico and across the north-east flank of Puebla, lesser rebel bands continued to be active

well into 1816. Basilio Ramírez, who led a small band in 1813, which
laid waste the haciendas and *ranchos* of the Pachuca region, had already
been twice amnestied. He was caught and executed by Royalist defence
forces from Zumpango.[79] The Llanos de Apan, which, as we have seen,
had been a scene of intense insurgent activity from 1810, were only
reported to be at peace in the late summer of 1816. The recession in the
Pachuca–Real del Monte mining zone and the impact of several years'
dislocation of the hacienda and village economies had left many of the
local people without a livelihood. Accordingly, a number of these
unemployed found a new occupation by assisting Royalist troops in
their pursuit of the remnants of the rebel bands. Military commanders
in these strategically located areas formed amnestied insurgents into
fifty-man companies. Their leaders became officers in government
service and were given the name, '*guardacampos*' or Field-Guards. Since
only the *pulque* trade yielded any revenue at that time, the cost of
government forces there had to be supplemented by an allocation of
30,000 pesos from the treasuries of Mexico City and Pachuca. The
position was eased somewhat by the fact that many insurgents had
presented themselves for amnesty along with their arms and horses, so
that they could be transformed almost automatically into Royalist
auxiliary forces. Local Royalist detachments operated in conjunction
with those in Puebla. Several key positions had by late October 1816
already been garrisoned by troops from a division of the Army of the
South – Pachuca itself, Tulancingo, parts of the Llanos, the Tlaxcala
towns of Huamantla and Nopalucan, and San Juan de los Llanos in
Puebla.[80]

The intention behind the government's amnesty policy was to win
back population for the official power. In general, terms were lenient.
Repentant insurgents would usually be permitted to return to their
original places of residence, so that they could once more resume their
previous occupations, where possible, in reorganised areas under the
surveillance of government forces.[81] The amnesty lists compiled by
army commanders tell us a great deal about the age and social groups
from which insurgency recruited. A striking phenomenon was the short
duration of much individual participation. Among the thirty-two rebels
amnestied in the Puebla district of Tochimilco in April 1816 was a
26-year-old married man from Atlixco, who had spent only six months
with the insurgents. A 30-year-old bachelor from Tochimilco had
fought with them for a year. Several other men were also natives of the
district. A group of them were young villagers, described as '*indios*', few
of them listed as married, who had spent between six months and two

years with the rebel bands. Many participants were either in their twenties or late teens: such was the case with rebels from Atlixco and Tlayacapam. A number were hacienda resident workers from the Hacienda de la Sabana and the Hacienda de Xonaca in Atlixco. An 'indio' from the village of Amecac, a married man of 21 years, was granted leave to return to his village of origin. One of the oldest seems to have been a 36-year-old married man, who originated from the Rancho de Ahuehuello in the district of Izúcar. He had, however, spent only three months with the insurgents: he chose to return to his place of origin.[82] It is quite conceivable that the restless, but not overly committed, youth we have seen above may well have provided, in more normal times, recruitment into bandit groups, rather than insurgent bands. Unfortunately, these men appear only fleetingly in the documentation, which is, of course, not primarily interested in them. We do not know, for instance, whether they subsequently participated in counter-insurgency operations, whether they remained pacifically on the land after their amnesty, or whether at a later date such men as these actually did reappear in bandit groups. We know nothing, needless to say, about what their wives thought or did during this period.

Artisan participation in insurgent bands appears clearly from the Tlaxcala amnesty lists. In Tlaxcala, the former occupations of amnestied rebels, listed in April 1816, included three muleteers, two weavers – one from the city itself and the other from Santa Ana Chiautempan – a shopkeeper from Chiautempan, a tobacco-guard, a soldier, a deserter from the mobile force of *volantes*, a religious, and a bell-founder.[83] The Puebla districts – Texmelucan, Huejotzingo, Atlixco and Cholula – showed in 1816 a broad range of artisan groups amnestied for participation in the insurgency. They included not only farmers ('*labradores*'), but weavers, tailors, blacksmiths, carpenters, barbers, sail-makers, bakers, shoemakers, button-makers, and tradesmen, as well as servants, saddle-makers, muleteers, and mineworkers. These artisans had probably worked not in Puebla itself, but in the country towns. Their motives for insurgency may have derived from the economic circumstances of recession or from social grievances such as the penetration of mercantile capital into their localities from the cities.[84]

Along the southern perimeter of Puebla, details of those amnestied in the Cuautla zone in March 1817 indicated that the rebel bands chiefly consisted of local villagers and hacienda workers.[85] Armijo reported from the southern Pacific zone in June 1818, that 4,371 individuals had presented themselves for amnesty and that a further 1,600 families were in the process of doing so. What these numbers actually signify is difficult to say. Even if they were grossly inflated, they would still give some indication of the extent to which insurgency had petered out in a formerly active region, one which for a time had been Morelos' base area of operations. According to Armijo, the local population was eager to change sides and assist the army to mop up the rebel bands, because of the depredations it had suffered at their hands throughout the insurgency. Such an argument suggests the villagers had succeeded in persuading Armijo, initially not known for his clemency, that they had been innocent all along. Viceroy Apodaca instructed him to reorganise the villages in the region, fourteen of which had already been restored to Royalist allegiance in the Acapulco district, and to form defence companies in them.[86]

Llano remained sceptical of the immediate results of the amnesty policy and dubious of the motives of both civil and military administrators. In his judgement, the villages which were full of amnestied rebels were precisely those which abounded with crime and unruliness. Neither magistrates nor military commanders showed any interest in combating such disorders, since they derived no personal profit by doing so.[87] Llano suspected that amnestied rebels were continually involved in schemes to launch a fresh insurrection. A priest from Puebla claimed to have heard as much through the confessional. Rumours of conspiracies among amnestied insurgents drifted in from as far afield as Tepejí de la Seda and even from Misantla in Veracruz. The passage of silver convoys from Mexico City to Jalapa and Veracruz through still exposed outlying districts concentrated the mind. Llano urged that complacency should not prevent effective military escort.[88]

Morelos' inability to take the city of Puebla was crucial to the outcome of his strategy. The tactical explanation lay in his failure to control Atlixco, the decisive position to the south of the city, at a time when the defences of the provincial capital had not been completed. Royalist commanders themselves were sceptical of their own ability to retain their hold on New Spain's second city. Morelos' hesitation before Atlixco may perhaps be explained by receipt of news of Calleja's advance with the main body of the Royalist army. Insurgent forces under Morelos had not yet encountered a large regular force, still less an army fresh from its successes on the north-central plateau and before Zitácuaro. It was probably tactical considerations that encouraged Morelos not to press his luck in the vicinity of Puebla, at least until the Royalist force had been deflected. If Calleja's army had caught the insurgent forces beyond the northern limits of their base of support in the *tierra caliente* and its mountainous hinterland, they would have been cut off from their sources of supply and reinforcement. In this sense, logistics entered into insurgent calculations. Evidently Morelos did not believe that a combination of local rebel bands around the perimeter of Puebla was sufficiently strong to take the city or reliable enough to hold it. The Royalist advance, moreover, faced him with the possibility of having to defend the city himself, if it had actually fallen to him, before Calleja arrived in the vicinity. It is feasible to argue that such calculations influenced Morelos' decision to fall back on Izúcar and Cuautla, as his two advance bases. A further factor may also have been Morelos' shortage of men at crucial moments in his campaigns. At Cuautla, this lack of manpower precluded effective occupation of outlying hacienda buildings as defensive positions against a Royalist assault. Shortage of firepower similarly impeded swift action on the plateau. When the force of 2,000 men entered Chilapa in September 1811, there were only 530 rifles between them, chiefly those captured from Royalist bands or brought over from deserters. Morelos at that time had eighteen cannons with him. When the insurgents entered Izúcar, they brought six or seven with them. In January 1812, the insurgents were reported to be melting church bells in Apizaco, donated by eighteen Tlaxcalan villages, in order to forge artillery weapons. It is not clear, however, whether insurgent artillery was in any way effective or not: the available documentation rarely, if ever, suggests so. The strength of the insurgents lay more in the mobility that could be expected from irregular forces. The horses that made this possible were frequently plundered from the haciendas that lay in the insurgents' path. Combined with mobility was the insurgent capacity for holding for long periods strategically located natural positions, usually in remote locations or in the vicinity of major transit routes. The itinerant nature of the rebel bands, even of Morelos' forces, should, however, be stressed. The geographical span of Morelos' five campaigns between 1810 and 1814 was enormous, encompassing a range of differing regions from Michoacán to Veracruz and Oaxaca. It is doubtful whether priority could be given for a consistent period to any one of them. With the disparate nature of insurgent support across these regions in mind, we can appreciate the difficulty of effective co-ordination between the operating bands. Insurgents fed themselves, while on campaign, by robbing grains and cattle from the haciendas. In this way they not only reduced estate owners' capital, but also deprived resident workers, who may not themselves have been tempted by the prospect of insurgency or coerced into it, of their prospects of work and food. Such depredations opened the possibilities of a popular based counter-insurgency. Insurgent bands traded in estate products, such as the sugar, spirits and honey of Izúcar, collected district taxes, as if they themselves were the official power, and exacted transit dues and protection money from merchants. By such methods they financed their campaigns. Some rebel bands grew rich from these activities.

# 7

## Local conflict and provincial chieftains

The Villagrán, the Osorno, the Galeana, the Bravo – these clans we have already encountered. They were among the many that operated during the insurgency, several, if not most of them, thrown into prominence by the war itself. Perhaps the two most celebrated in their particular regions at the time were Albino García and Gordiano Guzmán. Certainly not far behind would be Pedro Moreno, 'El Amo' Torres, Manuel Muñiz, Encarnación Rosas, P. Luciano Navarrete, Miguel Borja, or P. Miguel Torres. There were many more. They signified the early and irreversible fragmentation of command within the insurgent camp. A comparable decentralisation took place within government-held territory. The division of the viceroyalty into warring zones broke apart the hierarchy of command that had characterised colonial rule, and pushed the hitherto predominant civilian administrator into the background.[1] Despite Viceroy Calleja's efforts to retain central control, military commanders in the regions took virtually autonomous actions. This *de facto* regionalisation of authority left unprotected the exposed border zones, generally of difficult terrain, between the provinces. Rebel chieftains continued to thrive for long periods in such areas. Ineffective government control on the perimeters of one province left neighbouring provinces exposed to rekindled insurgent action. As a result, military commanders frequently did not know which direction to face. Their problem, as they saw it, was continually one of insufficient manpower.[2]

Local chieftains and provincial commanders, whether Royalist or insurgent, or oscillating between sides, represented, at the most blatant, the rule of force. At their most acceptable, they stood at the head of descending lines of clientage and kinship. Royalist amnesty policy facilitated the transfer of insurgent bands into the government fighting forces, and thereby enabled the survival of these networks of

Map 4  The centre-north-west (Michoacán and Guanajuato), 1813–16

personal allegiance. In such a way formerly rebel bands continued to pursue, in a different guise, similar objectives, frequently illegal, to those they had pursued while officially outside the law. If Royalism failed to satisfy their aspirations, defection back to the rebel cause always existed as a possibility. This legacy of naked power continued after Independence, when it subsisted alongside civilian efforts to restore constitutional legality. The two forces of private power and constitutionality competed together in nineteenth-century Mexico in a complex dialectical relationship.

## Albino García – guerrilla chieftain in Guanajuato

Nothing appears to be known, as yet, concerning the family of Albino García Ramos, described as a pure Indian, born sometime between 1775 and 1780. He came from Cerro Blanco in the district of Salamanca. A cowhand, who rose to become overseer of the hacienda work force on estates near Valle de Santiago, García acquired riding skills and earned a local reputation as an expert *charro*. After he broke his left arm in a fierce burst of horse-breaking, he gained the popular nickname, *'el manco García'*. On the sidelines, Albino devoted his attention to the profitable contraband trade, usually in tobacco and gunpowder, both royal monopolies. This activity gave him over the years an intimate knowledge of the Bajío and its surrounding areas. Travel throughout the region in his official capacity as work-foreman in charge of selling estate products brought him into contact with his fellow overseers and estate managers, a personal network of associations upon which he would draw in the years of the insurgency. With a few cowhands, Albino García joined Hidalgo's rebel forces in Salamanca less than ten days after the *Grito de Dolores*. Along with Albino went his cousin, Pedro García, known as *'Garcilita'*, and Andrés Delgado, known as *'El Giro'*, an Indian of repulsive aspect, who had earned his nickname through his habit of dressing in a manner regarded as superior to his social station. He came from the Salamanca barrio of Nativitas, and was a skilled horseman and roper. He gained particular notoriety especially after 1817.[3]

By the summer of 1811, insurgent bands across Guanajuato had begun to regroup following the defeat of the official leadership. The district of Pénjamo became a lasting centre of rebel activity. Navarrete's band regrouped there with the co-operation of *'Garcilita'*. Toribio Huidobro made Pénjamo his operational base, and by mid-June, Torres, Muñoz and Albino García had made their way there.[4] García, with a force of up to 1,000 men, sacked the district capital in August. His forces were mostly well-armed cavalry. He had by then begun to perfect his characteristic style of warfare, the surprise attack on Royalist-held villages and on convoys by his cowboy cavalry, often *mestizos*. Alamán, at that time a Royalist supporter, described the composition of Albino's forces as 'folk from the villages and hamlets along the trade routes'. Albino's sack of Lagos on 31 August 1811 made him for the first time appear to be a particularly dangerous threat. Former contrabandist though he was, Albino García particularly venerated the Virgin of Guadalupe, a devotion which apparently encouraged him to spare the houses of clergymen during the sack of Lagos. This generosity did not extend to Royal administrators and Royalist sympathisers. In the assault on Dolores, less than two weeks after the Lagos attack, Albino's force killed the subdelegate and four government supporters.[5]

García's band could count on considerable clandestine support in the villages of the Pénjamo, Piedragorda, Irapuato and León districts. In León the number of identified insurgents was large in these early days of the insurrection: some fifty-seven were listed in 1811 from the Hacienda de Cuerámaro and the Rancho de Santa Ana, while those of Jalpa were described as too 'innumerable' to be listed at all. Royalist forces managed to hold on to Irapuato, while rebel bands operated in the countryside. García took control of the Hacienda de Zurumuato in August 1811 in the middle of the rainy season. There is, it appears, no evidence that physical occupation of such estates involved land distribution whether among supporters or among any other candidates. Further bands operated on Pantoja and Cuerámaro, and posed a threat to both Silao and Celaya. At the same time, the Royalists were trying to form extemporary defence forces on the estates they controlled and elsewhere in the localities in government hands. Their aim was to patrol the highways and apprehend suspects.[6]

Albino operated on his own account, and, like Iriarte before him, recognised no higher authority than himself. He certainly had no respect for Rayón and the Junta of Zitácuaro, which at that stage claimed exclusive leadership of the insurrection. He is supposed to have commented that only the mountains were above him. When Calleja opened his campaign to reduce Zitácuaro, García and the other rebel bands in the centre-north renewed their threat to the principal cities. Although García with 1,000 men sacked Aguascalientes on September 1811, local Royalist forces drove the insurgents out eight days later. Guanajuato, however, remained similarly exposed. The band led by Tomás Baltierra, and consisting of up to 500 men, broke into the city on 18 November, only to leave shortly afterwards. Baltierra was generally known as 'Salmerón' for his huge size, which reminded local people of a veritable giant of the same name who had created a sensation in the city in 1792. Albino García entered Guanajuato himself on 23–4 November only to be promptly forced out by relief troops under Captains Luis Quintanar and Antonio Linares sent from Guadalajára by Cruz. As in other instances, the city and mining populace welcomed the insurgent bands. García went into Guanajuato with possibly 5,000 men and occupied virtually its entire extent, in spite of resistance from the defence forces commanded by the Conde de Pérez Gálvez. Albino's men also sacked Royalist-held Dolores, San Miguel and San Felipe. Royalist defence forces kept rebel bands out of León and Silao. Further attacks came on Guanajuato on 6 January 1812, on Irapuato on 11–12 January and 1 and 11 May, and on Celaya on 5 May.[7]

The principal Royalist commanders in the area, Diego García Conde and Pedro Celestino Negrete, opened an ultimately successful campaign in mid-May 1812 to finish off Albino García and reduce his stronghold in Valle de Santiago. At that time, García had gathered together several bands into a total force of some 6,000 men.

García Conde selected Iturbide as the rising young officer most suitable for the task of eliminating Albino. Iturbide broke into the town on 4 June, taking García's men by surprise, killing 200 of them in the fighting and executing a further 150 insurgent prisoners in the central square. García himself was captured. Although Iturbide was promoted to the rank of Lieutenant-Colonel two days later in recognition of this achievement, his career continued to be plagued thereafter by a sinister reputation. The Royalist forces conducted Albino García and his brother Francisco to Celaya.[8] Albino wrote to his father from confinement in the Carmelite convent there that both of them were well looked after and even well thought of by the Royalist soldiery. The García brothers were brought before a firing squad in Celaya on 8 June 1812. The death of García removed a major danger, but it did not stop insurgent attacks on exposed targets.[9]

Rebel bands, for instance, attacked the Valenciana mine in July 1812, when the bulk of the defence force was operating elsewhere. The rebels inflicted heavy damage, but they did not bring the mine to a standstill. Pérez Gálvez, defence force commander, complained of government failure to send sufficient troops into the area to dislodge rebel formations in the sierra to the north of the mining district. Continued rebel threats had combined with recession to throw much of the mining population of Valenciana out of work. Instead, they filled the streets of Guanajuato, and presented a repeated danger to the Royalist authorities, which with justification feared their further collaboration with insurgent bands.[10] Dr Cos attacked the city on 27 November, after raising forces in Dolores and operating in company with Ramón Rayón. Iturbide's appearance, however, pushed them back beyond Dolores itself. Another rebel band reached the limits of Guanajuato on 17 February 1813. Not until January 1814 did the authorities manage to fortify the city to some effect, a testament not only to their shortage of resources, but also to the repeated threat posed by the rebel bands. Fortification enabled the Royalists to beat back yet another attack on 2 April 1815, and a further assault, led by the rebel chieftains, Miguel Borja and Santos Aguirre, on 25 August.[11] Apart from the main towns themselves, several of which over a four or five year period still remained vulnerable, a continued state of lawlessness persisted throughout the countryside. Much of this activity could scarcely be described as part of a conscious and ideologically motivated Mexican Independence movement. Given the pre-revolutionary ante-cedents as well, rebel band activity was in many respects thinly disguised criminality. Taken together, it presented a powerful chal-lenge to the civilians who sought through the medium of the Consti-tution of 1812 to reassert the supremacy they had enjoyed under colonial absolutism.

## The later Guanajuato chieftains and their men

Alamán dated the spread of the fame of the 'Pachones' from November 1812. They took their name from the Rancho de la Pachona in the Pinos district of Zacatecas. The most notable among them were Matías and Encarnación Ortiz.[12] Matías Ortiz, known as 'El Pachón', operated across northern Guanajuato and into Aguascalientes. Ortiz formed part of the group of Bajío rebel bands, a total force of more than 1,500 men, which attacked the Hacienda de Ciénega de Mata on 8 February 1814. Along with Ortiz were Rafael Rayón, Fernando Rosas, Ignacio Franco and other chieftains. The Royalists, however, had organised defence forces on the estate. This Patriot Company killed forty of the assailants and chased them off, after they had robbed considerably.[13] Even so the situation in Guanajuato continued to be serious. 'El Pachón' swept into San Miguel on 17 April in company with Rafael Rayón and some 800 men. A rebel band known as the 'Nogaleños', which had threatened the weak Royalist positions in Michoacán, moved from Los Reyes across the undefended border zone into Guanajuato. The districts of Pénjamo, Piedragorda and Valle de Santiago once more remained rebel strong-holds, under the control of 'El Pachón', in company with Padre Torres, who had already tried to seize Salamanca with an estimated force of 2,480 men. 'El Pachón's' band of some 400 men attacked León on 13 December 1814. Rafael Rayón, Encarnación Rosas and the other Ortiz were installed in northern Guanajuato with a force of 1,500 men and a potential for recruitment of a further 1,200 from the *rancherías* incapable of absorbing the available labour supply. In western and southern Guanajuato, bands led by P. Uribe, Lucas Flores, Rosales, and

Hermosillo contained an estimated force of 1,300 men, while in Michoacán, Navarrete, Manuel Villalongín, Joaquín Arias, and Nájar, continued to operate with villagers' co-operation. Bands in Guanajuato and Michoacán often consisted of the *ranchero* population, tenants or sharecroppers. In the Bajío especially, they were usually not 'Indian' in the colonial classification, and were not primarily engaged in the defence of eroded village lands since, as Brading has shown, most Guanajuato villages had already lost their lands by the end of the eighteenth century.

The tenuous Royalist hold in Michoacán, well into 1814 contributed to the weakening of the government position in Guanajuato, especially since the vital border zones between the two Intendancies and New Galicia remained predominantly in rebel hands. The Royalists, increasingly aware of the implications of these anomalies, found themselves faced with the problem of committing adequate resources to the conquest of either one or the other province, rather than half commit themselves to both. The latter course, preferred as a result of personal rivalries among military commanders and chosen due to a shortage of manpower and equipment, ensured that the Royalists would be victorious in neither and that the insurgency of the rebel bands would continue in both. Though Iturbide, appointed to the military command of Guanajuato on 27 April 1813, Negrete and Colonel José Antonio Andrade conferred at La Piedad on 10–11 June 1814 with those problems in mind, little effective action resulted. Calleja complained in December 1815 that a similar conference between Iturbide and Cruz at the Hacienda de Arandas on 22 July, had produced few positive results. From the border zones and unpacified districts, rebel bands remained in a powerful position to frustrate government counter-insurgency strategy.[14]

Royalist inability to recover full control of cereal-producing estates in the southern and western Bajío deprived government representatives in the province of Guanajuato of much needed revenues and food supplies. This, in turn, delayed the fortification of the main towns and left them vulnerable. There is considerable evidence to suggest that, even by 1815–16, Royalist commanders in the region had still not discovered how to defeat the rebel bands. Iturbide's increasingly high-handed actions alienated not only villagers, whose sympathies the government needed to win back, but also the creole proprietors who resented his frequently arbitrary exactions.[15] Although Calleja rebuked Iturbide for his application of civil revenue to military purpose, the appropriations did not cease. On 5 October 1815, for instance, Iturbide imposed a

## Fortified positions in Guanajuato in 1815

| | Defence Forces | | |
| --- | --- | --- | --- |
| | Infantry | Cavalry | Artillery |
| Capital + mining districts | 881 | 244 | 98 |
| CELAYA + two haciendas | 352 | 44 | 27 |
| IRAPUATO | 190 | 85 | 63 |
| SILAO + two haciendas | 187 | 116 | 82 |
| SAN MIGUEL EL GRANDE | 182 | 32 | 25 |
| SALAMANCA | 165 | 76 | 31 |
| LEÓN | 122 | 75 | 24 |
| APASEO | 27 | 29 | 5 |
| CHAMACUERO | 21 | 44 | 5 |
| SAN JUAN DE LA VEGA | | 48 | 5 |

*Note*: Defence forces frequently consisted not only of local rural smallholders or tenants and agricultural workers, usually organised by proprietors, but also groups of amnestied insurgents, which only a few weeks previously had been raiding the same properties and localities.

*Source*: AGN OG 430, f. 482, Iturbide, Irapuato 19 April 1815

forced loan on the province of Guanajuato, in order to raise the sum of 60,000 pesos for the upkeep of his troops. He had received no prior government authorisation. For several years afterwards, persons subjected to payment, such as the Condes de la Valenciana and Pérez Gálvez, the Condesa de Casa Rul, and the Marqués de San Juan de Rayas, among the most influential mine and estate owners of the region, appealed to the authorities in Mexico City to order their reimbursement. Calleja repudiated the forced loan and on 10 June 1816 ordered collection to cease. The case for repayment, however, dragged on into 1820.[16] Merchants in Valladolid similarly complained of Iturbide's attempts to raise funds for his troops at their expense, and drew attention to the depressed condition of urban trade.[17]

A series of major towns in the province of Guanajuato had been fortified by mid-April 1815, as the accompanying table illustrates. Even so, the rebel chieftains in the countryside remained undefeated. *El Pachón* penetrated into Valenciana on 10 August 1817, only to be pushed out.[18] In Michoacán, however, the Royalist position was considerably worse. Rival bands still held sway throughout the whole of the *tierra caliente*, while in the central highland zone rebel control continued from Zacapu and Chilchota southwards. Francisco Chivilini controlled Ario, Manuel Suárez operated from Urecho and Mariano Figueroa from Uruapan. The most serious threat, nevertheless, was posed by Padre Miguel Torres, who often acted in consort with *El Giro* and Miguel Borja. The official leadership of the insurgent cause in Michoacán, however, was disputed between Rayón and the priest, Dr José Sixto Verduzco, both natives of the province. Neither succeeded in establishing effective control over virtually autonomous chieftains. Verduzco had been parish priest of Tuzantla in the south-east. Negrete's campaigns from mid-June 1812 had forced him from key positions such as Uruapan, Apatzingán and Huetamo. However, when Negrete returned to Zamora, drawn back by the continuing rebel pressures in the Jiquílpan – Lake Chapala zone, the insurgents recovered much of what they had initially lost. One Royalist thrust did not signify long-term control. Without waiting for Rayón, who claimed to be supreme commander, Verduzco brought together an array of rebel chieftains, such as Muñiz, P. Carvajal, Victor Rosales, and P. Navarrete from Pátzcuaro, in a vain effort to seize the city of Valladolid with a force of some 6,000 men in January 1813. This defeat, accompanied by heavy losses, worsened relations between Verduzco and Rayón, who sought to bring the former to account for alleged disobedience. A minor civil war followed among the official leaders in Michoacán.[19] Although five insurgent attacks were repulsed between May 1811 and December 1813, the city of Valladolid still remained exposed. Twice in 1814, the municipal syndic, alarmed that 'this province has been a theatre of insurrection right from the first instant', feared the imminent collapse of urban defences through shortage of funds. He identified the source of the problem to be the inability of government troops to push outwards from the provincial capital and establish control step by step over the countryside by a process of fortification of towns and villages.[20] Negrete and other Royalist commanders repeatedly complained of insurgent appropriation of revenues and their receipt of supplies from villages. Both phenomena frustrated the methods and goals of 'pacification'.[21] In Pátzcuaro, for instance, the insurgents collected the tobacco revenue during their seven-year control until 1817. Similarly, they seized livestock and foodstuffs from private estates, such as the Hacienda de Coapa, in Tiripitío, formerly the property of a city shop-keeper, Manuel de Valdovinos.[22]

Torres operated both in Michoacán and Guanajuato. In the latter province, swift cavalry thrusts by Bustamante and Márquez Donallo across the countryside and into the hills had not eliminated rebel bands by 1817–18. Well into these later years of the decade, the districts of

Valle de Santiago and Pénjamo had still not been brought effectively under government control. Even so, Bustamante had begun the process of driving rebel bands from the principal haciendas – Zurumuato, Huanímaro, Pantoja and La Calle.[23] In this later period, Torres rose to prominence. Originating from the Michoacán town of Cocupao, he had been parish administrator in Cuitzeo at the time of the Hidalgo revolt. Alamán described him as the scourge of the southern districts. Like Pedro Moreno from the sierra above Lagos, Torres had operated in conjunction with the ill-fated expedition of the Spanish Liberal adventurer, Javier Mina, in Guanajuato in 1817. Torres sponsored the formation of the rebel Junta of Jaujilla in Michoacán, though few other chieftains, among them *El Indio* Candelario, recognised it, still less, outside the province. Like Albino García before him, Torres himself recognised no other authority but himself, least of all that of the Jaujilla Junta. When the official leadership attempted to reconstitute a provisional government in Huetamo, its members bestowed upon *El Giro* the task of dealing with Torres, whom he forced into hiding. Divisions such as these among rival chieftains and authorities enabled local Royalist commanders to move to the offensive against the guerrilla bands. Linares sent Bustamante against *El Giro*, who was finally killed near Chamácuero on 3 July 1819. Márquez Donallo forced Torres into the sierra. The former cleric was killed in a dispute among rebels over a horse won in gambling. Torres' death obliged Borja to withdraw into the Sierra de Jalpa, part of the Sierra Gorda. Brigadier Melchor Álvarez, who had recovered Oaxaca for the Royalists in March 1814, opened a campaign for the reduction of the remaining redouts in these mountains in June 1819. He adopted counter-insurgency techniques already applied elsewhere, with varying degrees of success by Llano, Iturbide, Linares and Bustamante. These involved the clearance of exposed or disputed areas by the burning of scattered settlements, the destruction of sowings, and the resettlement of population in places under government surveillance. Royalist commanders frequently combined such policies with offers of amnesty, which enabled former rebels to return to their estate or village of origin, and thereby contribute to the recovery of food production. Amnesties often, though, enabled former rebels to change sides and continue as fighting men. Late in the 1810s, the Pachones, among several other notable instances, accepted royal amnesty. It was precisely amnestied insurgents that hunted down Borja and enabled his execution late in December 1819. Alamán pointed to Linares' role in organising the companies of amnestied insurgents, usually consisting of ordinary country folk, and called them *'rurales'* or '*auxiliares*'. He estimated their total to be as high as 6,000 men. In his judgement, they contributed in no small way to the extinction of insurgency in Guanajuato.[24]

Examination of the many lists of amnestied insurgents drawn up by Royalist commanders throws light on the social origins of members of rebel bands in the Guanajuato region though, of course, says little about the problem of their motivation. The list of twenty-four such cases drawn up in Salvatierra on 28 March 1816 by the district mobile detachment commander is representative. This list gives places of birth and residence, age, occupation and racial group. With regard to the latter, we find that only one of the twenty-four is described as an '*indio*' and only one as a '*mulato*'. Nine were categorised as '*mestizo*' and the remainder as 'Spanish' or 'white'. In effect, these pseudo-ethnic terms probably disguised the fact that all were *mestizos*, but did not wish to be downgraded through fear of either social disdain or some future restoration of Indian tribute. Their occupation was, with only two exceptions, that of '*labrador*' or farm-worker. The remaining individuals were cow-hands. The largest single group came from the Hacienda de la Zanja, given as their place of birth and origin. Two others came from the Hacienda de la Magdalena, and the rest from Amoles, Valle de Santiago, Jaral, El Zavino and Culiacán. Apart from one lad of eighteen years, a 'white' farm-worker on La Zanja, the age group of the remainder ranged from 20 years to 40 years of age, though only two men fell in the latter category. This, then, was the revolt of men in early maturity, born generally between 1780 and 1790, *mestizo* farm hands, born and resident on estates or moving from villages to live on them.[25] By way of comparison, Hermenegildo Revuelta's list of rebel guerrillas who presented themselves for amnesty in Lagos late in 1817 showed how many of the thirty-nine men passed over into the Royalist defence forces – twenty-two of them.[26] Linares in Guanajuato informed Viceroy Apodaca in 1819 that all of the fifty-nine men who applied for amnesty in León in November and December were either hacienda workers or came from local villages. Similarly, all seventeen who applied for amnesty in Silao in December were of the same provenance, with several as well from the cities of Guanajuato or San Luis Potosí.[27]

## Suspects, participants and by-standers

Armed conflict produced not only fighting men, but temporary participants, defectors, onlookers, suspects and innocent victims. It functioned also alongside other levels of violence, such as banditry,

highway robbery, and common criminality, which were not intrinsi-
cally connected to insurgency. As we have seen, however, these distinct
levels could overlap. It may even have been that they shared common
preconditions, but constituted separate consequences. Crime, of course,
was a permanent social phenomenon, whereas insurgency was not. Even
so, the latter had its own rhythm and varied in intensity according to
local circumstances. The repeated risings that followed the defeat of
Hidalgo suggest that popular behaviour followed its own pattern,
irrespective of any course determined by an official leadership. Local
risings took place in the period, 1811–16, at recurrent intervals in
specific districts, such as the La Barca–Atotonilco zone of eastern
Guadalajara, the Zacoalco–Zapotlán zone, and around the shores of Lake
Chapala. These were all areas of relatively dense and ancient settlement,
in which Indian villagers struggled to survive in an environment of
increasing competition for grain land, not only with private proprietors,
but also with one another. It is possible, though not proven as yet, that
parish priests in some localities themselves became the spokesmen of
popular discontent and the leaders of armed dissent. Early in March
1811, for instance, the parish priest of La Piedad, led an insurgent band
into nearby Atotonilco and provoked, thereby, the flight of his
pro-government counterpart, the district administrator, and a number
of Royalist clergy and laymen. An insurgent prison break-out in
mid-June resulted in further risings in Arandas, La Barca and Atotonilco, even though villagers had previously been amnestied for past
conduct. The repercussions travelled as far as León.[28]

It seems probable that the possibilities and motives for revolt existed
in particular areas independent of any general leadership call for a
national struggle to overthrow Spanish rule. These preconditions,
moreover, antedated the highly disruptive effects of the subsistence
crisis of 1809–10. There is no necessary indication, however, that the
existence of such 'causes' of revolt actually did lead to revolt. We are left
so often with the problem of the relation of cause and supposed effect,
largely through the difficulty of finding concrete evidence of individual
or collective motivation for insurgent affiliation. The preconditions of
peasant or lower-class revolt have a way of frequently not providing the
consequences that they are expected to. As a result, we cannot speak of
inevitability or predictability, but must content ourselves with sugges-
tive relationships between (1) worsening social and economic conditions, pressures from private proprietors or *gachupín* merchant–
investors, dislocation through dearth, temporary loss of political
control, disarray within the armed forces, and (2) opportunities for

group revindication. The case of the Lake Chapala villages illustrates the dilemma, particularly with respect to the relation between long and short-term causes of popular action. The turbulent situation there in 1812 and 1813 – a second phase, as it were, after the initial '*El Amo*' Torres phase, points to a close overlap between conditions such as we have discussed in chapter two and consequently. It appears that clumsy government efforts to seize the locally popular chieftain, Encarnación Rosas, son of a lake fisherman and native of Mescala, sparked off a rising. Rosas had fought with Hidalgo at Puente de Calderón. The appearance of troops in his village provoked such hostility that Rosas was able to raise a band of some 200 men there and from the neighbouring villages of Tizapán, Tlachichilco and San Pedro Ixicán. In this latter village, the hitherto pacific inhabitants joined Rosas. Another parish priest, Marcos Castellanos in Ocotlán, a native of Sahuayo, proved at this stage to be a decisive influence for continued revolt. Castellanos suggested that the rebels should occupy and fortify the Island of Mescala in Lake Chapala and hold it as their operational base, which they did from late December 1812. Thence they raided government positions on the shore and secured provisions from sympathetic villagers, usually operating by canoe under cover of night. It took the Royalists until 27 November 1816 to reduce this dangerous stronghold, and even then only by offer of an amnesty to the insurgent band and a provision for land distribution along the shore. Both Rosas and Castellanos accepted amnesty. It seems evident, given the historical antecedents in such long land disputes as the Vizcarra and Porres Baranda suits and the mutual rivalry of local villages, that in the theatres of conflict in the 1810s in the Zacoalco–Zapotlán zone and around Lake Chapala, land rights and land pretensions acted as motives for insurgent allegiance or sympathies. Even so, we are not, as far as the archival evidence shows, dealing with instances of large-scale popular action against private properties, but with the efforts of small peasant groups to preserve their village identity both from private proprietors, chiefly resident in the city of Guadalajara, and from other villagers, their own neighbours. How village political allegiances followed this pattern of local rivalries appears difficult, if not impossible, to determine. Nevertheless, it is a key question. Cruz attached major importance to the elimination of Mescala and his reputation suffered through his failure to take it. A strongly entrenched position, with well-known popular support, Mescala sapped manpower and wasted government time. Both, of course, were essential purposes of insurgency. All principal commanders reiterated complaints of shortage of manpower. Rebel bands, small in number as they generally became, probed government weaknesses and stretched its forces to the limit. Cruz believed that the long survival of Mescala weakened the Royalist position throughout the whole of New Galicia. He described both the Mescala groups and those operating beneath the Colima volcano in the south as '*indios*' from the local villages.[29]

Desertion and reluctance to serve never ceased to plague Cruz' efforts to raise militia forces to man the launches for use on the lake against Mescala. Within Guadalajara itself, the city council appeared unenthusiastic in the impressment of young men of the better classes. In July 1816, Cruz tried to draft amnestied deserters and press-ganged vagrants. A list of ninety-eight names on 29 July showed the clientele from which the government recruited. Anastasio Vásquez, for instance, a mulatto farm-worker from Masatepec aged 30 years, was sentenced to six months' service on the lake. A married man, he had been imprisoned for the theft of four cargas of chile and two horses in Jocotepec. A group of '*indios*' from Nestipac had been sentenced for the robbery of some muleteers in transit through their village.[30] Frustration produced policies that alternated between desperate violence and hopeful conciliation. Negrete, operating through the Guadalajara–Michoacán border zone of the Valle de Peribán and Los Reyes in 1815, set fire to several sugar mills there, including those of San Rafael and San Pedro, which belonged to the Indian community of Los Reyes. In doing so, he had sought to deprive the insurgents of any benefits that could be derived from them and to remove Los Reyes as a base for rebel incursions into New Galicia. This action, however, revealed the essence of the problem, continued failure to reduce Mescala, which in itself delayed the fortification of Los Reyes, once tried abortively in 1812, until December 1816.[31] In July 1816, Cruz ordered Quintanar, commander of the New Galicia Fourth Division, to fortify Jiquilpan, to the south-east of the lake, as a front-line position, with the object of depriving the Mexcala band of the food supplies of the shore. Special patrols (*cuerpos volantes*) were to scour the lake zone. In this, however, the watchword was to be conciliation of the local population through the maintenance of strict discipline among the troops. Villagers' sympathies, however, would scarcely be gained by government counter-insurgency techniques of clearing the lakeside zone of livestock, foodstuffs and clothing not immediately required by their owners, in order to deprive rebels of the opportunity of provisionment. Troops were instructed to conduct lakeside villagers into fortified positions such as Ocotlán, Poncitlán or Jocotepec. Such a policy demonstrated government suspicion of collaboration. Cruz, in particular, suspected the '*indios*' of the village of San

Luis, who, despite 'repeated clemency', had continued to supply the Mescala rebels.[32]

The presence of rebel bands produced a variety of reactions among local villagers, by no means universally favourable. In the district of León, *'indios'* of the villages of San Miguel de la Real Corona and San Francisco del Coecillo, with general support, requested protection in 1811 from bands formed within the same district. The latter were reputed to have killed 300 people in Irapuato. It was rumoured that they had threatened to kill anyone in León who opposed them. In August 1817, the farm workers of Sanjuanico and La Cantera, in Lagos, themselves resisted and killed the marauder, Simón de Espinosa, and three of his band, when they tried to rob them. These were by no means isolated cases.[33] Even so, insurgent sympathies often remained deeply rooted in other villages. Late in June 1819, Revuelta commented that local people, particularly around Pueblo Grande, still remained hostile towards Royalist troops, appeared unwilling to live under the authority of the Royal government, and were reluctant to co-operate in the process of fortification of villages and estates against marauding bands. Rebels could still count on villagers to supply them. The overstretched nature of all New Galicia forces delayed the establishment of effective control over the Lagos district.[34]

Military retaliation against suspected villagers, however, could earn a severe rebuke from the civil authorities, which sought, often in vain, to reassert their primacy in the later stages of the counter-insurgency. The village authorities of Chilchota, in highland Michoacán, complained in July 1818 to Intendant Merino that the military commander in Tangancícuaro had seized their livestock and the products of their mill, alleging complicity with insurgent bands. He charged them specifically with having taken part in the burning of Tangancícuaro. Evidently, anxious to win over peasant opinion, the fiscal in Valladolid warned him to restore what he had taken, and stressed that the Spanish Crown had always sought to preserve Indian property.[35]

Re-establishment of government control meant the return of official tax collectors. Rarely, if ever, did peasant producers welcome them, least of all, where the tithe was concerned. Accordingly, the tithe administrator of Zinapécuaro encountered, in 1817, difficulties in collecting the tax in all areas previously under insurgent occupation. When, in the following year, he took a body of Royalist troops with him, an insurgent band attacked the convoy in the Tarímbaro area and killed several members of the escort. After several days, insurgents set light to the houses and fields of the chief haciendas, consuming in the first much of the grain in storage.[36] A combination of repeated insurgent action and shortage of government funds delayed the fortification of Uruapan until May 1818. Thereafter, the tithe collector took a Royalist band to accompany him through the sierra, where the '*naturales*' continued to resist payment. He nearly lost his life, however, when rebels surprised his escort in Taretán.[37] In February 1819, the subdelegate of the mining district of Tlalpujahua complained that his life was in danger, because insurgents still dominated the countryside. In April, a rebel band kidnapped him in return for food and forrage.[38]

## Counter-insurgency bands in Zacatecas and Aguascalientes

Frequently, chaos and inefficiency characterised military attempts to organise self-defence forces even in areas where insurgency had begun to recede. During the period, 1817 to 1820, for instance, the Patriot Companies formed on the estates and in the towns of Zacatecas still remained ill-armed and undisciplined. These counter-insurgency bands were composed of the cowmen, shepherds and farmers who worked on the private properties. As the insurgency began to peter out in the central northern zones, the authorities managed to increase marginally the number of troops in the province of Zacatecas from 5,416 early in September 1817 to 5,812 by the end of April 1820. The 1817 total did not include a further 713 men of the Third Division of the Army of New Galicia, raised in Zacatecas itself, and the 495 men of the provincial reserve division, which guarded the Hacienda de Ciénega de Mata.[39] Brigadier José de Gayangos, the military commander in Zacatecas, formed a new section of 300 infantry and cavalry troops, when instructed to do so by Cruz, his superior. This body was also to be distributed among the estates and villages of the region, with its headquarters at the Hacienda del Pabellon. Its task would be to patrol the countryside from Ojuelos at the northern tip of the Altos de Jalisco near the Guanajuato border and the Villita de la Encarnación between Aguascalientes and Lagos and to operate in conjunction with Revuelta's forces from León and with the other village forces and detachments, in order to prevent fresh rebel incursions.[40]

Whether because of such measures as these or for internal reasons of its own, the insurgency petered out in Zacatecas, and remained virtually confined to the southern border zones which were mountainous areas of difficult access. Early in 1820, Gayangos felt confident enough to withdraw the section of 150 men stationed on the Hacienda del Pabellón between Zacatecas and Aguascalientes by way of economy.[41]

The rich cereal and livestock zone of Aguascalientes, however, was situated a good deal closer to the original heartlands of the insurrection in the Bajío. The Pachones' band threatened this region and the San Luis Potosí border area from its redouts in Guanajuato. Accordingly, in April 1818 Gayangos formed a Mobile Section, based in the Villa de Lagos, to patrol the district of Aguascalientes and cover the border areas in conjunction with other sections operating out of Lagos and from the north-east Guanajuato town of San Felipe. The ultimate objective would be the penetration of the sierra. Revuelta, who knew the terrain, would take command of this body of 394 men, sixty-four of them veteran troops from the Provincias Internas, and the rest almost equally divided between loyalist cavalrymen (*Fieles Realistas*) and infantrymen.[42] In the later years, 1819–20, we are really dealing with the aftermath of insurgency, rather than with any concerted or ideologically motivated impulse. Nevertheless, the memory of rebel support recruited from among hacienda workers and the continued danger of marauders discouraged the district commander, José Ruiz, from abandoning the self-defence policy. Ruiz proposed to form a total force of 950 men, fifty each in the nineteen hacienda and rancho groupings of Aguascalientes. Only those persons under sixteen years of age or over fifty, or otherwise unfit for service, would be ineligible for recruitment into these 'rural companies'. The government hoped to economise by persuading private proprietors to pay for the cost of mounting and arming this force, which was designed to protect their estates both from 'bands of thieves' and from 'internal upheavals'.[43]

## The rebel stronghold in the south

By 1821 government forces were obliged to leave the entire southern zone of Michoacán and Guadalajara under the control of insurgent bands, the principal of which were led by Gordiano Guzmán, a native of the Zapotlán district, who had made Aguililla his personal stronghold. Guzmán remained in contact with the other principal *caudillos* of the south, Juan Álvarez and Vicente Guerrero, in the hinterland of Acapulco, the heirs of Morelos. In effect, the entire region from Colima eastwards across Michoacán to the mountains between Chilpancingo and the Pacific coast continued to be effectively out of government control. It would remain so into the middle of the nineteenth century. Neither Negrete nor Quintanar succeeded in eliminating Guzmán: their failure during the 1810s had transcendent significance. It allowed the formation of a series of *cacicazgos*, which constituted *de facto* independent states within the national polity. Bustamante, Santa Anna and other Mexico City leaders tried at various intervals to eliminate them, but with little lasting success. Yet, the survival of Guzmán's domain and of the celebrated Álvarez realm posed no real threat to central government or the established power, since neither of their leaders proposed either to extend his personal empire at the national expense or to revolutionise society through a general insurrection. As a result, it was possible for the central power to accommodate the chieftains in a balance of mutual interests. Álvarez, in particular, only posed a threat, when the central power sought to undermine his *cacicazgo*. Guzmán, for his part, rarely acted beyond his domain after the unsuccessful attempt in 1829–31 to sustain Guerrero's presidency and to avenge his overthrow and murder. Understandably, both Álvarez and Guzmán were strong supporters of federalism.[44]

Guzmán, whose parents were mulattos, was born in 1789 on a *ranchería* belonging to the sugar-producing Hacienda de Contla. He was caught up in the early insurgency and joined a band of peons attacking the haciendas in southern Guadalajara and focussing their action on the mercantile town of Sayula. Local horsemen and skilled ropers, armed only rarely with rifles, formed his troop. Even when bands joined together, they rarely amounted to more than 400 men. Initial Royalist counter-offensives drove him to seek temporary refuge in the surrounding mountains, the Sierra del Tigre, the Sierra de Mazamitla, and the ravines of Atenquique. It appears that Guzmán fought alongside Morelos in the siege of Acapulco's San Diego fortress in 1813. Until his transfer into southern Michoacán in 1816, these areas formed Gordiano's base of operations. Thence he attacked positions such as Zapotiltic, near Zapotlán. The fall of Mescala late in 1816, however, provided the Royalists with the opportunity to push finally into these southern zones. Quintanar took command of this only partially effective counter-offensive. Gordiano made the Valley of Aguililla his new base, and consistently refused an amnesty. He populated the small town of Aguililla with his own kin and clientage. His control by 1817–19 stretched over the vast territory of Coahuayana, Coalcomán and Tepalcatepec, regions of scant population and remote location. Thence he remained in contact with Álvarez and the other chieftains in the south, Juan José Codallos and Isidoro Montes de Oca. No Royalist commander was ever able to deliver the final blow. Cruz attached priority to the destruction of Guzmán's band but his location was never easy to determine. As late as October 1818, Cruz concluded that Gordiano's force 'increases in strength in proportion to the support he receives from the negroes of the coast'. At the same time, José María Huerta's band threatened Uruapan and *El Indio* Candelario with 600 men, half of them armed with rifles, posed a danger to the area between Apatzingán and Tamazula. Continued rebel activity from the south, threw into jeopardy the entire Royalist effort in central Michoacán. With alarm, the authorities realised that the intention of the rebel bands was to join forces for the seizure of Sayula. Rapid counter-action from Zapotlán, however, frustrated this attempt, which would have endangered the safety of Guadalajara itself. Although Guzmán fell back, Royalist commanders recognised the impossibility of pursuit through the hostile terrain of his base areas, especially since other government forces were engaged in pursuit of Guerrero in Temascaltepec. Even the information provided in August 1819 by the amnestied chieftain, Trinidad Campos, failed to turn the tide. It did, however, reveal that Rosales, who led a band of 150 men, had refused to submit to Guzmán's authority.[45]

Negrete's offensive late in 1819 ground to a halt in the Zapotlán area, through shortage of funds and basic equipment, especially serious since both men and officers had fought until then with no pay. A campaign into the Coalcomán and Aguililla areas was out of the question; many soldiers had already succumbed to disease. The logic of his situation was withdrawal before having defeated the rebel bands. The latter, for their part, had taken advantage of Royalist paralysis to burn fortified villages in the Tamazula area.[46] The re-establishment of constitutionalism in 1820 provided the authorities with the opportunity to offer Guzmán a truce. Accordingly, the municipality of Apatzingán, a town which alone among those of southern Michoacán, contained a number of wealthy property-owners, appealed to Guzmán to end the long years of bloodshed. Gordiano, however, rejected any compromise founded upon mutual recognition of the Spanish Constitution of 1812. Instead, he argued that the rising of the Americas, beginning with the revolution in Caracas, had been no crime, in view of the imposition of a Bonaparte usurper upon the Spanish throne. He compared the struggle of his people to that of Israel, denounced the metropolitan government's disregard for rights or liberty, and dismissed the Constitution as the same oppression under a new guise. A personal appeal from Cruz, who himself had done his utmost to undermine the Constitution in the years 1812–14, fell on deaf ears. Guzmán replied by attacking Santa Ana Amatlán on 4 November. The war in the south continued.[47] Guzmán similarly rejected compromise with Iturbide on the basis of the Plan of Iguala in February 1821, despite the adherence of Guerrero. Equally, in 1823, Guzmán resolutely refused to co-operate with Quintanar, the chief protagonist of federalism in Guadalajara, in view of his counter-insurgency identification during the 1810s. This division within the federalist camp prevented in 1823–4 the tacit alliance between local *caciques* and regional politicians, which came to be a characteristic feature of the federalist-centralist struggle. The survival of *cacicazgos*, such as those of Álvarez and Guzmán, provided the material for Bulnes' celebrated dictum that federalism signified the institutionalisation and apogee of the *cacique* system.[48]

## Rebel bands and revolution

Many rebel chieftains were *mestizos*, mulattos or Indians. Even so, the social composition of the rebel bands varied widely, in accordance with the specific local problems to which insurgency provided a response. In the Bajío, where racial distinctions had become less pronounced than in Puebla or Guadalajara, it tended to be smallholders, tenants and other such groups, which composed the clientele of rebel bands. These individuals were generally, for want of a better word, *mestizo* rather than Indian. They might even describe themselves as creole or white. In many respects they constituted a rural middle sector, especially if compared to the peasant villagers of upland Michoacán or the Guadalajara lakes basin zone. Within their own region, however, it would be less easy to describe them as such, in view of the general absence in Guanajuato of the land-holding peasant village. We can have no definite proof of their motivations for insurgent allegiance, since few, if any of them, left written records substantiating their case histories. It is, however, important to make the connection between the pre-revolutionary social and economic changes in the Bajío and the insurgent action of specific groups and localities during the 1810s. It would be quite wrong to submerge the particular instances within a generalised concept of amorphous 'mass' action. If we do that, we shall lose sight of the concrete instances provided by the uneven and all too tantalising archival documentation. While the first instances of insurrection took place in and around Dolores and San Miguel el Grande, two different towns with different social structures, the initial impact of the revolt in the Bajío occurred in the principal cereal-producing districts, Celaya, Irapuato, Silao, Salamanca, as far as Querétaro. Several insurgent chieftains, among them Albino García, Andrés Delgado '*El Giro*', and possibly Tomás Baltierra '*Salmerón*', came from those districts. Insurgent actions, beyond the attempts of the official leaders to seize major cities, took the form of attacks on haciendas. Such attacks, however, present a problem. They do not appear to have been followed by tenant or worker land occupation, redistribution or exploitation. At least, the documentation does not suggest that this was the case. Similarly, we encounter throughout the insurgency statements to the effect that insurgent bands controlled or occupied certain private estates. We hear of them making use of hacienda resources, grains and livestock, trading in estate products, appropriating royal and ecclesiastical revenues, and making extortionate demands upon whichever proprietors happened to remain in the locality. We do not, however, read that insurgent chieftains either dispossessed the private proprietors and took over the properties themselves or distributed the lands among their own supporters. In view of the frequently mentioned pressures of population in many of the areas in which insurgency arose, these are, indeed, strange occurrences. They suggest that land hunger was not a prime motive of support for rebel bands. This is not, however to suggest, under any circumstances, that land and water rights were not issues in late colonial New Spain. We have seen from chapters three and four that they most certainly were.

It seems clear that we have to make several important distinctions in order to understand the insurgency phemonenon. In the first place, only extreme economic conditions provided incentives for the uprooting of small farmers and tenants. These conditions did appear in several areas of the Bajío in 1809–10. Without them, such cultivators would have usually remained on the land, whatever the pressures imposed upon them from above in the form of increased dues, enclosures, and removal of customary rights. More than likely their protest would have been, as we have seen in chapter three, localised and of short duration, if it did not give rise to the formation of bandit groups. We have, so far, concentrated upon the social and economic aspects, but the generally high level of urbanisation in the Bajío and the tendency towards cultural homogeneity suggests the parallel importance of ideological and political factors. Certainly these latter were evident among the provincial bourgeoisie. The connection between this latter group and those who later were to become the chieftains and members of rebel bands is not an easy one to make. Much of the evidence is tenuous. Yet, it appears that failure to subvert the regular army obliged the dissident bourgeoisie to contact local chieftains, since they could mobilise effective support among their kin and clientele. In this way the uneasy and worsening relationship between the urban professional men, on the one hand, and the violent chieftains of the countryside, came into being. None of the official leaders, not even Morelos, a former muleteer himself, could establish lasting control over these chieftains. As a result, the original ideological and nationalist superstructures of revolt rapidly disintegrated.

This broader appeal in the Hidalgo phase of revolt may have provided a unifying motivation for a few months, though we have no indication from the documentation that the parish priest of Dolores was regarded as a messianic figure. It is only secondary sources that suggest such a thing. Similarly, it is only conjecture to posit a millenarian character for the Hidalgo revolt. We are left, then, without a convenient motivation for generalised revolt. Hence, it is better that we stop searching for one, and return to the local instances that yield, possibly, more fruitful evidence. The conditions of dearth in 1809–10 were not by their nature permanent. Once the rains revived the land, conditions for exploitation returned. It seems probable that rebel bands consisted of those individuals who had nothing to return to and who hoped, in consequence, to make a living out of marauding rather than cultivating. Conditions in the late eighteenth-century Bajío, with their pressures on the labour force, too abundant in numbers to be absorbed by capital-conscious producers, provided many instances of such marginalisation. Apart from those who saw no hope for themselves in settled society, and thereby, filled the itinerant rebel bands, the original insurrection in the eastern Bajío proved to be a temporary phenomenon. This was especially so, since the city of Querétaro never fell to the insurgents. The western Bajío, however, was a different case. This was an area of less productive land and larger estates. Precisely in the districts of Piedragorda, Pénjamo and Valle de Santiago the insurgent bands managed to gain a lasting hold. They were not finally expelled until 1818–20.

In Guadalajara, insurgency arose from different circumstances to those in Guanajuato. These resulted from the survival of village communities of pre-Columbian origin on the central plateau and the lakes basin zone, and the competition for land rights, particularly with regard to the many disputed tracts between one village and another, or between villages and private estates, and again, as in the Bajío, over customary rights. The lakes basin towns were, as we have seen, areas of mercantile penetration from the city of Guadalajara. Since a number of these merchants were from the Spanish peninsula, they were particularly conspicuous among communities that consisted primarily of Indians and *mestizos*. In Michoacán insurgency remained deeply rooted among the highland villages of the Tlalpujahua–Zitácuaro zone and in the plateau district of hacienda penetration between Valladolid and Zamora. The insurgency in the Jiquílpan district remained connected to the continuing resistance of Mescala and the Chapala lakeside towns. The delayed counter-insurgency throughout Michoacán, in the border zones and in southern Guadalajara resulted from a number of factors, not the least of which was the long failure of Royalist military commanders to eradicate rebel bands from western Guanajuato. The vast areas of southern Michoacán which remained unsubdued in 1821 differed markedly in character from the zones which before 1819 had been the principal foci of rebellion in the central and highland areas. The *tierra caliente*, in which there had been small settled communities in the pre-Columbian era, remained a region of weak government authority throughout the colonial period. In some districts merchants had sought to establish control over the cotton trade, often produced not so much by Indian villagers, but by coastal negroes and mulattos. Guzmán received support from the latter: he was himself a Zapotlán mulatto. Yet we do not know what motivated the coastal negroid population to join his band. Available documentation does not tell us whether the motive was reaction to mercantile penetration or the promise of plunder at the expense of haciendas in the plateau regions. Similarly, we do not know the reason why Guzmán and the rebel chieftains of the south so frequently raided private properties, most, if not all of them, owned by Americans, rather than Spaniards. Once again, it does not appear that they sought to control these estates on a lasting basis and distribute the lands among their supporters. The counter-insurgency was not such an effective and permanent feature in these zones that peasant or rural worker land occupation could have been systematically eradicated, once it had been solidly established. It does not seem, however, that this was the objective of the rebel bands, which, on the contrary, remained mobile and, once threatened, withdrew into the hills or to their remote operational bases. Such behaviour patterns suggest that these bands did not consist of land hungry peasants, but of instinctive itinerants with nothing to lose, but a life of plunder to pursue. In this way, their raids posed a threat equally to villagers and smallholders as well as to creole hacienda owners. The village insurgents of the Guadalajara plateau and the lakes basin zone, however, were an entirely different category, since their revolt remained localised and responded to complex local circumstances.

The evident unwillingness or inability of rebel bands to retain permanent control of haciendas diminishes the social revolutionary character of the insurrection. Perhaps their actions reflected more 'social banditry' than social revolution. This absence of a redistributory intent opened the way for the re-occupation of country properties by government forces and the consequent reconstitution of as much of the pre-revolutionary structure of ownership as could be salvaged. Government policy, accordingly, began in a sporadic fashion, to emphasise the importance of winning over peasant support, as a precondition of continued social stability and of the recovery of agricultural production. Although for a long time small armed nuclei were capable of harassing, halting and even defeating government forces, particularly in areas of remote location, the rebel base zones never effectively became centres of an alternative political structure. The very strength of the rebel bands lay in their mobility and autonomy. Such factors, however, were precisely the opposite of those required to construct a recognisable authority which could claim a rival legitimacy to that of the central government. It seems that in Mexico in the 1810s we are witnessing a classic case of failed revolution.

# 8

## Conclusion

The revolutionary movement launched by Hidalgo and led subsequently by Morelos briefly transformed scattered, sporadic local conflicts into the semblance of a national movement. It is feasible to argue that *Guadalupanismo*, which symbolised Mexican national identity, constituted a surrogate ideology. The roots of insurgency, though, lay precisely in the localised tensions which the broader movement often subsumed. When the official leadership receded, the revolutionary movement fragmented into its component elements. In some regions, this process led to an insurgency of long duration. It was not inevitable, though, that local conflicts would in themselves generate an insurgency. It did not necessarily follow that *all* such conflicts became subsumed into the broader insurgency. Many did, although it is impossible to determine in what proportion. Several localities remained trouble spots of long duration, in view of their specific problems. Such recurrence of conflict suggests that transition to the status of independent nation in 1821 involved no concurrent resolution of the type of popular grievances, upon which the insurgency of the 1810s had once thrived. Not for another hundred years, however, until the Mexican Revolution of the 1910s, did a broad enough range of grievances on many levels combine with central government political failures to produce a generalised insurrection. In 1810 a variety of circumstances, long-term and short-term factors, dearth and dislocation, political loss of control and military lack of preparedness, came together. By doing so, an opportunity for insurrection was created, such as had not existed previously. The dearth of 1808–10 produced serious social and economic dislocation in the relatively high population areas of the centre-north-west, where popular living standards had deteriorated in the long term. However, the peculiar potentiality of this combination of long-term and short-term factors could not have been actualised without the political crisis of the central government. Loss of government control in several key provinces enabled insurgency to flourish in specific localities, once the initial impact of insurrection had died down. A leadership for insurrection was available in 1809–10, which was willing and able to exploit economic grievances, social dislocation, political crisis, and desire for personal advancement.

The origins of the insurrection of September 1810 cannot be explained uniquely in terms of the discrepancy between rising prices and relatively constant wages. In themselves such factors were not pre-conditions of revolution. Similarly, the sudden collapse of already deteriorating living standards did not automatically produce revolution. It is doubtful, in any case, whether the majority of the dispossessed and unemployed actually rebelled. Other factors had to be present capable of transforming the perceptions of a broad enough range of social groups for an insurrectionary movement to take root. Even then, it was not in any way inevitable that the either *ex post facto* causes of revolt or the supposed preconditions of revolution in fact produced the revolutions required of them. Large-scale violence was an exceptional occurrence in colonial New Spain, which had not experienced a rebellion such as that of Tupac Amaru and Tupac Catari in Upper and Lower Peru in the early 1780s. This alone suggests not only a greater social and cultural integration in New Spain than in Andean Peru, but also the possibility of a greater flexibility in administrative practices than has traditionally been appreciated. Conflict, moreover, was not the only element in social relationships, even in a colonial situation such as that of New Spain with its wide economic and ethnic disparities. There is no reason, founded in fact, that conflict should be regarded as the principal motivating factor in historical development. To focus upon conflict may well distort the interpretation of the historical process in the interests of a search for a ready answer to the problems of the origins of revolutionary movements. It should not necessarily be assumed, however, that when we are dealing with evident conflict it is first and foremost economic in origin. Conflict over perceived or ascribed status, juridical position, possession of authority, or integration into patronage or kinship networks – all characteristics of pre-modern or *ancien régime* societies – may well be uppermost. Rarely, if ever, did social and economic factors in themselves explain the outcome of events. Insurgent action in the 1810s might be just one of several popular responses to local problems. Varying conditions in the peasant villages, on the private estates, in the mining communities, among textile producers of town or country, and among the broad array of itinerants, underemployed, seasonally employed, and unemployed may well explain why some individuals or groups opted for insurgency and others did not. Altered circumstances during the course of the struggle may explain why previous insurgent groups became responsive to counter-insurgency. Fear of both rebels and Royalists would have explained passivity or collusion with different sides at different times. There could be a thin dividing line between the self-preservation that led to insurgency and that which led to non-insurgency. Unwillingness to take part in revolt suggested that a counter-insurgency might well become a possibility. This, from the point of view of the official power, would be the prerequisite of the post-insurgency situation. Determining pressures in the option for insurgency could well have been community preceptions that effective judicial redress through the established channels was not forthcoming over a long period in cases of estate pressures on land, labour, water usage or customary rights. This involved more than material disadvantage; such failure threatened the identity of historic peasant communities and their view of the cosmos.

It is virtually impossible to know at what point large segments of the population decided to – or realised they already had – opted for a course of action which could be described as insurrection. Perhaps this is a long process that, since it is rarely articulated, requires a long time to mature. Perhaps the social dislocation and sense of despair that result from natural causes, such as dearth, serve to crystallise these deeply rooted feelings of alienation. They can only do so, however, if other factors are present at the political level, since insurrection is a political act. Two crucial elements need to be operative if transition to the political plane of activity is to be realised. These are (1) the availability of leadership to articulate and direct grievances, that in their origins may be local, and (2) a crisis at the centre and the existence of political uncertainty in provincial capital cities. Such elements were present in New Spain in 1808–10. The conjunction of social, economic and political factors enabled the mental transition from local grievance or sense of alienation to outright revolt. In his discussion of the origins and implications of the Vendée rebellion in western France in 1793, Barrington Moore describes a process that we may well employ as a test model for New Spain in 1810. It poses remarkably similar dilemmas: 'in revolutions, as well as counter-revolutions and civil wars, there comes a crucial point when people suddenly realise that they have irrevocably broken with the world they have known and accepted all their lives. For different classes and individuals this momentary flash of new and frightening truth will come at successive points in the collapse of the prevailing system. There are also unique moments and decisions ...

after which there is no return . . . Huge sections of the population become part of a new social order.'[1] It may well be that the *Grito de Dolores* provided one such unique and decisive moment. Hidalgo's historical significance lay in his capacity to bind together, at least for a short time, disparate social groups in a combined attack on the European position in New Spain. Since the ultimate objective was the furtherance of the political ambitions of the frustrated 'provincial bourgeoisie' this revolutionary coalition of rural workers, villagers, dispossessed tenants, unemployed urban or mine workers, rancho-owners, muleteers, estate administrators, small town lawyers, lower clerics, provincial intellectuals, local *caciques*, men on the make, bandits and criminals suffered internal contradictions right from the start. Yet, the initial shock and breadth of the insurrection, followed by a series of entrenched local insurgencies, ensured that the official armed forces would have to undertake the difficult task of territorial reconquest.

The appeal to the lower classes in September 1810 transferred the locus of the revolutionary movement from the limited conspiratorial circles in the cities of Valladolid de Michoacán and Querétaro to the small town, village, and countryside. Once insurgency took root in the localities, the object of the struggle between government forces and rebel bands would be control of the local populace, available resources and the sources of information. The uncertain position of the numerous social groups, such as *arrimados* and other seasonal workers, which had no clear status in relation to the private estates or the village communities, became crucial. It was, moreover, vital for both Royalist forces and guerrilla bands to establish control over or collusion with the muleteer groups that provided the contacts between localities and provinces. Muleteers appear frequently in the documentation concerning insurgent bands and suspected rebels during the 1810s. Their contacts and their information made them invaluable allies of both sides in any armed conflict. Rebel bands consisted of individuals drawn from peasant communities in conflict with estates, as in the Guadalajara lakes basin zone in the period 1810–16, or from the farm workers and cowhands of the private estates, as in the case of the Bajío and adjacent zones in the period 1816–20. Puebla rebels included rural artisans as well. The participation of such social groups comes as no surprise. Given the itinerant nature of insurgency, moreover, it tended to be younger men who joined the bands, some of them only for short periods of time. This suggests either a low level of commitment followed by rapid disillusionment or transition to other competing pursuits, such as return to the land, option for amnesty and incorporation into a rival counter-insurgency band, or return to a life of vagrancy and crime. This mobility both of rebel bands across territory and of individuals in and out of them deflected any social revolutionary potential the insurgency might initially have possessed. This was especially so, in view of the rapid disintegration of its political front.

Counter-insurgency defence forces consisted, in the main, of the same social groups that fuelled insurgency. Apart from the hardened core of irreconcilables or unpardonables, it seems that the bulk of insurgent supporters tired of active participation before long. Patriot Companies on private estates contained farm-workers, cowmen and shepherds. The proprietors themselves organised, generally under army pressure, rural defence forces consisting of smallholders, tenants and estate workers. These often included amnestied insurgents. Formation of hacienda defence forces suggests that in sufficient instances the estate workforce remained more or less intact despite the impact of local insurgencies. This, in turn, implies that, where operative, a successful patron-client network on the private properties might have been sufficient to withstand – and eventually reverse – the impact of local insurgency. In cases where, as the available documentation shows, insurgency did recruit support among resident workers, the possibility exists that in due course the old patron-client network reconstituted itself by the later 1810s to a degree resilient enough to sustain counter-insurgency operations. In cities such as Puebla and Guadalajara, municipal government unwillingness to support guild efforts to subordinate independent artisans may have contributed to calming the social tensions between guild and non-guild workmen in the years immediately preceding the insurrection of 1810. Whatever the case, Royalist counter-revolutionary companies were formed partly from artisan recruitment during the 1810s. Such militia companies usually under merchant command held the rearguard behind the armies in the field.

Traditional histories of the Independence movements have focussed largely on the national dimension and have dealt considerably with both ideology and creole alienation. The approach adopted in this present study has been regional and local. Nevertheless, we have tried throughout to relate regional tensions and conflicts to the broader level. Insurgency developed from the failed revolutionary attempt of September 1810 to January 1811. Yet, neither the decision of Hidalgo to opt for insurrection nor the long-lasting insurgency in the provinces represented the only option for Mexicans anxious to modify or remove Spanish peninsular rule during the 1810s. It is important to bear in mind that insurgency operated within a broader political context in which shifting ideologies and alignments had become a characteristic feature. Although Hidalgo's movement later became the unique symbol of the movement of Independence, it had not been generally regarded as such at the time. This had been the later creation of nationalist historians and politicians. In this present study, we have tried to unscramble the national superstructure, and view the insurrection as but one response among a number of other no less important potential solutions to the late colonial crisis of New Spain. For this reason the history of the ensuing insurgency was also relative to the outcome of the other options at play during the 1810s and early 1820s. Neither insurrection in September 1810 nor the fragmented insurgency thereafter should be viewed in abstraction from their historical context. Still less, should they be regarded exclusively as the prerequisite for the attainment of independence or as the basis for the development of the modern Mexican nation. To distort the historical process in such a way, would be to ignore (1) the dilemma of the 'Mexican or resident élite', caught between Royalist militarism and marauding insurgency; (2) the fears of the 'provincial bourgeoisie' once the popular orders had been galvanised into action; (3) the Royalist régime's capacity for military and political recovery; (4) the efficacy of much Royalist counter-insurgency on the plateau and fringe zones; (5) the prospect of political participation offered by Spanish constitutionalism in 1810–14 and 1820–2; (6) the ability of American Royalist officers, such as Iturbide, to forge, with the assistance of the ecclesiastical hierarchy, a sufficiently broad coalition to bring New Spain to independence without recourse to another insurrectionary movement. Indeed, the six points outlined above indicate in themselves the full extent of the failure of Hidalgo and Morelos to seize control of the central political processes whether by a swift revolutionary act, or through a sustained revolutionary war. The fragmentation of the insurgency similarly pointed to the loss of political momentum – and certainly of co-ordination – within the revolutionary camp.

Since the insurrectionary movement never became a national independence movement that included the American élites, it found that it had to define its relationship to those who held aloof from it. Part of this process involved the explanation of its political aims. Since Hidalgo initially conceived of this movement as a Mexican national movement, there appeared to be little necessity to make its political goals explicit. These were implicit in the very nature of the movement itself: independence from Spanish rule. Once it became clear that the popular element in the revolutionary movement had divided Americans anxious to displace peninsular rule, the movement of 1810 was perceived by the élites not to be a national movement, but to consist of the insurrection of disparate lower class elements in co-operation with dissident members of the 'professional bourgeoisie', themselves often dependent upon local *caciques*. Impressive as Hidalgo and Morelos were in their capacity to rally popular support, they, nevertheless, failed to build a consensus broad enough to displace the existing régime. This was not accomplished until Iturbide accomplished it, in collaboration with the ecclesiastical hierarchy, in 1821. Since the insurrection itself strove to become the movement that would take New Spain to independence, it was essential for its intellectual leadership to make explicit the movement's aims. This was not achieved until September 1812 – October 1814, that is, one year after the Spanish constitutional system had been established in New Spain. Between 1812 and 1814, then, the Spanish régime and the insurgent leadership were engaged in a political struggle – apart from the military conflict – to determine which could provide the constitutional alternative to (a) viceregal absolutism, and (b) exclusive peninsular supremacy. In the end, the rising power of the Royalist military ensured that neither constitutional alternative would become a practical option. Ferdinand VII's nullification of the Constitution of 1812 and closure of the Cortes put the final seal on that process. Spain's return to absolutism did not provide the insurgent movement with any immediate political or moral advantage, since the military defeat of the insurgency in the plateau regions was becoming evident by the time the insurgent leadership issued the Constitution of Apatzingán – a town significantly located deep within the rebels' Michoacán base in the *tierra caliente* – in October 1814. Although this document provided for the creation of an independent, sovereign republic, it could never take effect. The lesson was clear. Although rebel bands still remained highly dangerous right until 1820–2, the insurgent movement had lost the political struggle.

Once the insurgency had degenerated into marauding bands, the 'Mexican or resident élite' could re-emerge as a political group. Similarly, the dissident element in the 'professional bourgeoisie', denied the opportunity of popular insurgency as a means to power, would have to pursue its aims through conventional channels. Since the senior élite, however, stood in its way, it would either (a) have to seek accommodation with it as a dependent junior partner, deprived for the time being of the prospect of a popular base of support, or (b) have to confront it. To accomplish the latter, it would have either to rebuild this popular base in a peaceful struggle, or appeal to dissident military figures to further its ends and bypass the senior élite through limited acts of armed force. From this, it can be seen that many of Mexico's political conflicts as an independent nation derived not strictly from the fact of independence but from the social antagonisms and shifting political alignments of the late colonial period. This continuity is obscured by the traditional historiographical periodisation.

As we have said, the revolutionary movement of 1810 never ceased to exhibit internal contradictions. They were never successfully resolved. A fundamental contradiction continued to be that between the military arm and the civilians who sought to control it. In an important sense, Hidalgo's appeal to direct action had contributed to the rise of the military within the insurgent movement, and to the escalation of violence as an end in itself. The adoption of religious symbolism only served to reinforce the propensity to violence all the more. Military figures, such as Allende, Abasolo and Aldama, were present in the movement from the start, though their position was diminished by Hidalgo's decision to direct military policy himself as supreme commander of insurgent forces. Morelos' adoption of a similar role in 1812–14 further strengthened this *caudillo* element in the insurgent movement. Morelos, within the confines of his movement, was a *caudillo* who could control a multiplicity of *caciques* each with their own armed bands beneath them. Once that *caudillo* figure was removed, the *caciques* had a free reign, except in so far as mutual rivalries constrained their activities. In consequence, a movement which in 1810–11 had had neither a clear ideology nor precise political aims became by 1815–16 a faction-ridden alliance of armed bands and aspiring civilian politicians, much like any other during the period 1821–76. Particularly striking was the local and provincial base of the rebel bands and their leaders, brought into being, in part, by the social tensions of the pre-insurgency, and, in part, by the escalating disorder and opening possibilities for self-advancement and enrichment offered by the war itself. Since the original leadership had sought at the outset to work through such local *cacique* figures in a network of dissident personalities that stretched far beyond the 'professional bourgeoisie' itself, the final consequences of so doing should come as no surprise. Several of these local figures had already achieved a certain prominence within their regions even before the insurrection of 1810 magnified their importance. Such were the Villagráns of Huichapan, the Osorno clan of the Llanos de Apan and the north Puebla sierra, the Galeanas of the Pacific coast and the Bravos of the Chilpancingo region. Other figures rose to prominence with the insurgency and were generally consumed by it: 'el amo Torres', the

'Pachones', Encarnación and Matías Ortiz, Albino García, Rafael Iriarte, 'el cabo Leytón', Manuel Muñiz, and a number of minor clerical *caudillos* like Correa, Navarrete and Torres. Some leaders of rebel bands such as Vicente Guerrero, Guadalupe Victoria, Nicolás Bravo, Gordiano Guzmán, and Juan Álvarez, remained important figures after 1821. The two latter managed to construct a lasting political base in the areas of the insurgent activity during the 1810s. Others vanished from sight.

Despite Royalist recovery of the provincial capitals, insurgency remained deeply rooted in Guanajuato, Michoacán and Guadalajara. The survival of insurgent territorial pockets in the two latter regions, in the large geographical area between Taxco and the Pacific coast, and in the hinterland of Veracruz meant that, in effect, the counter-insurgency struggle had reached a stalemate by 1820–1. Accordingly, Royalist military commanders were obliged to recognise this situation. The political logic that followed from it was the incorporation of the undefeated rebel leaders into a new consensus designed to displace the peninsular 'bureaucratic élite' and to facilitate Mexico's transition to a sovereign state. This they accomplished in the course of 1821. Thereafter, the new balance of forces reflected this decision and, as a consequence of it, enabled certain popular insurgent chieftains to become political figures at the national level for a time during the 1820s and early 1830s. Their entry enabled the re-emergence of formerly insurgent segments of the 'provincial bourgeoisie', among whom were such figures as Carlos María de Bustamante and Andrés Quintana Roo. The return of constitutionalists such as Miguel Ramos Arizpe and Lorenzo de Zavala from the Spanish Cortes further reinforced this group, several members of which became proponents of early liberalism and federalism. Their political future, however, would be lived out in relationship to the former Royalist commanders who had risen to prominence through their participation in the counter-insurgency of the 1810s. This state of affairs did not radically alter until after the final fall of Antonio López de Santa Anna in 1855.

Few of the localised sources of conflict which had contributed to insurgency during the 1810s disappeared afterwards. Many of the component elements remained to a lesser degree. A central issue continued to be the problem of law and order, which the disruption caused by the insurgency had intensified. Even after the insurgency had abated, many hacienda owners found it necessary to form self-defence forces on their properties. Such was the case in the States of Mexico, Querétaro, San Luis Potosí, Zacatecas and Nuevo León. Already in San

Luis Potosí, from the 1830s, hacienda owners were using their work force successfully as auxiliary police. An explanation for such individual initiatives, which place the self-defence policies of the insurgency period into a broader context, was the inability of the central government to provide for a national rural police agency. The Supreme Executive Power, which took office in Mexico City following the collapse of the First Empire in March 1823 instructed the provincial deputations late in the same year to establish two companies of rural mounted police to patrol the localities. In view of the persistent tensions between provincial and central authorities, nothing resulted. Failure to cope adequately with problems of internal security encouraged the Centralist régime on 17 January 1843 to order *hacendados* and municipal officials to co-operate with their respective departmental authorities, in order to form a rural cavalry force to patrol the highways. Despite these legitimate objectives, few State or department governors trusted the loyalty of such armed bands. In the late 1840s and early 1850s, particularly after the disruptive effects of the war with the United States, banditry and highway robbery flourished. They proved to be particularly severe in the north, chiefly in the States of Durango and Zacatecas. In Durango in 1826, the State Government had transformed hacienda owners and lessees into rural police custodians. Their faculties extended in 1847 to criminal indictment of thieves. The central zones did not remain unaffected by this widespread disorder. In Puebla, for instance, bandits sold protection to city inhabitants, until a conjunction of government forces and armed men paid by the haciendas finally broke their power. In Jalisco, *hacendados* were permitted in May 1847 to arm their workforce for self-defence, as were those of Querétaro in Mexico in 1849. A rural police force came into being in Jalisco in 1852. The estates of San Luis Potosí, severely plagued by escalating robberies, were permitted in the 1850s to raise ten mounted rural guards, if the property included more than 200 workers and employees, and five on lesser estates. The proprietor or hacienda administrator would take command of these forces. Federal Government attempts to deal with such disorders, increasingly evident in the 1850s, finally culminated on 16 January 1857 in President Ignacio Comonfort's decree forming the Mexican rural police force. Nevertheless, law and order remained a central preoccupation throughout the Reform period, during which the political conflicts served to exacerbate the problem.[2]

The survival of unresolved local tensions between villagers and estate owners or between peasants and the outside taxing or recruiting power contributed to the escalation of violence at a time of weak central government during the 1840s and 1850s. Grievances in the Tlapa-Chilapa region in the rising of 1842 extended to the diversion of the water supply, prohibition of wood-cutting, and allegation of corporal punishment of offending villagers by hacienda personnel. Issues such as these were perennial. Throughout the zone between the Pacific coast and the southern borders of Puebla and Morelos (created in 1869), these local issues came to involve the relationship between the regional patriarch Juan Alvarez, and the central government, particularly in view of his hostility to Santa Anna, in power between 1841 and 1844. Neither side in any such dispute could be exactly sure where Álvarez stood. Three rebellions in 1842–3 spread through western Guerrero into Morelos, the Acatlán district of Puebla, and into eastern Oaxaca and the Mixteca. The unrest in this region eventually involved some 10,000 individuals, who were able to hold off an exhausted and unpaid army. Not until the former insurgent commander of the 1810s, General Nicolás Bravo, began a serious campaign of repression in November 1844 did the movement disintegrate, especially in view of the murder of the peasant leader, Miguel Casarrubias. Peasant villagers rose again in January 1849, in protest against exaction of rents by proprietors for lands which the former maintained were by right their own. Again the army proved unable to put down rebellion. In the Tula district north of Mexico City, some 20,000 Indians rebelled in 1847–8. Rebellions in central districts, such as Teotihuacán, Otumba and Pachuca in 1848, and Chalco and Texcoco in 1868, arose out of conflicts with *hacendados*. A number of rebellions were not only long-lasting, but also widespread and persistently recurrent. In Papantla, a rebellion broke out in 1836, under the leadership of Mariano Olarte, who became undisputed leader of a vast area of Veracruz with influence into the contiguous States. The origins of Olarte's rebellion lay in the invasion of Indian subsistence lands by landowners' cattle and in administrators' attempts to stamp out a peasant contraband trade in arms. The rebellion was politically complicated by the fact that Olarte was, in effect, a Veracruz protégé of Santa Anna, who had raised him to the rank of *teniente coronel*. Olarte used his authority to protect the local population from the abuses and exactions of both the civil and military powers. The guerrilla repercussions of the Papantla rebellion extended into the States of Mexico and Puebla. Several military attempts to crush the 5,000 rebels failed, until Olarte was killed in May 1838. By the end of that year, the rebellion petered out, since the peasants involved needed to return home to grow their crops. Rebellion broke out again in Papantla in January 1848, and peasants from the Puebla–Veracruz border zone joined it. Twelve villages took part in the Pánuco and Tampico movements to recover communal lands in 1845–9, and rebellions extended into Tuxpan in 1847, Huejutla in 1848–9, and Tamazunchale in San Luis Potosí in 1849. Misantla rose in July 1853 against military recruitment. In the Coatepec district, to the south of Jalapa, Juan Climaco Rebolledo, became virtual patriarch through his defence of the local peasantry. Rebolledo, who had an intimate knowledge of the countryside, had since 1821 been associated in some form or another with Santa Anna. In 1847, the latter employed him as a guerrilla commander in operations against the U.S. invasion force in the Veracruz–Perote zone. For the most part, local *rancheros* composed the guerrilla bands operating there and also in Tamaulipas and Puebla. Rebolledo in 1851 took the lead in the protest movements in opposition to the restoration of sales-tax. Inhabitants of the villages and *rancherías* of Orizaba and Córdoba supported his rebellion in 1852, which spread to Coscomatepec and Huatusco. In the Xichú rebellion of 1847–9 in the Sierra Gorda, the rebels under Eleuterio Quiróz, who originated from the mining village, demanded moderate rents, the end of obligations to pay out a portion of their harvest, and the formation of villages out of haciendas with more than 1,500 inhabitants in the *casco*. The federal army, under the command of the counter-insurgency chieftain of the 1810s, Anastasio Bustamante, finally put down the rebellion in October 1849. The Sierra Gorda movement had extended across the States of Hidalgo and Querétaro into north-eastern Guanajuato and had repercussions as well in San Luis Potosí. It originated in attempted military recruitment, fiscal pressures and local opposition to the tobacco monopoly. Army deserters, fugitives, and vagrants swelled rebel ranks. The rebellion, which had included attacks on haciendas, ended with a government undertaking to attend to peasant demands for village organisation with sufficient land endowments.[3] Such rebellions resembled those of the eighteenth century, though, if anything, were more frequent, perhaps because of stronger *hacendado* pressure, diminished official channels for the presentation of grievances in the post-colonial era, and the repeated weakness of central government at several decisive stages of national history from the mid-1840s until the mid-1870s. Liberal policy towards corporate property-ownership, chiefly the disamortisation begun under the Ley Lerdo of 1856, often provoked peasant communities into outright opposition.

# Notes

### Introduction

1 See, for instance, John Lynch, *Argentine Dictator. Juan Manuel de Rosas, 1829–1852* (Oxford 1981).

2 See E. R. Wolf, 'The Mexican Bajío in the Eighteenth Century', *Synoptic Studies of Mexican Culture*, no. 17, Middle American Research Institute of Tulane University Publications (New Orleans 1955); D. A. Brading, *Merchants and Miners in Bourbon Mexico, 1763–1810* (Cambridge 1971); Brian R. Hamnett, *Politics and Trade in Southern Mexico, 1750–1821* (Cambridge 1971); Reinhard Liehr, *Stadtrat und Städtische Oberschicht von Puebla am Ende der Kolonialzeit (1787–1810)* (Wiesbaden 1971); William B. Taylor, *Landlord and Peasant in Colonial Oaxaca* (Stanford 1972); John K. Chance, *Race and Class in Colonial Oaxaca* (Stanford 1978); Claude Morin, *Michoacán en la Nueva España del siglo XVIII. Crecimiento y desigualdad en una economía colonial* (Mexico 1979); Eric Van Young, *Hacienda and Market in Eighteenth-Century Mexico. The Rural Economy of Guadalajara, 1675–1820* (California 1981); John C. Super, *La vida en Querétaro durante la Colonia, 1531–1810* (Mexico 1983).

3 A recent effort to view the Independence movements as factors of continuity linking late colonial tensions to the issues and problems of the first half of the nineteenth century is Miguel Izard, *El Miedo a la Revolución. La Lucha por la libertad en Venezuela (1777–1830)* (Madrid 1979), and the same author's, 'Ni Cuartreros ni Montoneros, Llaneros', *Boletín Americanista*, XXIII no. 31 (1981), 83–142.

4 We still tend to identify, for instance, the emergence of *caudillaje* (the political dominance of regional bosses) and *caciquismo* (the power-broking of local notables) as a phenomenon of the post-independence period, rather than to seek their origins in colonial Latin America. For a discussion of related issues, see Woodrow W. Borah, 'Discontinuity and Continuity in Mexican History', *Pacific Historical Review*, 48 (1979), 1–25.

5 See especially, Fray Servando Teresa de Mier y Noriega y Guerra, *Historia de la revolución de Nueva España, antiguamente Anáhuac, o verdadero orígen y causas de ella con la relación de sus progresos hasta el presente año de 1813*, 2 vols. (London 1813); Lorenzo de Zavala, *Ensayo histórico de las revoluciones de México desde 1808 hasta 1830*, 2 vols. (Paris 1831–2); José María Luis Mora, *México y sus revoluciones*, 3 vols. (Paris 1836); Carlos María de Bustamante, *Cuadro histórico de la revolución mexicana iniciada el 15 de septiembre de 1810 por el C. Miguel Hidalgo y Costilla cura del pueblo de Dolores en el obispado de Michoacán*, 6 vols. (Mexico 1843–6); Lucas Alamán, *Historia de Méjico desde los primeros movimientos que prepararon su independencia en el año 1808 hasta la época presente*, 5 vols. (Mexico 1849–52).

6 Cf. Ida Altman and James Lockhart, *Provinces of Early Mexico. Variants of Spanish American Regional Evolution* (Los Angeles 1976) 8: 'a complex interplay went on at all times in which the capital, whether by its action or lack of action, affected the autonomy and self-containedness to which each province in and of itself tended'.

7 D. A. Brading, *Haciendas and Ranchos in the Mexican Bajío, León 1700–1860* (Cambridge 1978), pp. 19, 176–7. Population estimates vary for the Intendancy of Guanajuato. Fernando Navarro y Noriega, *Memoria sobre la población del reino de Nueva España* (Mexico 1943), gives 576,600 for 1810 and a total viceregal population of 6,122,354.

8 Van Young, *Hacienda and Market*, pp. 23, 26, 28, 39, 74. City population stood at 24,249 in 1793 and 46,804 in 1822; Puebla 1790, 52,717, and 1820, 61,157.

9 Sherburne F. Cook and Woodrow W. Borah, *Essays in Population History: Mexico and the Caribbean*, Vol. I (California 1971), pp. 300–375, pp. 301, 310, 312, 355, 373. This region encompassed the modern states of Jalisco, Nayarit, Colima, Aguascalientes, parts of Zacatecas from Jerez to Juchipila, and the Michoacán coastal district of Motines. Population stood at 43,950 in 1680; 70,150 in 1710; 136,750 in 1740; 286,800 in 1770; and 605,500 in 1800.

10 D. A. Brading, 'La Estructura de la producción agrícola en el Bajío de 1700 a 1850', *Historia Mexicana*, XXIII, 1973, 197–237, pp. 201–2, 228, 233.

11 Wolf, 'Mexican Bajío', 177–200.

12 John M. Tutino, 'Life and Labor on North Mexican Haciendas: The Querétaro–San Luis Potosí Region, 1775–1810', in Elsa Cecilia Frost, Michael C. Meyer and Josefina Zoraída Vázquez (eds.), *El trabajo y los trabajadores en la historia de México* (Mexico and Arizona 1979), pp. 339–78, pp. 341–43. A relatively dense and increasing population became 'ever more closely tied to the larger colonial society through the regular movement of goods and persons'.

13 Jan Bazant, *Cinco haciendas mexicanas. Tres siglos de vida rural en San Luis Potosí* (Mexico 1976), pp. 95–103. Guanajuato haciendas were generally much smaller than those in San Luis Potosí, approximately one-third of the average size.

14 Ramón Serrera Contreras, *Guadalajara ganadera. Estudio regional novo-hispano, 1750–1805* (Seville 1977), pp. 107, 217–24, 319–20.

15 Van Young, *Hacienda and Market*, pp. 67, 88, and the same author's, 'Hinterland y Mercado Urbano: el caso de Guadalajara y su Región', *Revista Jalisco*, I, no. 2 (julio–sept. 1980), 73–95, p. 76. For Guadalajara, see also Richard Lindley, *Haciendas and Economic Development – Guadalajara, Mexico, at Independence* (Austin 1983).

16 Brading, 'Estructura', 199.

17 Morin, *Michoacán*, pp. 24–32, 284–87.

18 José Díaz and Ramón Rodríguez, *El movimiento cristero. Sociedad y conflicto en los Altos de Jalisco* (Mexico 1979), see the introductory study by Andrés Fabregas, 'Los Altos de Jalisco: características generales', pp. 11–67, see pp. 14–18, where three subregions are identified according to rainfall patterns.

19 Van Young, *Hacienda and Market*, pp. 64–6.

20 Brading, *Haciendas and ranchos*, pp. 171–2, 198–200; Brading 'Estructura', 230–6; Morin, *Michoacán*, p. 288; Bazant, *Cinco haciendas*, 110–11, 167; Tutino, 'Life and labor', 341–3, 371–7.

21 Van Young, *Hacienda and Market*, pp. 109–10. Brading, 'Estructura', 199–203.

22 Brading, 'Estructura', 233–5.

23  Tutino, 'Life and Labor', 376–8.

24  Van Young, *Hacienda and Market*, pp. 176–80, 192–7, 207, 211, 213, 219, 274–84, 356.

25  *Ibid.*, 266–69, 344–50, 353–4, where it is also argued that no authentic relationship should be assumed between hardship and insurgency support.

26  Tutino, 'Life and Labor', 341, 374.

27  Super, *Querétaro*, pp. 22, 33–6.

28  Morin, *Michoacán*, pp. 250–3.

29  James D. Riley, 'Landlords, Laborers and Royal Government: The Administration of Labor in Tlaxcala, 1680–1750', in Frost, Meyer, Vázquez, *El Trabajo*, 221–41, pp. 223–5. Population of the province remained approximately the same at c.60,000 (of which 55,000 were Indians) between 1742 and 1793.

30  Liehr, *Stadtrat*, pp. 8–12. In such districts as those of San Juan de los Llanos (now Libres), there was also a range of lesser tenants, such as *terrazgueros*, who paid either in part of their crop or by personal services. The Intendancy of Puebla in 1810 contained an estimated 811,285 inhabitants, of whom 602,871 were listed as Indians and 124,313 as mixed. See also Ward Barrett, *The Sugar Hacienda of the Marqueses del Valle* (Minnesota 1970), and Cheryl English Martin, 'Haciendas and Villages in late Colonial Morelos', *HAHR*, 62, no. 3 (Aug. 1982), 407–27.

31  Taylor, *Landlord and Peasant*, pp. 143–52, 162–3.

32  Hamnett, *Politics and Trade*, see chapters 2 and 3, and pp. 140–2. According to the legal assessor of the Intendancy of Puebla in 1800, district administrators put pressure on leading village personalities to provide their financial guarantees (*fianzas*) and threatened them with harassment if they refused. Archivo General de la Nación, Mexico City, (AGN), Intendentes 8, f. 467, asesor, Puebla 5 April 1800; f. 478, Manuel de Flon (Intendant) to Viceroy Berenguer de Marquina, no. 194, Puebla 3 December 1800.

33  Cook and Borah, *Essays in Population History*, II (California 1974), pp. 189–90, 206–7.

34  William B. Taylor, *Drinking, Homicide and Rebellion in Colonial Mexican Villages* (Stanford 1979), pp. 20, 26–7.

35  Cook and Borah, *Essays*, II, pp. 47–8, 54–8.

36  Sherburne F. Cook and Woodrow W. Borah, *The Population of the Mixteca Alta, 1520–1960*, Ibero-Americana 50 (California 1968), pp. 42–7. Taylor's study of the Valley estimates a rise in the population from 70,000 in 1740 to 110,000 in the 1790s. The population of Antequera de Oaxaca, increased to a peak of 19,653 in 1777 and 19,069 in 1793, only to slacken off thereafter until a recovery set in after the 1820s. Cook and Borah show a population increase for all races in the twenty-three parishes of the Mixteca Alta from 54,016 in 1742 to 75,990 in 1803, but again a slackening off to a figure of 64,549 in 1826. Cook and Borah, *Essays*, II, pp. 54–5. Taylor, *Landlord and Peasant*, pp. 18–19, 89–91, 96–97, where a connection is suggested between growing birthrate and increasing conflict between villages over land encroachment.

37  Charles Gibson, *The Aztecs under Spanish Rule: A History of the Indians of the Valley of Mexico, 1519–1810* (Stanford 1964), pp. 200–9, 210, 217–19. According to AGN Tributos 26, Royal Treasury Officials in Oaxaca estimated that in 1799 only 83,065 pesos 1 real had actually been collected out of total due from the province of 170,417 pesos 3 reales and 7 granos.

38  Cook and Borah, *Essays*, II, pp. 189, 206–7, 258, 266. Married men and their wives

were full tributaries; widows, widowers, and unmarried men and women above sixteen years were half-tributaries. Caciques and their eldest sons, senior village officials and their wives, the aged and infirm, children up to the age of fifteen inclusive, were exempt.

39 AGN Tributos 34, *Pardos Milicianos de la costa de Jicayán, Oaxaca*, 1792–93. The negroid element was described as landless and living in abject poverty in an area of considerable Indian landownership.

40 Woodrow W. Borah, 'Race and Class in Mexico', *Pacific Historical Review*, 23, iv (1954), 331–42. Taylor, *Drinking, Homicide and Rebellion*, pp. 2–3. Jean Piel, 'The Place of the Peasantry in the National Life of Peru in the Nineteenth Century', *Past and Present*, 46 (Feb. 1970), 108–33, see p. 108.

41 See, for example, Pablo González Casanova, *El misoneísmo y la modernidad cristiana en el siglo XVIII* (Mexico 1948), pp. 186–7. Bernabé Navarro, *Cultura mexicana moderna en el siglo XVIII* (Mexico 1964), pp. 37–8, 83. John Leddy Phelan, *The Millennial Kingdom of the Franciscans in the New World. A Study of the Writings of Gerónimo de Mendieta (1525–1604)* (California 1956), pp. 44–58, 74, 90, 111–12. Jacques Lafaye, *Quetzalcóatl and Guadalupe. The Formation of Mexican National Consciousness, 1531–1813* (Chicago 1976), pp. 60–8.

42 Rubén Vargas Ugarte, S. J., *Historia del culto de María en Iberoamérica y de sus imágenes y santuarios más celebrados*, 2 vols. (Madrid 1956), II, pp. 82–3, 116–17, 163, 177–91, 201–3, 233–51. Luis González y González, 'Ciudades y Villas del Bajío Colonial', *Relaciones. Estudios de Historia y Sociedad*, 4 (otoño de 1980), 100–11.

43 Irving Leonard, *Baroque Times in Old Mexico. Seventeenth-Century Persons, Places and Practices* (Ann Arbor 1959: 1966 edn), pp. 124–9, 200. Lafaye, *Quetzalcóatl and Guadalupe*, pp. 60–8. See John Leddy Phelan, 'Neo-Aztecism in the Eighteenth Century and the Genesis of Mexico Nationalism', in Stanley Diamond (ed.), *Culture in History. Essays in Honor of Paul Radin* (Columbia 1960), pp. 760–71. Vargas Ugarte, *Historia del culto de María*, II, pp. 203–4.

44 Navarro, *Cultura mexicana*, pp. 21–36, 42–3, 76, 95–101, 106, 121–2.

45 González Casanova, *El misoneísmo y la modernidad cristiana*, pp. 198–203. Navarro, *Cultura mexicana*, pp. 46–57, 60–1, 193–5. The remodelled Oratory of St Philip Neri in San Miguel el Grande (now de Allende) played a major role after 1770 in the dissemination of the new learning.

46 Victor Turner and Edith Turner, *Image and Pilgrimage in Christian Culture. Anthropological perspectives* (Oxford 1978), pp. 46–103. See pp. 64–5, 69, 77–9, 90, 101. The tiny image of Remedios, for instance, was taken from its sanctuary on the hill of Toltepec, near San Bartolo Naucalpan, into Mexico City for veneration some seventy-five times between 1576 and 1911, when calamity threatened. See also Francisco de la Maza, *El Guadalupanismo Mexicano* (Mexico 1953).

47 Lafaye, *Quetzalcóatl and Guadalupe*, pp. 29, 118, argues that *Guadalupanismo*, a counter-culture, grew in response to Bourbon attempts to reassert control in New Spain from the 1760s.

48 Hugh M. Hamill, *The Hidalgo Revolt. Prelude to Mexican Independence* (Gainesville 1966), pp. 113–14.

49 Luis Villoro, *El proceso ideológico de la revolución de independencia* (Mexico 1967), pp. 85–6, 121–2.

50 Taylor, *Drinking, Homicide and Rebellion*, pp. 124, 146, involving some 2,000 peasants: this 'might qualify as an uprising against colonial rule'.

51 See chapter three of this work for a discussion of rebellion.

52 Jesús Amaya, *Hidalgo en Jalisco* (Guadalajara 1954), pp. 74–6.

53 Alamán, *Historia de Mégico*, IV, p. 666 – 'a rising of the lower orders against property and civilization'. Zavala, Ensayo histórico, in *Obras* (Mexico 1969), p. 54. Francisco Bulnes, *La Guerra de Independencia: Hidalgo–Iturbide* (Mexico 1910, 1965 edn), pp. 171–80. Hamill, *Hidalgo Revolt* pp. 187, 191.

54 Alamán, *Historia de Mégico*, II, pp. 228–9. Villoro, *El proceso ideológico*, pp. 85–6, 92–4.

55 Doris M. Ladd, *The Mexican Nobility at Independence, 1780–1826* (Texas 1976), p. 114.

56 *Ibid.*, pp. 119–25. Timothy E. Anna, *The Fall of the Royal Government in Mexico City* (Nebraska 1978), pp. 35–63.

57 See José Miranda, *Las Ideas é Instituciones políticas mexicanas, 1521–1821*, II (Mexico 1952), pp. 304–10. Anna, *Fall of Royal Government*, pp. 35–63.

58 Super, *Querétaro*, pp. 153, 228, suggests that by the 1790s, the sharpest social distinction in the city of Querétaro was between *peninsulares* and American creoles, both an economic and political divide. Young creoles, particularly, had few opportunities for advancement.

59 Brian R. Hamnett, 'Mexico's Royalist Coalition: the Response to Revolution, 1808–1821', *Journal of Latin American Studies (JLAS)*, 12, no. 1 (May 1980), 55–86.

60 Christon I. Archer, 'The Royalist Army in New Spain: Civil–Military Relationships, 1810–1821', *JLAS*, 13, no. 1 (May 1981), 57–82, p. 65.

61 See Brian R. Hamnett, *Spanish Politics in the Revolutionary Era, 1790–1820* (in press, Fondo de Cultura Económica, Mexico), and Brian R. Hamnett, *Revolución y contrarrevolución en México y el Perú: Liberalismo, separatismo y realeza 1800–1824* (Mexico 1978), pp. 45–50.

62 Hamnett, *Revolución y contrarrevolución*, pp. 50–7, 203–8, 234–48. Ladd, *Mexican Nobility*, pp. 123–5. Anna, *Fall of Royal Government*, pp. 98–139.

63 For a comparative discussion, see chapter 2 of this present work.

64 In particular, Christon I. Archer, *The Army in Bourbon Mexico, 1760–1810* (Albuquerque 1977).

65 Christon I. Archer, 'The Officer Corps in New Spain: the Martial Career, 1759–1821', *Jahrbuch für Geschichte von Staat, Wirtschaft und Gesellschaft Lateinamerikas (JGSWGLA)*, Band 19 (1982), 137–58, pp. 140–2. See chapter five, section three, of this present work for a discussion of the problem of loss of political control in Guadalajara between September 1808 and September 1810.

66 *Ibid.*, 143–4.

67 Archer, 'The Royalist Army', 59. The total force was about 30,000 men by 1810, one-fifth of which were regulars. Archer, *Army*, pp. 110–11.

68 Archer, *Army*, pp. 61, 65, and 'Officer Corps', 145. Cook and Borah, *Essays*, II pp. 180–269, estimate the European immigrant component of the population of New Spain at 0.75 per cent of the total in the late eighteenth century. Europeans represented around 3 per cent of the total estimated 'white' component of the population, which itself composed up to 25 per cent of the full total. D. A. Brading, 'Los españoles en México hacia 1792', *Historia Mexicana*, XXIII, (1973), 126–44, pp. 130–2, 135, 137, estimates a total peninsular population of 9,236 individuals, with the bulk concentrated in Mexico City, the Bajío, the mining towns, and Antequera de Oaxaca.

## 1. Social tensions in the provinces

1 For this, there are a number of useful recent works, namely Doris M. Ladd, *The Mexican Nobility at Independence, 1780–1826* (Texas 1976) and Timothy E. Anna, *The Fall of the Royal Government in Mexico City* (Nebraska 1978). My own, *Revolución y Contrarrevolución en México y el Perú: Liberalismo, Separatismo y Realeza, 1800–1824* (Mexico 1978), attempts a comparative approach.

2 See Public Record Office (Kew), FO 50/27 and 34, for conflict in the Zacatecas, Bolaños and Real del Monte mining zones in 1826 and 1827.

3 Serrera, *Guadalajara ganadera*, 217–24, 264–8.

4 Morin, *Michoacán*, 173-4.

5 Archivo General de la Nación (Mexico City), AGN Civil 896, discussed in Mexico City 18 and 21 June 1804. See, also, Hamnett, *Politics and Trade*, pp. 36–55, and Horst Pietschmann, 'Der Repartimiento-Handel der Distriktsbeamten im Raum Puebla im 18. Jahrhundert', *Jarhbuch für Geschichte von Staat, Wirtschaft und Gesellschaft Lateinamerikas* (JGSWGLA), 10 (1973), 236–50.

6 See Linda Greenow, 'Spatial Dimensions of the Credit Market in Eighteenth-Century New Galicia', in David J. Robinson (ed.), *Social Fabric and Spatial Structures in Colonial Latin America* (Ann Arbor 1979).

7 Luis Pérez Verdía, *Historia particular del estado de Jalisco, desde los primeros tiempos de que hay noticia hasta nuestros días*, 3 vols. (Guadalajara 1910–11), I, pp. 1–5.

8 Serrera, *Guadalajara*, p. 57.

9 Jaime Olveda Legaspi, *Gordiano Guzmán: un cacique del siglo XIX* (Mexico 1980) pp. 15–18, gives the town population for the 1790s: 2,794 'Spaniards'; 1,676 mulattos; 1,385 'Indians'; 719 'miscellaneous castes'. The district population of Sayula was estimated at 47,360 (i.e. including Zacoalco as well) in 1793; Zapotlán at 21,092. José Menéndez Valdés, *Descripción y Censo General de la Intendencia de Guadalajara, 1789–1793* (Guadalajara 1980), pp. 133–61.

10 Olveda, *Gordiano Guzmán*, p. 19. The Liberal régime of the *Reforma* renamed Zapotlán on 19 April 1856 as Cuidad Guzmán in honour of Gordiano Guzmán, *cacique* of the south.

11 Van Young, *Hacienda and Market*, pp. 67, 79–81, 88, 284.

12 Archivo de Instrumentos Públicos, Guadalajara, (AIPG), Protocolos 2, notario: José Antonio Mallén, 1793–94: ff. 50–50v, Guadalajara 14 March 1794; ff. 190–191, Guadalajara 27 December 1794; ff. 22v–28, Guadalajara 17 February 1793. De la Madrid had been the first husband of Doña María Antonia's mother before she married Andrés López de Lara. Doña María's assets, included in the above, totalled 12,827 pesos. Etzatlán was located in the district of Ahualulco (population, 10,714 in 1793, Menéndez Valdés, *Descripción y censo*, 133–61). The district population of Bolaños came to only 5,676 inhabitants.

13 AIPG, Protocolos 3, Mallén, 1796: ff. 6v–8, Guadalajara 4 February 1796, for his will, the executor of which he named as the Guadalajara merchant Julián de Arrazola.

14 AIPG Protocolos 11, Mallén, 1811: Guadalajara 5 July 1811. Archivo Judicial de la Audiencia de Nueva Galicia (AJANG) (located in the Biblioteca Pública del Estado de Jalisco, Guadalajara), Civil 267-7-3646.

15 AIPG Protocolos 2, Mallén: ff. 53v–54, Guadalajara 6 March 1793; AIPG Protocolos 11, Mallén: 26 clause will, Guadalajara 5 July 1811.

16 AIPG Protocolos 2, Mallén: f. 58v, Guadalajara 4 April 1793 – José Martínez, resident and merchant of Sayula, resident also in the city of Guadalajara. AIPG Protocolos 11, Mallén: Guadalajara 17 July 1811 – Isidro de la Fuente, resident of both Sayula and Guadalajara.

17 AIPG, Protocolos 3, Mallén, 1796: f. 36, Guadalajara 28 April 1796 – Juan Vigil (B. Gijón, Asturias, Spain), resident and merchant of both the Real del Roasrio and the city of Guadalajara.

18 AGN Civil 1947, *documentos sobre la práctica que deben observar las tiendas de pulperías con las prendas empeñadas, 1765–1790*, including regulations on the subject in the *Bando* of Viceroy Revillagigedo, 19 January 1790 which dealt with the use of *tlacos* and *señales*. Morin, *Michoacán*, pp. 160–6. Antonio Carrión, *Historia de la ciudad de Puebla de los Angeles*, 2 vols. (Puebla 1896–7, 1970 edn.), p. 326.

19 Archivo Histórico Municipal de Guadalajara (AHMG) Paquete 16 (1798), no. 16, total area of 22 *sitios* and 16 *caballerías*, see Alejo de la Cueva to Dr J. M. Gómez y Villaseñor, Zapotlán 21 January 1798.

20 Archivo Judicial de la Audiencia de Nueva Galicia (Biblioteca Pública del Estado) (AJANG), Civil 127–1–1360, no. 583, Guadalajara 1777–94. See also Richard B. Lindley, *Haciendas and Economic Development. Guadalajara, Mexico, at Independence* (Texas 1983), p. 32.

21 AHMG Paquete 26 (1812), no. 6, Agustín de Echaurri supplied 3,100 fanegas at 16 reales on 1 April 1812. Felipe and Francisco de Echaurri performed a similar function in 1823, and José María de Echaurri was one of the two commissioners of the granary in that year. AHMG 55, Caja no. 1137, no. 61, Guadalajara 8 June 1823, and nos. 71 and 72.

22 For the Porres Baranda succession, see AIPG Protocolos 3, Mallén, f. 22, Guadalajara 17 March 1796.

23 AJANG 216–24–2746.

24 AJANG 212–7–2677. AJANG 228–13–2975.

25 AJANG 231–1–3008.

26 AJANG 253–12–3388, indios principales del barrio de Santa Cruz (Tonalá) en los autos con los indios de aquel pueblo sobre varias pensiones que quieren imponerles.

27 José Ramírez Flores, *El gobierno insurgente en Guadalajara, 1810–11* (Guadalajara 1980, 2nd edn, 1st edn 1969), pp. 159–66. Ramón de Murua also had commercial interests in Colima, probably in the cotton trade, AIPG, Protocolos, 11, Mallén, Guadalajara, 29 October 1811.

28 Mallén, 159–66.

29 See Robert A. Potash, *El Banco de Avío de México. El fomento de la industria, 1821–46* (Mexico 1959), pp. 17–25. Jan Bazant, 'Evolución de la industria textil poblana', *Historia Mexicana*, 52, XIII, no. 4 (Apr.–June 1964), 473–516.

30 Archivo General de Indias (Seville), AGI Mexico 1739, cuaderno 13, superior órden, Viceroy Martín de Mayorga, Mexico 20 March 1781. AGI Mexico 3170, Consulado of Veracruz, no. 288, Veracruz 22 July 1806. AGI Indiferente General 2438, Villa de Carrión del Valle de Atlixco, sala capitular, 24 January 1794. AGN Industria y Comercio 20, exp. 5, ayuntamiento to Charles IV, Puebla 3 September 1798.

31 Cuautla became part of the Intendancy of Mexico in 1793.

32 See Hamnett, *Politics and Trade*, chapters 4, 5, 6, and the unpublished dissertation (Cambridge 1981) of T. J. Cassidy, 'Haciendas and Ranchos in Nineteenth-Century Oaxaca', 109–19, 125–6, 136.

33 AGN Virreyes 273, ff. 255–263v, Venadito to Minister of War, no. 761, Mexico 31 December 1818. Instituto Nacional de Antropología e Historia (Mexico City), Microfilm Collection of Provincial Archives: Zacatecas, Roll 7, Documentos del H. Ayuntamiento de Sombrerete: H. L. Heldt, *Historical Sketch of the Sombrerete Mines* (Sombrerete 1911), pp. 29–33. H. G. Ward, *Mexico in 1827*, 2 vols. (London 1828), I, pp. 362–71, 401. Luis de la Rosa, *Observaciones sobre varios asuntos concernientes a la administración pública del estado de Zacatecas* (Baltimore 1851).

34 See Potash, *Banco de Avío*, pp. 17–25, and Bazant, 'Evolución', *HM, passim*. In some villages, weavers accounted for more than 75% of the artisans: this was the case with the Tlaxcala villages of Santa María Nativitas, Santa Ana Chiautempan, and San Pablo Apetatitlán. See Wolfgang Trautmann, *Las transformaciones en el paisaje cultural de Tlaxcala durante la época colonial* (Wiesbaden 1981), p. 102.

35 Manuel Carrera Stampa, *Los gremios mexicanos. La organización gremial en Nueva España, 1521–1821* (Mexico 1954), pp. 51–3, 142–55, 193–4, 224–31, 261–5.

36 Reinhard Liehr, *Stadtrat und Städtische Oberschicht von Puebla am Ende der Kolonialzeit (1787–1810)* (Wiesbaden 1971), pp. 17–23, in Puebla in 1802 there were only thirteen guilds, which observed elections in accordance with their ordinances. For the broad range of economic activities see Hugo Leicht, *Las Calles de Puebla* (Puebla 1934), pp. 349–50, 385.

37 Potash, *Banco de Avío*, p. 23, 'the fact that mercantile capital organized production and distribution of primary materials and finished product, modifies fundamentally the fact that the characteristic unit of production was the small artisan workshop run by its owner'.

38 Carrera Stampa, *Gremios*, pp. 201–2, 265–6, 280, 286. For earlier *obrajes*, see Leicht, *Las Calles de Puebla*, pp. 16, 278–9, 369.

39 *Legislación del trabajo en los siglos XVI, XVII y XVIII* (Mexico 1938), pp. 111, 151.

40 Liehr, *Stadtrat und Städtische Oberschicht*, pp. 18, 120–3.

41 Archivo del Ayuntamiento de Puebla (AAP), *Expedientes sobre Gremios y oficios* (1744–1802), T. 234, f. 174.

42 AAP *Expedientes sobre Panaderías*, T. 231, ff. 248, 253–267, 8 January – 9 March 1843. AAP *Expedientes sobre Gremios de Artesanos* (1732–1804), T. 223, f. 231 (1803–06), f. 105 (1809). The *Gremio de tejedores e hilanderas de algodón* mentioned in 1803, did not appear amongst those in 1743, but was included as '*maestros de Gremio de tejer algodón*' in 1773, in AAP, *Expedientes sobre Gremios y oficios* (1744–1802), T. 234, f. 214; f. 220, lists forty-five members of the *Gremio de Tejedores de lo Angosto*, 7 October 1773.

43 AAP *Expedientes sobre obrajes y talleres* (1621–1809), T. 224, f. 226.

44 *Ibid.*, T. 224, ff. 234–235, *síndico personero del común*, Puebla 1 August 1807.

45 AGN Alcabalas 37, Rafael Mangino to Juan Navarro, Puebla 24 March 1793. Liehr, *Stadtrat und Städtische Oberschicht*, 21, the majority of the Puebla population worked in the textile trade, with possibly some 20,000 persons involved, as well as domestically employed female spinners.

46 AGN Alcabalas 37, Rafael Mangino to Agustín Pérez Quijano, Puebla 24 June 1793.

47 AAP *Expedientes sobre gremios y oficios* (1744–1802), T. 234, L. 2699, ff. 269–270v, Manuel José Herrera, *escribano*, Puebla 6 May 1803; f. 274v, *veedores*, Puebla 11 May 1803.

48 Archivo General de Tlaxcala (AGT), Instituto Nacional de Antropología e Historia, (INAH), Mexico City, Microfilm Collection. Rollo 9, no. 369, no. 18, *ordenanzas*

*del gremio de tejedores de algodón* (1744), sala capitular, Tlaxcala 28 February 1744; fiscal, Mexico 24 May 1844; Fuenclara, Mexico 29 May 1744.

49 *Ibid.*, no. 372, no. 1, *El gremio de tejedores se queja contra los alcaldes y veedores de aquel por falta de cumplimiento de sus obligaciones* (1746).

50 *Ibid.*, INAH, Rollo 30, no. 67, *fiscal de lo civil* (Alva), Mexico 14 April 1790; escrito de la fiel ejecutoria, Tlaxcala 6 August 1790; fiscal, Mexico 1, 20, 28 October 1790; Revillagigedo, Mexico 13 November 1790; Iturrigaray to Col Manuel Baamonde, Mexico 27 February 1806; Baamonde to Iturrigaray, Tlaxcala 20 May 1806. At the end of the eighteenth century, artisans constituted 58% of the population of the city of Tlaxcala, which in 1793 contained 42,878 inhabitants. Among the artisans, weavers formed more than 60% of the total. Some 40% of all 'Spaniards' were artisans and more than half the castizos and mestizos. Trautmann, *Las transforma-ciones*, pp. 78, 101–3.

51 AGN Alcabalas 37, no. 116, *Estado que manifiesta los obrajes y telares* . . . , Mexico 17 October 1801.

52 INAH, Rollo 30, no. 88, no. 7, Chiautempan 12 March 1794.

53 AGT INAH, Rollo 30, no. 79, no. 50, asesor Lic. Nicolás Micleses Altamirano, Tlaxcala 16 July 1793; Francisco de Lisa, Tlaxcala 16 July 1793.

54 See for instance, AAP *Expedientes sobre servicio militar*, 1810–11, L. 1288, ff. 240–256, Puebla 21 June 1811, and AAP *LC* 81 (1812), ff. 79–83, Puebla 18 April 1812.

55 AMG Paquete 11 (1790–91), leg. 5, ordenanzas para panaderías. AMG Paquete 17 (1799–1800), leg. 5, informe del juez de gremios (1803); leg. 16, gremios de Tonalá (1799). AMG Paquete 24, leg. 78, el gremio de silleros al presidente y vocales de la junta de policía: sobre estar a las disposiciones del superior gobierno 120 individuos, Guadalajara 26 September 1810. AMG Paquete 30 (1815), legs. 158–164, guild examinations for master-shoemaker and master-tailor, and legs. 156–157, election of *alcaldes* of the chandlers' and saddlemakers' guilds. AMG Paquete 31 (1817), legs. 44–50, elections for ten guild *alcaldes*, one for each guild.

56 Enrique Florescano and Isabel Gil Sánchez (eds.), *Descripciones económicas regionales de Nueva España: Provincias del Centro, Sudeste y Sur, 1766–1827* (DERNE) (Mexico 1976), pp. 121, 131. There were no *obrajes* in Guadalajara in the late colonial period. Serrera, *Guadalajara*, pp. 58–9.

57 AMG Paquete 21 (1807), legs. 54 and 57, Guadalajara 9 July and 20 August 1807.

58 *Ibid.*, leg. 60, Guadalajara 2 April 1807.

59 AMG Paquete 23 (1809), leg. 4, ff. 3–4, Guadalajara 8 May 1809; ff. 27–38, *apoderados* to ayuntamiento, Guadalajara 12 February 1810; ff. 39–44, *síndicos procuradores generales*, Guadalajara 26 August 1811; ff. 59v–63, *síndicos procuradores generales*, Guadalajara 20 April 1818; f. 63, *alcalde del gremio*, Guadalajara 3 February 1819.

60 AMG Paquete 17 (1799–1800), leg. 16, ff. 4–10, *oidor fiscal*, Guadalajara 31 March 1800.

61 AMG Paquete 31 (1817), no. 167, José Lorenzo Peredo, alcalde de gremio de zapateros. AMG Paquete 32 (1818), exp. 56, los oficiales de zapateros, sent by Cruz to the Guild Inspectors, Guadalajara 17 August 1818.

62 AMG Paquete 32 (1818), exp. 56, ff. 17–18v, José Gutiérrez, Hilario Flores, Pablo Barba, and Nepomuceno Núñez, received by Cruz, Guadalajara 16 September 1818.

63 *Ibid.*, ff. 19–22, Arias and Andrade, sent by Cruz to *asesor* Guadalajara 1 October 1818.

64 *Ibid.*, ff. 24–26, síndicos procuradores generales, Manuel García Sancho and Lic. Jesús Moreno, Guadalajara 14 December 1818.

65 *Ibid.*, exp. 108, no date (1818).

## 2. Insurgency – characteristics and responses

1 Studies of rebellions include Roland Mousnier, *Fureurs paysannes: Les Paysans dans les révoltes du XVIIe siècle* (Paris 1968); Guy Fourquin, *Les Soulèvements populaires au Moyen Age* (Paris 1972); Antonio Domínguez Ortiz, *Alteraciones andaluzas* (Madrid 1973); Perez Zagorin, *Rebels and Rulers, 1500–1660*, 2 vols. (Cambridge 1982), 1, pp. 175–274.

2 Chalmers Johnson, *Revolutionary Change* (London 1968), pp. 5, 139, referring specifically to the form of change that occurred in France in 1789, Russia in 1917, and China in 1949. See also Perez Zagorin, *Rebels and Rulers*, 1, pp. 3–27.

3 David Galula, *Counter-Insurgency Warfare. Theory and Practice* (New York 1964: third edn 1966), pp. 4–14. For a controversial view, see Ernesto 'Che' Guevara, *Guerrilla Warfare* (New York 1968), where two propositions are put forward: that insurrection itself can create the conditions of revolution; that 'in underdeveloped America the countryside is the basic area for armed fighting'.

4 Richard Clutterbuck, *Guerrillas and Terrorists* (London 1977), p. 33.

5 An exception is John Ellis, *A Short History of Guerrilla Warfare* (London 1975).

6 An attempt to compare and contrast twentieth-century movements that included studies of the Mexican and Cuban Revolutions, was made by E. R. Wolf, *Peasant Wars of the Twentieth Century* (London 1969). For the first Nicaraguan insurgency (1926–33), see Neill Macaulay, *The Sandino Affair, 1928–33* (Texas, 1964), and for the second (1977–79), see for instance, George Black, *Triumph of the People. The Sandinista Revolution in Nicaragua* (London 1981), pp. 100–81. For El Salvador, see James Dunkerley, *The Long War. Dictatorship and Revolution in El Salvador* (London 1982), pp. 132–205.

7 Leon G. Campbell, *The Military and Society in Colonial Peru, 1750–1810* (Philadelphia 1978), and the same author's 'Recent Research on Andean Peasant Revolts, 1750–1820', *Latin American Research Review*, 14, no. 1 (1979), 3–49, and 'Social Structure of the Tupac Amaru Army in Cuzco, 1780–81', *HAHR*, 61, no. 4 (Nov. 1981), 654–93. J. R. Fisher, 'La rebelión de Tupac Amaru y el programa de la reforma imperial de Carlos III', *Anuario de Estudios Americanos*, 28, (1971), 405–21. Mario Castro Arenas, 'La rebelión de Juan Santos Atahualpa', *Cuadernos Americanos*, 199 (1975), 125–45. Scarlett O'Phelan Godoy, 'Elementos étnicos y de poder en el movimiento Tupacamarista, 1780–81', *Nova Americana*, 5, (1982), 79–101. Oscar Cornblit, 'Society and Mass Rebellion in Eighteenth-Century Peru and Bolivia', in Raymond Carr (ed.), *St Antony's Papers*, no. 22 (Oxford 1970), 9–44. Anthony McFarlane, 'Civil Disorders and Popular Protests in Late Colonial New Granada', *HAHR*, 64, no. 1 (Feb. 1984), 17–54.

8 See Charles W. Arnade, *The Emergence of the Republic of Bolivia* (Gainesville 1957), pp. 12–28.

9 Hugh M. Hamill, Jr, *The Hidalgo Revolt. Prelude to Mexican Independence* (Gainesville 1966).

10 Juan Uslar Pietri, *Historia de la rebelión popular de 1814. Contribución al estudio de la*

*historia de Venezuela* (Caracas 1962), Miguel Izad, *El Miedo a la Revolución. La Lucha por la libertad en Venezuela, (1777–1830)* (Madrid 1979), and Miguel Izard, 'Ni Cuartreros ni Montoneros, Llaneros', *Boletín Americanista*, 23, no. 31, (Barcelona 1981), 83–142.

11 Jorge Cornejo Bouroncle, *Pumacahua. La revolución del Cuzco de 1814. Estudio documentado* (Cuzco 1956). J. R. Fisher, 'Royalism, Regionalism, and Rebellion in Colonial Peru, 1808–1815', *HAHR*, 59, no. 1 (Feb 1979), 232–57. Hamnett, *Revolución y Contrarrevolución*, pp. 188–99.

12 José Santos Vargas, *Diario de un comandante de la independencia americana, 1814–25*, Gunnar Mendoza, ed. (Mexico 1982). See also John Lynch, *The Spanish American Revolutions, 1808–1825* (London 1973), pp. 118–19.

13 Osvaldo Díaz Díaz. *Los Almeydas. Episodios de la resistencia patriótica contra el ejército pacificador de Tierra Firme* (Bogotá 1962).

14 Gustavo Vergara Arias, *Montoneros y guerrillas en la etapa de la emancipación del Perú (1820–1825)* (Lima 1973). See also John Miller, *Memoirs of General Miller*, 2 vols. (London 1828).

15 See Émile de Kératry, *La Contre-Guérrille française au Mexique* (Paris 1869), pp. 5–6, 9–18, 24, 86, 92–4. J. F. Elton, *With the French in Mexico* (London 1867), pp. 76–80, 88–9, 109–10, 161–2, 175. Jack Autrey Dabbs, *The French Army in Mexico, 1861–1867* (The Hague 1963), pp. 99, 104–5, 235–6, 266–70, points to the repeated emergence of irregular bands in the Guerrero–Michoacán area even at the height of Imperial power in the winter of 1864–5. This zone, as we shall see in chapter seven had remained for a long time outside effective central control through the Independence period and for decades thereafter.

16 Paul J. Vanderwood, 'Response to Revolt: The Counter-Guerrilla Strategy of Porfirio Díaz', *HAHR*, 56, no. 4 (Nov. 1976), 551–9.

17 Galula, *Counter-Insurgency Warfare*, pp. 89–90.

18 Charles Tilly, *The Vendée* (Cambridge, Mass., 1964), p. 316. See also Jaime Torras Elías, *La guerra de los Agraviados* (Barcelona 1967), pp. 15, 27, 35–40, for Catalan rural discontent in 1827, in which the clergy were able to mobilise large sectors of the population at a time of peak wheat price rises.

19 See chapters three and seven of this work.

20 Tilly, *The Vendée*, pp. 317–19, 324, 327–8. By June 1793, the government had to send in some 30,000 troops, part of them veterans, against the rebels.

21 Galula, *Counter-Insurgency Warfare*, p. 32.

22 In French Indo-China, for instance, only 10,776 regular French troops, 16,218 Indo-Chinese militiamen, and 507 French policemen held down a Vietnamese territory with a population of 19 million inhabitants, before 1940. In contrast, by 1954, it was evident that seven years of warfare had exposed the failure of 140,000 Franco-African troops and 280,000 indigenous troops to retain control of North Vietnam. In Algeria, in 1954, at the time of the outbreak of the insurrection, there were only 50,000 policemen, a force scarcely larger than that of Paris, for a population of 10.5 million and a total area of 115,000 square miles or four times the size of France. See John J. McCuen, *The Art of Counter-Revolutionary War: The Strategy of Counter-Insurgency* (London 1966), pp. 121, and John T. McAlister, Jr, *Vietnam. The Origins of Revolution* (London 1969), p. 50.

23 Christon I. Archer, *The Army in Bourbon Mexico, 1760–1810* (New Mexico 1977), pp. 22–4, 35.

24 *Ibid.*, pp. 68, 108–10, 120–2.

25 *Ibid.*, pp. 93–101.

26 Colin M. MacLachlan, *Criminal Justice in Eighteenth-Century Mexico. A Study of the Tribunal of the Acordada* (California 1974), pp. 32–6.

27 For a study of such mediators, see E. R. Wolf, 'Aspects of Group Relations in a Complex Society: Mexico', *American Anthropologist*, 58, no. 6 (1956), 1065–78, pp. 1075–8, where in colonial Mexico, 'leaders of Indian corporate communities and royal officials' are included, and later, 'local entrepreneurs, such as the owners of haciendas'. In one sense, they provided the means by which population was incorporated into the broader political system, but in another sense, their position depended upon close control of the localities, which often resulted from village factional politics and ongoing vendettas between kinship networks.

28 See for a discussion of such issues, E. R. Wolf and Edward Hansen, 'Caudillo Politics: A Structural Analysis', *Comparative Studies in Society and History*, 9, no. 2 (1966–7), 168–79, where a salient feature is the armed patron-client network, bound by personal ties of dominance and submission, and by a common desire to obtain wealth and position by recourse to violence. For Indian authorities, see the discussion in Karen Spalding, 'The Colonial Indian: Past and Future Research Perspectives', *Latin American Research Review*, 7 (1972), 46–76.

29 See chapter seven.

30 An illustrative study is S. F. Scott, *The Response of the Royal Army to the French Revolution. The Role and Development of the Line Army, 1787–93* (Oxford 1978), see pp. 46–70.

31 See Hamill, *Hidalgo Revolt*, pp. 89–126.

32 Tulio Halperín Donghi, 'Revolutionary Militarization in Buenos Aires, 1806–1815', *Past and Present*, 40 (July 1968), 61, 92–6.

33 See Clutterbuck, *Guerrillas and Terrorists*, pp. 27–32, for a discussion of the rural–urban dichotomy in revolutionary thinking.

34 For discussion, see Barrington Moore, Jr, *Social Origins of Dictatorship and Democracy. Lord and Peasant in the Making of the Modern World* (London 1967), p. 215.

35 See chapter seven.

36 Sir Robert Thompson, *Defeating Communist Insurgency. Experiences from Malaya and Vietnam* (London 1967), p. 24. John Dunn, *Modern Revolutions: An Introduction to the Analysis of a Political Phenomenon* (Cambridge 1972), p. 129.

37 For studies of these problems, see Brian R. Hamnett, 'Anastasio Bustamante y la Guerra de Independencia, 1810–1821', *Historia Mexicana*, XXVIII, no. 4 (1979), 515–45, and the same author's 'Royalist Counter-insurgency and the Continuity of Rebellion: Guanajuato and Michoacán, 1813–20', *HAHR*, 62, no. 1 (Feb. 1982), 19–48.

38 Ellis, *Short History of Guerrilla Warfare*, pp. 80–2. Che Guevara, *Guerrilla Warfare*, p. 7, argues that guerrilla warfare 'is one of the initial phases of warfare and will develop continuously until the guerrilla army in its steady growth acquires the characteristics of a regular army ... Triumph will always be the product of a regular army, even though its origins are in a guerrilla army.'

39 A first-hand reaction to Spanish partisan warfare is M. de Rocca, *Mémoires sur la Guerre des Français en Espagne* (London 1815). José María Iribárren, *Espoz y Mina. El Guerrillero* (Madrid 1965). José Luis Comellas, *Los Realistas en el Trienio constitucional* (Pamplona 1958).

40 Douglas Dakin, *The Greek Struggle for Independence, 1821–1833* (California 1973), pp. 58–60, 66–7, 91, 124–37. D. A. Zakythinos, *The Making of Modern Greece. From Byzantium to Independence* (Oxford 1976), 70–87.

41 The concept of parallel hierarchies has given rise to much discussion. The Greek

insurgents of 1946–50, for instance, ultimately failed to seize control of a major town in which rebel government authority could be established, and took a fatal decision to turn to full scale warfare at the wrong time and place. See C. M. Woodhouse, *The Struggle for Greece, 1941–1949* (London 1976), pp. 212–21, 243, 257, 276–7. In contrast, the Chinese Communists by 1945 controlled 350,000 sq. miles of national territory and a population of 95 millions. Their regular army came to 900,000 men and their militia force to 2.4 million. Galula, *Counter-Insurgency Warfare*, p. 35.

42 A point developed by McAlister, *Vietnam*, p. 12.

43 See Woodhouse, *The Struggle for Greece*, p. 163, on the Greek klephts and the surviving tradition. Ellis, *Short History of Guerrilla Warfare*, pp. 83–4, shows that Garibaldi's movement in 1860, could count on the assistance of South Italian brigand bands, which the regular army had subsequently to suppress.

44 MacLachlan, *Criminal Justice*, pp. 50–5.

45 Archer, *Army*, 91–2.

46 AGN Civil 1418, exp. 15, ff. 201–202v., Flon to Viceroy Flores, no. 23, Puebla 25 August 1787.

47 British Museum, Egerton Manuscripts, vol. 1801, ff. 128–129v, Felipe Díaz de Ortega, Valladolid l August 1792; f. 130, no. 3, Díaz de Ortega, 4 October 1972; f. 131, no. 4, Diaz de Ortega, 11 October 1792; f. 132, no. 5, Díaz de Ortega, 11 October 1792; f. 134, no. 7, Manuel Gómez Carrasco to Díaz de Ortega, Valle de Santiago 26 October 1792.

48 Luis González y González, *Pueblo en vilo. Microhistoria de San José de Gracia* (Mexico 1968), p. 69. William B. Taylor, 'Sacarse de Pobre. El Bandolerismo en la Nueva Galicia, 1794–1821', *Revista Jalisco*, (Jan.–June 1981), no. 1–2, vol. II, 34–45.

49 British Museum, Eg. 1801, ff. 152–161 v, Bruno Díaz de Salcedo to Revilla-gigedo, San Luis Potosí 4 December 1792.

50 AGI Estado 43, Juan Cruz Ruiz de Cabañas, Bishop of Guadalajara, to Príncipe de la Paz, no. 30, Villa del Sacramento to Ojocaliente 20 October 1797. AGI Guadalajara, 543, Ruiz de Cabañas to Crown, Guadalajara 17 January 1805.

51 Van Young, *Hacienda and Market*, pp. 266, 269.

52 AGI Mexico 1885, Flon to Pedro de Acuña, no. 2, Puebla 1 February 1793.

53 AGI Indiferente General 2438, Cabildo, Justicia y Regimiento de la Villa de Atlixco, 24 January 1794, at the request of the *cuerpo de labradores*.

54 AAP *Libros de Cabildo* 83 (1814), Díaz de Ortega to Ayuntamiento, Puebla 25 April 1814. This official was the son of Felipe Díaz de Ortega, lately Intendant of Michoacán.

55 AAP *LC*, 92/1 (Jan.–June 1823), ff. 218–220, Vivanco to Ayuntamiento, Puebla 6 March 1823. Cf. AMG, Caja no. 1129, paquetes 9 and 10, and Caja no. 1140, paquetes 85 and 87 on night patrols in 1825.

56 AAP *LC*, 92/2 (July–Dec. 1823), f. 562, circular of *jefe superior político interino*, Puebla 21 November 1823.

57 See E. J. Hobsbawm, *Bandits* (Harmondsworth 1969), a study which, in effect, opened contemporary discussion of the problem.

58 Paul J. Vanderwood, *Disorder and Progress. Bandits, Police and Mexican Development* (Nebraska 1981), pp. 6, 16–17, and the same writer's 'Genesis of the Rurales; Mexico's Early Struggle for Public Security', *HAHR*, 50, no. 2 (May 1970), 323–44.

59 Waddy Thompson, *Recollections of Mexico* (New York 1846), p. 24, draws attention to the gentlemanly leadership of a bandit group in the Puebla region in the 1840s.

60 Anton Blok, *The Mafia of a Sicilian Village, 1860–1960* (Oxford 1974), p. 190, several landowners came to terms with bandit groups and employed them as private guards on their estates in the post-war years after 1943.

61 Hobsbawm, *Bandits*.

62 See Anton Blok, 'The Peasant and the Brigand: Social Banditry Reconsidered', *Comparative Studies in Society and History*, 14, no 4 (Oct. 1972), 494–503, pp. 496–7, 499–500. Blok argues that bands tended to obstruct efforts to mobilise peasants into revolutionary movements.

63 Hamnett, 'Counter-Insurgency', 46–7.

64 Christon I. Archer, 'Banditry and Revolution in New Spain, 1790–1821', *Bibliotheca Americana*, 1:2 (Nov. 1982), 59–89, p. 81. See also complaints made to Morelos, AGN Operaciones de Guerra (OG), 917, Esteban Pérez and Pedro José de Mercado to Morelos, ff. 76–8v, Campo de Zimatepec 23 July 1811.

65 In the Puebla district of Tepejí, villagers showed hostility to the insurrection as a result of depredations by rebel troops, AGN OG 292, Llano to Venegas, ff. 334–334v, no. 53, Puebla 28 November 1812.

66 Ladd, *Nobility*, pp. 115, 260.

67 AGN OG 923. F. González de Cossío, *Xalapa. Breve reseña histórica* (Mexico 1957), p. 134.

68 AGN Historia 338, cuaderno 3, ff. 140–141v, Convoy Commander Col. Luis del Aguila to Viceroy Calleja, Jalapa 17 November 1814; ff. 258–259v, Aguila to Calleja, Jalapa 31 January 1815; ff. 260–261v, Calleja to Aguila, Mexico 9 February 1815; ff. 493–498v, Calleja to Brig. Francisco Miyares, Mexico 17 July 1815.

69 AGN OG 462[2], Ten. Cor. Francisco de Villaldea, commander of Royalist auxiliaries, Supreme Military Commander in Pachuca from 29 April, to Col. Bernardo de Villamil, Mexico 13 April 1814.

70 Archer, 'Banditry', 85–6.

71 Archivo de la Catedral de Puebla (ACP), *Libros de Cabildo*, 61, f. 12, 10 February 1824.

72 Discussed in Galula, *Counter-Insurgency Warfare*, p. 32.

73 McCuen, *Counter-Revolutionary War*, pp. 152–3, 196–205, where the French failure to control fully the countryside in the Red River and Mekong Delta after 1946 contributed substantially to their military defeat in the north in 1952. The political argument at that time was between wide dispersal of forces or concentration in specific zones.

74 McCuen, *Counter-Revolutionary War*, illustrates this argument from the Malayan and Algerian case.

75 *Ibid.*, pp. 212–14, which discussed the role of the Philippine Constabulary, organised in August 1901 to take over the task of defeating guerrilla bands from the regular army.

76 François Chevalier, *Land and Society in Colonial Mexico* (California 1966), 149–50, 169. See also, Max Moorhead, *The Presidio. Bastion of the Spanish Borderland* (Norman, Oklahoma, 1975).

77 AGN OG 186, *Reglamento político-militar* ..., 8 June 1811. AGN OG 201, ff. 370–1, *Reglamento político-militar*, Mexico 5 March 1813. AGN Virreyes 268A, Calleja to Minister of War, Mexico 15 March 1813. AGN OG 426, ff. 51–5v, Calleja to Iturbide, Mexico 27 April 1813; ff. 63–4, Iturbide to Calleja, Irapuato 28 May 1813. AGN OG 428, ff. 53–60, Iturbide, *Diario de Operaciones*, 8 November 1813.

78 AGN OG 431, ff. 112–16v, Iturbide to Calleja, no. 452, Irapuato 28 June 1815.

79 For the Spanish military's application of this policy in Cuba in 1896–98, see Philip S. Foner, *Antonio Maceo. The 'Bronze Titan' of Cuba's Struggle for Independence* (New York 1977), pp. 138–9, 226–51, 307–11. The brunt of the struggle fell upon the country people caught in the fighting.

80 There are many reports of these problems: see, for instance, AGN Historia 152, Viceroy Apodaca to Minister of War, ff. 111–16v, no. 1, Mexico 31 October 1816.

81 See Hamnett, 'Bustamante', 520–33. For twentieth-century instances of similar tactics, see McCuen, *Counter-Revolutiónary War*, pp. 119–21, and Woodhouse, *The Struggle for Greece*, pp. 238–9.

82 Christon I. Archer, 'The Royalist Army in New Spain: Civil–Military Relationships, 1810–1821', JLAS, 13, no. 1 (May 1981), 57–82, see pp. 65–82.

83 For general points, see Galula, *Counter-Insurgency Warfare*, pp. 89–90.

84 R. M. Johnston, *The Napoleonic Empire in Southern Italy and the Rise of the Secret Societies*, 2 vols. (New York 1973), pp. 32–51, 91–5, 102–5, 127–63.

85 Antonio Carrión, *Historia de la ciudad de Puebla de los Angeles*, 2 vols. (Mexico 1970), II, p. 106. By the end of August 1816, the total auxiliary armed forces (infantry, cavalry and artillery) came to 44,098 men. AGN Historia 485, *Ejército-organización Feb. 1818–1821*, f. 19, 'Estado que manifiesta la fuerza de los cuerpos y compañías sueltas de urbanos y Realistas fieles de todas las armas auxiliares del Exército de Nueva España', ... José Joaquín Peláez, Mexico 31 August 1816.

86 See Hamnett, 'Counter-insurgency', 33–4.

87 Jan Bazant, *Cinco haciendas mexicanas. Tres siglos de vida rural en San Luis Potosí* (Mexico 1975), p. 98.

88 François Chevalier, 'The North Mexican Hacienda: Eighteenth and Nineteenth century', in Archibald R. Lewis and Thomas R. McGann, *The New World Looks at its History* (Texas 1963), pp. 95–107.

89 AGN OG 712, Manuel de la Hoz to Venegas, ff. 140–141v, Cuautla 23 November 1810, and de la Hoz to Venegas, ff. 153–7, Cuautla 24 November 1810. The nine estates were Buenavista, Casasano, Guadalupe, Santa Inés, Calderón, Hospital, Mapaxtlán, Tenestepec, and Cuahuista. Large amounts of capital were invested in refining mills, as at Casasano, which was owned by the Mexico City merchant, Lieut Col. Lorenzo García Noriega. In 1814, he sold the estate to Antonio González Alonso, the Marqués de Santa Cruz de Inguanzo, for 250,000 pesos. AGN Civil 45, exp. 11, ff. 3–8.

90 AGN OG 285, Llano to Venegas, ff. 240–241v, Texcoco 21 October 1811; ff. 287–287v, Llano to Venegas, San Cristóbal Ecatepec 28 October 1811. AGN OG 286, Llano to Venegas, ff. 13–14, Apam 3 November 1811.

91 AGN OG 289, Llano to Venegas, ff. 158–159v, no. 43, Puebla 10 February 1812.

92 See chapter six and seven. Van Young, *Hacienda and Market*, pp. 335, points to the fielding of their own defence forces led by local *hacendados* in the Guadalajara region from the same group of estate labourers and retainers that were *supposed* to have provided a major component of Hidalgo's forces. We need to know, if this is the case, at what stage of the struggle it took place and why and whether such groups consisted of amnestied rebel bands reconstituted as 'field guards'. See Hamnett, 'Counter-insurgency', 46–7.

### 3. Conflict, protest and rebellion

1 Paul Friedrich, *Agrarian Revolt in a Mexican Village* (Chicago 1970: 1977 edn) , pp. 2–4, 43–47. See also Raymond Buve, 'Movimientos campesinos mexicanos: algunos apuntes e interrogantes sobre sus orígenes en la sociedad virreinal', *Anuario de Estudios Americanos*, 28 (1971), 423–57.

2 Taylor, *Landord and Peasant*, *passim*.

3 For a stimulating comparison, see James C. Scott, *The Moral Economy of the Peasant. Rebellion and Subsistence in Southeast Asia* (Yale 1976), pp. 193–5: 'there is good reason ... for holding that rebellion is one of the least likely consequences of exploitation'.

4 John Womack, *Zapata and the Mexican Revolution* (New York 1968), p. 144. In late May 1912, for instance, many rebel soldiers returned to their villages to plant during the rainy season. Robert P. Millon, *Zapata: the Ideology of a Peasant Revolutionary* (New York 1969: 1979 edn), Zapata's army regularly disintegrated at planting times. 'In order to feed the troops and the villages, the Army of the South regularly alternated its men between three-month periods of active service and of agricultural labours in the villages. The objective of this system was to maintain in the field a permanent army composed largely of peasants without at the same time disrupting the economic life of the peasant villages.'

5 Scott, *The Moral Economy of the Peasant*, p. 203. See also, Buve, 'Movimientos campesinos mexicanos', 17–18, 24, which argues that many peasant uprisings were explosions of native consciousness, since the loss of land involved not only agrarian conflict, but loss of group identity.

6 See John Leddy Phelan, *The People and the King. The Comunero Movement in New Granada, 1780–1781* (Wisconsin 1978); Scarlett O'Phelan Godoy, 'Elementos étnicos y de poder en el movimiento Tupacamarista, 1780–81', *Nova Americana*, 5 (1982), 79–101; and Anthony McFarlane, 'Civil Disorders and Popular Protests in Late Colonial New Granada', *HAHR* 64, no. 1 (Feb. 1984), 17–54.

7 According to Brading, *Merchants and Miners*, p. 8, 'it was the system of *repartimientos* rather than debt peonage which provoked unrest and riot'.

8 AGI Mexico 600, *expediente sobre el punto de reforma de los alcaldes mayores e inquietudes en Tehuantepec (1642–1678)*, consulta de la audiencia, Mexico 27 September 1660; oidor Montemayor de Cuenca to Viceroy Conde de Baños, Mexico 20 December 1660; Dr Alonso de Cuevas Dávalos (Bishop) to Crown, Oaxaca 12 March 1661; Montemayor to Crown, Oaxaca 25 March 1661.

9 Archer, *Bourbon Army*, pp. 94–8. Taylor, *Drinking, Homicide and Rebellion*, pp. 137, 149.

10 AGN Historia 338, camino militar de Perote a Veracruz, 1813–15. AGN OG 292, ff. 297–298v, Juan Valdés to Ciriaco de Llano, Real Fuerte de San Carlos de Perote 23 November 1812. AGN Historia 152, f. 211, Viceroy Apodaca to Minister of War, no. 28, Mexico April 1817.

11 AGN Civil 1649 (1800–1801), Captain Francisco Viana to Viceroy Berenguer de Marquina, Papantla 28 July 1801. Viana, captain of a schooner captured off Tuxpan by a British frigate, commented on the open trading along the coast by British ships with the full co-operation of local inhabitants. AGN Intendentes 80, exp. 10, *siembras clandestinas de tabaco en Papantla* (1797), ff. 182–182v, Antonio de Cárdenas (intendente interino) to Viceroy Branciforte, Veracruz 1 March 1797. AGN OG 273 (Brig. Ramón Díaz de Ortega, 1810–15), ff. 143–145, Capt. José Vidal de Villamil

(of the Papantla Patriot Company) to Viceroy Calleja, Tesiutlán 13 December 1813; ff. 149–149v, Capt. Juan Francisco de Ateaga (Cavalry Captain in Tesiutlán), Tesiutlán 16 April 1814. Vidal's father had spent thirty-one years in Papantla as a Militia Captain, thirteen as Postal Administrator, and five as Tobacco Monopoly Administrator.

12 Leticia Reina, *Las rebeliones campesinas en México (1819–1906)* (Mexico 1980), pp. 343–59. Acayucan: population (1806), 30,000, see Florescano and Gil Sánchez, *DERNE, Centro*, 97–9.

13 AGN OG 296, ff. 53–54v, Pablo Escandón to Llano, Puebla 17 November 1812; ff. 55–55v, Llano to Venegas, Puebla 20 January 1813.

14 Florescano and Gil Sánchez, *DERNE*, 63–5, Quirós, Veracruz 18 August 1814. Although labour shortages had pushed the daily wage from 2 reales to 4 reales in cotton zones such as Tlalixcoyán, the annual rent required of *colonos* on estates in Boca del Río, Alvarado and Antigua had risen from 4 pesos to 25 pesos p.a. since 1768.

15 Reina, *Rebeliones campesinas*, pp. 348–9, 358.

16 Florescano and Gil Sánchez, *DERNE*, 179–80.

17 Reina, *Rebeliones campesinas*, pp. 348–9, 358.

18 Archivo Judicial de Puebla, antiguo archivo de intendencia, corregimiento y alcaldía, ramo I (1623–1887), *INAH*, Roll 2, Independencia (1811–35), procesos a sospechos de insurgencia, Tlapa (1811), no. 1, Dr J. I. Berqueta, Puebla 28 November 1810; Juan José de Ortega y Chacón to Berqueta, Tlapa 25 January 1811.

19 Ernesto Lemoine Villicaña, *Morelos: su vida revolucionaria a través de sus escritos y de otros testimonios de la época* (Mexico 1965), p. 51.

20 Reina, *Rebeliones campesinas*, pp. 348–9, 358, sees the expansion of the haciendas as a cause of discontent. The issues were diversion of the water supply, prohibition of wood-cutting in the *montes*, and corporal punishment of offenders by hacienda employees. The rebellion of 1842–3 extended, just as the Morelos movement had done thirty years earlier, into Acatlán in southern Puebla and into eastern Oaxaca.

21 Taylor, *Drinking, Homicide and Rebellion*, pp. 124–5.

22 AGN Civil 215, exp. 3, ff. 1–12v, Joseph Andrade y Guevara to Juan Navarro (Director General de Alcabalas), Apan 24 February 1802. AGN Civil 184, ff. 20–24, Estéban González de Cosío to Viceroy Iturrigaray, Tulancingo 26 September 1807. AGN Virreyes 268c, ff. 380–386, Calleja to Campo Sagrado, no. 11 res, Mexico 6 September 1816.

23 AGN OG 462/2, Villaldea to Calleja, Pachuca 8 November 1813; Villaldea to Calleja, Pachuca 2 February 1814; Villaldea to Col Bernardo de Villamil, Mexico 13 April 1814; Villaldea to Calleja, Pachuca 11 May 1815. Reina, *Rebeliones campesinas*, pp. 61–82.

24 Tutino, 'Life and Labour', 341–3. Lino Gómez Canedo, *Sierra Gorda. Un típico enclave misional en el centro de México (Siglos XVII–XVIII)* (Pachuca 1976), pp. 6–8, 11. For the rebellions of 1847–9, 1854–5 and 1877 in the Sierra Gorda, see Reina, *Rebeliones campesinas*, pp. 291–304.

25 Taylor, *Drinking, Homicide and Rebellion*, pp. 115–16, 124, 146.

26 Guy Fourquin, *Les Soulèvements populaires au Moyen Age* (Paris 1972), pp. 36–7. See also the identification of the 'enemy' by a village community in the encroaching outside, in E. Le Roy Ladurie, *Montaillou, village occitan, de 1294 à 1324* (Paris 1975), pp. 34–44.

27  Riley, 'Landlords, Laborers', pp. 225–6, 228, 240.

28  Archivo General de Notarías (Puebla) (AGNP), leg. 238, años 1770–79, notaría 3, escribano Joseph de Castillo: Registro del año de 1777, ff. 48: Juan Domingo Capitán, Juan Bartholomé hijo de Cristóbal, Juan Antonio, Manuel de la Cruz hijo de Miguel Cristóbal, Miguel Antonio por mí y por mi padre Josef Moreno, Hermenegildo Dionisio por mi padre Santos de la Cruz, Josef de la Cruz, Juan de la Cruz, Mathias Josef, Antonio Paulino por mi padre Matheo Antonio, Felipe Santiago, Marcos Antonio, Francisco Javier por mi padre Miguel Gerónimo.

29  Archivo Judicial de Puebla (Cerro de Loreto, INAH), leg. for 1782, no. 2651. 30 April 1782, Los indios gañanes de la hacienda de Puchingo contra D. Miguel de Arroyo, su amo sobre liquidación de cuentas. The *gañanes* owed the estate the sum of $558, whereas the latter owned them the greater sum of $768.

30  AGI Mexico 1739, Audiencia to Crown, Mexico 23 July 1785, with 18 cuadernos. AGN Bandos 8, f. 72. AGN Bandos 13, ff. 344–347. According to Herbert J. Nickel, *Soziale Morphologie der Mexikanischen Hacienda* (Wiesbaden 1978), p. 183, the daily wage of the *gañanes* stood at 1.5 – 2 reales. According to Van Young, *Hacienda and Market*, p. 250, the wage in Guadalajara at the end of the eighteenth century stood at two reales per day.

31  Archivo Judicial de Puebla (INAH, Roll 68), *levantamiento de gañanes de la Hacienda Virreyes* (1779) and *Hacienda de San Miguel* (1780), San Juan de los Llanos. In this latter case the majordomo and his assistant were the focus of worker hostility.

32  AGI Mexico 1739, landowners of Tlaxcala and San Juan de los Llanos, 21 December 1785; cuad. 2 (1778), according to Felipe Santiago, spokesman for the *gañanes*, a *gañan* on the Hacienda de San Diego Tlachialoya (Tepeaca) received 4 pesos plus one fanega of maize (valued at 12 reales) for thirty days' labour (i.e. 5 pesos 4 reales), or 2 pesos less than *gañanes* elsewhere, who worked less days, and where the lowest salary was 7 pesos, 4 reales. See also Trautmann, *Tlaxcala*, pp. 85–6, 157–9. Tlaxcala estates suffered a notoriously low profitability and not infrequently made a loss.

33  AGN Civil 1418, exp. 15, sobre provisión de maizes en Puebla, ff. 208–209, *alcalde mayor* Lázaro Josef Figueroa Yáñez, Izúcar 10 May 1787; ff. 210–211, *fiscal*, Alva, Mexico 19 June 1787. AGN Tierras 1385, exp. 2 (1806). AGN Tierras 1404, exp. 6 (1809). There were four sugar refineries and three mills in Izúcar.

34  AGI Mexico 1739, *ibid.*, *consejo*, Madrid April 1778.

35  AGN Tierras 1296, exp. 6 (1798), *los indios gañanes radicados en la hacienda de San Miguel Villanueva sobre que allí se funde pueblo*, Sagarzurrieta, Mexico 31 August 1799; Viceroy Azanza, decree of 9 October 1799. This estate formed part of the *mayorazgo-vínculo* founded in 1613 by the grandson of Pedro de Villanueva, one of the *conquistadores*. Fifty-six families paid an annual rent of 200 pesos. The owners suggested the transportation of surplus population to California or the Provincias Internas, which needed settlers. Nickel, *Sociale Morphologie*, p. 37, the 1567 provision that each village had a right to 500 varas' circumference, had been extended in 1687–95 to 600–1,000 varas.

36  AGN Tierras 1366, exp. 3, ff. 119. Similar petitions recurred during the 1810s and 1820s, perhaps symptomatic of a trend that had not abated, in spite of the insurgency, e.g. *gañanes* of the Hacienda de Santa Lucía Nocemaluapan (Atlixco), 1820, AGN Tierras 1903, exp. 6.

37  AGN Tierras 1370, exp. 1 (1806), ff. 92–94, *fiscal protector* Robledo, Mexico 7 April 1807.

38  AGN Tierras 1404, exp. 19 (1809), ff. 2–3, Conde de la Cadena (Flon) to

Archbishop-Viceroy Lizana, no. 33, Puebla 2 September 1809; f. 7, Viceroy to Flon, Mexico 13 October 1809.

39 AGN Intendentes 73, Juan Antonio de Riaño to Viceroy, ff. 42–43v, Guanajuato 25 October 1809.

40 Archivo Histórico de Hacienda (AGN, Mexico City), (AHH) Comunidades indígenas, leg. 441, exp. 16, *incidente del expediente sobre alboroto de los indios de Xichú (Sierra Gorda)*, ff. 3–5, sent to the *fiscal de lo civil*, Mexico 7 April 1793; f. 7, *ibid.*, 8 April 1794; ff. 7–10 *fiscal de lo civil* (Alva), Mexico 14 April 1794; ff. 12–12v, Joseph Ignacio Machiel (Subdelegate) to Revillagigedo, San Luis de la Paz 7 May 1794; ff. 15–17v (1794–5), Governor of the three missions subject to the pueblo of San Juan Bautista de Xichú to Viceroy.

41 Brading, *Haciendas and Ranchos*, pp. 198–200.

42 AGN Tierras 1373, exp. 3, 1st expediente, ff. 68–70v, Septién to audiencia. San Luis de la Paz 7 July 1806; 2nd exped., f. 11, Pedro García Coana (owner of the Hacienda del Salitre), 27 June 1808, stated that incursions took place on 20 June 1808 on his rancho de la Simona; ff. 19–20v, José María López (owner of the Hacienda de Palmillas), Guanajuato 30 June 1808, stated that villagers had dispossessed his tenants; ff. 33–36v, Joaquín Pérez Gavilán for the Indians. Also affected was the Hacienda de Capulín, owned by the Mexico City councillor, Manuel de Luyando, who also owned the Hacienda de Jofré in San Miguel el Grande. Capulín formed part of the *mayorazgo de Guerrero*, AGN Tierras 1385, exp. 4 (1807).

43 AGN Tierras 1385, exp. 7 (1807), *expediente formado a pedimiento del común de naturales del pueblo de Mezquitic (San Luis Potosí)* 2nd. exp., f. 3, Mexico 27 Auguast 1807; ff. 8–9, 15–17, *fiscal protector* Robledo, Mexico 17 September 1807. AGN Tierras 1412, exp. no. 2, ff. 1–4v, Bachiller, Mexico 31 July 1808.

44 AGN Tierras 1412, exp. 4 (1813), los naturales del pueblo de San Miguel Mezquitic sobre poder eligir república y posesión de tierras (San Luis Potosí), ff. 1–5, *apoderado* of the *república* and *común* to viceroy, San Luis Potosí, 12 July 1813; ff. 14–18, Torres Torja, Mexico 8 March 1814. For the estates, see Jan Bazant, *Cinco haciendas mexicanas: tres siglos de vida rural en San Luis Potosí (1600–1910)* (Mexico 1975), pp. 16, 18, 41–2.

45 AGN Tierras 1408, exp. 3 (1810), 1st exp., ff. 1–7v, Subdelegate of San Felipe, 30 April 1810; alcalde de primer voto, 7 May 1810; f. 36, común de naturales, 10 May 1810; ff. 37–43, Real Provisión de la Audiencia to Intendant of Guanajuato (Juez Privativo de Tierras), Mexico 6 June 1810; 2nd exp., f. 3, apoderado del marqués, Mexico 16 June 1810; ff. 18–24v, apoderado, 24 May 1810; ff. 26–26v, audiencia 1 June 1808.

46 For estimates of population growth and relationship to available food supply, see Hérmes Tovar Pinzón, 'Insolencia, Tumulto e Invasiones de la Naturales de Zacoalco (México) a fines del siglo XVIII', *Cuadernos de Historia Social y Económica*, 10 (1985), 1–18, p. 7, where the total population of the five villages is placed at over 8,000 persons, who needed 3–4,000 hectares of land to feed themselves, but possessed under 1,000 hectares, including useless land.

47 AJANG 127–1–1360, cuaderno 9, *autos de D. Agustín de Echaurri contra los naturales de Zacoalco, 1777–81*; ff. 77–77v, Audiencia de Guadalajara 31 August 1780, on the statement by the Zacoalco legal representative. See also AJANG 128–1–1360.

48 AJANG 252–14–3370, ff. 2–3v, *fiscal protector de indios*, Guadalajara 27 August 1807; f. 5, Intendant Roque Abarca to *Regente* Antonio de Villaurrutia, Guadalajara 27 March 1810.

49 Tovar, 'Insolencia', 10–11.

50 AJANG 127–1–1360, no. 583, ff. 1–3v, Audiencia de Guadalajara 21 March 1791; ff. 33–41v, *Real Provisión*, Guadalajara 26 March 1791.

51 Tovar, 'Insolencia', 14–15.

52 Richard L. Garner, 'Problèmes d'une ville minière mexicaine à la fin de l'époque coloniale: Prix et salaires à Zacatecas (1760–1821)' *Cahiers des Amériques Latines*, 6 (1972), 75–112, p. 108.

53 Luis Chávez Orozco (ed.), *Conflicto de trabajo con los mineros de Real del Monte. Año de 1766* (Mexico 1960), pp. 12–21. Between 250 and 300 workers were involved in the demonstrations of 1766. The workers' petition to the royal financial officials of Pachuca on 28 July drew attention to declining receipts from mine labour. The original *partido* had not corresponded to the amount dug per man-shift. The workers had reluctantly agreed to a change: for each three sacks in the work-shift, the miner was entitled to one in *partido*: this had recently been altered to four, leaving the miner only the lowest quality ore.

54 Morin, *Michoacán*, p. 297.

55 Chávez Orozco (ed.), *Conflicto de trabajo*, pp. 205–11. Toribio Esquivel Obregón, *Biografía de D. Francisco Javier Gamboa. Ideario político y jurídico de Nueva España en el siglo XVIII* (Mexico 1941), p. 165.

56 See Archivo Histórico Guanajuatense (INAH, Rollo 9, alcaldía mayor, ramos de gobierno y civil, 1611–1792), Superior Gobierno (1766), no. 26, testimonio de los autos fechos sobre la conmoción acaecida en la Ciudad de Santa Fe, Real y Minas de Guanajuato por los operarios de ellas por la causa que se expresa.

57 Priestley, *Gálvez*, pp. 211–28, 232. Hamill, *Hidalgo Revolt*, pp. 90–2.

58 D. A. Brading, 'Government and Élite in Colonial Mexico', *HAHR*, 53, no. 3 (Aug. 1973), 389–414, pp. 391–2. D. A. Brading and Harry E. Cross, 'Colonial Silver Mining in Mexico and Peru', *HAHR*, 52, no. 4 (Nov. 1972), 549–79, p. 558.

59 Garner, 'Problèmes', 110–11.

60 See chapter 5, section one of this present work.

61 This was the case with the virtually accidental riot in Puebla in August 1744. See Eugenio Sarralbo Aguareles, 'Una conmoción popular en el México Virreinal del Siglo XVIII', *Anuario de Estudios Americanos*, 7 (1950), 125–61.

62 Cf. Torcuato di Tella, 'The Dangerous Classes', 82–5, 89–95.

## 4. Dearth and dislocation

1 Enrique Florescano, *Precios del maíz y crisis agrícolas en México, 1708–1810* (Mexico, 1969), pp. 46, 50–6, 92–4. Liehr, *Stadtrat und Städtische Oberschicht*, pp. 124–30, 44–52. Morin, *Michoacán*, pp. 156–7. Van Young, *Guadalajara*, pp. 75, 88–90. AAP *Libros de Cabildo*, 80 (1811), ff. 40–3, sala capitular to Venegas, Puebla 5 January 1811. For a comparable case, see Brooke Larsen, 'Rural Rhythms of Class Conflict in Eighteenth-Century Cochabamba', *HAHR* 60, no. 3 (Aug. 1980), 407–30.

2 See for broader discussion, Sherburne F. Cook, *Soil Erosion and Population in Central Mexico* (California, 1949), and *The Historical Demography and Ecology of the Teotlalpan* (California 1949). Gibson, *Aztecs*, pp. 307–17, refers to the declining soil fertility of the Valley of Mexico.

3 Humboldt, *Essai Politique*, III, pp. 11, 76.

4 For instance, AGN Consulados 3, ff. 1–16, Tehuacán (1805).

5 Van Young, *Hacienda and Market*, p. 68. Liehr, *Stadtrat und Städtische Oberschicht*, p. 13. John C. Super, 'Pan, alimentación y política en Querétaro en la última década del siglo XVIII', *HM*, 118, xxx, no. 2 (Oct.–Dec. 1980), 247–72.

6 AGN Civil 1418, exp. 8, el ayuntamiento de Guadalajara solicita dispensación de alcabalas para las harinas que introduce con destino a vender a los pobres al menudeo: f. 1, f. 4, Guadalajara 4 October 1780, 14 February 1786. AMG Paquete 22 (1808), leg. 2, remate del abasto de carnes (1808). AMG Paquete 23 (1809), legs. 4 and 5, libros formados sobre calicata del pan (1804–19). AMG Paquete 24 (1810), legs. 82, 82, 85, on city maize supplies; leg. 95, orden de Antonio Villaurrutia a los deueños de haciendas y administradores del distrito sobre envíen a la alhóndiga todo el sobrante de semilla que tengan, Guadalajara 3 November 1810. AAP *LC* 80 (1811), ff. 31–2. AAP *LC* 82 (1813), f. 34v, Puebla 12 February 1813: Lorenzo Muñoz, owner of the Hacienda de San Cristóbal in Huejotzingo, sold 1,000 cargas of top quality maize to the city commissioners at the rate of 7 pesos 6 reales per carga, and received from them the sum of 7,750 pesos.

7 Florescano, *Precios del Maíz*, pp. 150–2.

8 AMG Paquete 22, leg. 1, ff. 36, Guadalajara 29 March 1808; ff. 40–3, jueces de pósito, Guadalajara 2 May 1808; ff. 45–49v, cabildo, Guadalajara 9 May 1808.

9 AMG Paquete 24, leg. 53, José de Monasterio, Antonio Pacheco Calderón and Francisco Fernández to Abarca, sala capitular del ayuntamiento de Guadalajara 30 October 1810.

10 R. C. Cobb, *The Police and the People. French Popular Protest 1789–1820* (Oxford 1970), vol., XVII, pp. 249–84.

11 George Lefèbvre, *The Great Fear of 1789. Rural Panic in Revolutionary France* (London 1973: orig. publ. as *La Grande Peur de 1789*, Paris 1932), pp. 7–11.

12 *Ibid.*, pp. 25–32, 40–9, 89–90, 94–117, 142.

13 S. F. Scott, *The Response of the Royal Army to the French Revolution, The Role and Development of the Line Army, 1787–93* (Oxford 1978), pp. 46–70.

14 Humboldt, *Essai Politique*, III, p. 58.

15 Torcuato di Tella, 'The Dangerous Classes in Early Nineteenth-Century Mexico', *JLAS*, 5, no. 1 (May 1973), 79–105.

16 Lucio Marmolejo, *Efemérides guanajuatenses, o datos para formar la historia de la ciudad de Guanajuato*, 4 vols. (Guanajuato 1883–84), II, pp. 22–4.

17 D. A. Brading and Celia Wu, 'Population Growth and Crisis: León, 1720–1860', *JLAS*, 5, no. 1 (May 1973), 1–36, pp. 26–8, 32–4.

18 AGI Mexico 1506, Revillagigedo to Ensenada, no. 47, Mexico 27 November 1749.

19 AGI Mexico 1506, testimonio de los autos fechos a consulta del Col J. Escandón sobre lo acaecido en la ciudad de Querétaro con motivo de la escasez de maíz que se ha experimentado (1749).

20 Specific study of the 1785–6 dearth may be made from the data provided in Enrique Florescano (comp.), *Fuentes para la historia de la crísis agrícola de 1785–86*, 2 vols. (Mexico 1981).

21 AGN Civil 1817, exp. 7, ff. 15–16, justicia mayor to viceroy, Pachuca 1 October 1785.

22 AGN Civil 1646, exp. 6, ayuntamiento to viceroy, Sombrerete 4 December 1785; diputación de minería to viceroy, Sombrerete 5 December 1785; fiscal de real hacienda (Posada), Mexico 29 December 1785 and 23 February 1786.

23 Garner, 'Problèmes d'une ville minière', 78–80, 84–90, 87.

24 AGN Intendentes 59, exp. 4, ff. 18–19, Felipe Cleere (intendant) to viceroy, no. 57, 25 December 1789; ff. 20–1, subdelegate to intendant, Aguascalientes 15 December 1789; f. 24, Revillagigedo to subdelegate, Mexico 12 January 1790. Zacatecas suffered a smallpox epidemic in 1798 and 1799, AGN Intendentes 71.

25 AGN Civil 1817, exp. 4, ayuntamiento to viceroy, San Luis Potosí 20 September 1785; Alva (fiscal), Mexico 9 October 1785. AGN Civil 1465, exp. 10, cabildo to viceroy, San Luis Potosí 29 May 1786; Alva, Mexico 11 July 1786.

26 British Museum, Eg. 1801, ff. 152–161v, Intendant to viceroy, San Luis Potosí 4 December 1792. The flour price had fallen from between 12 and 24 pesos per carga to between 6 and 9 pesos.

27 Brading and Wu, 'Population Growth and Crisis', 24–5, 33–4. Florescano, *Precios del maíz*, p. 152, states that the Guanajuato mining zone consumed annually 350,000 fanegas of maize and 26,000 cargas of flour.

28 Marmolejo, *Efemérides guanajuatenses*, II, pp. 76, 279–83.

29 AGN Civil 1817, exp. 6, ff. 8–12v, diputación de minería to viceroy, Tlalpujahua 28 September 1785. See also AHMM Caja 163 (1809), IV (leg. 167), no. 22, José María Galán (tithe administrator) to subdelegate's lieutenant, Tlalpujahua 16 November 1809.

30 Van Young, *Hacienca and Market*, pp. 94–103.

31 AGN Civil 1465, instrucción completa que D. Manuel Calixto Cañedo . . . ministra hoy a su apoderado y procurador . . ., Hacienda del Cabezón 4 September 1787.

32 AGN Civil 1418, exp. 8, f. 4, ayuntamiento, Guadalajara 14 February 1786; ff. 71–2, *ibid.*, to viceroy, Guadalajara September 1786.

33 Van Young, *Hacienda and Market*, pp. 99–100. For the varying conditions within the valley of Mexico, see AGN Civil 1646, exp. 10, and AGN Civil 1708, exp. 1.

34 AGN Intendentes 59, ff. 105–11, Zempoala 17 February 1787.

35 AGN Civil 1817, exp. 12, consulta del gobernador de Colotlán sobre socorro de maizes para contener la despoblación que por su falta se empieza a experimentar en aquellos pueblos.

36 AGN Intendentes 59, f. 3, Flon to viceroy, no. 24, Puebla 22 July 1786; f. 6, Flon to viceroy, no. 11, Puebla 19 July 1786.

37 AGN Civil 1646, exp. 8, alcalde mayor to viceroy, San Sebastián Tlacotepec 20 December 1785; alcalde mayor to viceroy, Tehuacán 9 February 1786; alcalde mayor to viceroy, Mexico 8 March 1786; Alva, Mexico 22 March 1786; viceroy, Mexico 20 April 1786.

38 AGN Intendentes 59, f. 8, Flon to viceroy, no. 15, Puebla 8 July 1786; ff. 36–7, Flon to viceroy, no. 49, Puebla 30 September 1786; f. 47, Flan to viceroy, no. 59, Puebla 21 October 1786.

39 AGN Civil 1465, exp. 8, Alva, Mexico 30 March 1786 and 13 May 1786.

40 AGN Civil 1827, exp. 2, ff. 1–10, junta de ciudadanos to viceroy, sala capitular de Mexico 11 July 1786; Alva and Posada, Mexico 18 July 1786.

41 AGN Civil 1827, exp. 2, ff. 1–10, Valladolid 25 November 1785; ff. 12–15, Alva, Mexico 16 December 1785.

42 AGN Civil 1418, exp. 15, ff. 197–8, Padre Francisco del Corazón de Jesús to Flores, Puebla 18 August 1787; ff. 199–200, común de pobres to Flores, Puebla 18 August 1787; ff. 203–6v, Flon to Flores, Puebla 25 August 1787.

43 AGN Intendentes 59, exp. 4, ff. 11–15, José Gómez Campos (almacenero del comercio de México, Otero's apoderado) to Revillagigedo, undated, but discussed and signed by the latter, Mexico 13 November 1789.

44 Florescano, *Precios del maíz*, pp. 150–2.

45 AGN Intendentes 73, exp. 4, Riaño to Viceroy Lizana, no. 15 reservada, Guanajuato 25 August 1809.

46 Cobb, *The Police and the People*, p. 263.

47 AHML, Caja 1809 (Rollo 28, INAH), exp. 18. AHML, Caja 1809 (Rollo 29, INAH), ff. 4–6, Subdelegate José María Mazorra to Riaño, León 30 January 1809.

48 AGN Intendentes 73, Riaño to Viceroy Lizana, no. 17 res., Guanajuato 25 August 1809.

49 AGN Intendentes 73, ff. 69–70v, Domínguez to Lizana, Querétaro 2 September 1809; exp. 9, ff. 9–11, Domínguez to Lizano, Querétaro 19 September 1809.

50 AGI Mexico 1830, Viceroy Apodaca to Minister of Finance, no. 35, Mexico 30 November 1816, sending *expendientes* on the 'suma escaséz de maíz' experienced by the villages of San Pedro Tolimán (1809).

51 AGN Intendentes 73, Josef de Peón Valdés to Lizana, no. 29, Zacatecas 1 September 1809.

52 John C. Super, 'Querétaro Obrajes', *HAHR*, 56, no. 2 (May 1976), 213. See also Florescano, *Precios del maíz*, 153.

53 Christon I. Archer, *The Army in Bourbon Mexico, 1760–1810* (Albuquerque 1977), pp. 293–4.

54 AGN Intendentes 73, exp. 8, *sobre proveer de maiz a México (1809)*, ff. 1–3, Francisco Robledo to Lizana, Mexico 17 November 1809; ff. 5–11, Francisco Robledo to Lizana, Mexico 20 November 1809; ff. 16–18v, fiscal de lo civil Sagarzurrieta, Mexico 22 November 1809; exp. 9, ff. 8–9v, Cuernavaca 26 August 1809.

55 AGN Intendentes 73, exp. 7, ff. 11v–23, Sagarzurrieta, Mexico 6 September 1809; fiscal, *ibid*, 6 October 1809; exp. 9, f. 102, Cempoala 1 September 1809; ff. 92–3v, Real de Zimapan 31 August 1809 ff. 15–15v, Pachuca 26 August 1809; ff. 32–4, Huichapan 18 January 1809, 10 July 1809, 26 August 1809; f. 34, Ixmiquílpan 1 September 1809.

56 Florescano, *Precios del maíz*, App. 1, 201–27, p. 224.

57 AHMM Caja 164 (1810 no. 1), no. 10, diligencias reservadas que se han practicado en el juzgado de Zinapécuaro: Terán to subdelegate, Valladolid 22 December 1809. AGN Intendentes 73, *teniente letrado* to Lizana, no. 5622, Valladolid 28 August 1809, for food prices at the end of June 1809.

58 AHMM Caja 165 (1810 no. 2), no. 12, expediente promovido por los naturales . . . Terán to protector de naturales (*teniente letrado*), Valladolid 26 April 1810; *promotor fiscal*, Valladolid 30 April 1810; *protector de naturales*, Valladolid 16 May 1810; Huaniqueo villagers appear to have retained their 600 *varas*, according to British Museum, Eg. 1801, f. 270, estado de los pueblos . . . Valladolid 24 December 1793.

59 AHMM Caja 164, no. 15, los indios de Junganícuaro sobre que se les exima del tributo: Terán to subdelegate of Puruándiro, Valladolid 24 July 1810. Individual testimonies, 8–9 May 1810.

60 AGN Arzobispos y Obispos 11 (1729–1809), Campillo *et al.*, to Iturrigaray, Puebla 5 September 1807.

61 AAP *Libros de Cabildo*, 78 (1809), 12–13 October 1809.

62 AAP *Expedientes sobre alhóndigas* (1800–10), 113, L. 1213, ff. 186–7, *síndico personero del común*, Lic. Joaquín Estévez, Puebla, no date but located with 19 May 1810.

63 AAP *LC* 80 (1811), ff. 31–2, Venegas to ayuntamiento of Puebla, Mexico 12 January 1811; ff. 40–3, sala capitular to Venegas, Puebla 5 January 1811.

64 AAP *LC* 80, ff. 122–5, junta municipal to ayuntamiento, Puebla 6 March 1811. The administrator of the *abasto de carnes* was Juan José Olabarrieta.
65 Archer, *Army*, pp. 293–5.
66 AGN OG 94/2, ff. 36–9, Cadena to Venegas, Querétaro 5 October 1810; ff. 43–4v, Calleja to Cadena, San Luis Potosí 2 October 1810; ff. 81–2, Cadena to Calleja, Querétaro 9 October 1810; ff. 93–4, Cadena to Venegas, Querétaro 12 October 1810; ff. 116–117v Cadena to Venegas , Querétaro 13 October 1810; ff. 178–80, Cadena to Venegas, San Miguel 25 October 1810.

### 5. Insurrection – recruitment and extension

1 Genaro García, *Documentos históricos mexicanos*, I, pp. 467–71.
2 Bulnes, *Independencia*, pp. 124–25.
3 For Zacatecas, see Richard L. Garner, 'Reformas borbónicas y operaciones hacendarias. La real caja de Zacatecas', *Historia Mexicana*, 108, XXVII, no. 4, (April–June 1978), 542–87, pp. 542–8, 582–4. See also the same author's 'Problèmes d'une ville minière mexicaine à la fin de l'époque coloniale: prix et salaires à Zacatecas (1760–1821)', *Cahiers des Amériques Latines*, 6 (1972), 75–112, pp. 78–9. Ernesto de la Torre Villar, *La constitución de Apatzingán y los creadores del estado mexicano* (Mexico 1964), doc. 4, pp. 152–3. AIPG. Protocolos 11, *ibid* (1810–1811), Guadalajara 17 September 1810, 9 November 1815.
4 AGN OG 178, no. 4, ff. 17–19, Calleja to Venegas, Guadalajara 4 February 1811. AGN Minería 29, Tribunal to Venegas, Mexico 27 July 1811. AJANG 115–6–1233, civil (Zacatecas 1793).
5 Jesús Amaya, *Hidalgo en Jalisco* (Guadalajara 1954), p. 41.
6 AGN OG 179, ff. 103–103v, Calleja to Venegas, no. 68, Guadalajara 27 January 1811.
7 Amaya, *Hidalgo en Jalisco*, pp. 41–2.
8 *Ibid.*, pp. 190–2. Alejandro Villaseñor y Villaseñor, *Biografías de los héroes y caudillos de la independencia*, 2 vols. (Mexico 1910), I, pp. 111–14.
9 Alamán, *Historia de Méjico*, II, 250–251.
10 See, 'Revolución en San Luis Potosí formada por Fray Luis Herrera, lego de San Juan de Dios, la noche del 10 al 11 de noviembre de 1810', in *Archivos de Historia Potosina*, 42, XI, no. 2 (December 1979), 187–95.
11 José de J. Núñez y Domínguez, *La virreina mexicana, Doña María Francisca de la Gándara de Calleja* (Mexico, 1950), pp. 162–64.
12 Amaya, *Hidalgo en Jalisco*, pp. 190–2. Villasenor, *Biografías*, I, pp. 111–14.
13 Pérez Verdía, *Jalisco*, I, pp. 431, 447–53.
14 *Ibid.*, II, pp. 8–10, 33–6. Abarca, at this stage, took measures in conjunction with the municipality to assess the quantity of maize and other grains in the city, in face of the insurgent approach. Similarly, the Intendant and city council sought to raise men for the defence of the city and to guard against the transit of suspicious persons. AMG Paquete 24 (1810) legs. 53, 83, 85, 95, 96, 97.
15 José Ramírez Flores, *El gobierno insurgente en Guadalajara, 1810–1811* (Guadalajara 1980: 1st published 1969), pp. 25, 30, 37–9, 41–2.
16 *Ibid.*, pp. 12–13. Alamán, *Historia de Méjico*, II, pp. 251–2.
17 AGN OG 179, ff. 179–180, Vicente Velázquez de León to Calleja, no. 100, Guadalajara 3 February 1811.
18 See *Colección de acuerdos, órdenes y decretos sobre tierras, casas y sobres de los indígenas, bienes*

*de sus comunidades y fundos legales de los pueblos del estado de Jalisco*, Tome 2 (Guadalajara 1868), 5, no. 1.

19 Ramírez Flores, *El gobierno insurgente*, pp. 42–3; Pérez Verdía, *Jalisco*, pp. 38–42. The municipality on 20 November explained to Torres its practice in October, November and December of making anticipated maize purchases for the supply of the *pósito*, and that such purchases were, as a consequence of the fighting, overdue. Torres agreed to their continuation. AMG Paquete 24, leg. 83, ayuntamiento to Torres, Guadalajara 20 November 1810; Torres to city council, Guadalajara 22 November 1810.

20 AJANG 259–12–3513, El Teúl (1814), ff. 11–19, fiscal protector de indios, Guadalajara 26 November 1802.

21 AGN OG 143, Cruz to Calleja, Valladolid 31 December 1810, ff. 96–97.

22 AGN OG 179, ff. 145–146, *Regente* de Guadalajara, 31 January 1811.

23 Pérez Verdía, *Jalisco*, II, pp. 50 (gives 200). Ramírez Flores, *El gobierno insurgente*, pp. 107–09, suggests 61 documented cases and states that at his trial Hidalgo's own estimate was 350. Hamill, *Hidalgo Revolt*, pp. 181–2, 194.

24 AJANG Criminal 17, no. 11, sumaria contra el Br. D. J. A. Díaz, acusado del delito de infidencia: ff. 2, 4v–8v, 16–17, 74–76v.

25 AJANG Criminal 17, no. 18, Junta de Seguridad Pública, Guadalajara 8 May 1812. AJANG Civil 255–10–3427, no. 48, Junta de Seguridad Pública, Guadalajara 23 Oct. 1811, Gutiérrez, a merchant, received licence to journey to Mexico City in pursuance of his affairs and to carry arms for self-defence on the roads.

26 AGN OG 176, ff. 80–83v, Calleja to Venegas, no. 22, Pueblo de San Pedro 20 January 1811; ff. 86–87v, Calleja to Venegas, no. 24, Guadalajara 21 January; ff. 102–105, Calleja to Venegas, no. 30, Guadalajara 23 January 1811.

27 AGN OG 176, ff. 120–122, Calleja to Venegas, Guadalajara 26 January 1811; ff. 123–126, Calleja to Venegas, no. 34, Guadalajara 27 January 1811; ff. 142–143v, Calleja to Venegas, no. 37 res., Guadalajara 29 January 1811.

28 AGN OG 178, ff. 7–16v, no. 3, Calleja to Venegas, Guadalajara 3 February 1811. AGN OG 179, ff. 179–180, Velázquez de León to Calleja, no. 100, Guadalajara 3 February 1811; ff. 181–182v, Bernardino de la Fuente (subdelegate) to Calleja, no. 101, Sayula 4 February 1811; ff. 237–237v, Francisco Ventura y Moreno to Calleja, Sayula 8 February 1811; ff. 239–240, Rafael Murguía to Calleja, Sayula 8 February 1811.

29 AJANG Criminal 16 (1813), no. 7, La Real Audiencia; sobre el levantamiento de los indios de Zacoalco y otros pueblos: fiscal Andrade, Guadalajara 13 February 1811.

30 Anastasio Zerecero, *Memorias para la historia de las revoluciones en México* (Mexico 1975), pp. 210–14. The parish priest, Nicolás Santos Verdín, was at the centre of the plot against the rebels. Mercado's father was hanged on 14 February.

31 AGN OG 146, ff. 77–81, Porlier to Cruz, 4 March 1811. See also Alamán, *Historia de Méjico*, pp. 251–252, and Luis Pérez Verdía, *Apuntes históricos sobre la guerra de independencia de Jalisco* (Guadalajara 1953), pp. 58–63. Repression in Colima appears to have been severe. Colonel Manuel del Río in one day shot 81 individuals. In the action of 21 August the cavalry killed 700 and executed up to a further 800 persons. In the Autlán and Mascota area 'many villages were in a state of insurrection'. AGN OG 146, ff. 106–107, exp. 32, Cruz to Venegas, Guadalajara 26 August 1811.

32 AGN OG 922, ff. 249–250v, Cárdenas to José Sixto Verduzco, Cojumatlán 23 October 1812.

33 AGN OG 178, ff. 34–34v, Venegas to Calleja, Mexico 11 February 1811. AGN OG 146, ff. 103–104v, exp. no. 31, Cruz to Venegas, Guadalajara 19 July 1811; ff. 106–107, exp. 32, Cruz to Venegas, Guadalajara 26 August 1811.

34 I am very grateful to Christon I. Archer for kindly letting me read his manuscript study, 'Banditry and Revolution in New Spain, 1790–1821', from which I have greatly benefited.

35 AGN Alcabalas 37, no. 116, Santiago Joseph de Cortázar to Juan Navarro, *director general de alcabalas*, Huichapan 30 March 1793, enclosing *padrón* of 1 May 1785.

36 AGN Civil 1418, exp. 10 and exp. 11, *fiscales de real hacienda* (Posada) and *civil* (Alva), Mexico 29 November 1786, 20 March 1787, 1 April 1787.

37 Villaseñor, *Biografías*, I, 141–6, 147–9. 'El Chito' was executed on 14 May and Julian on 21 June 1813. See Genaro García, *Documentos históricos mexicanos*, V, xlii, 454–6, *lista de las personas de la familia del jefe insurgente Villagrán capturadas en Ixmiquílpan*, Huichapan 14 October 1813.

38 AGN OG 745, ff. 48–48v, Fausto de Elhuyar to Venegas, Mexico 14 December 1810.

39 AGN Historia 105, no. 28, Pedro Rodríguez Argumosa to Venegas, Ixmiquílpan 20 September 1811. AGN Historia 103, no. 23, Pedro Rodríguez Argumosa to Venegas, Ixmiquílpan 6 September 1811.

40 Carrión, *Puebla*, II, pp. 82–85. René Cuellar Bernal, *Tlaxcala a través de los siglos*, (Mexico 1968), pp. 184–7.

41 AGN OG 285, ff. 50–51, Ciriaco de Llano to Venegas, 14 September 1811.

42 AGN OG 285, ff. 100–101, Llano to Venegas, Tulancingo 24 September 1811; ff. 112–115, Llano to Venegas, Chinahuapan 27 September 1811; ff. 125–126v, Manuel Aráoz to Llano, Tlaxco 30 September 1811; ff. 127–132, Llano to Venegas, Tetela 30 September 1811; ff. 303–304, Manuel del Valle to Llano, Zacatlán 14 October 1811.

43 Carrión, *Puebla*, II, pp. 87–91.

44 AGN OG 285, ff. 72–73v, Llano to Venegas, Apan 20 September 1811; ff. 175–176, Llano to Venegas, Mazaquiagua 10 October 1811; ff. 214–216v, Llano to Venegas, Apan 18 October 1811; ff. 240–241v, Llano to Venegas, Texcoco 21 October 1811.

45 AGN OG 285, ff. 156–157, Bernabé de Santa Cruz to Venegas, Texcoco 5 October 1811; ff. 253–254v, Llano to Venegas, Teotihuacán 23 October 1811. AGN OG 30, ff. 283–283v, junta del vecindario de Zimapan to Calleja, 3 June 1813. AGN, Historia 445, ff. 134–138, Ramón Gutiérrez del Mazo to Calleja, Mexico 9 July 1813.

46 Cuellar, 186–90. Osorno during the early 1820s became a close associate of Nicolás Bravo in Tulancingo and Tlaxcala. He died in 1824 and was buried in the church of Chinahuapan in north Puebla.

47 Lemoine Villicaña, *Morelos: su vida revolucionaria*, pp. 42–4. Morelos (b. Valladolid 1765) worked until the age of twenty-five as an hacienda labourer on his uncle's property near Apatzingán. Ordained in 1797, he received the parish of Carácuaro in 1799.

48 *Ibid.*, pp. 43–51.

49 An insurgent force of about 2,000 men entered Iguala on 19 November. Royalists tried in vain to raise adequate forces from local haciendas and from those in the Cuautla zone. AGN OG 712, ff. 73–74v, José Antonio de Andrade to Venegas, Hacienda de San Gabriel 15 November 1810; ff. 116–117, de Andrade to Venegas

20 November 1810; ff. 140–141v, Manuel de la Hoz to Venegas, Cuautla 23 November 1810.

50 Lemoine, *Morelos*, pp. 48, 162–3.

51 Luis Chávez Orozco, *El sitio de Cuautla* (Mexico 1976), pp. 30–2, 95–9. José María del Pilar Galeana had accumulated considerable tracts of land in the ranchos of El Real, Boca de Coyuca, San Jerónimo, Coyuquilla and Cuacoyal, this latter a cotton estate. At the beginning of the nineteenth century, four-fifths of the inhabitants of the rancho of hacienda de San Jerónimo were negroes.

52 Carlos Alvear Acevedo, *Galeana* (Mexico 1958), pp. 10–12. Hermenegildo Galeana, b. April 1762.

53 AGN Historia 74, Manuel de Flon, Puebla 18 March 1794.

54 Alvear Acevedo, *Galeana*, pp. 14–16.

55 *Ibid.*, pp. 22–7.

56 Leonardo Bravo, aged forty-six, became Morelos' second in command until his capture following the break-out from the siege of Cuautla. He was executed in Mexico City on 14 September 1812. Miguel Bravo was captured near Chilac in March 1814, sentenced to death in Puebla, and executed on 15 April. Nicolás Bravo became Vice-President of the Mexican Republic between 1825 and 1829. Chávez Orozco, *El sitio de Cuautla*, pp. 31–2. Carrión, *Historia de la ciudad de Puebla*, II, pp. 160–2. Fernando Díaz Díaz, *Caudillos y caciques. Antonio López de Santa Anna y Juan Álvarez* (Mexico 1972), pp. 30–100.

57 AGN OG 918, ff. 61–62v, Nicolás Bravo to Col. Vicente Bravo, no. 45, sending the appeal of eight Indian villages, 26 January 1812.

58 Torre Villar, *Constitución de Apatzingán*, no. 65, Tecpan 13 October 1811, pp. 335–6; no. 69, to contain thefts, 9 December 1812, p. 347.

59 AGN OG 917, ff. 253–254, no. 145, José María Liceaga to Morelos, Palacio Nacional de Zitácuaro 18 December 1811.

60 AGN OG 917, ff. 248–249v, no. 142, Miguel Bravo to Morelos, Tlapa 16 December 1811. Bravo arrived in Tlapa on 15 December and was waiting for Trujano.

61 Archivo Judicial de Puebla (AJP) *Independencia (1811–35)*: procesos a sospechos de insurgencia, Tlapa (1811), Rollo 2, Puebla, INAH, no. 1, 20 November 1810, asesor ordinario, Puebla, Dr J. I. Berqueta; Juan José de Ortega y Chacón to Berqueta, Tlapa 25 January 1811.

62 AGN Historia 105, no. 41, Mariano Ortiz to Venegas, Huajuapan 18 September 1811.

63 AGN OG 286, ff. 171–171v, Venegas to Miguel de Soto y Maceda, Mexico 28 November 1811. AGN OG 919, no. 22, f. 31, Pedro José Figueroa to Trujano, hacienda de San Francisco 9 February 1811; no. 24, ff. 33–34.

64 AGN OG 917, ff. 76–78v, Esteban Pérez and Pedro José Mercado to Morelos, Campo de Zimatepec, 25 July 1811. AGN OG 918, ff. 31–34v, Miguel Bravo to Morelos, no. 24, Cuartel subalterno de Ayutla, 13 January 1812.

## 6. The struggle for Puebla 1811–13

1 AGN Virreyes 268A, ff. 1–7, no. 1, Calleja to Minister of War (in Cádiz), Mexico 15 March 1813.

2 AGN Historia 103, no. 22, Juan Torquemada y Veristáin (interim subdelegate to Mariscal del Campo Dávila (Governor-Intendant of Puebla), Tetela 3 September 1811.

3 AGN OG 285, *Correspondencia de Ciriaco de Llano, Sept-Oct 1811*, ff. 125–6v, Manuel Aráoz to Llano, Tlaxco 30 September 1811.

4 AGN Historia 103, no. 493, Dávila to Venegas, Puebla 7 September 1811.

5 Carrión, *Historia de la ciudad de Puebla*, II, pp. 86–9. Llano became division commander in Toluca in 1813. In December, Calleja sent him, along with Iturbide from Guanajuato, to reinforce the beleaguered garrison of Valladolid, facing its fifth insurgent assault.

6 AGN OG 285, ff. 100–1, Llano to Venegas, Tulancingo 24 September 1811; ff. 112–15, Llano to Venegas, Chinahuapan 27 September 1811; ff. 127–32, Llano to Venegas, Tetela 30 September 1811; 303–4, Manuel del Valle to Llano, Zacatlán 14 October 1811.

7 AGN Historia 105, no. 7, Tomás Rodríguez, Huejotzingo 5 September 1811.

8 AGN Historia 103, no. 24, Juan Valdés to Venegas, Real Fuerte de San Carlos de Perote 12 September 1811. AGN Historia 105, no. 44, Carlos de Urrutia to Venegas 18 September 1811. Urrutia believed the garrison of Orizaba sufficiently strong to resist any threat. M. Rivera Cambas, *Historia antigua y moderna de Jalapa y de las revoluciones del estado de Veracruz*, 5 vols. (Mexico 1869–71), I, pp. 297–300.

9 AGN OG 286, ff. 245–6, Llano to Venegas, Puebla 11 December 1811. The cleric Herrera, b. Huamantla (Tlaxcala), became vicar general of Morelos' forces in 1812, signed the Act of Independence at Chilpancingo on 6 November 1813 and the Constitution of Apatzingán on 22 October 1814. See Torre Villar, *Constitución de Apatzingán*, p. 64.

10 AGN OG 286, Declaración de Juan de Dios Guerrero, f. 260; ff. 271–271v, Llano to Venegas, Puebla 18 December 1811. Llano became second-in-command in Puebla on 1 November 1811, ff. 1–2v, Venegas to Llano, Mexico 1 November 1811.

11 Carlos María de Bustamante, *Cuadro histórico de la revolución mexicana*, 4 vols. (Mexico 1961), II, p. 351. Domingo Díez, *Bosquejo histórico-geográfico de Morelos* (Cuernavaca 1967), p. 61, where Jantetelco is described as a 'village hemmed in by the lands of the hacienda de Santa Clara Montefalco'.

12 Gómez Haro, *Puebla en la guerra*, pp. 27–9.

13 Liehr, *Stadtrat und Städtische Oberschicht*, p. 186.

14 AGN OG 30, Bravo to Venegas, ff. 184–8v, Puebla 15 January 1813; Calleja to ayuntamiento of Puebla, f. 297, Mexico 25 June 1813. Gómez Haro, *Puebla en la guerra*, p. 58.

15 AAP *LC* 80 (1811), ff. 274–5, Venegas to ayuntamiento of Puebla, Mexico 3 November 1810: this force included the guards of Puebla, Tlaxcala, Jalapa, Papantla, Zacatlán, San Juan de los Llanos, Tesiutlán and Chalchicomula.

16 AAP Expedientes sobre servicio militar (1810–1811), T. 117, L. 1281, ff. 168–74, Juan Andrés Azcárate, Puebla 24 December 1810. Azcárate was also a city merchant. AAP *LC* 81 (1812), ff. 36–43v.

17 AAP *LC* 80, ff. 158–9v. Venegas to ayuntamiento of Puebla, Mexico 10 March 1811.

18 AAP *LC* 80, f. 99, Puebla 20 February 1811.

19 AAP *LC* 80, ff. 200–11, Venegas to ayuntamiento of Puebla, Mexico 16 April 1811.

20 AAP *LC* 80, ff. 326–9v, García Dávila to ayuntamiento, Puebla 26 April 1811.

21 AAP *LC* ff. 151–6, Sala capitular to Venegas, Puebla 16 March 1811.

22 AAP *LC* 80, ff. 215–17v, Dávila to ayuntamiento, Puebla 1 May 1811.

23 AAP Expedientes sobre servicio militar, T. 117, L. 1288, ff. 206, 209–11,

214–18v, 240–1, 247, 249, 256. They included the city councillors Ovando y Rivadeneyra and the Marqués de Monserrate, and the militia officers Captain José María Lafragua and José Flon, son of the late Intendant.

24 AAP *LC* 80, ff. 300–1, Francisco Jiménez Saavedra (volunteer commander) to ayuntamiento, Puebla 28 June 1811; Francisco Jiménez Saavedra to ayuntamiento, ff. 436–7, Puebla 2 October 1811.

25 AAP *LC* 80, f. 495, Dávila to ayuntamiento, Puebla 28 November 1811.

26 AAP *LC* 80, ff. 495–6, ayuntamiento of Puebla 28 November 1811. AAP *LC* 81, ff. 13–15, Puebla January 1812; Venegas to ayuntamiento of Puebla, Mexico 22 January 1812.

27 AGN OG 286, encargado de justicia de Tlacotepec, f. 261, 12 December 1811.

28 AGN OG 286, ff. 162–3, Llano to Venegas, Puebla 27 November 1811; ff. 194–5, Llano to Venegas, Puebla 3 December 1811; f. 251, Venegas to Llano, Mexico 14 December 1811.

29 AGN OG 286, ff. 268–268v, declaración del capt. de Patriotas, Antonio Estevas, sent by Llano, 15 December 1811.

30 AGN OG 286, ff. 123–123v, Llano to Venegas, Puebla 23 November 1811; f. 184, Llano to Venegas, Puebla 1 December 1811.

31 Lemoine Villicaña, *Morelos*, pp. 52–3.

32 AGN OG 289, ff. 92–92v. Venegas to Llano, Mexico 25 January 1812. On 25 January 1812 the city of Puebla was defended by 1,031 regular troops, of whom 400 were in the vanguard at Atlixco and 500 had arrived from Spain with the Battalion of Asturias. These forces did not include urban irregulars. See Carrión, Historia de la ciudad de Puebla, II, p. 108, and Chávez Orozco, *Sitio*, pp. 7–8, 24, 73.

33 At his trial Morelos maintained that he had not planned to take Toluca during this operation, but had merely intended to dislodge Porlier from Tenancingo, since the Royalists there threatened the rebel forces on the cerro de Tenango. Chávez Orozco, *Sitío*, pp. 3–4.

34 AGN OG 289, ff. 111–111v, Ten. Col. José Antonio de Andrade to Llano, no. 34, Atlixco 25 January 1812. Chávez Orozco, *Sitío*, pp. 15–16, 27–8.

35 AGN OG 289, ff. 158–9v, no. 43, Llano to Venegas, Puebla 10 February 1812; f. 180, Venegas to Llano, Mexico 14 February 1812. Carrión, *Historia de la cuidad de Puebla*, II, pp. 124–5, lists pro-insurgents within the city.

36 AGN OG 289, ff. 2–3 no. 1, Llano to Venegas, Puebla 1 January 1812; ff. 6–7, no. 3, Llano to Venegas, Puebla 2 January 1812; ff. 64–64v, no. 23, Llano to Venegas, Puebla 15 January 1812; ff. 74–78v, Lieut. Diego Ruiz Herrera to Llano, San Martín Texmelucan 15 January 1812.

37 AGN OG 289, ff. 30–3, no. 11, Agustín González del Campillo to Venegas, Puebla 12 January 1812. Carrión, *Historia de la ciudad de Puebla*, II, pp. 114–15. An insurgent force of 2,000 men attacked Huamantla on 18 March 1812.

38 AGN OG 289, ff. 85–85v, Antonio García del Casal (Patriot commander in Huamantla) to Llano, Huamantla 17 January 1812; ff. 87–8, Llano to Venegas, Puebla 19 January 1812.

39 AGN OG 289, ff. 79–79v, no. 27, Llano to Venegas, Puebla 17 January 1812; ff. 131–131v, no. 39, Llano to Venegas, Puebla 2 February 1812; ff. 168–9v, no. 47, Llano to Capt. César Castillo (in Tepeaca), Puebla 5 February 1812.

40 AGN OG 289, ff. 54–5, no. 19, Llano to Venegas, Puebla 12 January 1812; ff. 62–62v, no. 22, Llano to Venegas, Puebla 15 January 1812.

41 AGN OG 293, ff. 8–8v, Mariano Ramírez de la Cuesta to Venegas, Puebla 8 February 1812. The rebels in Huejotzingo heard on 3 February that 700 armed

men garrisoned Atlixco and that on the previous day 400 European soldiers from an estimated total force of 7–8,000 men in four divisions entered Puebla. AGN OG 918, ff. 81–2, no. 57, Josef Felipe Rodríguez to Col Francisco de Ayala, Huejotcingo 3 February 1812. Between 14 and 19 February 1812, Llano organized the *División del Sur*, Carrion, *Historia de la cuidad de Puebla*, II p. 109.

42 AAP *LC* 81, ff. 36–43v, Puebla 8 February 1812.

43 AGN OG 289, f. 180, Venegas to Llano, Mexico 14 February 1812; ff. 189–199, no. 56, Llano to Calleja, Izúcar 25 February 1812. AGN OG 290, ff. 17–20v, no. 11, Llano to Venegas, Campo del Calvario (near Izúcar) 25 February 1812.

44 AGN OG 289, f. 201, Calleja to Llano, Campo de Cuatlixco 23 February 1812. For the siege, see Chávez Orozco, *Sitío*, Alamán *Historia de Méjico*, II, pp. 534–5, refers to a 'counter-revolution', in Chilapa in March 1812, in which 'that town's citizens who had always been fervently Royalist' expelled Morelos' subdelegate, Francisco Moctezuma. A similar movement took place also in Tixtla. To date, however, we have little information on these events, and are in no position to determine their exact significance.

45 A large insurgent force with five cannons attacked Atlixco from Izúcar on 23 April 1812, and might have taken the town, had not 200 men and a cannon arrived in time from Puebla. Twenty defenders died in the fighting. Another rebel band attacked the city of Tlaxcala on 11 May. Alamán, *Historia de Méjico*, II, pp. 573–4. Carrion, *Historia de la cuidad de Puebla*, II, pp. 119–20.

46 AAP *LC* 81, ff. 79–83, Puebla 18 April 1812; Dávila to ayuntamiento, Puebla 24 April 1812; ayuntamiento to Dávila, Puebla 27 April 1812. Castro Terreño became interim Governor Intendant early in June 1812, while Dávila left to repair his health. Terreño vacated these offices early in September 1812, and entrusted them on an interim basis to Llano, *ibid*, f. 200.

47 Alamán, *Historia de Méjico*, III, pp. 162–3.

48 Bustamante, *Cuadro histórico de la revolución mexicana*, I, pp. 408–9.

49 AGN OG 69, ff. 11–11v, Armijo (division commander) to Venegas, Ozumba 1 June 1812; ff. 28–29v, Armijo to Venegas, Yautepec 11 June 1812. Armijo (b. 1774) later became a vigorous opponent of Nicolas Bravo whom he defeated and captured at Tlalchapa in 1817, and Vicente Guerrero, who defeated him at Tamo in September 1818. Ayala, formerly Captain of the Acordada, refused to join in the Royalist defence of Cuautla early in 1812, and instead, joined Morelos' forces at Tepecuacuilco and operated in conjunction with Trujano. Díez, *Bosquejo histórico-geográfico de Morelos*, pp. 59–60. AGN OG 918, no. 49 (document missing, but summarised), Morelos to Ayala, 29 January 1812.

50 AGN OG 69, 37–38v, Armijo to Venegas, Yecapixtla 19 June 1812; ff. 79–81v, Armijo to Venegas, Yecapixtla 26 July 1812. Armijo reported that Yautepec had remained loyal to the crown, ff. 43–4, Yecapixtla 29 June 1812; ff. 143–144v, Armijo to Venegas, Yecapixtla 25 September 1812.

51 AGN OG 293, f. 2, Teniente Coronel José Antonio de Andrade to Francisco Trasgallo (Subdelegate of Atlixco), Atlixco 30 January 1812. AJP (INAH), *Independientes*, no. 2, *Robos*, Izúcar 1812, discussed in Puebla 22 May 1812, see Rollo 2. AGN OG 69, ff. 112–117v, Armijo to Venegas, Yecapixtla 11 September 1812; ff. 143–144v, Armijo to Venegas, Yecapixtla 25 September 1812.

52 AGN OG 72, ff. 41–42v, Armijo to Venegas, Izúcar 26 January 1813.

53 AGN OG 292, ff. 334–334v, Llano to Venegas, no. 53, Puebla 28 November 1812.

54 AGN OG 296, ff. 4–16, Joaquín Palafox y Hacha (parish priest) to Llano, Orizaba

20 June 1812. AGN OG 290, ff. 139–140v, Llano to Venegas, no. 71, Puebla 28 June 1812; ff. 148–167v, no. 77, Llano to Venegas, Puebla 2 July 1812. P. Sánchez de la Vega, who had risen in Tlacotepec on 9 January and led 500 men from the local villages, threatened the Tehuacán haciendas, and entered Nopalucan with Osorno on 26 April. Carrion, *Historia de la ciudad de Puebla*, II, pp. 106, 118.

55  AGN Historia 338, *Camino militar de Perote a Veracruz*. AAP *LC* 81, Sala capitular to ayuntamiento of Puebla, Veracruz 14 July 1812.

56  AGN OG 291, ff. 12–13, Llano to Venegas, no. 5, Puebla 14 September 1812, ff. 109–12, Llano to Venegas, no. 18, Puebla 15 October 1812; ff. 156–157v, Llano to Venegas, Puebla 29 October 1812. AGN OG 292, ff. 163–4, no. 26, Llano to Venegas, Puebla 1 November 1812; f. 176, Mariano Rivas to Llano, Tepeaca 2 November 1812. AGN OG 289, ff. 443–443v, no. 1 23, Llano to Venegas, Puebla 3 November 1812.

57  AGN OG 289, ff. 306–315v, no. 84, Llano to Venegas, Jalapa 10 August 1812. F. González de Cossío, *Xalapa. Breve reseña histórica* (Mexico 1957), pp. 127–9, 132.

58  AGN OG 292, ff. 234–5, Llano to Venegas, Puebla 16 November 1812; ff. 277–8, no. 48, Puebla 23 November 1812; f. 262, Luis de Aguilar to Llano, Tehucán 20 November 1812; ff. 327–8, Jose Basilio de las Rosas (acting administrator) to Llano, Chietla 23 November 1812.

59  Biblioteca Lafragua (University of Puebla), *Cartas de Morelos, 1812–1815*, Morelos to Rayón, no. 4, Hacienda de Viguera (near Oaxaca) 24 November 1812, in INAH, Rollo 68, Puebla. Bravo was beaten back on 21 November.

60  AGN OG 292, ff. 260–2, Aguila to Llano, Tehuacán 20 and 21 November 1812; ff. 297–298v, Juan Valdés to Llano, Real Fuerte de San Carlos, Perote 23 November 1812. Despite Royalist success in the Puebla valleys, rebel forces consolidated their hold in Veracruz, a clear indication that the war, increasingly transferred to other theatres, was by no means over.

61  AGN OG 292, ff. 311–5, no. 50, Llano to Venegas, Puebla 25 November 1812.

62  AGN OG 69, ff. 201–4, Armijo to Venegas, Izúcar 20 December 1812.

63  See the present writer's *Politics and Trade*, pp. 135–9.

64  Alamán, *Historia de Méjico*, III, pp. 250–2. Bustamante, *Cuadro histórico de la revolución mexicana*, I, pp. 504–8, 533–5. Lemoine, *Morelos*, pp. 75–8.

65  Biblioteca Lafragua (INAH, Rollo 68, Puebla), Morelos to Rayón, no. 7, Oaxaca 15 January 1813.

66  Hamnett, *Politics and Trade*, pp. 14–54. Taylor discusses motives for insurgent support in the city of Oaxaca in 1812 in Lockhart, *Provinces*, pp. 91–4.

67  Lemoine, *Morelos*, pp. 400–3, doc. 125, Bustamante to cabildo eclesiástico of Oaxaca 13 October 1813.

68  Lemoine, *Morelos*, p. 385.

69  Biblioteca Lafragua INAH, Rollo 68, Puebla, Morelos to Rayón, no. 46, cuartel general de Aguadulce 14 July 1814; Morelos to Rayón, no. 47, date torn away.

70  AGN OG 921, ff. 222–3, no. 156, Joseph Osorno to Rayón, Atlamaxac 24 April 1814.

71  For details of the Congress, see Torre Villar, *Constitucion de Apatzingán*.

72  AGN OG 289, ff. 444–444v, Llano to Venegas, Puebla 30 December 1812.

73  AGN OG 163, f. 179: the troops that arrived from Spain in January 1812 consisted of the Third Asturias Regiment, the First Lovera Battalion and the First *Battalón Americano*. Royalist forces in Puebla consisted of the following: a Division of 2,493 men under Olazábal; a Division of 500 under Col Agustín de la Viña; a Division of

500 under Col. José Antonio Andrade; a Division of 400 under Armijo: 1,310 troops in the Puebla city garrison; 1,000 men with the First *Batallón Americano* under Terreño; 791 in the Puebla urban defence forces; 504 stationed in fixed positions.

74 AGN OG 463, Captain Antonio Zubieta to Calleja, Cuautla 21 November 1814.

75 AGN Virreyes 268A, ff. 1–7, no. 1, Calleja to Minister of War, Mexico 15 March 1813.

76 AAP *LC* 82, ff. 441–442v, Dávila to ayuntamiento constitucional, Puebla 5 August 1813. AAP, Expedientes sobre servicio militar, (1812–20), T. 118, ff. 71–72v, 91–105v, Castro Terreño, Puebla 27 September 1813; ayuntamiento, Puebla 14–16 October 1813.

77 AAP *LC* 83, f. 60, Calleja to ayuntamiento of Puebla, Mexico 20 January 1814. AAP, Expedientes sobre servicio militar, T. 118, ff. 112–13, 118–122v, *Bando* of 5 March 1814. Brigadier José Moreno Dáoiz replaced Ortega.

78 AAP *LC* 84, f. 301, Saavedra, Puebla 17 May 1815.

79 AGN OG 462/2, Villaldea to Calleja, Pachuca 4 September 1813.

80 AGN Historia 152, ff. 111–116v, Apodaca to Minister of War, no. 1 *reservada*, Mexico 31 October 1816.

81 AGN Virreyes 273, ff. 255–263v, Venadito to Minister of War, no. 761 *reservada*, Mexico 31 December 1818.

82 AGN OG 296, ff. 106–113v, Captain Rafael de la Luz Segura of *Realistas* (Subdelegate and Military Commander), Tochimilco 7 April 1816.

83 AGN OG 296, no. 77, f. 102, Ramón Quintana, Tlaxcala 13 April 1816.

84 AGN OG 296, ff. 136–45, José Montero, Puebla 31 May 1816; ff. 165–72, *ibid.*, Puebla 14 April 1816, when 192 amnesties were granted; ff. 193–201v, *ibid.*, Puebla 19 November 1816, when there were 125; ff. 203–208v, Llano, Puebla 3 December 1816, with 139 granted.

85 AGN OG 463, Zubieta to Apodaca, Cuautla 13 March 1817.

86 AGN Historia 152, ff. 334–48, Apodaca to Minister of War, no. 57, 30 June 1818.

87 AGN OG 293, ff. 233–234v, no. 1177, Llano to Apodaca, Puebla 13 January 1818.

88 AGN OG 293, ff. 186–7, no. 945, Llano to Apodaca, Jalapa 28 April 1818.

## 7. Local conflict and provincial chieftains

1 See Christon I. Archer, 'The Royalist Army in New Spain: Civil-Military Relationships, 1810–1821', *JLAS*, 13, no. 1 (May 1981), 57–82. For Calleja's policy, see AGN OG 201, ff. 370–371, Reglamento político-militar . . . Mexico 5 March 1813.

2 For a discussion of these issues, see my article, 'Royalist Counter-insurgency and the Continuity of Rebellion: Guanajuato and Michoacán, 1813–20', *HAHR*, 62, no. 1 (Feb. 1982), 19–48.

3 Fernando Osorno Castro, *El insurgente Albino García* (Mexico 1982), 23–9. Villaseñor y Villaseñor, *ibid.*, II, 13–20.

4 AHML Caja 3, exp. 2 (INAH Rollo 32), Subdelegate José Estéban de Rozas to Capt. Manuel Gutiérrez de la Concha, Royalist Commander in the Villa de León, Rincón de Leon 15 March 1811; *ibid.*, exp. 5, Manuel Ignacio García to Concha, Silao 30 March 1811. AGN OG 733, ff. 207–208, no. 66, Casa Rul to Calleja, Guanajuato 10 June 1811; ff. 223–224, no. 72, Casa Rul to Calleja, Guanajuato 17 June 1817.

5 Osorno Castro, *Albino García*, pp. 39–43, 49, 93. Alamán, *Historia de Méjico*, II, pp. 395–8.

6 AHML Caja 1, exp. 1 (INAH Rollo 32), Rozas to Concha, Rincón de León 26 December 1810; Pedro Menezo to Concha, Hacienda de Pantoja 18 August 1811; Pedro Menezo to Concha, Irapuato 22, 28, 31 August, 6, 15, 16 September 1811; exp. 3, *artáculos correspondientes a la formación de compañías en las haciendas y ranchos*, Aguascalientes 8 June 1811; exp. 4, Intendant Fernando Pérez Marañón to Concha, Guanajuato 17 November 1811. AHML, Caja 2, exp. 21.

7 Osorno, *Albino García*, pp. 49–50, 67, 72–8, 83–4, 136–7. Alamán, *Historia de Méjico*, II, pp. 395–9. Marmolejo, *Efemérides guanajuatenses*, II, p. 340; III, p. 125.

8 AHML Caja 5, exp. 1 (INAH Rollo 33), García Conde to Luis Berrara (Military Commander in León), Celaya 8 June 1812. Osorno, *Albino García*, pp. 137–8, 150–8, 160, 223–6. William Spence Robertson, *Iturbide of Mexico* (Durham, N.C., 1952), pp. 20–1.

9 AHML Caja 1, exp. 14 (INAH Rollo 34), José Albino García to Miguel García, Celaya 8 June 1812 (copy), concluding, 'padrecito, por amor de dios, le pido a Vd. perdón de todo lo que le hubiere injuriado, y a todos los vecinos me hará Vd. favor de decirles que me perdonen'.

10 Archivo Histórico Guanajuatense (AHG) (INAH Rollo 16), Independencia (1810–21): Guanajuato (1813), testimonio literal del expediente . . . , Pérez Gálvez to Pérez Marañón, Guanajuato 4 August 1812.

11 Alamán, *Historia de Méjico*, III, pp. 356–7. Marmolejo, *Efemérides guanajuatenses*, III, pp. 128–37.

12 Alamán, *Historia de Méjico*, III, pp. 356–7. Villaseñor y Villaseñor, *Biografías*, II, 213–22.

13 AHML Caja única (1814), exp. 14 (INAH Rollo 34), Rafael Flores to Pérez Gálvez, Lagos 11 February 1814.

14 AGN OG 428, ff. 291–294v. Iturbide to Calleja, no. 200, Corralejo 10 May 1814; f. 311, Iturbide, no. 6, La Piedad 4 June 1814. AGN OG 430, ff. 471–476, Col. Antonio de Soto (Military Commander) to Iturbide, León 18 December 1814. AGN OG 431, ff. 191–194v, Iturbide, Hacienda de Arandas 22 July 1815. AGN OG 432, ff. 204–6, Calleja to Iturbide, Mexico 31 December 1815.

15 AGN OG 426, ff. 57–58, Domínguez to Calleja, Querétaro 6 May 1813; ff. 230–233v, Otero to Calleja, Guanajuato 12 August 1813.

16 AHG (INAH Rollo 16): Guanajuato (1816): expediente formado a consecuencia de varios superiores órdenes relativos a la satisfacción de los 60,000 pesos de préstamos que exigió en esta provincia el Señor Coronel D. Agustín de Iturbide: ff. 1–5v, Calleja to Pérez Marañón, Mexico 10 June 1816; ff. 24–24v, Cristóbal Ordóñez to Pérez Marañón, Irapuato 2 April 1817; ff. 39–41, *asesor ordinario*, Guanajuato 6 May 1817. AHML Caja (1820), exp. 22 (INAH Rollo 39).

17 AHMM loose papers (1816–17), no. 7, Iturbide to Intendant Manuel Merino and Ayuntamiento, Valladolid 27 March 1816; Iturbide to ayuntamiento, Valladolid 30 March 1816; Sala Capitular to interim-Intendant, Valladolid 6 June 1816.

18 Marmolejo, *Efemérides guanajuatenses*, III, 143.

19 AJANG Criminal 17, no. 11, sumario contra el Br D. José Antonio Díaz, acusado del delito de infidencia, ff. 24–25, Verduzco to Cristóbal Cobián, 'Palacio Nacional' de Uruapan 9 October 1812; ff. 38–39, Verduzco to Díaz, 'Palacio Nacional' en Pátzcuaro 10 December 1812. Villaseñor y Villaseñor, *Biografías*, II, 21–6.

20 AHMM Caja 169 (1814), no. 21, síndico procurador to ayuntamiento, Valladolid

30 July and 13 August 1814. AHCM Diezmatorios leg. 1 (1800–19), Linares to Vicente Amesqua, Uruapan 28 February 1812, on the weakness of the militia.

21 AGN OG 150, ff. 172–175v, Negrete to Cruz, La Piedad 5 March 1814.

22 AHMM Caja 164/1 (1810), no. 14, Eusebio Pérez de Cosío (factor) to Intendant, Valladolid 12 March 1819. AHMM Caja 166/1 (1811), no. 1.

23 AGN OG 477, ff. 185–187v, f. 214, Bustamante to Linares, Pueblo Nuevo 31 March 1818.

24 AGN OG 153, no. 35, Declaración tomada del secretario de los rebeldes, Antonio Basilio Vargas, por el señor Coronel, D. Juan Josef Recacho, Guadalajara 30 December 1817. Vargas said that he had joined the rebellion through horror at Negrete's mass executions. Alamán, *Historia de Méjico*, IV, pp. 688–92; Villaseñor y Villaseñor, *Biografías*, II, 209–12.

25 AGN OG 434, ff. 102–103v, Antonio de Larragoiti, Salvatierra 28 March 1816.

26 AGN OG 153, ff. 10–10v, no. 8, Revuelta to Cruz, Lagos 25 December 1817.

27 AGN OG 399, ff. 170–171, Linares to Apodaca, León 30 November and 27 December 1819. AGN OG 476, ff. 95–96v, f. 178, Reynoso, Silao 3 January 1820.

28 AHML Caja 3 (1811), exp. 2, (INAH Rollo 32), Rozas to Concha, Rincón de León 7 March 1811; Rozas to Concha, Rincón de León 19 June 1811. Even as late as July 1820, the town of Santa Clara del Cobre, in Michoacán rose in rebellion. In August 1820, the villagers of Comachuén rose to join the defeated rebel chieftain, Villareal. No one in Peribán in mid-September attempted to oppose an insurgent band that entered the area. AGN OG 157, ff. 175–188, Cruz to Venadito, no. 428, Guadalajara 30 July 1820; ff. 245–245v, Cruz to Venadito, no. 439, Guadalajara 12 August 1820; ff. 281–282v, Cruz to Venadito, Guadalajara 13 September 1820.

29 AGN OG 149, ff. 1–1v, Cruz to Venegas, Guadalajara 6 January 1813; ff. 30–30v, Cruz to Venegas, Guadalajara 6 February 1813; f. 50, Cruz, Guadalajara 16 March 1813. Pérez Verdía, *Historia Particular*, II, pp. 110–12. For a recent study, see Eric Van Young, 'Conflict and Solidarity in Indian Village Life: The Guadalajara Region in the Late Colonial Period', *HAHR*, 64, no. 1 (Feb. 1984), 55–79.

30 AMG Paquete 25 (1811), leg. 17, no. 79, ff. 1–1v, Cruz to Ayuntamiento, Guadalajara 23 March 1811. AMG Paquete 27 (1813), leg. 84, Cruz: expediente sobre préstamo de maderas para una batería flotante en la Laguna de Chapala, Guadalajara 8 October 1813. AJANG 263–4–3583, Expediente sobre aprehensión de vagos para el servicio de los buques de la laguna (1816), Cruz to Hernández de Alva, Guadalajara 15 March 1816; Cruz to Hernández, Guadalajara 9 July 1816; audiencia, Guadalajara 27–9 July 1813.

31 AHMM Caja 170 (1817), no. 10, ff. 21–22, Negrete, Guadalajara 26 April 1819.

32 AGN OG 151, f. 204, Cruz to Calleja, no. 121, Guadalajara 24 July 1816; ff. 206–208, Cruz to Quintanar, Guadalajara 5 July 1816; ff. 250–257, Cruz, Guadalajara 30 July 1816.

33 AHML Caja 4 (1811), exp. 13, (INAH Rollo 33), AGN OG 152, ff. 34–34v, Revuelta to Cruz, Lagos 9 August 1817.

34 AGN OG 158, ff. 20–20v, Revuelta to Cruz, Lagos 30 June 1819; ff. 129–129v, no. 2 Revuelta to Linares, Lagos 25 August 1819; f. 179, Cruz to Venadito, no. 175, Guadalajara 14 September 1819.

35 AHMM Caja 169 bis (leg. 176) (1816), no. 16, Gobernador, alcaldes y república to Intendant, Chilchota 29 July 1818; teniente coronel José Antonio García Rojas to *encargado de justicia*, Tangancícuaro 26 July 1818; *fiscal protector de indios*, Valladolid 30 October 1818.

36  AHCM Diezmatorios leg. 1, Cuenta que presenta de Tribunal de Hacedería . . . (1817), cuaderno 1, Zitácuaro 31 August 1819.

37  AHCM Diezmatorios leg. 2 (1817–40), subdelegate to *jueces hacedores*, Uruapan 22 November 1820.

38  AGN OG 585, ff. 147–148, no. 425, Merino to Venadito, Valladolid 24 February 1819; ff. 149–150, Montiel to Merino, Tlalpujahua 18 February 1819; ff. 171–171v, Merino to Venadito, no. 437, Valladolid 9 March 1819. AGN OG 587, ff. 12–13v, Subdelegate to Merino, Tlalpujahua 29 April 1819.

39  AGN OG 399, ff. 85v, 105, 232v. Late in December 1818, there were 192 troops on the Hacienda de Ojuelos, and 520 in Lagos.

40  AGN OG 399, ff. 170–171, Gayangos to Venadito, no. 1154, Zacatecas 24 December 1819.

41  AGN OG 399, ff. 206–206v, Gayangos to Venadito, no. 1235, Zacatecas 2 March 1820.

42  AGN OG 400, ff. 133–137, Gayangos to Venadito, Aguascalientes 16 April 1818.

43  AGN OG 399, ff. 186–187v, Ruiz to Venadito, no. 20, Aguascalientes 5 February 1820.

44  Olveda, *Gordiano Guzmán*, pp. 83, 100, 109, 112, 121–44, where the social conflict aspect of Guzmán's career is stressed.

45  AGN OG 150, f. 212, Cruz, no. 12, Guadalajara 10 February 1814. AGN OG 153, no. 133, Capt. Martín Manrique to Ten. Cor. Domingo Chavarino, Tecalitlán 27 June 1818. AGN OG 155, ff. 13–13v, Ten. Cor. José María Vargas to Ten. Cor. Mariano Urrea, Apatzingán 25 September 1818; ff. 49–50v, Cruz to Apodaca, no. 214, Guadalajara 8 October 1818; ff. 164–165v, Chavarino to Cruz, Zapotlán el Grande 29 October 1818; ff. 272–273, J. B. Delgado to Guzmán, Coalcomán 8 December 1818. AGN OG 156, ff. 29–45, Urrea to Cruz, Río Grande en el Pirú 2 January 1819. AGN OG 158, ff. 40–40v, Juan Antonio Fuentes to Cruz, Colima 10 July 1819; f. 108, Venadito to Cruz, Mexico 15 September 1819; ff. 107–109v, Cruz to Venadito, Guadalajara 13 August 1819.

46  AGN OG 157, ff. 19–20v, Negrete and Urrea to Cruz, no. 1, Zapotlán el Grande 25 December 1819; ff. 17–18, Cruz to Venadito, no. 19, Guadalajara 19 January 1820.

47  AGN OG 580, ff. 149–50, ayuntamiento to Guzmán, no. 1, Apatzingán 29 August 1820; ff. 151–152, Martín Guzmán to ayuntamiento, no. 2, Aguililla 11 September 1820, AGN OG 157, ff. 384–386v, Gordiano Guzmán to ayuntamiento, Potrero 19 October 1820; ff. 388–388v, Cruz to Guzmán, Guadalajara 28 October 1820. AGN OG 580, ff. 158–160, sala capitular de Apatzingán to Merino, 13 November 1820. Olveda, *Gordiano Guzmán*, pp. 114, 117.

48  Bulnes, *Juárez y las revoluciones*, 306.

## 8. Conclusion

1  Barrington Moore, *Social Origins*, p. 100.

2  Moisés González Navarro, *Anatomía del poder en México (1848–1835)* (Mexico 1977), pp. 118–25. Paul J. Vanderwood, *Los Rurales Mexicanos* (Mexico 1982), pp. 23–4, 27. Richard N. Sinkin, *The Mexican Reform, 1855–1876. A Study in Liberal Nation Building* (Texas 1979).

3  Leticia Reina, *Las rebeliones campesinas de México (1819–1906)* (Mexico 1980), pp. 45–57, 61–82, 85–110, 117–20, 157–9, 289–99, 303–04, 325–54. González

Navarro, *Anatomía*, pp. 33, 38, 166, 261–68. Bazant, *Cinco Haciendas*, pp. 68–70, 112–19. María Elena Galaviz de Capdevielle, 'Eleuterio Quiróz y la rebelión de 1847 en Xichú', *Archivos de Historia Potosina*, 41, XI, no. 1 (Sept. 1979), 5–27. Jean Meyer, 'Los movimientos campesinos en el occidente de México en el siglo XIX', *Boletín del Archivo Historico de Jalisco*, III, no. 2 (May–Aug. 1979), 2–12. T. G. Powell, *El liberalismo y el campesinado en el centro de México, 1850–1876* (Mexico 1974).

# Bibliography

## PRIMARY SOURCES

### 1. MEXICO

*A. Mexico City*

**Archivo General de la Nación (AGN)**

Alcabalas: 37

Alhóndigas: 1

Arzobispos y Obispos: 11

Bandos: 8, 13

Civil: 45, 100, 184, 189, 215, 896, 1418, 1465, 1646, 1649, 1708, 1817, 1827, 1947, 2041, 2154, 2243

Consolidación: 2, 4, 5, 6, 14, 20, 27, 28

Consulados: 3

Gobernación: leg. 1954

Historia: 49, 74, 103, 105, 122, 152, 269, 270, 307, 325, 338, 485

Industria y Comercio: 20

Infidencias: 108, 157, 35 (1816), 1043 (1811)

Inquisición: 1454 (1811), 1463 (1816)

Intendentes: 8, 16, 17, 47, 48, 59, 60, 68, 72, 73, 78, 80, 81

Minería: 29, 30

Operaciones de Guerra (OG): 1, 19, 20, 30, 69, 70, 72, 94/2, 101, 140, 141, 143, 144, 146, 147, 148, 149, 150, 151, 152, 153, 154, 155, 156, 157, 158, 159, 160, 163, 176, 177, 178, 179, 186, 201, 272, 273, 274, 275, 285, 286, 289, 290, 291, 292, 293, 294, 295, 296, 372, 399, 400, 426, 427, 428, 429, 430, 431, 432, 433, 434, 445, 459, 460, 461, 462/2, 463, 464, 474, 475, 476, 477, 478, 580, 581, 582, 583, 584, 585, 586, 587, 675, 676, 677, 678, 704, 705, 706, 707, 709, 712, 733, 745, 809, 810, 811, 812, 906, 907, 917, 918, 919, 920, 921, 922, 923, 1013, 1014

Tierras: 1110, 1154, 1183, 1202, 1205, 1208, 1225, 1239, 1261, 1296, 1323, 1324, 1335, 1343, 1366, 1370, 1373, 1382, 1385, 1395, 1404, 1408, 1412, 1420, 1446, 1903, 2817, 2934

Tributos: 26, 34

Vínculos: 5, 48, 57, 59, 80, 137, 146, 149, 213, 214, 219, 251, 261, 285

Virreyes: 268A, 268B, 268C, 273, 280

**Archivo Histórico de Hacienda (AHH)**
Alcabalas: leg. 42, leg. 73, leg. 75
Comunidades Indígenas: leg. 441
Diputaciones foráneas: leg. 463
Intendentes: leg. 1043, leg. 1044
Primer Imperio: leg. 1871

**Biblioteca Nacional (BN)**
MSS 58

B. *Guadalajara*

**Archivo Histórico Municipal (AHMG)**
**Paquete:**

| | |
|---|---|
| 11 (1790–1) | 55 (1823) |
| 17 (1799–1800) | 16 (1798) |
| 22 (1808) | 21 (1807) |
| 24 (1810) | 23 (1809) |
| 26 (1812) | 25 (1811) |
| 29 (1814) | 27 (1813) |
| 31 (1817) | 30 (1815) |
| 32 (1818) | 35 (1819) (Caja 1115 |
| 36 (1820) | 38 (1812–21) |
| 45 (1822) | 47 (1825) |

**Archivo de Instrumentos Públicos (AIPG)**
Tierras y Aguas: 53 (1821–3)
Protocolos: José Antonio Mallén (1790–1818): 2 (1793–4), 3 (1795–6), 9 (1806–07),
    11 (1810–11), 13 (1814), 17 (1818)

**Archivo Judicial de la Audiencia de Nueva Galicia (AJANG)**
Civil:

| | |
|---|---|
| 115–6–1233 | 119–13–1286 |
| 127–1–1360 | 128–1–1360 |
| 212–7–2677 | 216–24–2746 |
| 223–11–2909 | 226–2–2945 |
| 228–13–2975 | 231–1–3008 |
| 235–13–3091 | 246–4–3276 |
| 252–14–3370 | 253–12–3388 |
| 255–10–3427 | 259–6–3507 |
| 259–12–3513 | 260–2–3524 |
| 260–6–3528 | 260–9–2531 |
| 263–4–3583 | 264–12–3606 |
| 265–3–3615 | 267–7–3646 |
| 267–8–3647 | 267–15–3654 |

Criminal: leg. 1 (1791–1812), leg. 2 (1815–16), leg. 4 (1812–16), leg. 5 (1819), leg.
    8 (1813), leg. 9 (1813), leg. 10, leg. 12 (1812), leg. 16 (1813), leg. 19 (1820),
    leg. 17 (1815)

*C. Puebla*

**Archivo del Ayuntamiento de Puebla (AAP)**
Libros de Cabildo: 77 (1808), 78 (1809), 79 (1810), 80 (1811), 81 (1812), 82 (1813),
    83 (1814), 84 (1815), 85 (1816)
    90/1 (January–June 1821)
    92/1 (January–June 1823)
    92/2 (June–December 1823)
    93/1 (January–June 1824)
Expedientes sobre Abastos (1810–66) 169
Expedientes sobre Alhóndigas (1800–10) 113
Expedientes sobre Gremios de Artesanos (1732–1804) 223
Expedientes sobre Gremios y Oficios (1744–1802) 234
Expedientes sobre Obrajes y Talleres (1621–1807) 224
Expedientes sobre Panaderías (1803–1751) 231
Expedientes sobre Policía (1792–1831) 194
Expedientes sobre Sanidad (1713–1813) 78
Expedientes sobre Servicio Militar (1810–11) 117, (1812–20) 118

**Archivo General de Notarías (ANP)**
Legajo 213 (1727–9) notaría 3
Legajo 235 (1759–65 notaría 3
Legajo 238 (1770–9) notaría 3
Legajo 241 (1786–8) notaría 3
Legajo 145 Caja I   (1806–07) notaría 2
Legajo 146 Caja 2   (1806–07) notaría 2
Legajo 152 Caja I   (1811–12) notaría 2
Legajo 170 Caja I   (1822–3)
Legajo 171 Caja II (1822–3) notaría 2
Atlixco 68 leg.         (1772–90)
Atlixco 75              (1772–90)
Atlixco 75 Caja I     (1810–19)
Atlixco 76 Caja II   (1810–19)

**Archivo del Registro Público de la Propiedad (ARPP)**
Libros de Censos: 40 (1811–15), 41 (1816–21)

**Archivo del Poder Judicial (APJ)**
Legajo 1810

**Archivo Judicial de Puebla (AJP)**
Legajo 1781, 1782
INAH (Mexico City), Rollos 2, 1811–35; 38, 1786–1825; 68, 1779–82

**Archivo de la Catedral de Puebla (ACP)**
Libros de Cabildo: 55 (1805–08), 56 (1809–12), 57 (1813–15), 58 (1816–18), 59
    (1818–21), 60 (1822–4), 61 (1824–6), 62 (1826–9), 63 (1829–32)

**Biblioteca Lafragua (University of Puebla)**
Cartas de Morelos, 1812–15, INAH (Mexico City), Rollo 68

## D. *Morelia*

**Archivo Histórico Municipal (AHMM)**
Caja:149 (1807, leg. 154); 151 (1807, leg. 155); 156 (1807–08, leg. 160); 157 (1808, leg. 161); 158 (1808, leg. 162); 159 (1808, leg. 163); 160, 161, 162, 163 (1809); 164, 165 (1810); 166, 167 (1811); 167 bis (1812); 168 (1813); 169 (1814): 169 bis (2 legs., 175 (1815) and 176 (1816)); 170 (1817)
 leg. suelto (1816–17); 171 (1818); 172 (1819); 173 (1820); 174 (1820); 175 (1821–2) (2 legs. 182 (1821) and 183 (1822)); 176 (1823–4) (2 legs., 184 (1823) 185 (1824); 177 (1825) (2 legs., 186 and 187 (1825))

**Archivo Histórico de la Ciudad de Morelia del Archivo del Antiguo Arzobispado de Michoacán (ACM) (Casa de Morelos: Museo)**
Diezmatorios: legajo 1 1800–19, legajo 2 1817–40

E. *Microfilm Collection of Provincial Archives (Instituto Nacional de Antropología e Historia, Mexico City)*

**Archivo General de San Luis Potosí**
Rollo 44 (1810–12)

**Archivo General de Tlaxcala**
Rollo 9 (1740–51), 30 (1792–1806), 31 (1810), 32 (1811)

**Archivo Histórico Guanajuatense**
Rollo 9 (1611–1792), 16 (1810)

**Archivo Histórico Municipal, Léon**
Rollo 28–34 (1809–14), 39 (1820–1)

## 2 SPAIN

### A. *Seville*

**Archivo General de Indias (AGI)**
Audiencia de Mexico: 600, 1141, 1142, 1144, 1300, 1310, 1503, 1506, 1540, 1544, 1545, 1548, 1630, 1632, 1675, 1739, 1751, 1780, 1781, 1791, 1809, 1812, 1814, 1815, 1818, 1819, 1829, 1830, 1862, 1866, 1879, 1885, 1973, 1974, 1976, 2026, 2028, 2374, 2375, 2376, 2438, 2505, 2506, 2507, 2513, 2850, 2896, 2902, 3170
Audiencia de Guadalajara: 543
Estado: 28, 30, 43
Indiferente General: 2438

### B. *Madrid*

**Archivo Histórico Nacional (AHN)**
Consejos: 20,727; 21,390

## 3 GREAT BRITAIN

*London*

**British Museum (BM)**
Eg. Mss. 1801
Add. Mss. 17,557

## SECONDARY SOURCES

*HAHR*    *Hispanic American Historical Review*
*HM*    *Historia Mexicana*
*JLAS*    *Journal of Latin American Studies*
*JGSWGLA*    *Jahrbuch für Geschichte von Staat, Wirtschaft und Gesellschaft Lateinamerikas*

Alamán, Lucas, *Historia de Méjico desde los primeros movimientos que prepararon su independencia en el año 1808 hasta la época presente*, 5 vols. (Mexico 1849–52).

Altman, Ida and Lockhart, James, *Provinces of Early Mexico. Variants of Spanish American Regional Evolution* (Los Angeles 1976).

Alvear Acevedo, Carlos, *Galeana* (Mexico 1958).

Amaya, Jesús, *Hidalgo en Jalisco* (Guadalajara 1954).

Anderson, Rodney D., *Guadalajara a la consumación de la Independencia: estudio de su población según los padrones de 1821–1822* (Guadalajara 1983).

Anna, Timothy E., *The Fall of the Royal Government in Mexico City* (Nebraska 1978).

Archer, Christon I., *The Army in Bourbon Mexico, 1760–1810* (New Mexico 1977).

   'The Royalist Army in New Spain: Civil–Military Relationships, 1810–1821', *JLAS*, 13, no. 1. (May 1981), 57–82.

   'The Officer Corps in New Spain: the Martial Career, 1759–1821', *JGSWGLA*, Band 19 (1982), 137–58.

   'Banditry and Revolution in New Spain, 1790–1821', *Bibliotheca Americana*, 1:2 (Nov. 1982), 59–89.

Arnade, Charles W., *The Emergence of the Republic of Bolivia* (Gainesville 1957).

Bancroft, H. H., *History of Mexico*, 6 vols. (San Francisco 1883–8).

Barrett, Ward, *The Sugar Hacienda of the Marqueses del Valle* (Minnesota 1970)

Bataillon, Claude, *Les régions géographiques au Mexique* (Paris 1967).

Bazant, Jan, *Historia de la deuda exterior de México (1823–1946)* (Mexico 1968).

   *Alienation of Church Wealth in Mexico: Social and Economic Aspects of the Liberal Revolution, 1856–1876* (Cambridge 1971).

   *Cinco haciendas mexicanas. Tres siglos de vida rural en San Luis Potosí* (Mexico 1975).

   'Evolución de la industria textil poblana', *HM*, XIII, no. 4 (Apr.–June 1964), 473–516.

Benson, Nettie Lee, *La diputación provincial y el federalismo mexicano* (Mexico 1952).

   (ed.), *Mexico and the Spanish Cortes, 1810–1822. Eight Essays* (Austin 1966).

Blok, Anton, *The Mafia of a Sicilian Village, 1860–1960* (Oxford 1974).

   'The Peasant and the Brigand: Social Banditry Reconsidered', *Comparative Studies in Society and History*, 14, no. 4 (Oct. 1972), 494–503.

Borah, Woodrow W., 'Race and Class in Mexico', *Pacific Historical Review*, 23, no. 4 (1954), 331–42.

   'Discontinuity and Continuity in Mexican History', *Pacific Historical Review*, 48 (1979), 1–25.

Brading, D. A., *Merchants and Miners in Bourbon Mexico, 1763–1810* (Cambridge 1971).

*Haciendas and Ranchos in the Mexican Bajío. León, 1700–1860* (Cambridge 1978).

'Mexican Silver Mining in the Eighteenth Century. The Revival of Zacatecas', *HAHR*, 50, no. 4 (Nov. 1970), 665–81.

'Government and Élite in Colonial Mexico', *HAHR*, 53, no. 3 (Aug. 1973), 389–414.

'La estructura de producción agrícola en el Bajío de 1700 a 1850', *HM*, XXIII (1973), 197–237.

'Los españoles en México hacia 1792', *HM*, XXIII (1973), 126–44.

'El clero mexicano y el movimiento insurgente de 1810', *Relaciones*, 2: V (1981), 5–26.

Brading, D. A., and Cross, Harry E., 'Colonial Silver-Mining in Mexico and Peru', *HAHR*, 52, no. 4 (Nov. 1972), 545–79.

Brading, D. A., and Wu, Celia, 'Population Growth and Crisis: León, 1720–1860', *JLAS*, 5, no. 2 (May 1973), 1–36.

Bravo Ugarte, José, *Historia sucinta de Michoacán;*, 3 vols (Mexico 1964).

Bulnes, Francisco, *Juárez y las revoluciones de Ayutla y de la reforma* (Mexico 1905).

*La guerra de independencia; Hidalgo–Iturbide* (Mexico 1910, 1965 ed.)

Burkholder, Mark A., and Chandler, D. S., *From Impotence to Authority. The Spanish Crown and the American Audiencias, 1687–1808* (Missouri 1977).

Bustamante, Carlos María de, *Historia del Emperor D. Agustín de Iturbide, hasta su muerte y sus consecuencias, y establecimiento de la República Popular Federal* (Mexico 1846).

*Cuadro histórico de la revolución mexicana iniciada el 15 de septiembre de 1810 por el C. Miguel Hidalgo y Costilla cura del pueblo de Dolores en el obispado de Michoacán*, 6 vols. (Mexico 1849–52, 2nd edn).

Buve, Raymond, 'Movimientos campesinos mexicanos: algunos apuntes e interrogantes sobre sus orígenes en la sociedad virreinal', *Anuario de Estudios Americanos*, 28 (1971), 423–57.

Cabrera Ipiña, Octaviano, *El Real de Catorce* (Mexico 1970).

Campbell, Leon G., *The Military and Society in Colonial Peru, 1750–1810* (Philadelphia 1978).

'Recent Research on Andean Peasant Revolts, 1750–1820', *Latin American Research Review*, 14, no. 1 (1979), 3–49.

'Social Structure of the Tupac Amaru Army in Cuzco, 1780–81', *HAHR*, 61, no. 4 (Nov. 1981), 654–93.

Cardozo Galué, Germán, *Michoacán en el siglo de las luces* (Mexico 1973).

Carrera Stampa, Manuel, *Los gremios mexicanos. La organización gremial en Nueva España, 1521–1821* (Mexico 1954).

Carrión, Antonio, *Historia de la ciudad de Puebla de los Angeles*, 2 vols. (Puebla 1896–97, 1970 edn).

Castañeda, Carmen, 'Fuentes para la historia de la educación en la Nueva Galicia y en el estado de Jalisco', *HM*, 113, XXIX, no. 1 (July–Sept. 1979), 180–95.

Castro Arenas, Mario, 'La rebelión de Juan Santos Atahualpa', *Cuadernos Americanos*, 199 (1975), 125–45.

Céspedes del Castillo, Guillermo, *América Latina colonial hasta 1650* (Mexico 1976).

Chance, John K., *Race and Class in Colonial Oaxaca* (Stanford 1978).

Chávez, Ezequiel A., *Agustín de Iturbide. Libertador de México* (Mexico 1962).

Chávez Orozco, Luis (ed.), *Conflicto de trabajo con los mineros de Real del Monte. Año de 1766* (Mexico 1960).

*El sitio de Cuautla* (Mexico 1976).

Chevalier, François, *Land and Society in Colonial Mexico. The Great Hacienda* (California edn, 1966).

'The North Mexican Hacienda: Eighteenth and Nineteenth Century', in Archibald R. Lewis and Thomas R. McGann, *The New World Looks At Its History* (Texas 1963).

Clavero, Bartolomé, *Mayorazgo. Propiedad feudal en Castilla (1369–1836)* (Madrid 1974).

Clutterbuck, Richard, *Guerrillas and Terrorists* (London 1977).

Cobb, R. C., *The Police and the People. French Popular Protest, 1789–1820* (Oxford 1970).

*Colección de acuerdos, órdenes y decretos sobre tierras, casas y sobres de los indígenas, bienes de sus comunidades y fundos legales de los pueblos del estado de Jalisco*, 2 vols. (Guadalajara 1868).

Comellas, José Luis, *Los Realistas en el Trienio constitucional* (Pamplona 1958).

*Constitución política de la monarquía española* (Cádiz 1812).

Cook, Sherburne F., *Soil Erosion and Population in Central Mexico* (California 1949).

*The Historical Demography and Ecology of the Teotlapan* (California 1949).

Cook, Sherburne F., and Borah, Woodrow W., *The Population of the Mixteca Alta, 1520–1960*, Ibero-Americana 50 (California 1968).

*Essays in Population History: Mexico and the Caribbean*, 3 vols. (California 1971, 1974, 1979).

Cordero, Enrique, *Diccionario biográfico de Puebla*, 2 vols. (Mexico 1972).

Cornblit, Oscar, 'Society and Mass Rebellion in Eighteenth-Century Peru and Bolivia', in Raymond Carr (ed.), *St. Antony's Papers*, no. 22 (Oxford 1970), 9–44.

Cornejo Bouroncle, Jorge, *Pumacahua. La revolución del Cuzco de 1814. Estudio documenta-do* (Cuzco 1956).

Cuellar Bernal, René, *Tlaxcala a través de los siglos* (Mexico 1968).

Dabbs, Jack Autrey, *The French Army in Mexico, 1861–1867* (The Hague 1963).

Dakin, Douglas, *The Greek Struggle for Independence, 1821–1833* (California 1973).

De la Peña, Guillermo, *(et al.)*, *Ensayos sobre el Sur de Jalisco* (Mexico 1977).

Díaz, José, and Rodríguez, Ramón, *El movimiento cristero. Sociedad y conflicto en los Altos de Jalisco* (Mexico 1979).

Díaz Díaz, Fernando, *Caudillos y caciques. Antonio López de Santa Anna y Juan Álvarez* (Mexico 1971).

Díaz Díaz, Osvaldo, *Los Almeydas. Episodios de la resistencia patriótica contra el ejército pacificador de Tierra Firme* (Bogotá 1962).

Díez, Domingo, *Bosquejo histórico-geográfico de Morelos* (Cuernavaca 1967).

Domínguez Ortiz, Antonio, *Alteraciones andaluzas* (Madrid 1973).

*Sociedad y estado en el siglo XVIII español* (Barcelona 1976).

Dunn, John, *Modern Revolutions: An Introduction to the Analysis of a Political Phenomenon* (Cambridge 1972).

Ellis, John, *A Short History of Guerrilla Warfare* (London 1975).

Elton, J. F., *With the French in Mexico* (London 1867).

Esquivel Obregón, Toribio, *Biografía de D. Francisco Javier Gamboa. Ideario político y jurídico de Nueva España en el siglo XVIII* (Mexico 1941).

Farriss, N. M., *Crown and Clergy in Colonial Mexico, 1759–1821. The Crisis of Ecclesiastical Privilege* (London 1968).

Fisher, John, 'La rebelión de Tupac Amaru y el programa de la reforma imperial de Carlos III', *Anuario de Estudios Americanos*, 28 (1971), 405–21.

'Royalism, Regionalism and Rebellion in Colonial Peru, 1808–1815', *HAHR*, 59, no. 1 (Feb. 1979), 232–57.

Fisher, Howard T., and Fisher, Marion Hall (eds.), *Life in Mexico. The Letters of Fanny Calderón de la Barca* (New York 1970).

Florescano, Enrique, *Precios del maíz y crísis agrícolas en México, 1708–1810* (Mexico 1969).

(ed.), *Fuentes para la historia de la crísis agrícola de 1785–86*, 2 vols., (Mexico 1981).

Florescano, Enrique, and Gil Sánchez, Isabel (eds.), *Descripciones económicas generales de Nueva España, 1784–1817* (Mexico 1973). *Descripciones económicas regionales de Nueva España: Provincias del Centro, Sudeste y Sur, 1766–1827* (Mexico 1976). *Provincias del Norte, 1766–1827* (Mexico 1976).

Foner, Philip S., *Antonio Maceo. The 'Bronze Titan' of Cuba's Struggle for Independence* (New York 1977).

Fourquin, Guy, *Les Soulèvements populaires au Moyen Age* (Paris 1972).

Friedrich, Paul, *Agrarian Revolt in a Mexican Village* (Chicago 1977).

Frost, Elsa Cecilia, Meyer, Michael C., and Vázquez, Josefina Zoraída (eds.), *El trabajo y los trabajadores en la historia de México* (Mexico-Arizona 1979).

Fuentes Mares, José, *Santa Anna. El hombre* (Mexico 1982).

Galaviz de Capdevielle, María Elena, 'Eleuterio Quiróz y la rebelión de 1847 en Xichú', *Archivos de Historia Potosina*, 41, XI, no. 1 (Sept. 1979), 5–27.

Galula, David, *Counter-Insurgency Warfare. Theory and Practice* (New York 1964: third edn 1966).

Gamas Torruco, José, *El federalismo mexicano* (Mexico 1975).

García, Genaro, *Leona Vicario. Heroína Insurgente* (Mexico 1910). *Documentos históricos mexicanos*, 7 vols. (Mexico 1971). *Documentos inéditos y muy raros para la historia de México* (Mexico 1974).

García Cubas, Antonio, *Diccionario geográfico, histórico y biográfico de los estados unidos mexicanos*, 5 vols. (Mexico 1888–91).

Garner, Richard L., 'Problèmes d'une ville minière mexicaine à la fin de l'époque coloniale: Prix et salaires à Zacatecas (1760–1821)', *Cahiers des Amériques Latines*, 6 (1972), 75–112.

'Reformas borbónicas y operaciones hacendarias. La real caja de Zacatecas', *HM*, XXVII, no. 4 (Apr.-June 1978), 542–87.

Gibson, Charles, *The Aztecs under Spanish Rule: A History of the Indians of the Valley of Mexico, 1519–1810* (Stanford 1964).

Gómez Canedo, Lino, *Sierra Gorda. Un típico enclave misional en el centro de México (Siglos XVII–XVIII)* (Pachuca 1976).

Gómez Haro, Eduardo, *La ciudad de Puebla y la guerra de Independencia* (Puebla 1910).

González de Cossío, F., *Xalapa. Breve reseña histórica* (Mexico 1957).

González y González, Luis, *Pueblo en vilo. Microhistoria de San José de Gracia* (Mexico 1968).

*Nueva invitación a la microhistoria* (Mexico 1982).

González Navarro, Moisés, *Anatomía del poder en México (1848–1853)* (Mexico 1977).

González Sánchez, Isabel, *Haciendas y ranchos de Tlaxcala en 1712* (Mexico 1969).

Greenow, Linda, *Credit and Socioeconomic Change in Colonial Mexico: Loans and Mortgages in Guadalajara, 1720–1820* (Boulder, Colorado, 1983).

'Spatial Dimensions of the Credit Market in Eighteenth-Century New Galicia', in Robinson, David J. (ed.), *Social Fabric and Spatial Structures in Colonial Latin America* (Ann Arbor 1979).

Guevara, Ernesto 'Che', *Guerrilla Warfare* (New York 1968).

Hale, Charles A., *Mexican Liberalism in the Age of Mora, 1821–1853* (Yale 1968).

Halperín Donghi, Tulio, 'Revolutionary Militarization in Buenos Aires, 1806–1815', *Past and Present*, 40 (July 1968), 84–107.

Hamill, Hugh M., *The Hidalgo Revolt. Prelude to Mexican Independence* (Gainesville 1966).

'Royalist Counterinsurgency in the Mexican War for Independence: the Lesson of 1811', *HAHR*, 53, no. 3 (Aug. 1973), 470–89.

Hamnett, Brian, R., *Politics and Trade in Southern Mexico, 1750–1821* (Cambridge 1971).

*Revolución y contrarrevolución en México y el Perú. Liberalismo, realeza y separatismo, 1800–1824* (Mexico 1978).

'Mercantile Rivalry and Peninsular Division: The Consulados of New Spain and the Impact of the Bourbon Reforms, 1789–1824', *Ibero-Amerikanisches Archiv*, NF. Jg.2, H4 (1976), 273–305.

'Anastasio Bustamante y la guerra de independencia, 1810–1821', *HM*, XXVIII, no. 4 (1979), 515–45.

'The Economic and Social Dimension of the Revolution of Independence in Mexico, 1800–1820', *Ibero-Amerikanisches Archiv*, NF. Jg.6, H1 (1980), 1–27.

'Mexico's Royalist Coalition: The Response to Revolution, 1808–1821' *JLAS*, 12, no. 1 (May 1980), 55–86.

'Royalist Counter-insurgency and the Continuity of Rebellion: Guanajuato and Michoacán, 1813–1820', *HAHR*, 62, no. 1 (Feb. 1982), 19–48.

Harris, Charles R., *A Mexican Family Empire. The Latifundo of the Sánchez Navarro Family, 1765–1867* (Texas 1975).

Hobsbawm, E. J., *Bandits* (Harmondsworth 1969).

Humboldt, Alexander von, *Essai politique sur le royaume de la Nouvelle Espagne*, 5 vols. (Paris 1811).

Iribárren, José María, *Espoz y Mina. El Guerrillero* (Madrid 1965).

Izard, Miguel, *El Miedo a la Revolución. La Lucha por la libertad en Venezuela (1777–1830)* (Madrid 1979).

'Ni Cuartreros ni Montoneros, Llaneros', *Boletín Americanista*, XXIII, no. 31 (1981).

Johnson, Chalmers, *Revolutionary Change* (London 1968).

Johnston, R. M., *The Napoleonic Empire in Southern Italy and the Rise of the Secret Societies*, 2 vols. (New York 1973).

Katz, Friedrich, 'Labor Conditions in Haciendas in Profirian Mexico: Some Trends and Tendencies', *HAHR*, 54, no. 1 (Feb. 1974), 1–47.

Kératry, Émile de, *La Contre-Guérrille française au Mexique* (Paris 1869).

Ladd, Doris M., *The Mexican Nobility at Independence, 1780–1826* (Texas 1976).

Ladurie, E. Le Roy, *Montaillou, village occitan, de 1294 à 1324* (Paris 1975).

Lafaye, Jacques, *Quetzalcóatl and Guadalupe: the Formation of Mexican National Consciousness, 1531–1813* (Chicago 1976).

Lafuente Ferrari, Enrique, *El virrey Iturrigaray y los orígenes de la independencia de Méjico* (Madrid 1941).

Larsen, Brooke, 'Rural Rhythms of Class Conflict in Eighteenth-Century Cochabamba', *HAHR* 60, no. 3 (Aug. 1980), 407–30.

Lefèbvre, George, *The Great Fear of 1789, Rural Panic in Revolutionary France*, (London 1973).

*Legislación del trabajo en los siglos XVI, XVII y XVIII* (Mexico 1938).

Leicht, Hugo, *Las Calles de Puebla* (Puebla 1934).

Lemonie Villicaña, Ernesto, *Morelos: su vida revolucionaria a través de sus escritos y do otros testimonios de la época* (Mexico 1965).

Lerdo de Tejada, Miguel, *Apuntes históricos de la heróica ciudad de Veracruz*, 3 vols. (Mexico 1850–8).

Liehr, Reinhard, *Stadtrat und Stätische Oberschicht von Puebla am Ende der Kolonialzeit (1787–1810)* (Wiesbaden 1971).

*Ayuntamiento y oligarquía en Puebla, 1787–1810*, 2 vols. (Mexico 1976).

'Die Soziale Stellung der Indianer von Puebla während der Zweiten Hälfte des 18 Jahrhunderts', *JGSWGLA*, 8 (1971), 74–125.

Lindley, Richard, *Haciendas and Economic Development – Guadalajara, Mexico, at Independence* (Austin 1983).

Lockhart, James, 'Encomienda and Hacienda: The Evolution of the Great Estate in the Spanish Indies', *HAHR*, 49, no. 3 (Aug. 1969), 411–29.

Lynch, John, *The Spanish American Revolutions 1808–1825* (London 1973).

McAlister, John T., Jr, *Vietnam. The Origins of Revolution* (London 1969).

McCuen, John J., *The Art of Counter-Revolutionary War: The Strategy of Counter-Insurgency* (London 1966).

McFarlane, Anthony, 'Riot and Rebellion in Colonial Spanish America', *Latin American Research Review*, 17 (1982), 212–21.

'Civil Disorders and Popular Protests in Late Colonial New Granada', *HAHR*, 64, no. 1 (Feb. 1984), 17–54.

MacLachlan, Colin M., *Criminal Justice in Eighteenth-Century Mexico. A Study of the Tribunal of the Acordada* (California 1974).

Marmolejo, Lucio, *Efemérides guanajuatenses, o datos para formar la historia de la ciudad de Guanajuato*, 4 vols. (Guanajuato 1883–4).

Marshall, C. E., 'The Birth of the Mestizo in New Spain', *HAHR*, 19 (1939), 161–184.

Martin, Cheryl English, 'Haciendas and villages in late colonial Morelos', *HAHR* 62, no. 3 (Aug. 1982), 407–27.

Martínez de Lejarza, Juan José, *Análisis estadístico de la provincia de Michoacán en 1822* (Morelia 1974).

Maza, Francisco de la, *El Guadalupanismo Mexicano* (Mexico 1953).

Mecham, J. Lloyd, 'The Origins of Federalism in Mexico', *HAHR*, 18 (1939) 164–182.

Mejía Zúñiga, Raúl, *Valentín Gómez Farías, hombre de México, (1781–1858)* (Mexico 1982).

Menéndez Valdés, José, *Descripción y Censo General de la Intendencia de Guadalajara, 1789–93* (Guadalajara 1980).

Meyer, Jean, 'Los movimientos campesinos en el occidente de México en el siglo XIX', *Boletín del Archivo Histórico de Jalisco*, III, no. 2 (May–Aug. 1979), 2–12.

Mier y Noriega y Guerra, Fray Servando de, *Historia de la revolución de Nueva España, antiguamente Anáhuac, o verdadero orígen y causas de ella con la relación de sus progresos hasta el presente año de 1813*, 2 vols. (London 1813).

Miller, John, *Memoirs of General Miller*, 2 vols. (London 1828).

Millon, Robert P., *Zapata: the Ideology of a Peasant Revolutionary* (New York 1979).

Miranda, José, 'El liberalismo mexicano y el liberalismo europeo', *HM*, 8, no. 4, (Apr.–June 1959), 512–23.

Moore, Barrington, Jr *Social Origins of Dictatorship and Democracy. Lord and Peasant in the Making of the Modern World* (London 1967).

Moorhead, Max, *The Presidio. Bastion of the Spanish Borderland* (Norman, Oklahoma 1975).

Mora, José María Luis, *Obras sueltas*, 2 vols. (Mexico 1963).

   *México y sus revoluciones*, 3 vols. (Mexico 1965).

Morin, Claude, *Michoacán en la Nueva España de siglo XVIII. Crecimiento y desigualdad en una economía colonial* (Mexico 1979).

Mörner, Magnus, *Estratificación social hispano americana durante el período colonial* (Institute of Latin American Studies, Stockholm) Paper no. 28 (Jan. 1981).

Mousnier, Roland, *Fureurs paysannes: Les Paysans dans les révoltes du XVIIe siècle* (Paris 1968).

Muría, José María, *La Historia SW Jalisco* (no date).

   (ed.) *El federalismo en Jalisco, (1823)* (Guadalajara 1973).

   (*et al.*), *Historia de Jalisco*, 4 vols. (Guadalajara 1980–2).

Navarro, Bernabé, *Cultura mexicana moderna en el siglo XVIII* (Mexico 1964).

Navarro y Noriega, Fernando, *Memoria sobre la población del reino de Nueva España* (Mexico 1820, 1943 ed.).

Nickel, Herbert J., *Soziale Morphologie der Mexikanischen Hacienda* (Wiesbaden 1978).

Núñez y Domínguez, José de J., *La virreina mexicana, Doña María Francisca de la Gándara de Calleja* (Mexico 1950).

Olveda Legaspi, Jaime, *El Iturbidismo en Jalisco* (Mexico 1974).

   *Gordiano Guzmán: un cacique del siglo XIX* (Mexico 1980).

O'Phelan Godoy, Scarlett, 'Elementos étnicos y de poder en el movimiento Tupacama-rista, 1780–81', *Nova Americana*, 5 (1982), 79–101.

Ortega y Pérez Gallardo, Ricardo, *Historia genealógica de la más antiguas familias de México*, 3 vols. (Mexico 1908).

Ortiz de la Tabla, Javier, *Comercio exterior de Veracruz, 1778–1821: crísis de dependencia* (Seville 1978).

Osorno Castro, Fernando, *El insurgente Albino García* (Mexico 1982).

Palomino y Cañedo, Jorge, *La casa y mayorazgo de Cañedo en Nueva Galicia*, 2 vols. (Mexico 1947).

Parry, J. H., *The Audiencia of New Galicia in the Sixteenth Century. A Study in Spanish Colonial Government* (Cambridge 1948, 1968 ed.).

Pérez Verdía, Luis, *Historia particular del estado de Jalisco, desde los primeros tiempos de que hay noticia hasta nuestros días*, 3 vols. (Guadalajara 1910–11).

   *Apuntes históricos sobre la guerra de independencia de Jalisco* (Guadalajara 1953).

Phelan, John Leddy, *The People and the King. The Comunero Movement in New Granada, 1780–1781* (Wisconsin 1978).

Piel, Jean, 'The Place of the Peasantry in the National Life of Peru in the Nineteenth Century', *Past and Present*, 46, (Feb. 1970), 108–33.

Pietschmann, Horst, 'Der Repartimiento-Handel der Distriktsbeamten im Raum Puebla im 18. Jahrhundert', *JGSWGLA*, 10 (1973), 236–50.

Popkin, Samuel L., *The Rational Peasant. The Political Economy of Rural Society in Vietnam* (California 1979).

Potash, Robert A., *El Banco de Avío de México. El fomento de la industria, 1821–46* (Mexico 1959).

Powell, T. G., *El liberalismo y el campesinado en el centro de México, 1850–1876* (Mexico 1974).

Priestley, Herbert I, *José de Gálvez: Visitor-General of New Spain, 1765–1771* (Berkeley 1916).

Ramírez Flores, José, *El gobierno insurgente en Guadalajara, 1810–11* (Guadalajara 1980, 2nd edn; 1st edn 1969).

Reina, Leticia, *Las rebeliones compesinas en México (1819–1906)* (Mexico 1980).

Riley, James D., 'Landlords, Laborers and Royal Government: The Administration of Labor in Tlaxcala, 1680–1750', in Elsa Cecilia Frost, Michael C. Meyer, and Josefina Zoraída Vázquez (eds.), *El trabajo los trabajadores en la historia de México* (Mexico and Arizona 1979), 221–41.

Rivera Cambas, M., *Historia antigua y moderna de Jalapa y de las revoluciones del estado de Veracruz*, 5 vols. (Mexico 1869–71).

Roa, Victoriano, *Estadística del Estado Libre de Jalisco* (Guadalajara 1825, 1981 ed.).

Roberts, Bryan, 'Estado y Región en América Latina', *Relaciones. Estudios de Historia y Sociedad*, 4 (Otoño 1980), 9–40.

Robertson, William Spence, *Iturbide of Mexico* (Durham, N.C. 1952).

Rocca, M. de, *Mémoires sur la Guerre des Français en Espagne* (London 1815).

Romero, José Guadalupe, *Noticias para formar la historia y la estadística del Obispado de Michoacán* (Mexico 1862).

Romero Flores, Jesús, *Iturbide pro y contra* (Morelia 1971).

Santos Vargas, José, *Diario de un comandante de la independencia americana, 1814–25* Gunnar Mendoza, ed. (Mexico 1982).

Sarfati, Magali, *Spanish Bureaucratic Patrimonialism in America* (Berkeley 1966).

Sarralbo Aguareles, Eugenio, 'Una conmoción popular en el México Virreinal del siglo XVIII', *Anuario de Estudios Americanos*, 7 (1950), 125–161.

Scott, James C., *The Moral Economy of the Peasant. Rebellion and Subsistence in Southeast Asia* (Yale 1976).

Scott, S. F., *The Response of the Royal Army to the French Revolution. The Role and Development of the Line Army, 1787–93* (Oxford 1978).

Serrera Contreras, Ramón, *Guadalajara ganadera. Estudio regional novo-hispano, 1750–1805* (Seville 1977).

Sinkin, Richard N., *The Mexican Reform, 1855–1876. A Study in Liberal Nation-Building* (Texas 1979).

Smith, Robert S., 'The Puebla Consulado, 1821–1824', *Revista de Historia de América*, 21, (1946), 150–61.

Smith Robert S., and Ramírez Flores, José, *Los consulados de comerciantes de Nueva España* (Mexico 1976).

Spalding, Karen, 'The Colonial Indian: Past and Future Research Perspectives', *Latin American Research Review*, 7 (1972), 46–76.

Super, John C., *La Vida en Querétaro durante la Colonia, 1531–1810* (Mexico 1983).

'Querétaro Obrajes: Industry and Society in Provincial Mexico, 1600–1810', *HAHR*, 56, no. 2 (May 1976), 197–216.

'Pan, alimentación y política en Querétaro en la última decada del siglo XVIII', *HM*, 118, XXX, no. 2 (Oct.–Dec. 1980), 247–72.

Taylor, William B., *Landlord and Peasant in Colonial Oaxaca* (Stanford 1972).

*Drinking, Homicide and Rebellion in Colonial Mexican Villages* (Stanford 1979).

'Sacarse de Pobre. El Bandolerismo en la Nueva Galicia, 1794–1821', *Revista Jalisco*, no. 1–2, II, (Jan.–June 1981).

Tella, Torcuato di, 'The Dangerous Classes in Early Nineteenth Century Mexico', *JLAS*, 5, no. 1 (May 1973), 79–105.

Tena Ramírez, Felipe, *Leyes fundamentales de México, 1808–1864* (Mexico 1964).

Thompson, Sir Robert, *Defeating Communist Insurgency. Experiences from Malaya and Vietnam* (London 1967).

Thompson, Waddy, *Recollections of Mexico* (New York 1846).

Tilly, Charles, *The Vendée* (Cambridge, Mass., 1964).

Torras Elías, Jaime, *La guerra de los Agraviados* (Barcelona 1967).

Torre Villar, Ernesto de la, *La Constitución de Apatzingán y los creadores del estado mexicano* (Mexico 1964).

   *Los Guadalupes y la Independencia* (Mexico 1966).

Tovar Pinzón, Hérmes, 'Insolencia, Tumulto e Invasiones de los Naturales de Zacoalco (México) a fines del siglo XVIII', *Cuadernos de Historia Social y Económica*, 10 (1985), 1–18.

Trautmann, Wolfgang, *Las transformaciones en el paisaje cultural de Tlaxcala durante la época colonial* (Wiesbaden 1981).

Tutino, John, 'Hacienda Social Relations in Mexico: The Chalco Region in the Era of Independence', *HAHR*, 55, no. 3 (Aug. 1975), 496–528.

   'Life and Labor on North Mexican Haciendas: The Querétaro-San Luis Potosí Region: 1775–1810', in Elsa Cecilia Frost, Michael C. Meyer, and Josefina Zoraída Vázquez (eds.), *El trabajo y los trabajadores en la historia de México* (Mexico and Arizona 1979), 339–79.

Uslar Pietri, Juan, *Historia de la rebelión popular de 1814. Contribución al estudio de la historia de Venezuela* (Caracas 1962).

Vanderwood, Paul J., *Disorder and Progress; Bandits, Police and Mexican Development* (Nebraska 1981).

   *Los rurales mexicanos* (Mexico 1982).

   'Genesis of the Rurales: Mexico's Early Struggle for Public Security', *HAHR*, 50, no. 2 (May 1970), 323–44.

   'Response to Revolt: The Counter-Guerrilla Strategy of Porfirio Díaz', *HAHR*, 56, no. 4 (Nov. 1976), 551–79.

Van Young, Eric, *Hacienda and Market in Eighteenth-Century Mexico. The Rural Economy of Guadalajara, 1675–1820* (California 1981).

   'Conflict and Solidarity in Indian Village Life: The Guadalajara Region in the Late Colonial Period', *HAHR*, 64, no. 1 (Feb. 1984), 55–79.

Vergara Arias, Gustavo, *Montoneros y guerrillas en la etapa de la emancipación de Perú (1820–1825)* (Lima 1973).

Villaseñor y Sánchez, José Antonio de, *Theatro Americano, descripción general de los reynos y provincias de la Nueva España y sus jurisdicciones*, 2 vols. (Mexico 1746–8).

Villaseñor y Villaseñor, Alejandro, *Biografías de los héroes y caudillos de la independencia*, 2 vols. (Mexico 1910).

Villoro, Luis, *El proceso ideológico de la revolución de independencia* (Mexico 1967).

Ward, H. G., *Mexico in 1827*, 2 vols. (London 1828).

Wolf, E. R., *Peasant Wars of the Twentieth Century* (London 1969).

   'The Mexican Bajío in the Eighteenth Century', *Synoptic Studies of Mexican Culture*, no. 17, Middle American Research Institute of Tulane University Publications (New Orleans 1955).

   'Aspects of Group Relations in a Complex Society: Mexico', *American Anthropologist* 58, no. 4 (1956) 1065–78.

Wolf, E. R., and Hansen, Edward, 'Caudillo Politics: A Structural Analysis', *Comparative Studies in Society and History*, 9, no. 2 (1966–7), 168–79.

Womack, John, *Zapata and the Mexican Revolution* (New York 1968).

Woodhouse, C. M., *The Struggle for Greece, 1941–1949* (London 1976).

Zagorin, Perez, *Rebels and Rulers, 1500–1660*, 2 vols. (Cambridge 1982).

Zakythinos, D. A., *The Making of Modern Greece. From Byzantium to Independence* (Oxford 1976).

Zavala, Lorenzo de, *Ensayo histórico de las revoluciones de México desde 1808 hasta 1830*, 2 vols. (Paris 1831–2).

   *Obras* (Mexico 1969).

Zerecero, Anastasio, *Memorias para la historia de las revoluciones en México* (Mexico 1975).

# Index

# CAMBRIDGE LATIN AMERICAN STUDIES